T0133109

Advanced Wireless Sensing Techniques for 5G Networks

Advanced Wireless Sensing Techniques for 5G Networks

Edited by

Ashish Bagwari
Geetam Singh Tomar
Jyotshana Bagwari

CRC Press
Taylor & Francis Group
Boca Raton London New York

CRC Press is an imprint of the
Taylor & Francis Group, an **informa** business

A CHAPMAN & HALL BOOK

CRC Press
Taylor & Francis Group
6000 Broken Sound Parkway NW, Suite 300
Boca Raton, FL 33487-2742

Printed on acid-free paper

International Standard Book Number-13: 978-0-8153-7837-2 (Hardback)

Library of Congress Cataloging-in-Publication Data

Names: Bagwari, Ashish, editor. | Tomar, Geetam, editor. | Bagwari, Jyotshana, editor.
Title: Advanced wireless sensing techniques for 5G networks / editors, Ashish Bagwari, Geetam Singh Tomar, Jyotshana Bagwari.
Description: Boca Raton : Taylor & Francis, a CRC title, part of the Taylor & Francis imprint, a member of the Taylor & Francis Group, the academic division of T&F Informa, plc, 2019. | Includes bibliographical references and index.
Identifiers: LCCN 2018046896| ISBN 9780815378372 (hardback : acid-free paper) | ISBN 9781351021746 (ebook)
Subjects: LCSH: Wireless sensor networks. | Cognitive radio networks. | Radio--Receivers and reception.
Classification: LCC TK5103.4815 .A38 2019 | DDC 621.3845/60285625--dc23
LC record available at https://lccn.loc.gov/2018046896

Visit the Taylor & Francis Web site at
http://www.taylorandfrancis.com

and the CRC Press Web site at
http://www.crcpress.com

Dedicated to our real GOD our Parents, Baba Kedarnath,
and Anshul, Anushka, and Agrim

Ashish Bagwari, Jyotshana Bagwari

Contents

Part I Introduction of 5G Networks

Part II Various Spectrum Sensing Techniques

Part III Advanced Wireless Sensing Techniques

Part IV Energy Efficient Routing Protocols

Part V Challenges in 5G Networks

Part VI 5G Networks with Ad hoc Networks

Part VII Applications of 5G Networks

Preface

Cognitive radio is considered one of the main tools in combating the problem of spectrum availability for future mobile communications systems. It utilizes innovative technologies that increase the efficiency of spectrum usage, and therefore, solve the problem of bandwidth requirements for highly demanding applications. In this book, we present the state-of-the-art on advanced wireless sensing techniques for cognitive radio networks' operations. This includes various sensing algorithms for configuring radio networks to meet the perfect requirements and applications in the real world.

The focus of this book is on efficient resources allocation sensing algorithms, present and advanced wireless sensing techniques, how much work has been done up until now, and also summarizes recent advances in the sensing techniques. Also discussed are the energy efficient routing protocols, existing issues with 5G networks, applications of 5G networks, and the usages of 5G networks with Adhoc networks.

This book is intended for engineers (who are practicing cognitive radio-related developments), researchers, and higher degree students that are working on radio scene analysis for cognitive radios and sensing techniques. For researchers, this book serves as a starting point for research in areas such as algorithms for detectors, sensing techniques, challenges, collaboration with other networks, and applications of radio networks. It may serve as a comprehensive tutorial or be used as the basis for new research projects. For practitioners, this book contains many sensing algorithms, protocols, and experiments that will prove useful in the design and deployment of sensing techniques for radio networks.

This book is organized into seven parts. The first part provides the introduction of this book and gives a background on 5G networks. The second part presents the motivation and the overview of the various spectrum sensing techniques. The third part is arranged into four chapters and presents many advanced wireless sensing algorithms/techniques for 5G networks. This includes efficient sensing techniques, two-phase detection techniques, multiple antennas-based collaborative sensing techniques, and compressive sensing techniques. The fourth part presents the energy efficient routing protocols for 5G networks. The fifth part discusses the challenges or issues related to 5G networks. The sixth part discusses the role of 5G networks with Adhoc wireless networks. The seventh part presents 5G network applications and illustrates how 5G networks may be used. The momentum for applications has also gained a further step forward with the latest technologies such as Wi-Fi and Li-Fi networks.

Ashish Bagwari
Geetam Singh Tomar
Jyotshana Bagwari
India

Acknowledgments

We express our deep gratitude to our parents, Mr. Pradeep Kumar Bagwari and Mrs. Saraswati Bagwari, who have been encouraging and supporting us throughout the tenure of our research work, and the grace of Baba Kedarnath to achieve this goal. We also wish to acknowledge our family members, both personal and professional (WIT), for their continuous support, help, and encouragement without which this research work would not have been completed in time. Last, but not least, special thanks to our lovely nephew, Anshul Semwal, niece, Anushka Gaur, and our son, Agrim Bagwari, for their true love.

Ashish Bagwari
Jyotshana Bagwari
India

Editors

Dr. Ashish Bagwari received his B. Tech. (Hons.), M. Tech. (Hons. and Gold Medalist), and Ph.D. in Electronics and Communication engineering. He is currently Head of Electronics and Communication Engineering Department, Women's Institute of Technology (WIT) (Institute of State Government) Dehradun, Constituent College of Uttarakhand Technical University (State Government Technical University), Dehradun, India. He has published more than 90 research papers in various international journals (including ISI/SCI indexed) and IEEE international conferences. His current research interests include wireless communications, sensor networks, 5-G Technology, Digital communication, and Mobile Adhoc networks. He is a member of IEEE USA, MIR Laboratories India, IETE, ACM, and IAENG. He has also been an editor, an advisor, and a reviewer of several well-known international journals published by IEEE, Taylor & Francis, Springer, Elsevier, IJCCN, ISTP, IJATER, JREEE, JCSR, and JNMS, CICN-2011, 2013, 2015, 2016, 2017, 2018, CSNT-2014, 2015, 2016, 2017, 2018, ICMWOC-2014, I4CT'2014, and ICEPIT-2014, 17, 18. He has two patents, and written three books and a few book chapters for CRC Press and other publishers.

Geetam Singh Tomar received his UG, PG, and PhD degrees in electronics engineering from the universities of India and PDF from the University of Kent, UK. He is the director of THDC Institute of Hydropower Engineering and Technology, Tehri, India and is also the director of Machine Intelligence Research Labs, Gwalior, India. He is associated with professional societies such as IEEE as a Senior Member and IETE and IE (I) as a Fellow. He also served at the Dept. of Electrical Computer Engineering, University of West Indies, Trinidad and Tobago, and Univ. of Kent, Canterbury, UK. Research areas of interest are air interface and advanced communication networks, sensors and sensor networks, and digital design. He is actively involved in IEEE activities and has organized more than 25 IEEE International conferences in India and other countries and has delivered keynote speeches in many conferences abroad. He is a Visiting Professor in Hannam University, Korea, Thapar University Patiala, and many other institutes of repute. He is chief editor of 5 International Journals, has published more than 170 research papers in international journals/conferences, and has written 6 books and book chapters for IGI Global and CRC Press.

Jyotshana Bagwari received the Bachelor of Technology degree (Hons.) and Master of Technology degree in Computer Science and Engineering from Uttarakhand Technical University, Dehradun, India. Presently, she is pursuing her Doctor of Philosophy in cognitive radio network from Uttarakhand Technical University, Dehradun, India. She has published several research papers in various reputed international SCI/ISI indexed journals such as Springer, Taylor & Francis, Elsevier, Oxford UK Publications, and conferences including IEEE international conferences. She has also written one book.

Contributors

M.F.L. Abdullah
Department of Communication
    Engineering
University Tun Hussein
    Onn Malaysia
Batu Pahat, Johor, Malaysia

S. Arunmozhi
Department of Electronics and
    communication Engineering
Manakula Vinayagar Institute of
    Technology
Madagadipet, Puducherry, India

Ashish Bagwari
Department of Electronics and
    communication Engineering
Women's Institute of
    Technology
Uttarakhand Technical University
Dehradun, Uttarakhand, India

Jyotshana Bagwari
Department of Computer Science and
    Engineering
Uttarakhand Technical University
Dehradun, Uttarakhand, India

Debnath Bhattacharyya
Department of Computer Science and
    Engineering
Vignan's Institute of Information
    Technology (Autonomous)
Visakhapatnam, Andhra Pradesh, India

Robin Singh Bhadoria
Department of Computer Science and
    Engineering
Indian Institute of Information
    Technology Nagpur
Nagpur, Maharastra, India

P.T.V. Bhuvaneswari
Electronics Engineering
Madras Institute of Technology campus
Anna University
Chennai, Tamil Nadu, India

Rabia Bilal
Usman Institute of Technology
Electrical Engineering Department
Karachi, Sindh, Pakistan

M.S.M. Gismalla
Department of Communication
    Engineering
University Tun Hussein Onn Malaysia
Batu Pahat, Johor, Malaysia

A.N. Ibrahim
Department of Communication
    Engineering
University Tun Hussein Onn Malaysia
Batu Pahat, Johor, Malaysia

A. Jayanthiladevi
School of Computer Science
Jain University
Bangalore, karnataka, India

Poonam Jindal
Electronics and Communication
    Engineering Department
National Institute of Technology
Kurukshetra, Haryana, India

Pooja Joshi
Department of Computer Science
Uttarakhand Technical University
Dehradun, Uttarakhand, India

P. Magesh Kannan
Department of Electronics and
    Communication
Pondicherry Engineering College
Pillaichavadi, Pondicherry, India

Bilal Muhammad Khan
National University of Sciences and
    Technology
Electronic and Power Engineering
    Department
Karachi, Sindh, Pakistan

Shadab Pasha Khan
Department of Information Technology
Oriental Institute of
    Science & Technology
Bhopal, Madhya Pradesh, India

Tai-hoon Kim
Department of Convergence Security
Sungshin Women's University
Seongbuk-gu, Seoul, South Korea

Anu Mangal
Department of Electronics &
    Communication Engineering
University Institute of Technology
Rajiv Gandhi Technical University
Bhopal, Madhya Pradesh, India

G. Nagarajan
Department of Electronics and
    Communication Engineering
Pondicherry Engineering College
Pillaichavadi, Puducherry, India

R. Narmadha
School of Electrical and Electronics
    Engineering
Sathyabama Institute of Science and
    Technology
Chennai, Tamil Nadu, India

Ashish Negi
Department of Computer Science &
    Applications
G.B. Pant Engineering College
Pauri Garhwal, Uttarakhand, India

N.P. Pathak
Electronics & Communication
    Engineering
Sant Longowal Institute of Engineering &
    Technology
Sangrur, Punjab, India

T. Perarasi
Department of Electronics and
    Communication Engineering
Karpaga Vinayaga College of Engineering
    and Technology
Chennai, Tamil Nadu, India

M. Hassanein Rabah
Components and Systems-LEOST
The French Institute of Science and
    Technology for Transport,
    Development and Networks (IFSTTAR)
Villeneuve d'Ascq, Nord, France

N. Thirupathi Rao
Department of Computer Science and
    Engineering
Vignan's Institute of Information
    Technology (Autonomous)
Visakhapatnam, Andhra Pradesh, India

M.A. Rizvi
Department of Computer Engineering and
    Applications
National Institute of Technical Teachers'
    Training and Research, Bhopal
    (NITTTR)
Bhopal, Madhya Pradesh, India

Divitha Seetharamdoo
Components and Systems-LEOST
The French Institute of Science and
    Technology for Transport,
    Development and Networks (IFSTTAR)
Villeneuve d'Ascq, Nord, France

Brahmjit Singh
Electronics and Communication
    Engineering Department
National Institute of Technology
Kurukshetra, Haryana, India

Surinder Singh
Electronics & Communication Engineering
Sant Longowal Institute of Engineering &
    Technology
Sangrur, Punjab, India

Geetam Singh Tomar
T.H.D.C.I.H.E.T.
Tehri, Uttarakhand, India

Pankaj Verma
Electronics and Communication
    Engineering Department
National Institute of Technology
Kurukshetra, Haryana, India

Vinod Kumar Verma
Computer Science and Engineering
Sant Longowal Institute of
    Engineering & Technology
Sangrur, Punjab, India

Part I

Introduction of 5G Networks

1

5G Disruptive Technologies and Architecture

Anu Mangal, M.A. Rizvi, and Shadab Pasha Khan

CONTENTS

1.1 Communication Overview

The era of communication technology led to one of the major catalysts in developing modern human society. Transfer of information from one place to another is called communication. It is a process of conveying messages over a distance. In communication systems, a physical message such as pictures, sound, words, and so on are converted into electrical signals and transmitted through a medium and then reconverted into the physical message at the receiver. This medium is defined as a communication medium and it can be wired or wireless, but wireless communication has changed the way in which society operates. The transmission path of mobile communication spans the distance from mobile phones to the Base Station (BS) of the radio cell in which the caller is basically located. In wireless communications, a communication radio spectrum has been used which, until now, has typically referred to the full frequency range from 3 KHz to 300 GHz.

The advancements which have been done in wireless technologies have greatly improved people's abilities to communicate and live in both business operations and social functions. Mobile radio communication was started in the twentieth century for military communications (such as car-based mobile telephone systems). Mobile telecommunications have had both phenomenal and transformational impacts on society. Mobile wireless communication started with analog voice calls in 1G which had to be continuously nurtured, then 2G, 3G, and 4G were developed, and finally technology has reached the 5G era and more evolutions are taking place each day. The future of wireless communication will be unbounded; this means unlimited access of data and information will be ubiquitously available to everyone.

1.2 Overview of Existing and Past Wireless Technologies

Table 1.1 provides the services offered, key factors, and the drawbacks of all the wireless generations at a glance; the technologies that connected, are connecting, and will connect us to the world.

There is a drastic change in the generations of mobile communication starting from the analog 1G to the very fast and digital 4G. Now 5G is on its way to provide the user with real time experiences in technology and ease the issues related to the present technology in order to make human life much easier. From 1991, when 2G was first realized to the 3G system launched in 2001, a huge transformation has taken place in wireless

TABLE 1.1

Comparison between Past and Existing Wireless Technologies

Generation	Primary Services	Key Factor	Drawbacks
1G(AMPS)	Analog phone calls, circuit switching	Mobility	Limited connectivity, poor security
2G(GSM)	Digital phone calls, messaging, circuit switching	More efficient on spectrum, greater mobile phone penetration	Limited data rate-difficult to support internet demands, security was not enough
2.5G(GPRS)	MMS and mobile internet with WAP	More speed as compared to 2G, applies packet switching along with circuit switching	Speed was not enough
2.75G(EDGE)	8 PSK modulation	Faster internet up to 128 kbps	Slower data rate
3G(W-CDMA, UMTS)	Phone calls, video calls, messaging, data	Better internet experience, global roaming, improved voice quality	Coverage, WAP failure for internet access, 3G handsets require more power as compared to 2G counterparts
3.5G(HSPA)	Phone calls, messaging, mobile data	Broadband internet applications	Tied to legacy, architecture and protocols are mobile-specific
3.75G (LTE/OFDMA)	Phone calls, mobile data, messaging	Better coverage with improved performance for less cost	Tied to legacy, architecture and protocols are mobile-specific
4G(LTE-A)	Designed for data, IP based protocols	Faster mobile broadband, lower latency, high throughput	Not optimized for IoT scaling; limited flexibility to support bespoke services across industry verticals; inadequate for next generation services
5G	All-IP services, new technology sectors, verticals and end-users	Pervasive Networks, Group Cooperative Relay, higher data rates and better support for IoT. Lower latency, faster, and higher capacity broadband internet	

mobile networks. It has changed from a pure telephony system to a network that can support video calls and transport high speed data-rich multimedia content, and has revolutionized the Internet experience. 4G systems contain an advanced radio interface which incorporates orthogonal frequency-division multiplexing (OFDM), link adaptation, and multiple-input multiple-output (MIMO) technologies. The data rates supported by 4G wireless networks can be up to 1 Gb/s for low mobility such as nomadic access and up to 100 Mb/s for high mobility, such as mobile access [2]. Long-Term Evolution (LTE) and its advanced systems are deployed or will soon be deployed around the globe as practical 4G systems.

However, the number of mobile broadband users is increasing exponentially and will continue to increase as per recent trends. As the world is growing and people are getting more technologically advanced, they crave much faster Internet access, trendier and advanced mobile communication, and faultless and smooth connectivity. In a nutshell, the world today wants wonderful connectivity and instant access to information. As a result, more powerful laptops and smart phones are becoming popular nowadays, demanding advanced multimedia capabilities. This has led to the explosion of new wireless mobile devices and services.

1.3 Issues Related to Existing Systems

Technologies advance day by day and regular improvements are made based on the problems related to the existing applications. Some of them are listed below:

- *Scarcity of spectrum*: Spectrum is the most crucial element as far as wireless communication is concerned. Cellular frequencies utilize an ultra-high frequency band which ranges from several megahertz to gigahertz. Due to the increasing demand and exponential growth in the number of users, this frequency spectra is heavily crowded, making it very difficult for the wireless operators to explore it further. Thus, the need for new innovative technology that uses other frequency spectra (apart from those which are already in use) and new techniques which could further use those spectra effectively are increasing.

- *High energy consumption*: Energy conservation is the need of the day as the world is taking steps toward "Green Communication." It has been realized by cellular operators that the base station consumes much electricity and is approximately responsible for 70% of the electricity bill, which is huge [7]. The increase in energy consumption increases the amount of carbon dioxide in the atmosphere which is a threat for the environment. When 4G was introduced, energy efficiency was not a concern, but later on it became a big issue. Therefore, researchers are going on to make 5G energy efficient or "green."

- *Low data rates and QoS*: Apart from spectral efficiency and energy consumption, Quality of Service (QoS) provided by the operator and data rates are also major concerns. With the advent of changing the communication scenario, users want a real time experience which requires very high data rates. A larger network capacity is also needed to accommodate more new users without much degradation in the QoS. All of the above-mentioned issues demand high data rates and improvements in quality by wireless service providers. Moreover, these demands cannot be met by

4G as it has already reached its theoretical limit on data rates using existing technologies. Hence, 4G is insufficient to address the above challenges [2].

- *Unable to meet increasing traffic demands*: The wireless communication industry is observing an incremental increase in all domains. There is an enormous increase in the number of new users along with which there is also an increase in the amount of usage required by existing users. This tremendous increase has caused an overwhelming amount of traffic in the communication spectra. LTE enhancements have provided some of the methods such as heterogeneous networks, advanced MIMO, coordinated multipoint, and carrier aggregation (CA) to meet these traffic needs, but it will be unable to solve the problems caused by an increase of a hundred times more traffic demands by year 2020 and beyond, which is now called the 5G era [4].

1.4 Demystifying 5G: An Introduction

The mobile wireless industry has witnessed tremendous growth in recent years with the advancements in LTE which have brought together the entire mobile industry. These innovations have not been experienced before. Still there is a continuous demand for higher throughput, lower latency, and more data capacity to provide better broadband services. But these are only a few of the potential needs of 5G. Massive machine type communications and real Internet of Things (IoT) experiences require a new technology which needs to contain great improvements over its predecessors.

Necessity is the basis of new inventions, hence the drawbacks of LTE have led to the development of 5G. LTE is OFDM-based so it is very sensitive to frequency and clock offsets. Also, it has a high peak to average power ratio and spectral spikes are also present. With the increasing rise in the demands of users, 4G now will be replaced by 5G using Beam Division Multiple Access (BDMA). For operators, the quest for faster and higher-capacity mobile broadband, plus the opportunities for IoT, will remain the key drivers for 5G.

Apart from meeting the demands of the network capacity, traffic, and power consumption, 5G technology also includes many disruptive technologies such as including millimeter waves (mm-waves) and the visible light spectrum for communication purposes in order to increase the overall bandwidth of the system. This will increase the channel capacity by tens to hundreds of times compared to the existing 4G system. mm-waves and visible light communication (VLC) are not currently in use as they have problems such as a short range and non line of sight coverage issues. Such problems are effectively addressed using 5G technologies which are later discussed in Section 1.5.1. Re-allocation of bandwidth and network function virtualization are also techniques designated to meet the spectra needs. 5G is also a potential technology for IoT, which includes the interconnectivity of billions of devices and 5G will provide new ways to access and use IoT [1].

To meet these growing demands, it is essential for the 5G wireless network to use an efficient radio access technology along with the addition of the spectrum of mm-waves and VLC technology [5]. The 5G cellular system should also be capable of providing high data rates and the cell capacity has to be improved to meet increasing traffic demands. Specifically, from the data rates perspectives, 5G is expected to offer a minimum rate of 1 Gb/s anywhere and up to 5 and 50 Gb/s data rates for pedestrian and high mobility users, respectively [4].

The aim is to connect the entire world and achieve seamless and ubiquitous communications between everyone (people to people) and anything (people to machine, machine to machine), wherever they are (anywhere), whenever they need it (anytime), and by whatever electronic devices/services/networks they wish (anyhow) [2]. 5G promises a leap in technological capabilities, unleashing new opportunities to digitalize more segments of everyday life. For operators, 5G is an opportunity to make a big step beyond connectivity and capture value from the Internet of Things (IoT), optimized services, and mobile broadband. In this chapter, the proposed architecture of 5G is explained in detail. Along with that, technologies such as VLC, mm-wave communication, distributed antenna system (DAS), and spatial modulation are also elaborated on. This chapter provides detailed analysis of the features and characteristics of 5G and beyond.

1.5 Architecture of 5G

To contemplate the 5G network, the present multiple access techniques require improvements. Present techniques like OFDMA are effective, but some of their drawbacks need to be eliminated to meet user requirements. To meet the challenges that are being put forward for 5G, a change in the strategy of designing the 5G cellular architecture is the need of the day.

1.5.1 Key Technologies Emerging as a Base for 5G

1. *Distributed Antenna System (DAS)*: We know that wireless users stay indoors for ~80% of the time, while they only stay outside ~20% of the time [11]. In the present cellular architecture, if a mobile user wants to communicate inside or outside, an outside base station will perform the task because the technique which is used consists of a centralized or an outdoor base station, thus there is no discrimination between indoor and outdoor signals. The signals have to go through building walls, which causes penetration loss, no matter whether the signal is indoor or outdoor. This significantly damages the rates, energy efficiency, and spectral efficiency of the transmission.

   In a distributed antenna system, there are both active and passive elements. For example, when a signal comes from an outside tower and reaches a building, it gets attenuated and suffers from penetration loss. In DAS, a base station is installed in the building and the DAS element (master unit) is equipped with that capability. Then in the complete building, remote units are located at different places which coordinate with the master unit. This remote unit provides its signals to the other elements. So, the DAS consist of many antennas which are all distributed throughout a building. Hence, the user is much closer to the area from where the signal is coming. This provides a much better user experience.

2. *mm-wave and VLC technologies*: The spectrum which is used by communication systems is overcrowded. The same spectrum is shared by many operators and various technologies making it complex. Therefore, a new idea could be the introduction of higher frequency ranges in communication so that the spectrum which has not been utilized until now could be efficiently utilized, making more bandwidth available so that overcrowding of the signals and any accompanying interferences could

be avoided. Higher frequency bands are used by mm-wave and VLC technologies, which have not been traditionally used for cellular communications. This leads to an improvement in the quality of signals.

However, these high frequency mm-waves have their own disadvantages. These waves are absorbed by rain and gases. Also, they do not penetrate well through solid materials. Thus, it is a difficult task to use them for outdoor and long-distance applications. But mm-wave and VLC technologies provide a larger bandwidth for the transmission of signals. Some of the new techniques such as small cells are being employed in 5G to eliminate such problems. Besides finding the new spectrum through techniques which are not conventionally used such as mm-wave and VLC, spectrum utilization could be optimized using some technologies such as cognitive radio (CR) networks which are discussed later in this chapter in the section 1.5.1 [12].

3. *Small Cell*: The mm-wave communication which is discussed above has the problems of absorption by rain, loss of signal when it collides with buildings or any other object, foliage losses, and so on. To solve all these problems, small cells can be implemented in which more base stations at shorter distances are employed. These are called low power mini BS. As the user (mobile station) moves behind an obstacle, the device will automatically switch to the BS which is in better range of the device (Figure 1.1).

4. *Massive MIMO*: Conventional MIMO technology is used in 4G, but 5G uses massive MIMO technology. It is also known as a large-scale antenna system, very large MIMO, hyper MIMO or full dimensional MIMO. While conventional MIMO uses a small number of antennas, massive MIMO utilizes larger arrays of antennas. This is done to exploit the potentially large capacity gains. The extra antennas of massive MIMO focus energy in the smaller regions of space (more directivity) and this brings huge improvements in throughput and energy efficiency.

In massive MIMO, the number of antennas is much larger, providing directivity to the signals. More directivity leads to less interference and more spectrum efficiency. Outdoor base stations are equipped with large antenna arrays and are connected to indoor base stations via optical fiber which is again distributed among different antennas of a complete building (a unit) called a DAS. Outdoor mobile users are equipped with a limited number of antennas, but their collaboration

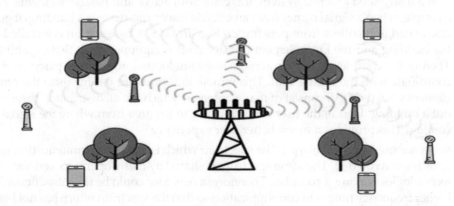

FIGURE 1.1
Small Cell.

FIGURE 1.2
Diagram of massive MIMO.

with each other forms a virtual large antenna array. Thus, a virtual MIMO link is established consisting of BS antenna arrays and a large antenna array. Large antenna arrays communicate with both outdoor base stations and stations and distributed antenna elements of BS and are installed outside every unit (building) (Figure 1.2).

As shown in Figure 1.2, MIMO consists of multiple antenna elements at both transmitter and receiver ends (typically tens to hundreds). More information data can be accommodated because of the addition of multiple antennas as a greater degree of freedom is obtained. A massive MIMO system contains all the benefits of a conventional MIMO and additionally enhances the performance of the system in terms of reliability and spectral and energy efficiency [8]. Also, in a massive MIMO, by using linear pre-coding and a detection method the effects of noise and fast fading could be mitigated. Hence, a massive MIMO system serves as a potential candidate for the 5G wireless communication system [2].

However, there are some challenges related to the above-mentioned technology. The fabrication of low cost and low precision components which work effectively is a major challenge in the MIMO technology. Synchronization of terminals and a reduction in internal power consumption are also some concerns of massive MIMO technology which are eliminated using spatial modulation, as discussed in Section 1.5.1.

5. *Beam forming*: The complications of massive MIMO can be alleviated using beam forming technology. Massive MIMO passes the information in every direction at once causing severe interference of signals. So, by analogy, beam forming is just like a traffic light over the base station. Instead of broadcasting in every direction, it focuses the stream in a particular direction avoiding interference and enabling more precise work (Figure 1.3).

6. *Mobile Femto Cell*: A mobile femto cell is another key technology of a 5G wireless system. 5G cellular architecture is heterogeneous, that is, it contains macro cells, micro cells, and relays. It combines the concepts of mobile relay and femto cells [9].

FIGURE 1.3
Diagram of Beamforming.

To accommodate high mobility users, that is, the users traveling in moving buses or trains, this concept can be used. The users inside the bus or car are connected to each other and they communicate with the antenna array placed outside the moving bus or car to communicate with outdoor BS. For the individuals inside the bus or train, it serves as a regular base station. A mobile femto cell and all the individuals associated with it are viewed as a single unit by the BS thus separating indoor and outdoor scenarios.

5G promises to provide flawless connectivity for users whether they are moving or stationary. A mobile femto cell can serve as the technology for providing such uninterrupted connectivity among the users traveling inside a moving vehicle. It consists of a small cell that moves around and dynamically changes its connection to the core network, making the mobile femto cell an intelligent transport system. The applications of mobile femto cells include deployment in public transport systems such as buses, trains, cars, and so on to enhance the end user experience, increasing the QoS, and improving the spectral efficiency of the overall system.

As compared to a direct transmission scheme, that is, when users inside any vehicle communicate with the BS, a mobile femto cell is much better as it increases the spectral efficiency. In addition to this benefit, a mobile femto cell offers many other advantages. Reductions in energy consumption and signaling overhead reduction are some of them. As the range of communication is reduced, less energy is consumed by the users inside a mobile femto cell. A mobile femto cell also performs handoff on behalf of its users which reduces the overhead of handoff from the serving BS [2].

7. *Spatial modulation (SM)*: To mitigate the problem related to massive MIMO, spatial modulation can be used apart from beam forming. Spatial modulation is a technique which mitigates the problems related to massive MIMO. A massive MIMO system faces three major issues: inter antenna synchronization; inter channel interference; and multiple radio frequency (RF) chains [10]. By using spatial modulation, low complexity MIMO systems can be established.

In spatial modulation, each part of the data to be transmitted is given a different spatial position and that part is encoded instead of simultaneously sending multiple data streams. For mobile communication, transmitting and receiving antennas are required. Suppose the first 4 letters of the alphabet, A, B, C, D, need to be transmitted and the way they need to be transmitted is by using signals. Now, these signals will be linked to the constellation diagrams. So, for 4 signals, you will have 4 constellation points. Different antennas are present at the transmitting end. The first antenna is related to symbol A, the next to B, and so on. Thus a single RF chain is required to transmit data in spatial modulation, whereas multiple RF chains are required in conventional MIMO for the transmission of data. Also, spatial modulation is significantly more energy efficient as compared to all the other MIMO systems.

Spatial modulation reduces the complexity of the device, since a low complexity SM system could be designed for any number of transmitting and receiving antennas. It also reduces power consumption and provides two data streams with a single RF chain. Thus, high data rates could be offered.

8. *Cognitive radio networks*: We have discussed the technologies such as mm-wave and VLC technology which increase the complete bandwidth of the system by using the spectrum which is not presently in use. A radio frequency signal is used in the existing system for the transmission, but a large part of this bandwidth is not utilized efficiently or it is underutilized. So, a CR network is innovative software designed to effectively utilize this radio spectrum [9].

   A CR network employs a secondary network along with the primary network. The secondary system can be either be on an interference-free basis or an interference-tolerant basis. The transmission in the CR network should be done by taking the surrounding environment into consideration. The CR network shares the spectrum band of the primary licensed system with a secondary system. In an interference-free CR network, the spectrum is allotted to the CR network when it is not in use by the primary user. Using spectrum sensing, the CR network first monitors and then allocates the resources to the secondary user if they are not used by the primary user and feeds this information back to the CR transmitter. This optimizes the spectrum capability as the spectrum is being used at the time when it becames "idle" [13].

   In an interference-tolerant CR network, the spectrum is shared with the secondary user even when the licensed or primary user is using it, keeping the threshold of interference within limits. An interference-tolerant CR system is more efficient in terms of spectrum and energy utilization as compared to interference-free CR networks. But small changes in user densities, interference threshold, and transmission behavior can affect the performance of a licensed system. In order to explore additional bands and increase the capacity, a hybrid cellular network has also been developed [2].

9. *Device-to-device Communication (D2D)*: In D2D, communication devices will be allowed to communicate with each other without using BS. This can be done in areas where the coverage is very poor. There are four types of D2D communication: Device relaying with operator-controlled link establishment, direct D2D communication with operator-controlled link establishment, device relaying with device-controlled link establishment, and direct D2D communication.

   D2D communication can revolutionize the user experience by reducing the latency and power consumption and increasing peak data rates. Dense spectrum reuse can be done using this technology. The BS and the traffic related to it will no longer be the area of concern for establishing a communication link between the source and the destination [3]. However, there are some challenges associated with D2D communication technology, such as the privacy and security of the users.

Peer discovery, that is, the device must be able to find a nearby device quickly and with low power consumption, is also a major task. Additionally, resource allocation is a critical task in D2D communication [6].

1.5.2 Working of 5G

The 5G network architecture consists of Radio Access Networks (RANs), an aggregator, an Internet protocol network, nano core, and so on. 5G offers remote management to the user, hence the user gets faster and better solutions.

As discussed in Figure 1.4, a flat IP concept is used by a 5G network so that different RANs can use the same single nano core for communication. RANs that are supported by 5G architecture include Global System for Mobile Communication (GSM), General Packet Radio Service (GPRS)/Enhanced Data for GSM Evolution (EDGE), Universal Mobile Telecommunications System (UMTS), Long Term Evolution (LTE), LTE-advanced, Worldwide Interoperability for Microwave Access (WiMax) Wireless Fidelity (WiFi), Code Division Multiple Access (CDMA2000), Evolution Data Optimized (EV-DO), Interim Standard (IS-95), and so on. The hierarchical architecture uses normal IP addresses for the identification of devices, whereas a flat IP architecture identifies devices using symbolic names.

This architecture reduces the overall cost to a great extent as it mitigates the number of network elements in the data path. It also helps in minimizing latency as different RANs are connected to a single nano core. Flat IP is the key concept which makes 5G acceptable and compatible for all existing technologies. Flat IP architecture also reduces the number of network elements in the data path which lowers capital expenditure and operation costs.

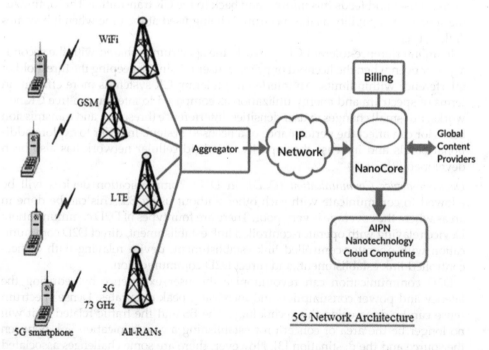

FIGURE 1.4
5G Network Architecture.

The architecture consists of mobile units, all-RANs, a network aggregator, and the 5G nano core. The mobile unit communicates with the RANs, which passes the signals toward the aggregator. It is the most essential unit as it aggregates the traffic coming from different RANs and routes it toward the gateway. The next component in the architecture is the 5G nano core. It consists of nanotechnology, cloud computing, and an all-IP architecture. Nanotechnology is the technology that works on nano materials, that is, between 0.1 and 100 nm. Nanotechnology will revolutionize the mobile communication industry by making it more intelligent and having an impact on sensors and security. In the 5G nano core, mobiles will be termed as nano-equipment (NE) and these will also lead to the next generation level having self-cleaning and powering capabilities. NE will be transparent and flexible; it will be able to sense the environment.

Cloud computing utilizes the Internet as well as centralized remote servers for the maintenance of data and applications of the users. In the 5G network, this remote sensor acts like a content provider. It permits the consumers to use applications without any installation and they can access their files from any computer across the globe with the use of the Internet. An all-IP network has many advantages. It mitigates the cost, provides universal access, and also enhances the users' experience.

1.6 Advantages of 5G Over the Existing Mobile Generations

5G, the next generation leap, will continue the trend by adding to the achievements of 4G and will bring more opportunities and facilities for customers and industry stakeholders.

- *Low (real time) latency*: Latency is the amount of time it takes for data transfer to take place. When you open a web page, it requires some time to open. The time it takes to open is its latency. A buffering period while watching a video is also a latency. Thus, from the examples, it can be stated that latency should be as low as possible. As there has been an increase in the number of users in the existing 4G system, latency has also increased. Latency of less than 1 ms can be achieved in the 5G mm-wave. The applications which need a real time environment such as live gaming and so on will be supported by 5G. This leads to immediate connection establishment and release with the 5G network by 5G smart phones. Hence, the traffic load is decreased on 5G base stations.

- *Higher spectrum efficiency*: 5G will provide higher spectrum efficiency as compared to its counterparts as it employs higher frequencies (e.g., VLC and mm-waves) and the unlicensed spectrum. It also uses technologies such as CR networks and network function virtualization (NFV) which work on the concept of optimizing the existing frequency. This will lead to the effective utilization of the present spectrum as well as efficient use of the spectrum which is not presently in use.

- *High data rates*: Data rates will be very high in 5G (near real time communication). The latencies provided by a 4G roundtrip currently are in the order of a 15 ms sub-frame time. This includes necessary overheads for resource allocation and access. 5G is expected to increase the data rates to beyond 1 Gb per second and will provide higher broadband density to users.

- *Green communications by 5G*: "Green" is the term related to a reduction in carbon dioxide emissions in the environment. Energy efficient wireless communication is the need of the day. A 5G wireless system must be designed in such a way to reduce the energy requirements in order to achieve a greener wireless communication system [7]. In 5G, indoor and outdoor communications are separated, which is a promising strategy in the deployment of energy consumption. This is because of the favorable channel conditions they can offer between the transmitters and receivers. When the indoor traffic is separated from the outdoor, the macro BS will have less pressure for the allocation of radio resources, hence it can transmit with less power requirements, thus reducing the overall energy consumption and resulting in a degradation in the level of CO_2 emissions. Therefore, 5G is considered "green." Also, the mm-wave and VLC technologies are also considered energy efficient in a 5G wireless communication system [2].

1.7 5G as a Foundation of Many Technologies

5G will be the foundation for various new technologies which will make life much easier and Hi-Tech (Figure 1.5).

5G will serve as a driving force and the basis of many intellectual and smart services such as IoT, wireless sensor networks, environment monitoring, virtual reality, autonomous driving, and many more things which we cannot even imagine. 5G will also serve as a basis of IoT which will interconnect smart things to Internet to camouflage real world. It will improve peoples' lives by creating new and interactive business opportunities, and making businesses, homes, cities, transportation, agriculture, traffic, industries, and medication smarter than ever before. IoT is the interconnection of things as well as humans to things. With the evolution of 5G, IoT will acquire new wings for flight.

Environment monitoring will allow the monitoring of tsunamis, earthquakes, cyclones, and so on so that damage caused by these in terms of lives could be minimized. Autonomous driving will lead to driverless and fully equipped cars and wireless sensor networks will enable doctors to examine the human body without injecting any physical device inside

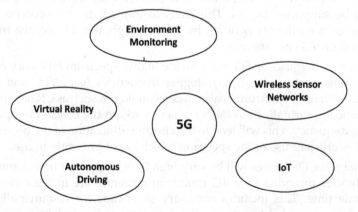

FIGURE 1.5
Various Technologies related to 5G.

it. Thus, interconnectivity between things and individuals to make life much easier and more comfortable will be guided by 5G wireless technology. All of these astonishing features could be readily achieved by 5G technology.

1.8 Beyond 5G

1.8.1 Future Challenges for 5G

- *Optimizing performance metrics*: There are various performance matrices such as energy efficiency, spectral efficiency, delay, QoS, reliability, fairness of users, implementation complexity, and so on that are associated with the communication system. Due to high complexity, evaluation in a wireless communication network is usually done using only two or three performance metrics, neglecting the others. Many other performance metrics should be considered from all different prospectives for an overall and fair assessment of 5G wireless systems and a trade-off must be maintained among all of them [2].

- *Realistic channel models for 5G wireless systems*: Realistic channel models for a typical 5G system such as massive MIMO and high mobility channels (buses, trains, etc.) with proper accuracy and complexity are needed. Compared to the conventional channels which have low mobility, the channels having high mobility suffer more severe fading and their characterization is also very challenging [2].

- *Reducing signal processing complexity for massive MIMO*: In massive MIMO, numerous signals are present and the main complexity lies in the processing of these signals. Transmitting and receiving signals are also very lengthy as far as massive MIMO is concerned. Thus, a search algorithm has to be performed over many possible permutations of signals which is also one of the biggest challenges for 5G technology [2].

- *Interference management for CR networks*: Interference is a major issue in CR networks especially in interference-tolerant CR networks. Regulation of the transmitting power is essential so that the CR network could efficiently exist along with the primary or licensed network. Various methods could be applied to face such a challenge. Interference cancellation techniques could be implemented at CR receivers. Proper feedback mechanisms should be employed which periodically inform the CR network about the recent interference status of the spectrum. Another solution could be a central unit and the interference state information could be sent from the primary spectrum to it. Then that central unit must be kept updated about every change that is being made in the licensed spectrum. Any CR network which wants a licensed spectrum should also update the central unit about itself and whether or not the interference will go above the threshold limit. The central unit would send a beacon signal which has to be followed by each CR network [2].

1.8.2 Conclusion

This chapter discusses the need for 5G, its architecture, applications, advantages, and what challenges 5G has to face. The performance requirements of 5G in terms of spectral efficiency, energy efficiency, data rate, cell average throughput, and capacity are also explained.

The architecture of 5G has been proposed with separated outdoor and indoor applications. Some technologies which will play a key role in the development of 5G include massive MIMO, DAS, mobile femto cell, spatial modulation, CR networks, D2D, VLC, and mm-waves. Green communication with 5G is also an important topic which is discussed. The advantages of 5G over existing technologies and various services which require 5G such as IoT, autonomous driving, and so on are mentioned. Finally, the challenges 5G has to face and the possibilities beyond 5G are taken into account [2].

5G will coexist with past wireless generations. It will make the lives of people faster, more efficient, and smarter. It is the next generation technology and will bring more innovative and realistic experiences. Apart from all the positive aspects that 5G has, each new technology has to face many challenges. 5G will be able to meet the needs of the changing communication system. On one hand, it will provide "green communication" (energy efficient communication) and on other it will increase spectrum efficiency by involving mm-wave and VLC technologies along with CR networks which will be employed in the present RF spectrum. 5G promises to provide real time or low latency and also very high data rates. Projects based on the innovative cases of 5G range from industries to agriculture to smart cities and transportation and are ongoing. However, there are some challenges related to 5G as discussed above. 5G, the next generation, will definitely add another color to the ever-growing telecommunication industry.

Acknowledgments

We thank our parents for their support and motivation. Also, we would like to thank our colleagues who helped us in the entire process of writing.

References

1. J. G. Andrews, S. V. Hanly, A. C. K. Soong, and J. C. Zhang, "What Will 5G Be?" *IEEE J. Sel. Areas Commun.*, vol. 32, no. 6, June 2014, pp. 1065–1082.
2. C.-X. Wang, F. Haider, Y. Yang, D. Yuan, H. M. Aggoune, H. Haas, S. Fletcher, and E. Hepsaydir, "Cellular Architecture and Key Technologies for 5G Wireless Communication Networks." *IEEE Commun. Mag.*, Vol. 52, Issue 2, February 2014, pp. 122–130.
3. N. Bhushan, J. Li, D. Malladi, R. Gilmore, D. Brenner, A. Damnjanovic, R. T. Sukhavasi, C. Patel, and S. Geirhofer, "Network Densification: The Dominant Theme for Wireless Evolution into 5G," *IEEE Commun. Mag.*, Vol. 52, Issue 2, February 2014, pp. 82–89.
4. W. Roh, J.-Y. Seol, J. Park, B. Lee, J. Lee, Y. Kim, J. Cho, and K. Cheun, "Millimeter-Wave Beamforming as an Enabling Technology for 5G Cellular Communications: Theoretical Feasibility and Prototype Results," *IEEE Commun. Mag.*, Vol. 52, Issue 2, February 2014, pp. 106–113.
5. T.S. Rappaport, S. Sun, R. Mayzus, M. Zhao, Y. Azar, K. Wang, G. N. Wong, J. K. Schulz, M. Samimi, and F. Gutierrez, "Millimeter Wave Mobile Communications for 5G Cellular: It Will Work!," *IEEE Access*, vol. 1, 2013, pp. 335–349.
6. A. Gupta, (Student Member, IEEE), and R. K. Jhaa, "Survey of 5G Network: Architecture and Emerging Technologies," *IEEE Access*, vol. 3, 2015, pp. 1206–1232.
7. C. Han et al., "Green Radio: Radio Techniques to Enable Energy Efficient Wireless Networks," *IEEE Commun. Mag.*, vol. 49, no. 6, June 2011, pp. 46–54.

8. F. Rusek et al., "Scaling Up MIMO: Opportunities and Challenges with Very Large Arrays," *IEEE Sig. Proc. Mag.*, vol. 30, no. 1, January 2013, pp. 40–60.
9. F. Haider et al., "Spectral Efficiency Analysis of Mobile Femtocell Based Cellular Systems," *Proc. IEEE ICCT '11*, Jinan, China, September 2011, pp. 347–351.
10. M. D. Renzo et al., "Spatial Modulation for Generalized MIMO: Challenges, Opportunities, and Implementation," *Proc. IEEE*, vol. 102, no. 1, January 2014, pp. 56–103.
11. V. Chandrasekhar, J. G. Andrews, and A. Gatherer, "Femtocell Networks: A Survey," *IEEE Commun. Mag.*, vol. 46, no. 9, September 2008, pp. 59–67.
12. X. Hong et al., "Secondary Spectrum Access Networks: Recent Developments on the Spatial Models," *IEEE Vehic. Tech. Mag.*, vol. 4, no. 2, June 2009, pp. 36–43.
13. X. Hong et al., "Capacity Analysis of Hybrid Cognitive Radio Networks with Distributed VAAs," *IEEE Trans. Vehic. Tech.*, vol. 59, no. 7, September 2010, pp. 3510–3523.

2

Basic of 5G Networks: Review

A.N. Ibrahim, M.F.L. Abdullah, and M.S.M. Gismalla

CONTENTS

2.1 Introduction

Mobile communication technology is a revolutionary paradigm shift undergoing extensive transformations and is used to connect people around the world. This technology is not only used for daily communication, but also for data transmission. The users of mobile devices need more advanced technology with many advantages. This requires a new design and innovations in network topology and the architecture of mobile communication technology to achieve these goals. Mobile communication technology was categorized as "Generation" because there is a big "Generation gap" in this technology [1]. The development of this technology, starting from supporting the analog voice only, has become the powerful system which provides countless different applications for the increasing demands of mobile users [2]. Subsequently, digital mobile communication systems are continuously on a mission to answer the growing needs of human beings [3].

2.2 The Evolution of Mobile Communication Technology

The first Generation (1G) mobile communication technology was introduced in the 1980s and was an analog system with speeds up to 2.4 kbps. It was used for transmitting voice signals. The mobile devices of 1G technology were very large and had limited capacity. Hence, a mobile device was usually mounted in trucks or cars and the smallest device was a brief-case model [4]. 1G technology was not user-friendly for future development because of the limited technology and capacity to serve and cover a large area [4]. This is because the operating range of those mobile devices was limited to ten meters from a single base station [5]. Additionally, the mobile devices of 1G technology were very large and carried high prices for devices and tariffs. Most of the 1G mobile devices could only access one channel and users could not do anything to avoid the interference from anyone nearby who was using the same channel [5]. To overcome this problem and to satisfy the exploding demand for this technology, the industry developed the second generation of mobile communication technology.

Second generation (2G) technology was introduced in the 1990s with speeds up to 14.4–64 kbps. This technology was different compared to the previous generation because it used digital transmission which is based on a digital system and network infrastructure. In addition, that technology could support short message service (SMS) text messages, which were a new variant of communication technology at that time. The digital system improved voice clarity and reduced noise in the line by using digital coding. In addition, the batteries of the mobile devices lasted longer because the digital systems required less battery power. The mobile devices of 2G technology employed digital speech transmission and had a dedicated channel for the exchange of control information between a terminal and base station during a call [5]. In addition, the mobile devices were able to communicate with more than one base station [5] and would automatically choose the best available radio channel [5]. 2G technology success and the ensuing massive demand ultimately led to the next generation technology.

Third generation (3G) succeeded 2G mobile communication technology and was introduced in the 2000s. This technology offered advanced services because it carried digital broadband packet data as compared to 2G which used a digital narrowband packet data. The main purpose of 3G was to develop a universal infrastructure able to support the existing and future services of mobile networks. This technology supported universal access and enhanced roaming with speeds up to 2 Mbps for local coverage area and 144–384 kbps for wide coverage area. This technology provided faster communication as compared to the previous generations. 3G also offered high speed web with more security, sending and receiving large emails or messages, television (TV) streaming, video conferencing, web browsing, and navigational maps. The limitation of this technology was the slow speed for multimedia data and to move beyond this problem, the fourth generation of mobile communication technology was proposed.

Fourth generation (4G) featured digital broadband packet data with high throughput and was introduced in 2011. Nowadays, the increasing demand for data requirements among mobile users has become one of the issues needed to upgrade the system. Therefore, improvements were made on downlink and uplink throughput rates by employing higher modulation techniques [6]. 4G technology not only overcame the problems and limitations of the previous generations, but this evolution also increased the bandwidth, enhanced the quality of services (QoS), and reduced the cost of resources. In addition, this technology offered high spectral efficiency, high voice quality, low latency, easy access to the Internet,

TABLE 2.1

The Evolution of 1G to 4G Mobile Communication Technology

Generation	Time Period	Definition	Characteristics	Data Rates
1G	1980–1990	Analog	Voice only	2.4 kbps
2G	1990–2000	Digital narrowband circuit data/packet data	Data analog voice, multimedia messaging service (MMS), web browsing	14.4–64 kbps
3G	2000–2011	Digital broadband packet data	Universal access, portability, video calling	2 Mbps
4G	2011–Present	Digital broadband packet data with high throughput	HD streaming, portability increased to worldwide roaming	200 Mbps–1 Gbps

streaming media, video calling, and so on with speeds of 200 Mbps to 1 Gbps [6]. However, this technology was very expensive and hard to implement because of the complex hardware required. Table 2.1 shows the evolution of 1G to 4G mobile communication technology.

Figure 2.1 shows the evolution of mobile technology over time. Based on Figure 2.1, 1G was an analog system and was comprised of the following technologies, which are Advanced Mobile Telephone System (AMTS), Improved Mobile Telephone Service (IMTS), Push to Talk (PTT), and Mobile Telephone System (MTS) [7]. 2G consisted of the following technologies, which are Global System for Mobile Communication (GSM), Enhanced Data Rates for GSM Evolution (EDGE), General Packet Radio Service (GPRS), and Code Division Multiple Access (CDMA) [7]. 3G was comprised of Universal Mobile Telecommunication System (UMTS), Wireless Local Area Network (WLAN), High Speed Downlink Packet Access (HSPDA), Wideband CDMA, and Bluetooth [7]. 4G was able to deliver faster service and provided better mobile broadband experiences in addition to providing mobile web access with high quality video and images. However, 4G LTE (Long Term Evolution) was introduced because 4G technology was not able to fully reach the required range. The download process, streaming, and browsing become faster with a better connectivity, hence it is closer to meeting the criteria of a standard technology. Next, LTE-Advanced was introduced which has more progressive technologies and standards in addition to being capable of delivering faster and bigger data. 4G technology is comprised of

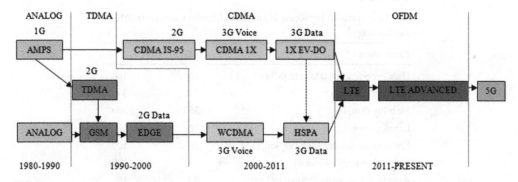

FIGURE 2.1

The evolution of mobile technology over time.

LTE, Multiple Input Multiple Output (MIMO) smart antenna technologies, Worldwide Interoperability for Microwave Access (WiMAX), Mobile Broadband Wireless Access (MBWA), and Orthogonal Frequency Division Multiplexing (OFDM).

2.3 Fifth Generation (5G) Technology

The exciting growth of laptops, smartphones, and other devices with improved applications that connect to the wireless network are expected to use up additional spectrum and need extra capacity because of the higher spectral efficiency of 4G technology [3]. Nowadays, 4G offers users access to the faster speed of data with a latency range of 40–60 ms. However, the numbers of mobile users in this world are increasing dramatically. In 2020, traffic sizes are estimated to grow 1000 times [8], hence the number of connected devices will increase 10 to 100 times more than that in recent times. As a consequence, high capacity and low energy consumption are required to overcome the limitations of the recent mobile communication technology. The researchers started searching and researching for solutions for the next wireless system to overcome the problems and to fulfill the expected massive demand in 2020 with the explosive growth of advanced devices.

5G technology will be the next generation of mobile communication technology, which must be based on enhanced services, system performance, and user experiences. 5G is expected to be launched in 2020 and is predicted to support new frequency bands with wider spectral bandwidth per channel. 5G technology will be implemented with 1–10 Gbps user data rates, superior spectrum frequency, up to 500 kilometers per hour (km/h) of mobility, a reduction in latency to as low as 1 ms, and a massive increase in the connection density which will be able to support up to 1 million devices per square kilometer (devices/km^2). The expected increment of energy efficiency is 100× times greater than that of the 1000 mW/ Mbps/s in International Mobile Telecommunication (IMT) -2000 [9]. In addition, the area of traffic capacity for 5G technology requirements is 10 Mbps/m^2 and the expected peak data rate is 20 Gbps. 5G technology will provide better coverage and be able to generate ultrahigh speeds to enhance the usability of mobile devices. Table 2.2 shows the comparison between 4G and 5G mobile communication technology.

TABLE 2.2

The Comparison between 4G and 5G Mobile Communication Technology

Parameters	4G	5G
User experienced data rate (Mbps)	10	100
Spectrum efficiency	1×	3×
Mobility (km/h)	350	500
Latency (ms)	10	1
Connection density (devices/km^2)	10^5	10^6
Network energy efficiency	1×	100×
Area traffic capacity (Mbps/m^2)	0.1	10
Peak data rate (Gbps)	1	20

The predecessors of mobile communication technology provided substantial increases in peak bit rates. 5G technology will have an additional substantial increase in peak bit rates, high capacity to support moving mobile devices, higher reality, lower battery consumption, and larger data volume per unit area [3]. The system of 5G technology will become more powerful and provide more efficiency and features to mobile users because this technology includes all types of advanced technology. 5G technology will fascinate users and lead to the increased use of mobile devices which offer more gaming options, global access, interactive media, and Internet and video with high resolution. In addition, 5G technology will provide lower cost per bit, large broadcasting of data, high speed, and high capacity, hence users will be able to download and upload any comprehensive multimedia with the finest QoS.

Research directions are important because they lead to fundamental changes and become a key technological driving force for future 5G architecture realization. Figure 2.2 shows the

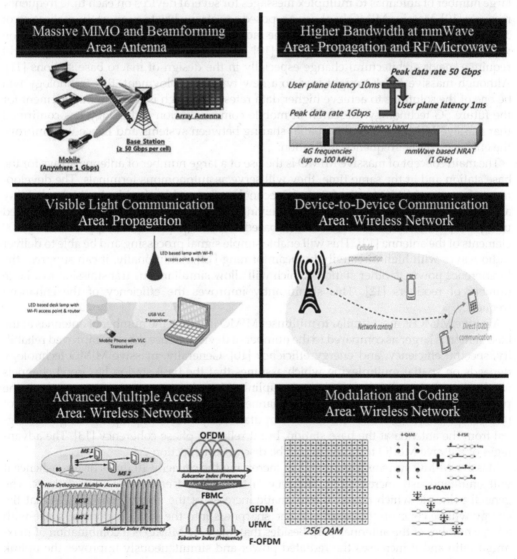

FIGURE 2.2
Research direction in 5G mobile communication technology.

research directions proposed in 5G mobile communication technology. Currently, there are six directions proposed in 5G technology which are massive MIMO and beamforming, higher bandwidth at millimeter wave (mmWave), visible light communication (VLC), Device-to-Device (D2D) communication, followed by advanced multiple access, and modulation. All of these proposed directions will be discussed in this chapter.

2.4 Massive MIMO and Beamforming

Massive MIMO is an emerging technology which involves high quality and an extremely large number of antennas to multiplex messages for several devices on each time frequency resource [10]. Massive MIMO has been proposed as a strong key to support the realization of 5G technology. This technology focuses the radiated energy toward the intended direction while minimizing the intercell interference [10]. However, massive MIMO technology might require a major architectural change especially in the design of macro base stations [11]. Although massive MIMO might lead to a new type of deployment, this technology will be one of the solutions to achieve higher data rates [10] which is the main requirement for the future 5G technology. Research in mobile communication technology has confirmed that massive MIMO will enable spatial sharing between systems and hence will improve the efficiency of the frequency utilization.

The main concept of massive MIMO is the use of a large number of antenna arrays for the base station and at the same time, they will serve as autonomous terminals. The development of massive MIMO for the future 5G technology is capable of achieving high reliability and high speeds for transmitting and receiving signals [12]. Terminals can be simplified using a sophisticated wireless entranced based station equipped with approximately 100 elements of the antenna [12]. This will enable simple signal processing and be able to deliver radio waves with high directivity by beamforming [12]. Additionally, it can suppress the interference power to other stations which will allow simultaneous transmission to a large number of receivers [12]. This significantly improves the efficiency of the enhanced frequency.

Massive MIMO is most similar to multiuser MIMO in which the number of antennas at the base station is larger as compared to the number of devices, hence there is improved reliability, spectral efficiency, and energy efficiency [10]. Generally, massive MIMO technology depends on spatial multiplexing which assumes that the base station has good channels for the downlink and uplink [10]. At the uplink side, when the user equipment sends the pilot signal, the base station will send a channel response for each of the different types of user equipment [10]. Massive MIMO is computationally a very simple processing of the signal from the antenna at the base station, but it relies on phase coherency [13]. The advantages of massive MIMO technology will be discussed in Section 2.4.

Massive MIMO systems are capable of increasing the capacity 10 times or more, hence it will simultaneously increase the efficiency of the radiated energy by 100s of times. The general principle which makes the dramatic increase of the energy efficiency is that the energy will be concentrated with extreme sharpness into the small regions of space with a large number of the antennas [13]. Besides that, massive MIMO is a combination of maximum ratio and it increases the radiated power and simultaneously improves the uplink spectral efficiency [10]. In addition, massive MIMO systems are combined with the base system of OFDM and each of the subcarriers in the massive MIMO will have approximately the same channel gain [10]. Hence, massive MIMO will also simplify the layers of multiple access.

Mobile communication technology is characterized by multipath fading. Fading will reduce the strength of the received signal at certain times [10]. This problem will happen when the waves resulting from the multiple paths interfere with the signal which is sent from the base stations through the multiple paths before it reaches the terminal [13]. Therefore, to overcome this problem, massive MIMO depends on the law of large numbers and beamforming to diminish the effect of latency which is produced by the multipath channel [10]. In addition, the expensive ultralinear 50 W amplifier which is used in the conventional systems will be replaced with hundreds of low cost amplifiers with output powers in the milliWatt range. Thus, this is one of the advantages of a massive MIMO system because it can be developed with low power components which are less inexpensive for the system [13].

However, there are certain limitations that need to be addressed before the deployment of the massive MIMO system. Generally, each terminal of the massive MIMO system is assigned an orthogonal uplink pilot sequence [10]. The maximum number of orthogonal uplink pilot sequences is limited by the channel delay spread. The effect of reusing pilots from one cell to another and the negative consequences of this are called pilot contamination [13]. The basic phenomenon of pilot contamination is not specific to the massive MIMO system, however, its effect on massive MIMO appears to be more radical than that on classical MIMO [13]. Another issue of limitation is the time division duplexing which is applied in the massive MIMO system and relies on channel reciprocity [13]. In addition, the other challenges that need to be overcome in order to implement the massive MIMO system are the synchronization of the antenna units, diminishing the computational complexity, and the realization of the distributed system [10].

A comprehensive review of massive MIMO is presented to describe the technology gaps and challenges that may inhibit the implementation of this emerging technology in the 5G network. Suggestions of solutions and discussion by academics and researchers is required in order to develop the technology [14,15,16]. The large numbers of antennas used in massive MIMO have produced a high and unlimited capacity in cellular networks [17,18]. The capacity of cellular networks can be computed by the third Shannon law as illustrated in [19], with the mathematical Equation given below:

$$C = B \log_2 (1 + \text{SNR}) \tag{2.1}$$

where C refers to the channel capacity, B is the bandwidth of the channel measured in Hertz, and signal to noise ratio (SNR) is the ratio of signal power to noise power measured in decibel units. Massive MIMO is characterized by a gold mine of study problems. As of now, massive MIMO technology is still lacking and faces more difficulties such as computational complexity, synchronization of antenna elements, cost-performance, and delayed power. This opens the minds of researchers in industry and academics to tackle and suggest new solutions to support the 5G networks.

2.5 Higher Bandwidth at mmWave

Currently, all of the electronic devices use the specific radio frequency spectrum which is commonly limited up to 30 GHz. This entire range of the radio frequency is currently highly congested because of the rapid increase in the number of mobile users. Hence, the future mobile communication standards are focusing more on standards in order to use more than 30 GHz of the radio frequency band. The mmWave spectrum recently attracted research interest among researchers and technologists since the extremely large available bandwidth could potentially lead to rates of multiple Gbps per users [20]. The broadcasting frequency of the mmWave spectrum is 30–300 GHz as compared to the currently broadcasting frequency used for mobile devices which is 6 GHz [20]. Additionally, there are several bands which have been considered, such as multipoint distribution service band (28–30 GHz), E-band (71–76 GHz, 81–86 GHz, and 92–95 GHz), and the license free band (60 GHz) [10]. If all of these bands were implemented, several tens of GHz would become available for the future 5G technology, which is also offering more bandwidth compared to the current systems [10].

There are many technical problem which need to be addressed in order to achieve the high potential rates of the mmWave band for the future 5G mobile communication technology [20]. Basically, the frequency bands have mostly been utilized for outdoor point-to-point line of sight (LOS) backhaul links due to the absence of a reasonable costs of the components and high propagation losses [10]. There are two issues that need to be addressed in order to fully exploit these unused frequency bands; they are support mobility in non-line of sight (NLOS) environments and sufficiently large coverage areas [10]. In addition, supporting NLOS communication links is important for cellular networks with high mobility and higher error free data rates [10]. In addition, to overcome the undesired path loss (which is an element needed to use the mmWave frequency bands for mobile communications), an appropriate beamforming scheme needs to focus the transmitting and the receiving powers in the desired direction. It is quite challenging to use the mmWave band in mobile network technology because it is possible to move the receiving and transmitting nodes, hence the coordination among multiple nodes are difficult and the channels will have a complicated structure [20].

The main reason the mmWave band has been idle until recently is because the mmWave band has been considered unsuitable for mobile networks because of its rather unfriendly propagation qualities [21]. This includes the strong path loss, low diffraction around obstacles, low penetration through objects, rain and atmospheric absorption, high equipment costs, and strong phase noise [21].

2.6 Visible Light Communication (VLC)

The optical band was suggested as a complementary technology to radio frequency (RF) in the short-range in order to deliver data with high rates by using white light emitting diodes (LEDs) [22]. The visible light communication founded on white LEDs represents a newly emerging practice for the optical wireless communication area, where practical implementation of the single node-to-node link is studied, and an acceptable bit error rate (BER) has resulted in a 1.5 m range for the VLC scheme [23]. The VLC with LED lights are considered to be both communication and illumination techniques in indoor environments. It has a low cost due to the solid-state element used and the VLC consists of multiple LEDs with several devices connected in an indoor environment [24]. The system was simulated and implemented, and the packet error rate (PER) and daylight effect were evaluated. The effect of daylight may require more studies in the future with colored wall paints and their reflections.

Recently, optical wireless communication (OWC) has garnered great attention in indoor communication systems, with VLC considered to be one of the key techniques that offer high data transmission in indoor communication for 5G networks. However, the same issues in the OWC must be considered in the design of proper indoor channels, such as direct LOS connection, multipath dispersion, field of view at the detector, and the link structure [25]. Unlimited free spectra with lower interference represent an ideal case for the communication system. This can be accomplished via installing a system to include the unlicensed electromagnetic spectrum (EM) through visible light. Three basic colors, red, green and blue, are evaluated based on wavelength of the photodiode (PD) fabricated from silicon material at the receiver of an optical communication system [26]. Signals of 1 Mbps are modulated by on-off keying (OOK) with non return zero (NRZ) and produced by a Pseudorandom binary sequence (PRBS) generator for the three wavelength colors. The signals are transmitted in the indoor short-range environment via OWC and the aperture diameters were assumed to be 0.5 and 1 cm for the transmitter and receiver, respectively. The results show that the red color produces high optical power at the receiver and a lower bit error rate (BER) compared to other colors, while white light was examined for different distances and the results showed that the received optical power decayed with increases in the distance between the transmitter and receiver.

One of the main problems affecting every VLC system is the restriction of the transmission bandwidth that is generated from the intersymbol interference (ISI) in the communication channel. The received optical signal at the receiver arrives several times when the transmitter broadcast multiples signals through the VLC system; this produces an inequality in the SNR at the receiver for all the applied LEDs due to the generation of ISI. A new approach for optimization that includes a matrix of LEDs was investigated and it called a selecting communication-LED. The new approach depends on choosing some LEDs of low delay and ISI in the communication. The evolutionary algorithm (EA) was applied to optimize the SNR of different LEDs; the authors discussed the effects of data rate and field of view on the proposed optimal approach. The BER and SNR for single and multiple users were calculated, and the simulation results show that the proposed approach has the ability to give a specific data rate and acceptable BER for all users when the EA program is applied [27].

2.6.1 Simulation Result and Analysis for Indoor Environment

The two important parameters of received power and SNR for any communication system are discussed in indoor environments in order to improve the link quality and satisfy the 5G network requirements. A room of $5 \times 5 \times 3$ m dimensions was simulated; the ceiling bounce propagation model was applied, and single and multiple LEDs arrays were mounted on the ceiling to provide both communication and illumination.

Figures 2.3 and 2.4 illustrated received power versus SNR of the single LEDs array at a semi-angle at half power 12.5° and 70°, respectively. The results showed the received power increases when the SNR decreases and vice versa. In addition, at a semi-angle at half power 12.5°, the maximum received power and SNR concentrate only at the center of the room. Because of this, a 4-LED array is proposed in order to provide acceptable link quality around the room.

Figures 2.5 and 2.6 illustrate the received power and SNR of a 4-LED array at a semi-angle at half powers 12.5° and 70°, respectively. In the 4-LED array, as shown in the results, the communication link is improved due to the uniform distribution of LEDs around the

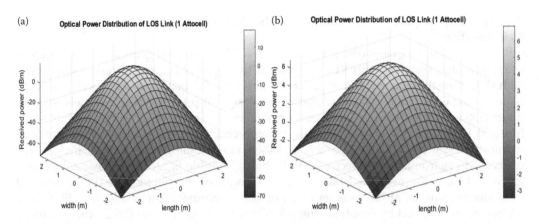

FIGURE 2.3
Received optical power at semi-angle at half power (a) 12.5° and (b) 70°.

room. The relationship between received power and SNR are the same as in a single LED array. The SNR can be used to compute the capacity by using the Shannon capacity law.

2.7 Device-to-Device (D2D) Communication

Due to the limitation of the RF spectrum in cellular communication systems, a new architecture was investigated by using a small base station to enhance the data rate of D2D in the Internet of things (IoT) ecosystem [28]. A huge number of devices will be connected with each other in the IoT ecosystem in order to deliver the data in a more efficient, smart, and suitable way. An overview of the VLC and D2D was discussed extensively as promising technologies to enhance the capacity of the 5G network. These are known as offloading techniques. D2D was suggested by the European 5G research project to be a backbone of huge

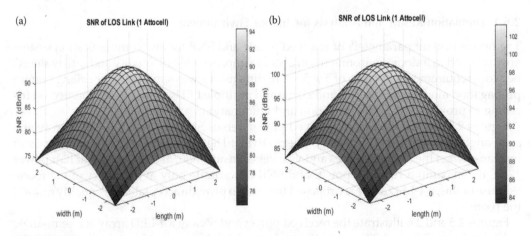

FIGURE 2.4
Signal-to-Noise ratio at semi-angle at half power (a) 12.5° and (b) 70°.

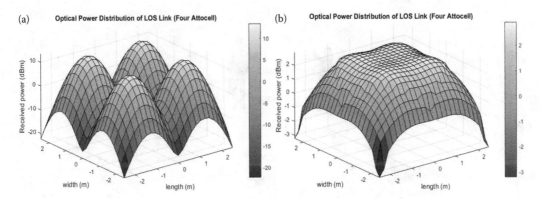

FIGURE 2.5
Received optical power at semi-angle at half power (a) 12.5° and (b) 70°.

services in 2020 [29,30]. D2D communication is proposed as a promising technology in 5G networks and beyond due to the fast growth of short-range communication, because recent reports show that more than 70% of communication traffic originates indoors [31,32]. Figure 2.7 displays the general concept of a direct conversation in human-to-human and D2D communication.

Additionally, another report showed that traffic will be growing extensively until 2020 compared to 2010 as illustrated in Figure 2.8 and will be 1000 times more than other forecasts. The D2D communication was used to mitigate the interference and improve the spectrum efficiency, and VLC may offer a huge spectrum of indoor communication for the IoT ecosystem [33].

D2D communication is defined as a novel model applied to facilitate the traffic congestion in 5G cellular networks. The movement of devices is considered to be one of the difficult issues in the D2D communication, and the solution of this issue will produce a successful transceiver system between devices. The synchronization content between D2D communications in the dynamic environment was proposed in [34], with a couple strategies of synchronization investigated in terms of delay in order to increase the energy efficiency. They are analyzed theoretically and simulated by applying the city section mobility model. In the

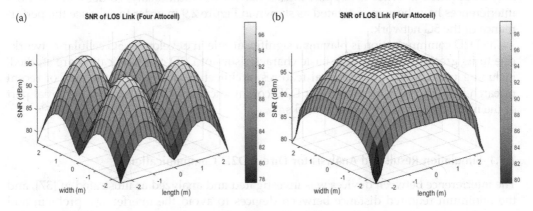

FIGURE 2.6
Signal-to-Noise ratio at semi-angle at half power (a) 12.5° and (b) 70°.

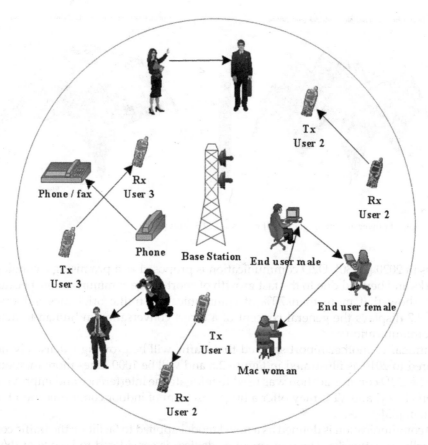

FIGURE 2.7
General concept of point-to-point or direct communication.

cellular system, the D2D communication uses the same frequency as the cellular equipment. An overview of D2D communication was presented in [35], and the conclusion showed that interference between D2D communication represents the main challenge. More suggestions may be required in order to support the 5G networks. Additionally, co-tier and cross-tier interferences have been investigated as shown in Figure 2.9 in order to enhance the performance of the 5G network.

The D2D communication is playing a significant role in developing 5G cellular networks due to its great advantages. The basic characteristics of D2D communication are studied, including usage scenarios, technical features, architecture design, and the area of recent research [36]. The authors expect that D2D communication will become a substantial part of the realization of 5G cellular networks.

2.7.1 Simulation Result and Analysis for Direct D2D Communication

The interference between devices was investigated and analyzed as illustrated in [37], and the minimum required distance between devices to avoid the interference problem and guarantee the SNR was studied in [38]. The green color indicates signals to the transmitter and the red color refers to the receiver. The simulation results showed a cellular network of

FIGURE 2.8
Forecasting of advanced communication and connectivity required in the next 10 years.

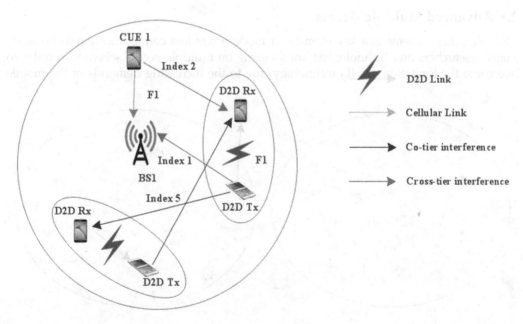

FIGURE 2.9
Types of interference in cellular networks.

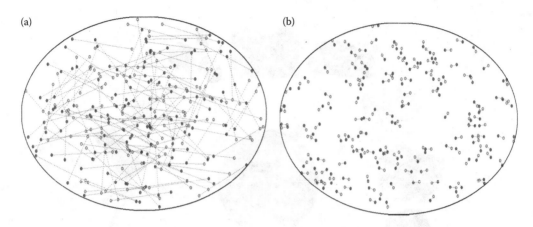

FIGURE 2.10
Cellular network scenario of 300 D2D communications with fixed link lengths (a) 500 m and (b) 50 m.

diameter 1 km. The number of connected devices in Figure 2.10 is 300 with variable distances between transmitters and receivers of (a) 500 m and (b) 50 m, respectively. The same parameters are also applied to Figure 2.11, but for 100 devices. From the two figures, the interference between devices increases when the distance between the transmitter and receiver increases and vice versa. In addition, when the number of D2D communications decreases in a cellular network, then the interference also decreases and vice versa. The green and red colors represent the transmitter and receiver, respectively.

2.8 Advanced Multiple Access

Multiple access scheme is a key element of modern wireless communication technology. Many researchers and technologists are focusing on multiple access schemes in order to overcome the limitations of 4G technology due to the increasing demands of the mobile

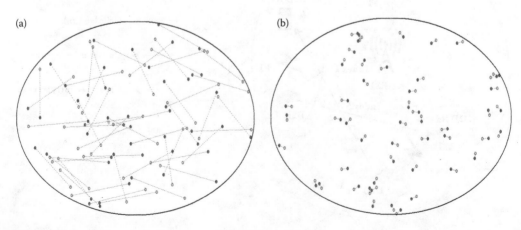

FIGURE 2.11
Cellular network scenario of 100 D2D communications with fixed link lengths (a) 500 m and (b) 50 m.

communication network. The multiple access scheme for 1G technology was Frequency Division Multiple Access (FDMA) which was based on analog frequency modulation. The FDMA scheme divided the medium bandwidth into individual channels, so users only got a small portion of bandwidth. 2G technology was commonly known as Time Division Multiple Access (TDMA) due to the innovation of time multiplexing, although it employed with both TDMA and FDMA [39]. TDMA divides a single band or channel into time slots. Each time slot in TDMA is used to transmit the digital signal in sequential serial data format. 3G technology applied CDMA, also in a digital technique. CDMA spread the digital version of the analog signal out over the wider bandwidth at a lower power level.

4G introduced the Orthogonal Frequency Division Multiplexing (OFDM) to overcome the spectrum resources' scarcity problem because of the increasing demands of mobile users [39]. OFDM became a popular method in wideband digital communication and used the technique of encoding the digital data on multiple carrier frequencies. This scheme is widely used to combat multipath fading and is already used over the world to produced high data rates which are needed for today's intensive data applications. The OFDM scheme is based on the idea of modulating each data stream on the subcarriers and dividing a high bit data rate into several lower bit data rates. Figure 2.12 shows the block diagram for the OFDM system.

Based on the description of the OFDM system's block diagram as shown in Figure 2.12, the modulated data is split into parallel data using a serial to parallel data converter. Next, the data is passed into the Inverse Fast Fourier Transform (IFFT) to generate a time sequence of the data streams. The time sequenced data streams of the OFDM system will be extended by adding the Cyclic Prefix (CP). Before it has been transmitted over the channel, the digital signal will be converted to analog form using the parallel to serial converter [40]. The OFDM system has already been used in the Wireless Fidelity (WiFi) arena (IEEE 802.11a, 802.11ac, etc.), however, the use of CP in the OFDM system will reduce the overall spectral efficiency [41]. Nowadays, the rapid development of mobile communication technology has attracted the attention of technologists and researchers all around the world [39]. The data traffic service diversity and device densities are expected to create a massive demand for the future 5G [42]. There are several ideas for the future 5G technology which could bring additional advantages to the new cellular system such as Filterbank Multicarrier (FBMC), Universal Filtered Multicarrier (UFMC), filtered Orthogonal Frequency Division Multiplexing

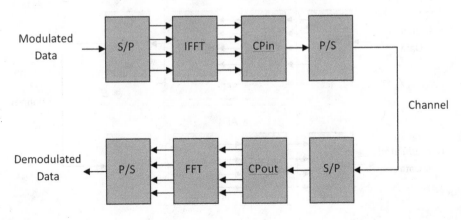

FIGURE 2.12
Block diagram of OFDM technique.

(f-OFDM), and Generalized Frequency Division Multiplexing (GFDM). These ideas are still under research [6]. All of these ideas will be discussed in Section 2.8.1.

2.8.1 Filterbank Multicarrier (FBMC)

FBMC, also known as the Orthogonal Frequency Division Multiplexing/Offset Quadrature Amplitude Modulation (OFDM/OQAM) [43], is an advanced version of the OFDM technique. FBMC is a multicarrier waveform which uses a set of analysis and synthesis filters that are employed at the receiver and transmitter, respectively [44,45]. FBMC is a combination of modulation and multiplexing with the ability to break the wideband channel into narrowband channels, which are also known as subchannels. Figure 2.13 shows the block diagram of the FBMC technique. Based on the block diagram illustrated in Figure 2.13, FBMC consists of a synthesis filterbank (SFB) at the transmitter side and an analysis filterbank (AFB) at the receiver side. At the transmitter side, the modulated data will be split into parallel using a serial to parallel converter. Next, the data will be passed through the SFB which contains IFFT and a polyphase network (PPN). There is no CP needed in the FBMC technique as compared to the OFDM, hence FBMC will have more spectral containment signals. FBMC uses the same size of the IFFT, however, the FBMC computes double the output signals at double the speed of the OFDM [46].

Figure 2.14 shows the graphical illustration of the FBMC transmitter and Figure 2.15 shows the graphical illustration of the FBMC receiver. Based on the FBMC transmitter shown in Figure 2.14, the high-speed input signal will be demultiplexed into N branches. Next, it will be modulated by different signal constellations as required [47]. The subsequent modulated branches are then upsampled to give N copies and the upsampled data will be sent through the set of synthesis filters, gk(n), where k = 1,2, … , N − 1. Subsequently, the output of all filters will be summed in order to produce the transmitted signal [47]. At the receiver side of the FBMC, as illustrated in Figure 2.15, the received signal, r(n), will be passed through to the analysis filterbank, fk(n), where k = 0,1, … , N − 1 in order to discover the different center frequencies of N subcarriers. The signal in every branch will be downsampled by N and demodulated and multiplexed to produce the estimate of the original signal, xr(n) [47].

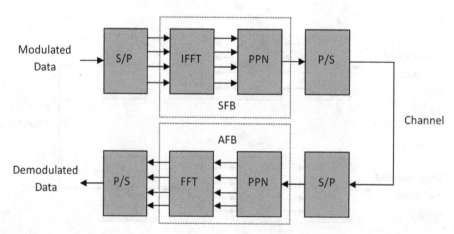

FIGURE 2.13
Block diagram of FBMC technique.

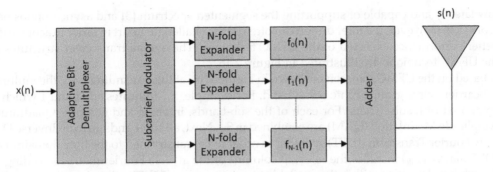

FIGURE 2.14
Graphical illustration of FBMC transmitter.

FBMC techniques have a few advantages as compared to OFDM. The fundamental change of FBMC is the replacement of CP with the filterbanks at the transmitter and receiver. The extension of CP will reduce the bandwidth efficiency and data capacity of OFDM. The OFDM technique is very sensitive to the carrier frequency offset (CFO), but the FBMC technique is less sensitive, hence it performs better with an increase in the number of mobile users. In addition, OFDM has large sidelobes of the frequency response as compared to FBMC. For the FBMC technique, the energy is concentrated within the frequency range of a single subcarrier, however, the OFDM technique has rather strong sidelobes due to its rectangular windowing [48].

2.8.2 Universal Filtered Multicarrier (UFMC)

UFMC is one of the techniques for future 5G technology. UFMC filters the successive subbands, hence it supports the sliced spectrum. The filter design of UFMC is an essential and challenging issue which is critical to the performance of this technique [49]. UFMC is a result of endeavors to overcome the inherent problems associated with FBMC [50]. This is because the FBMC technique requires a relatively long filter length, thus it may be difficult to implement because of the hardware complexity which may induce an extra delay and make it infeasible for short burst traffic [51]. UFMC can achieve a lower out of band (OOB) emission compared to OFDM by filtering a series of successive subcarriers [1]. In addition, UFMC is

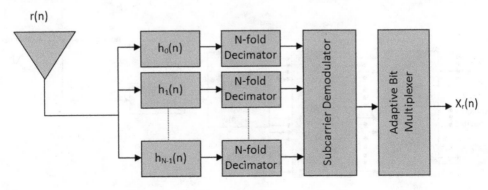

FIGURE 2.15
Graphical illustration of FBMC receiver.

low latency and capable of supporting the segmented spectrum [3] and asynchronous net-work [52]. However, the filter design can often be the challenging part in order to achieve the better performance expected of the UFMC technique. The overall transceiver structures of the UFMC technique are illustrated in Figure 2.16.

Based on the UFMC transceiver shown in Figure 2.16, at the transmitter part, the multiple subcarriers were grouped into a sub-band. For example, S_{1k} indicates sub-band 1 which is composed of k subcarriers. For each of the sub-bands, indexed and complex Quadrature Amplitude Modulation (QAM) are combined in S_{ik}. Next, all sub-bands go to an Inverse Discrete Fourier Transform (IDFT) spreader in order to be transformed to the time domain. The IDFT-matrix (V_{ik}) includes the relevant columns of the inverse Fourier matrix according to the sub-band position within the available frequency range [52]. The filter impulse response, which is composed a Toeplitz matrix (F_{ik}), performs the linear convolution [52]. Subse-quently, the outputs of each filter are combined and up-converted to the radio frequency and will be transmitted. There is no CP needed for the UFMC, but it is able to provide further improvement of the ISI protection [52].

One of the main criteria of the UFMC design is to accumulate the advantages of the FBMC and f-OFDM technique in addition to avoiding the disadvantages of these two techniques with the use of the filtering functionality [53]. Basically, the filtering of the UFMC technique is performed per sub-band comprised of the multiple subcarriers [53]. The advantage of fil-tering per sub-band as compared to the per sub-carrier is that the length of the filter can be significantly shorter as compared to the FBMC technique. Thus, the UFMC technique becomes an appealing technique which is also proposed for future 5G technology [53].

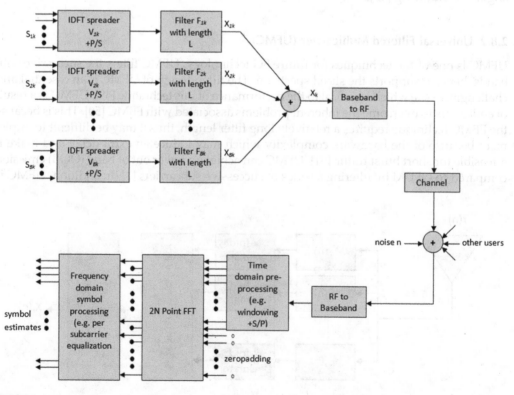

FIGURE 2.16
UFMC transceiver.

2.8.3 Filtered Orthogonal Frequency Division Multiplexing (f-OFDM)

f-OFDM has a structure similar to the UFMC transmitter structure [54,55]. Figure 2.17 shows the block diagram of an f-OFDM transceiver. The main difference of f-OFDM as compared to the UFMC is that f-OFDM requires the employment of CP which usually allows ISI [54]. At the receiver, the matched filter (MF) is applied instead of the Zero Padding (ZP) and decimation [56]. In addition, downsampling may be applied before the Discrete Fourier Transform (DFT) operation, thus it will significantly reduce the complexity since the CP diminishes most of the interference caused by the tail of the filter [56] and the leftover interference has much lower power, hence it can be treated as noise [55]. The filter of the f-OFDM may be longer compared to that of the UFMC and it has better attenuation outside the band [56]. The performance degradation, which is caused by residual interference in the f-OFDM technique, can be negligible with effective channel coding [56]. The soft-truncatedsinc filter is the most widely used for the f-OFDM technique [54] and is easily used in various applications with different parameters [56]. In addition, the f-OFDM technique is very flexible in frequency multiplexing [56].

2.8.4 Generalized Frequency Division Multiplexing (GFDM)

The GFDM scheme is designed to overcome the real-time and major broadband challenges for future 5G technology [53]. Figure 2.18 shows the block diagram of the GFDM and Figure 2.19 shows the block diagram of the GFDM receiver. In the GFDM scheme, multiple sub-symbols are used to transmit a data block and a symbol is composed of several subcarriers. Each of the subcarriers is a pulse shape with a transmission filter [57]. The impulse response of each sub-symbol is applied through the circular convolution in order to avoid spending additional samples on the ramp down and ramp up of the filter response [57]. The different pulse shapes can be used as prototype filters which introduce a new degree of freedom to the system [57]. The subcarrier filtering will reduce the OOB emissions [57], however, there may be inter-carrier interference among the adjacent subcarriers and ISI may arise if the combination of transmitting and receiving filters does not fulfill the Nyquist criteria [53].

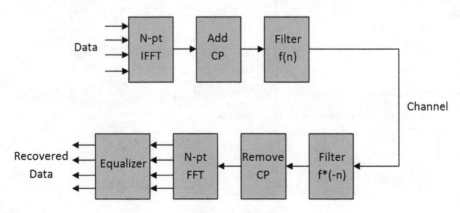

FIGURE 2.17
f-OFDM transceiver.

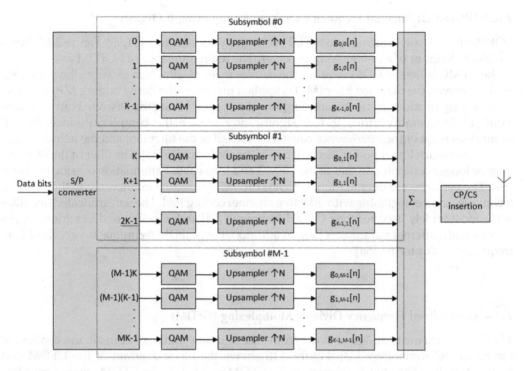

FIGURE 2.18
Block diagram of the GFDM transmitter.

2.8.5 Summary

The common OFDM system, which is based on Fast Fourier Transform (FFT), has encountered several challenges in an effort to fulfill the 5G requirements [39]. It is sensitive to the Doppler shift caused by high speed moving mobile stations [58]. Additionally, the existence

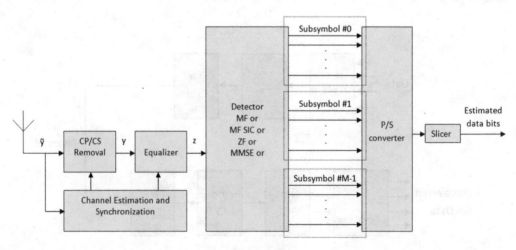

FIGURE 2.19
Block diagram of the GFDM receiver.

TABLE 2.3

The Comparison of the Proposed Techniques

Technique	Key Technology	Advantages	Disadvantages
FBMC	Multicarrier fitering	• Less sensitive, hence performs significantly with an increase in the mobile users [3] • Conserved the bandwidth efficiency [3] • High spectrum sensing resolution [3]	• Limited flexibility • Complex implementation [3]
UFMC	Block-wise filtering	• Low complexity • Small inteference between subcarriers	• Higher synchronization requirement than CP-OFDM
GFDM	Tx filtering FFT-based equalization	• Lower PAPR • Use of scattered spectrum resources • Ultra-low out of band radiation	• Complex receiver
f-OFDM	Soft-truncated sinc filter	• Flexible in multiplexing	• Complexity of structure and implementation

of the CP extension is inhibited by the effect of multipath fading channel propagation [58] and reduces the spectrum efficiency of the system. In addition, OFDM has a considerably high peak to average ratio (PAPR) which is caused by a linear superposition of a plurality of subcarriers' modulated signals [58]. There are several new techniques proposed to successfully produce future 5G technology, including FBMC, UFMC, f-OFDM, and GFDM.

All of these techniques have reduced the sidelobes because of the filtering functionality as compared to the OFDM [39]. However, these techniques also have some drawbacks. For the FBMC technique, the prototype filter is more complex, hence it is more difficult to develop. The length of the UFMC filter is relatively shorter, however, this technique is more sensitive to time differences. In addition, the UFMC technique may not suitable for applications which require loose time synchronization [39]. The subcarrier filtering of the GFDM technique can result in non-orthogonalsubcarriers, ICI, and ISI. However, all of these modulation techniques will be able to achieve the 5G requirements if they can reduce the complexity of the receivers and ICI [39]. Table 2.3 shows the comparison of the proposed techniques.

2.9 Quadrature Amplitude Modulation (QAM)

QAM is widely used in mobile communications and is mainly used in LOS for microwave systems, coaxial cables, and satellite communications. QAM transmits the information data by modulating the amplitudes of two carrier waves, using straight amplitude modulation for the analog signal and Amplitude Shift Keying (ASK) for the digital signal. QAM requires linear amplifiers and coherent detection [59]. QAM has a moderate energy efficiency, excellent bandwidth, and complexity on the receiver side because it needs to track the frequency, phase, and amplitude of the carrier and also track the sampling time and symbol rate [59]. Some of common forms of QAM include 16QAM, 32QAM, 64QAM and 128QAM. In QAM, the signal in two carriers is shifted in phase by 90°, hence it will be modulated and the output consists of both phase and amplitude variations which may also be considered as a mixture of amplitude and phase modulations [3].

One major challenge of future 5G technology is the high capacity demands of the users of mobile devices. Therefore, the spectral efficiency is very important to support all of the mobile devices beyond the era of 2020, which is believed to be rapidly increasing. Table 2.4 shows the constellation diagram and the forms of QAM which are used in digital radio communications. Based on Table 2.4, future 5G technology will propose to use 256QAM because it gives a better performance as compared to 64QAM. This is because the higher QAM numerology reflects the ability to represent more data with the same number of symbols [3]. However, the standardization of a new modulation for the future 5G is still under research.

TABLE 2.4

Form of QAM Used in Mobile Communications

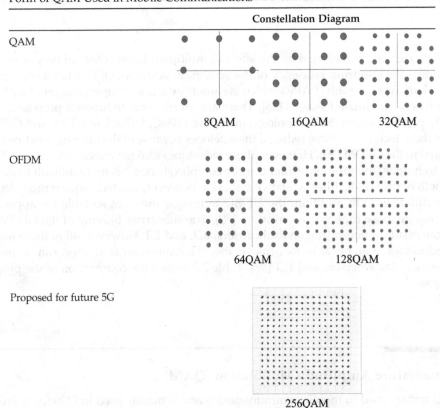

	Constellation Diagram		
QAM	8QAM	16QAM	32QAM
OFDM	64QAM	128QAM	
Proposed for future 5G	256QAM		

2.10 Conclusion

The biggest thing that will happen in the mobile communication industry is the advent of 5G mobile communication technology, which is on track for launch in 2020 in conjunction with the Winter Olympic Games in Korea. Most of the countries in the world, such as Japan, China, and those in Europe, have taken significant steps to lead global developments toward this strategy technology. Mobile communication is undergoing a revolutionary paradigm shift over the world because of the increase in the number of mobile users. Additionally, consumers will be able to download a 1080p high definition (HD) movie to their mobile phone in about one second and 50 GB video games within minutes with this 5G mobile communication technology. 5G mobile communication is the next step in the transformation of communication technology. The competence of 5G mobile communication must broaden far beyond those of the previous generations to facilitate connectivity for a wide range of applications. We provided an overview of several emerging technologies for future 5G mobile communication networks. In addition, to achieve future 5G technology, the technologies such as massive MIMO and beamforming, higher bandwidth at mm-Wave, VLC, D2D communication, advanced multiple access, and modulation will also impact the design and development of 5G networks.

Acknowledgments

We would like to express our special thanks of gratitude to UniversitiTun Hussein Onn Malaysia (UTHM) and the Malaysian Government—MyBrain15 scholarship for giving us the golden opportunity to embark on the research related to 5G Communication.

References

1. Mishra, A. R. 2004. *Fundamentals of Cellular Network Planning and Optimisation: 2G/2.5 G/3G… Evolution to 4G.* John Wiley & Sons, pp. 217–224.
2. Dahlman, E., Mildh, G., Parkvall, S., Peisa, J., Sachs, J., Selén, Y., and Sköld, J. 2014. 5G wireless access: Requirements and realization. *IEEE Communications Magazine*, 52(12), 42–47.
3. Ibrahim, A. N. and Abdullah, M. F. L. 2017. The potential of FBMC over OFDM for the future 5G mobile communication technology. In *AIP Conference Proceedings*, Vol. 1883, No. 1, September. Johor Bahru, Malaysia, AIP Publishing, p. 020001.
4. Seo, D. (Ed.). 2013. *Evolution and Standardization of Mobile Communications Technology.* IGI Global.
5. Goodman, D. J. 1991. Second generation wireless information networks. *IEEE Transactions on Vehicular Technology*, 40(2), 366–374.
6. Agrqwal, J., Patel, R., Mor, P., Dubey, P., and Keller, J. M. 2015. Evolution of mobile communication network: From 1G to 4G. *International Journal of Multidisciplinary and Current Research*, 3, 1100–1103.
7. Jain, V. S., Jain, S., Kurup, L., and Gawade, A. 2014. Overview on generations of network: 1G, 2G, 3G, 4G, 5G. *IOSR Journal of Electronics and Communication Engineering*, 9(3), 1789–1794.

8. Olsson, M., Cavdar, C., Frenger, P., Tombaz, S., Sabella, D., and Jantti, R. 2013. 5GrEEn: Towards Green 5G mobile networks. In *2013 IEEE 9th International Conference on Wireless and Mobile Computing, Networking and Communications (WiMob)*, October 7-9. Lyon, France, IEEE, pp. 212–216.

9. Abrol, A. and Jha, R. K. 2016. Power optimization in 5G networks: A step towards Green communication. *IEEE Access*, 4, 1355–1374.

10. Rawat, D. B., Rodrigues, J. J., and Stojmenovic, I. (Eds.). 2015. *Cyber-Physical Systems: From Theory to Practice*. CRC Press.

11. Boccardi, F., Heath, R. W., Lozano, A., Marzetta, T. L., and Popovski, P. 2014. Five disruptive technology directions for 5G. *IEEE Communications Magazine*, 52(2), 74–80.

12. Nakatsugawa, M. 2014. R&D efforts on wireless access systems toward realization of future networks. *NTT Technical Review*, 12(3), 1–6.

13. Larsson, E. G., Edfors, O., Tufvesson, F., and Marzetta, T. L. 2014. Massive MIMO for next generation wireless systems. *IEEE Communications Magazine*, 52(2), 186–195.

14. Rajoria, S., Trivedi, A., and Godfrey, W. W. 2018. A comprehensive survey: Small cell meets massive MIMO. *Physical Communication*, 26, 40–49.

15. Lu, L., Li, G. Y., Swindlehurst, A. L., Ashikhmin, A., and Zhang, R. 2014. An overview of massive MIMO: Benefits and challenges. *IEEE Journal of Selected Topics in Signal Processing*, 8 (5), 742–758.

16. Larsson, E. G., Marzetta, T. L., Ngo, H. Q., and Yang, H. 2017. Antenna Count for Massive MIMO: 1.9 GHz versus 60 GHz. arXiv preprint arXiv:1702.06111.

17. Björnson, E., Hoydis, J., and Sanguinetti, L. 2018. Massive MIMO has unlimited capacity. *IEEE Transactions on Wireless Communications*, 17(1), 574–590.

18. Haykin, S. 2001. Communication Systems, Engineering. Published by Wiley, p. 816.

19. Xiao, M., Mumtaz, S., Huang, Y., Dai, L., Li, Y., Matthaiou, M., ... and Ghosh, A. 2017. Millimeter Wave Communications for Future Mobile Networks. arXiv preprint arXiv:1705.06072.

20. Andrews, J. G., Buzzi, S., Choi, W., Hanly, S. V., Lozano, A., Soong, A. C., and Zhang, J. C. 2014. What will 5G be? *IEEE Journal on Selected Areas in Communications*, 32(6), 1065–1082.

21. Uysal, M. and Nouri, H. 2014. Optical wireless communications—An emerging technology. In *2014 16th International Conference on Transparent Optical Networks (ICTON)*, pp. 1–7.

22. Wang, J., Zou, N., Dong, W., Kentaro, I., Zensei, I. H. A., and Namihira, Y. 2012. Experimental study on visible light communication based on LED. *Journal of China Universities of Posts and Telecommunications*, 19, 197–200.

23. Warmerdam, K., Pandharipande, A., and Caicedo, D. 2015. Connectivity in IoT indoor lighting systems with visible light communications. In *2015 IEEE Online Conference on Green Communications (OnlineGreenComm)*, pp. 47–52.

24. Elgala, H., Mesleh, R., and Haas, H. 2011. Indoor optical wireless communication: Potential and state-of-the-art. *IEEE Communications and Magazine*, 49(9), 56–62.

25. Singh, V. K., Patel, D., and Dalal, U. D. 2016. A 100 Mbps visible light communication system using optical wireless channel for indoor application based on composite white light generated using RGB LEDs. *Procedia Computer Science*, 93, 655–661.

26. Wang, L., Wang, C., Chi, X., Zhao, L., and Dong, X. 2017. Optimizing SNR for indoor visible light communication via selecting communicating LEDs. *Optics Communications*, 387 (November 2016), 174–181.

27. Liu, X., and Ansari, N. 2017. Green relay assisted D2D communications with dual batteries in heterogeneous cellular networks for IoT. *IEEE Internet Things J.* 4(5), 1707–1715.

28. Buzzi, S., Chih-Lin, I., Klein, T. E., Poor, H. V., Yang, C., and Zappone, A. 2016. A survey of energy-efficient techniques for 5G networks and challenges ahead. *IEEE Journal on Selected Areas in Communications*, 34(4), 697–709.

29. Fodor, G. et al. 2016. An overview of device-to-device communications technology components in METIS. *IEEE Access*, 4, 3288–3299.

30. Bello O. and Zeadally S. 2015. Intelligent device-to-device communication in the internet of things. *IEEE Systems Journal*, 10(3), 1–11. Ieeexplore.Ieee.Org

31. Asadi, A., Wang, Q., and Mancuso, V. 2014. A survey on device-to-device communication in cellular networks. *IEEE Communications Surveys & Tutorials*, 16(4), 1801–1819.

32. Gismalla, M. S. M. and Abdullah, M. F. L. 2017. A survey on device-to-device communication with internet of things in cellular networks. *Journal of Applied Engineering and Technology*, 1(1), 1–7.

33. Li, W., Chen, X., and Lu, S. 2017. Content synchronization using device-to-device communication in smart cities. *Computer Networks*, 120, 170–185.

34. Gismalla, M. S. M. and Abdullah, M. F. L. 2017. Device to device communication for internet of things ecosystem: An overview. *International Journal of Integrated Engineering*, 9(4), 118–123.

35. Noura, M. and Nordin, R. 2016. A survey on interference management for Device-to-Device (D2D) communication and its challenges in 5G networks. *Journal of Network and Computer Applications*, 71, 130–150.

36. Kar, U. N. and Sanyal, D. K. 2017. An overview of device-to-device communication in cellular networks. *ICT Express*.

37. Meibergen, M. 2011. Device-to-device communications underlaying a cellular network.

38. Salih, M., Gismalla, M., and Eltahir, I. K. 2015. Interference reduction between Device to Device (D2D) communication underlying cellular networks. *International Journal of Scientific & Engineering Research*, 6(11), 410–414.

39. Yunzheng, T., Long, L., Shang, L., and Zhi, Z. 2015. A survey: Several technologies of non-orthogonal transmission for 5G. *China Communications*, 12(10), 1–15.

40. Tensubam, B. D., Chanu, N. L., and Singh, S. 2014. Comparative analysis of FBMC and OFDM multicarrier techniques for wireless communication networks. *International Journal of Computer Applications*, 100(19), 27–31.

41. Schaich, F. 2010. Filterbank based multi carrier transmission (FBMC)—evolving OFDM: FBMC in the context of WiMAX. In *Wireless Conference (EW), 2010 European*, April. IEEE, pp. 1051–1058.

42. Wang, J., Jin, A., Shi, D., Wang, L., Shen, H., Wu, D., ... and Wang, J. 2017. Spectral efficiency improvement with 5G technologies: Results from field tests. *IEEE Journal on Selected Areas in Communications*. 35(8), 1867–1875.

43. Sriyananda, M. G. S. 2014. Analysis and Performance of FBMC Techniques with Application to Relay Networks. Jyväskylä Studies in Computing, University JYVASKYLA, Finland, 199, 1456–5390.

44. Bogucka, H., Wyglinski, A. M., Pagadarai, S., and Kliks, A. 2011. Spectrally agile multicarrier waveforms for opportunistic wireless access. *IEEE Communications Magazine*, 49(6), 108–115.

45. Bellanger, M. G. 2001. Specification and design of a prototype filter for filter bank based multicarrier transmission. In *2001 IEEE International Conference on Acoustics, Speech, and Signal Processing (ICASSP'01). Proceedings*, 2001. IEEE, vol. 4, pp. 2417–2420.

46. Schaich, F., Ringset, V., Bellanger, M., Zhang, D., and Ruyet, D. L. 2009. Compatibility of OFDM and FBMC systems and reconfigurability of terminals. Physical Layer for DYnamicAccesS and Cognitive Radio (PHYDYAS) Project Report, D7.

47. Velamala, H. 2013. Filter Bank Multicarrier Modulation for Spectrally Agile Waveform Design. Doctoral dissertation, Worcester Polytechnic Institute.

48. Berardinelli, G., Pajukoski, K., Lahetkangas, E., Wichman, R., Tirkkonen, O., and Mogensen, P. 2014. On the potential of OFDM enhancements as 5G waveforms. In *2014 IEEE 79th Vehicular Technology Conference (VTC Spring)*, Seoul, South Korea, May. IEEE, pp. 1–5.

49. Zhang, Z., Wang, H., Yu, G., Zhang, Y., and Wang, X. 2017. Universal filtered multi-carrier transmission with adaptive active interference cancellation. *IEEE Transactions on Communications*. 65(6), 2554–2567.

50. Vakilian, V., Wild, T., Schaich, F., Ten Brink, S., and Frigon, J. F. 2013. Universal-filtered multi-carrier technique for wireless systems beyond LTE. In *2013 IEEE Globecom Workshops (GC Wkshps)*, December. IEEE, pp. 223–228.

51. Chen, Y., Schaich, F., and Wild, T. 2014. Multiple access and waveforms for 5G: IDMA and universal filtered multi-carrier. In *2014 IEEE 79th Vehicular Technology Conference (VTC Spring)*, May. IEEE, pp. 1–5.

52. Schaich, F. and Wild, T. 2014. Relaxed synchronization support of universal filtered multi-carrier including autonomous timing advance. In *2014 11th International Symposium on Wireless Communications Systems (ISWCS)*, August. IEEE, pp. 203–208.

53. Wunder, G., Jung, P., Kasparick, M., Wild, T., Schaich, F., Chen, Y., ... and Mendes, L. 2014. 5GNOW: Non-orthogonal, asynchronous waveforms for future mobile applications. *IEEE Communications Magazine*, 52(2), 97–105.

54. Abdoli, J., Jia, M., and Ma, J. 2015. Filtered OFDM: A new waveform for future wireless systems. In *2015 IEEE 16th International Workshop on Signal Processing Advances in Wireless Communications (SPAWC)*, June. IEEE, pp. 66–70.

55. Zhang, X., Jia, M., Chen, L., Ma, J., and Qiu, J. 2015. Filtered-OFDM-enabler for flexible waveform in the 5th generation cellular networks. In *2015 IEEE Global Communications Conference (GLOBECOM)*, December. IEEE, pp. 1–6.

56. Cai, Y., Qin, Z., Cui, F., Li, G. Y., and McCann, J. A. 2017. Modulation and Multiple Access for 5G Networks. arXiv preprint arXiv:1702.07673.

57. Gaspar, I. S., Mendes, L. L., Michailow, N., and Fettweis, G. 2014. A synchronization technique for generalized frequency division multiplexing. *EURASIP Journal on Advances in Signal Processing*, 2014(1), 67.

58. Zhou, W. and Lam, W. H. 2008. A novel method of Doppler shift estimation for OFDM systems. In *IEEE Military Communications Conference, 2008 (MILCOM 2008)*, November. IEEE, pp. 1–7.

59. Korn, I. and Fonseka, J. P. *Quadrature Amplitude Modulation*. Encyclopedia of Telecommunications, Wiley, 2003.

Part II

Various Spectrum Sensing Techniques

3

Various Sensing Techniques for Cognitive Radio

Debnath Bhattacharyya, N. Thirupathi Rao, and Tai-hoon Kim

CONTENTS

3.1 Introduction to Cognitive Radios

The radio spectrum is a compelling resource and has resulted in many additions in remote devices and applications. The assigned spectrum is not completely used due to the static dispersion of the spectrum. The normal approach to manage spectrum organization is that each remote overseer is doled out a particular allowance in a particular band. With an extensive bit of the radio spectrum being started distribution, it is hard to locate discharge gatherings to either pass on to new organizations or to improve those on hand. Remembering the true goals of mobile communication, we need to devise techniques for upgraded consumption of the spectrum by creating new open entryways [1,2].

The matter of remote correspondence can be settled better using the Cognitive Radio (CR) concept. Cognitive radios are created with the particular ultimate objective to provide extremely strong service to all customers of the framework anywhere and at any point necessary and to allow fruitful utilization of the radio spectrum. Figure 3.1 demonstrate the low utilization of the approved spectrum which is, all things considered, due to inefficient repeated designations instead of any physical absence of spectrum. The managerial bodies need to instigate a procedure where unlicensed structures are allowed to utilize the unused fundamental bands which, more often than not, are considered to be void zones.

Subjective radio can change its transmitter parameters by utilizing a coordinated effort. Subjective radio consolidates four guideline utilitarian needs: spectrum identification, spectrum organization, spectrum sharing, and spectrum flexibility. Range detecting plans are used to choose the spectrum openness and closeness for the approved customers (generally called basic customers). The range-assigning organization needs to determine to what degree the spectrum openings are going to be accessible for use by customers with no licensed permission (also called subjective radio customers or helper customers). Range sharing is proposed to allocate the spectrum holes among the discretionary customers. Range adaptability is needed to maintain predictable correspondence requirements in the midst of the advance to a better spectrum.

3.2 Issues and Challenges Observed in Sensing of the Spectrum

A few wellsprings of vulnerability, for example, channel vulnerability, clamor vulnerability, detecting obstruction restraints, and so forth should be addressed to provide understanding of the issue of spectrum detecting in psychological radio systems. These points are discussed in [3,4].

3.2.1 Channel Ambiguity

In distant communication frameworks, signal superiority develops due to channel obscuring or surveillance which may incorrectly determine that the fundamental system is out of the assistant customer's impedance spectrum had the basic banner which might experience a significant ambiguousness or be strongly shadowed by obstacles. Thus, cognitive radios may be more prone to perceive an obscured or shadowed basic banner from a clear spectrum. Any helplessness in the allocation of channel may cause the basic banner proselytes into a higher recognizable proof affectability essential.

3.2.2 Joined Intervention Ambiguity

In the future, due to the extensive use of discretionary structures, there will be a greater likelihood of various subjective radio frameworks working over the same approved band. Subsequently, range distinguishing will be exaggerated by a lack of power for all outside obstacles. If the basic system is out of hindrance spectrum of a discretionary structure, the collective impedance may provoke wrong revelation. This loss of power forms an obstacle for more fragile users, as a helper structure may have intruded into the fundamental system in the past and should have the ability to remember them.

3.2.3 Detecting Intervention Limit

The fundamental goal of identifying a spectrum is to recognize the spectrum's condition regardless of whether it is stationary or not, so it can be accessed by an unlicensed customer. The problem lies in the impedance estimation of the approved recipient caused by communications from customers without proper permission to use the spectrum. Initially, an unlicensed customer may not know the zone of the approved beneficiary which is required to process the impedance caused by its transmission. Second, if an approved beneficiary is a latent system, the transmitter may not "think" about the gatherer. Thus, these components require thought while discovering the obstacle.

3.3 Spectrum Mobility Issues

Spectrum versatility works in an intellectual radio system to enable an unlicensed client to progressively change its working spectrum in light of the spectrum conditions. These points can be observed in the following sections [5].

3.3.1 Seek the Finest Frequency Band

A subjective radio must screen open repeated bands so that if the licensed customer is engaged (e.g., an approved customer is remembered), it can change instantly to another repeated band. In the midst of transmission by an unlicensed customer, the condition of the repeated band must be known. Moreover, for spectrum distinguishing, this would clearly involve some overhead. The observation can be performed proactively or with an on-ask protocol.

3.3.2 Protocol Stack Version

Since the latency of the band as a result of spectrum handoff will possibly be high, the adjustment and change of various portions of the traditional range is requisite. For example, when a customer with no proper license switches the channel, the Transmission Control Protocol time at the vehicle layer can be lessened to avoid any additional wait caused for the primary message. A cross layer updated structure for traditional modification must be delivered to adjust spectrum adaptability.

3.3.3 Self Coexistence and Synchronization

When a discretionary customer performs spectrum handoff, two issues must be considered [6]. To begin with, the target channel must not at this moment be used by some other discretionary customer (i.e., the self-simultaneousness essential), and the other helper user must be informed with respect to the spectrum handoff (i.e., the synchronization need).

3.3.4 Spectrum Sensing

An important test in mental radio is that the discretionary customers need to perceive the proximity of fundamental customers in an approved spectrum and leave the repeated band as quickly as possible, which means the discretionary customers remember the true objective which is to avoid blocking basic customers. This framework is called spectrum identifying. Range identifying and assessment are the underlying steps to produce a Cognitive Radio structure [3]. We can characterize the spectrum recognizing methodology into an arranged system, which is considered to be a repeated region approach, where the assessment is done clearly from a banner with a distorted technique. Another technique depends upon the requirement of spectrum identifying as communicated under the perceived signal [2].

3.4 Spectrum Sensing for Spectrum Opportunities

3.4.1 Basic Transmitter Area

The disclosure of basic customers is performed in perspective of the spectrum sensing at cognitive radio customers. This approach joins the facilitated station (matched filter) based revelation, imperativeness-based area, covariance-based acknowledgment, waveform based recognizable proof, cyclostationary based disclosure, radio recognizing verification-based area, and the unpredictable Hough Transform based area.

3.4.2 Agreeable and Community Oriented Recognition

The essential signs for spectrum openings are identified by collaborating or participating with different clients, and the strategy could be executed as either access to a spectrum facilitated by a spectrum server or a dispersed method suggested by the spectrum stack smoothing calculation or outside recognition.

3.5 Spectrum Sensing for Interference Recognition

3.5.1 Interference Temperature Finding

In the current method, the cognitive radio framework fills in as in the ultra-wide band (UWB) innovation where the optional clients coincide with essential clients and are permitted to broadcast with small power but are limited by the impedance temperature height so as not to create harmful impedance for the essential clients.

3.5.2 Main Receiver Finding

In this technique, the impedance as well as spectrum open doors are distinguished in light of the essential recipient's neighborhood oscillator spillage control.

Classification of Spectrum Sensing Techniques: Figure 3.1 demonstrates the point by point grouping of spectrum sensing systems. They are comprehensively characterized into three

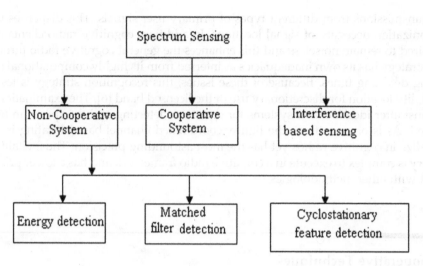

FIGURE 3.1
Classification of spectrum sensing techniques.

fundamental types, transmitter recognition or non-agreeable detecting, helpful detecting, and obstruction-based detecting. The transmitter recognition method is additionally divided into vitality discovery, coordinated channel identification, and cyclostationary highlight location [7].

3.6 Main Transmitter Recognition

3.6.1 Energy Detection

This is a non-intelligible recognition technique that identifies the necessary flags in light of the identified vitality [1]. Due to its straightforwardness and no necessity to have earlier information of the primary customer flags, energy detection is the most prominent identifying method used for energy detection [4,8]. In this strategy, the flag does not appear during data transfer, W, but is incorporated after some time interval.

The yield from the integrator piece is then contrasted with a predefined edge. This examination is utilized to find the presence of or absence of the essential client. The edge can be set to be settled or variable in light of the channel circumstances. The energy detection is known as the blind flag indicator since it disregards the organization of the flag. It assesses the nearness of the flag by contrasting the vitality and a known edge received from the clamor. Scientifically, flag discovery can be decreased to a basic recognizable proof issue.

3.6.2 Cyclostationary Feature Detection

This abuses the periodicity in the essential flag to distinguish the nearness of essential clients (Primary Users). Along these lines, cyclostationary highlighted discovery is robust to clamor vulnerabilities and is superior to anything else with vitality recognition in low signal to noise ratio areas. In spite of the fact that it requires earlier information of the flag attributes, the cyclostationary method includes the ability to recognize the cognitive radio transmissions from different types of primary user signals. This dispenses with the synchronization necessity of signal locations. In addition, cognitive radio clients may not be required to remain noiseless and this enhances the general cognitive radio throughput.

This strategy has its own inadequacies as inferred from its highly computational qualities and long detecting times. Because of these issues, this recognition strategy is less useful than vitality location for discretionary use of the licensed band [6]. The examination of various transmitter identification systems for spectrum detecting and the spectrum openings discussed. As is obvious from the figure, coordinated channel-based locating is difficult to actualize in cognitive radios yet has the most astounding precision. Thus, vitality-based discovery is complex to execute in a cognitive radio framework and has a lower precision in contrast with other methodologies.

3.7 Cooperative Techniques

Distinct topologies are presently used and are widely classifiable into three organizations as shown by their levels of investment [6,9].

3.7.1 Decentralized Uncoordinated Techniques

The individual customers in the framework who does not present any sort of joint effort infers that each cognitive radio customer will unreservedly perceive the channel, and if a cognitive radio customer recognizes the basic customer, it would clear the channel without prompting. Uncomfortable or insecure frameworks are temperamental in examination with formed procedures. Thus, cognitive radio customers that experience reduced channel recognition will recognize the channel incorrectly, causing problems for the basic customer.

3.7.2 Centralized Coordinated Techniques

An established association is acknowledged for cognitive radio customers. One cognitive radio that recognizes the proximity of a basic transmitter or authority prompts a cognitive radio controller which can be a wired stationary contraption or another cognitive radio customer. The cognitive radio controller identifies all the cognitive radio customers in its spectrum for a control message. Complex designs can be also assembled by their level of interest as partially accommodating where they sort out center points to aid in identifying the channel. Cognitive radio customers autonomously recognize the channel and entirely accommodating methods where center points take an interest in giving off each other's information despite pleasingly identifying the channel [5].

3.7.3 Decentralized Coordinated Techniques

The present type of coordination proposes preparing an arrangement of intellectual radios without using or considering the use of a controller. Various computations have been considered for the decentralized methodology among which are the squealing estimations or gathering designs, where mental customers collect in bundles, auto arranging themselves [10]. Range recognizing raises the necessity for a control channel, which can be executed as a submitted repeat channel.

3.7.4 Prosperity of Cooperation

Cognitive clients participating in detecting the channel have advantages: channel problems like various path blurring, investigating, and tailing infiltration occurrences force highly affected prerequisites that are naturally constrained by cost and influence the results. By utilizing the collaboration between nodes can radically diminish the affected results by up to 25 dBm. Also an additional decrease in the limitations can be observed by utilizing the above plan. Hence, all the topologies of helpful systems might decreases the location time in contrast with awkward networks [9].

3.7.5 Problems of Cooperation

The cognitive radio clients should perform occasional detection as detected data quickly become noticeably out of date because of components such as portability, channel impedances, and so on. This significantly increases the information overhead, vast tactile information as the cognitive radio can conceive any spectrum opening. The spectrum should examine a wide range of lot of information, throughput, affectability prerequisites and vitality utilization. Despite the fact that detecting information creates some of the difficulties, it could be completed without bringing about much overhead in light of the fact that exclusive rough detecting data is required, disposing of the requirement for complex flag preparation plans at the collector and decreasing the information stack. Additionally, despite the fact that a wide channel must be examined, just a part of it changes at one time which means refreshing only the changed data and not every one of the points of interest of the whole filtered band [9].

3.8 Interference-Based Recognition

In this segment, we introduce obstruction-based location with the goal that the cognitive radio clients would work in the spectrum underlying method.

3.8.1 Primary Receiver Detection

By and large, the primary collector produces nearby oscillator (Locally Optimum) spillage control from its Radio Frequency front end while accepting the information from the essential transmitter. This has been recommended as a strategy to identify the essential client by mounting a minimal effort sensor hub near an essential client's collector, keeping in mind that the end goal is to recognize the nearby oscillator (Locally Optimum) spillage control discharged by the Radio frequency front end of the essential client's recipients which are inside the correspondence spectrum of the cognitive radio framework clients. The neighborhood sensor at that point reports the detected data to the cognitive radio clients with the goal that they can distinguish the spectrum inhabitance status.

3.8.2 Intrusion Temperature Managing

Unlike the essential collector identification, the fundamental thought behind the obstruction temperature administration is to set up an upper impedance restriction for a given recurrence band in a particular geographic area with the end goal that the cognitive radio clients are not permitted to cause destructive obstruction while utilizing that particular band in that particular region. Ordinarily, cognitive radio client transmitters control their obstructions by directing their transmission control (their out-of-band emanations) in light of their areas with regard to essential clients. This strategy essentially focuses on measuring obstructions at the collector [7]. The working rule of this technique resembles a UWB innovation where the cognitive radio clients are permitted to exist together and transmit at the same time with essential clients by utilizing a little broadcast control that is limited by the obstruction temperature height in order to avoid creating hurtful impedance for essential clients.

3.9 Conclusion

Spectrum is a great resource in remote correspondence systems and it has been an imperative research subject for many years. Subjective radio is a promising development which enables distinguishing tricky spectrum use by giving a path to the void zones. Considering the problems encountered by scholarly radios, the use of a spectrum distinguishing system appears as an urgent need to provide results similar to the unencumbered use of an open spectrum and also confines impedance for the approved basic customers. As discussed in this chapter, the change of the subjective radio framework requires the commitment and association of many strategies, including, deterrent organization, scholarly radio reconfiguration organization, and pleasing correspondences.

Also, with the objective of totally comprehending the cognitive radio system in remote exchanges for the beneficial utilization of little used Radio frequency bands, the strategy of perceiving the block and in addition run systematic searches for impediments or interference should be tried and true so the fundamental customer will not encounter the problems of the cognitive radio structure. We introduced diverse flag preparing techniques by gathering them into three fundamental gatherings and discussed their points of interest. We have likewise introduced the advantages and disadvantages of various spectrum detecting techniques, and explained the correlations regarding operation, exactness, complexities, and executions.

References

1. Ariananda, D. D. et al., A survey on spectrum sensing techniques for cognitive radio, Second International Workshop on Cognitive Radio and Advanced Spectrum Management, pp. 74–79, 2009.
2. Chen, R. and Park, J.-M., Robust distributed spectrum sensing in cognitive radio networks, The 27th IEEE Conference on Computer Communications, pp. 1876–1884, 2008.
3. Force, S. P. T., Spectrum policy task force report, Federal Communications Commission ET Docket 02, 2002.
4. Ismail, R. et al., The beta reputation system, Proceedings of the 15th Bled Electronic Commerce Conference, pp. 324–337, 2002.
5. Ganesan, G. and Li, Y., Cooperative spectrum sensing in cognitive radio networks, IEEE International Symposium on New Frontiers in Dynamic Spectrum Access Networks, pp. 137–143, 2005.

6. Cabric, D. and Mishra, S. M., Implementation issues in spectrum sensing for cognitive radios, Thirty-Eighth Asilomar Conference on Signals, Systems and Computers, Vol. 1, pp. 772–776, 2004.
7. Cordeiro, C. et al., IEEE 802.22: The first worldwide wireless standard based on cognitive radios, First IEEE International Symposium on New Frontiers in Dynamic Spectrum Access Networks, pp. 328–337, 2005.
8. Huang, X. et al., Weighted-collaborative spectrum sensing in cognitive radio, Second International Conference on Communications and Networking in China, pp. 110–114, 2007.
9. Kaligineedi, P., Khabbazian, M., and Bhargava, V. K., Secure cooperative sensing techniques for cognitive radio systems, IEEE International Conference on Communications, pp. 3406–3410, 2008.
10. Lim, S. et al., Cooperative spectrum sensing for IEEE 802.22 wran system, 18th International Conference on Computer Communications and Networks, pp. 1–5, 2009.

4

Sensing Techniques in Cognitive Radio Networks: An Appraisal

Pankaj Verma, Poonam Jindal, and Brahmjit Singh

CONTENTS

4.1 Introduction

This chapter gives an exhaustive analysis of the various spectrum sensing methods, their advantages, and disadvantages. Spectrum sensing empowers the ability of a CR to measure and learn the radio's operating environment characteristics, such as spectrum availability, interference, and so on. The spectrum availability varies with time, location, and operating frequency, resulting in spectrum access opportunities. Thus, a Secondary User (SU) can access the available spectrum in an adaptive way. In this way, spectrum sensing aids SUs in achieving the goal of increasing the utilization of the spectrum, and concurrently assuring the protection of primary users (PUs) from any harmful interference. It also helps to determine if the PU has become active in the band currently used by the SU so that the band can be vacated immediately to avoid any harmful interference to the PU.

4.2 Hypothesis Testing

In binary hypotheses testing, a null hypothesis (H_0) corresponds to the absence of PU under which the received signal $y(n)$ is represented as

$$H_0 : y(n) = u(n) \tag{4.1}$$

An alternate hypothesis (H_1) indicates the presence of PU and the received signal in this case is represented as

$$H_1 : y(n) = h(n)s(n) + u(n) \tag{4.2}$$

Here, $h(n)$ is the channel gain at the nth time instant, $s(n)$ is the signal transmitted by PU, and $u(n)$ is the noise signal. In general, test statistics, X, is computed from the observation vector, $y = [y(1), y(2), \ldots, y(n)]$, comprising N observation samples. Test statistics (X) is equated to a predetermined threshold (λ) to resolve between the two hypotheses. If test statistics is greater than a given threshold, that is, $X > \lambda$, then hypothesis H_1 is true, which means the presence of the PU in the band, otherwise, H_0 is true, which implies the absence of the PU. The performance of any spectrum-sensing algorithm can be interpreted in terms of the probability of detection (P_d) and probability of false alarm (P_f). The term P_d may be described as the probability for which the SU claims the presence of the PU (decide H_1) when the PU is present (H_1 is true). The probability of a missed detection (P_{md}) is the probability of deciding H_0 when H_1 is true, that is, $P_d + P_{md} = 1$. The P_f may be described as the probability for which the SU claims the existence of a PU (decides H_1), when the PU is not using the channel (H_0 is true). Accordingly, the terms P_d and P_f can be represented as:

$$P_d = P(H_1/H_1) = P(X > \lambda | H_1) \tag{4.3}$$

and

$$P_f = P(H_1/H_0) = P(X > \lambda | H_0) \tag{4.4}$$

The probability of detections and false alarms are depicted pictorially in Figure 4.1. In this figure, the likelihood distributions for the non-existence and existence of a PU signal are assumed to be normally distributed having equal variance and means as μ_1 and μ_2, respectively. It can be seen from the graph that if the threshold is increased, P_{md} will increase and P_f will decrease. Similarly, if the threshold value is decreased, P_d will increase at the cost of an increase in the P_f. Therefore, there is a fundamental trade-off between detection and false alarm probabilities.

The detection probability should be on the higher side to ensure protection of the PUs from the harmful interference that could be caused by SUs' transmissions. At the same time, the P_f should as small as possible to increase the chances of utilization of any vacant spectrum. The probability of error in sensing is defined as

$$P_e = P(H_0)P_f + P(H_1)P_{md} \tag{4.5}$$

where $P(H_0)$ and $P(H_1)$ are the probabilities for which the hypotheses H_0 and H_1 are true, respectively.

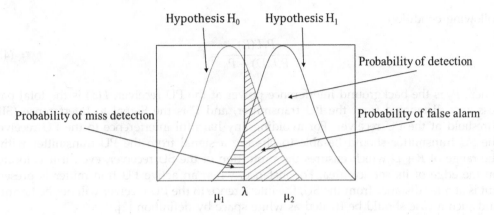

FIGURE 4.1
Illustration of detection and false alarm probabilities.

4.3 Primary Transmitter Detection

The transmitter detection model is established on identification of a feeble signal from the PU transmitter by the local observations of the SU. This model suffers from the drawback of its dependability on the detection of a PU transmitter to find vacant spectrum. At the same time, interference may occur at the PU receiver as well, so a detection margin has to be included to protect the PU [1]. This is illustrated in Figure 4.2. The interference also depends on the PU transmitter power in addition to the power transmitted by the SU transmitter for its own transmission. Let P_p and P_s denote the power transmitted by PU and SU, respectively, and R is the distance of the PU transmitter from the PU receiver. Then, the interference range of SU, 'D', is determined from the

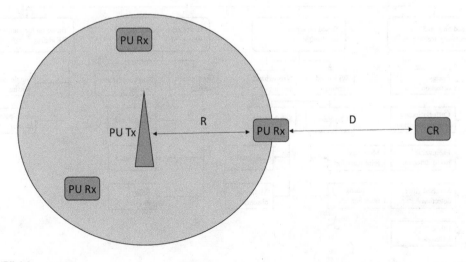

FIGURE 4.2
Illustration of interference to PU receiver.

following condition

$$\frac{P_p L(R)}{P_s L(D) + P_b} = \Gamma \qquad (4.6)$$

where P_b is the background interference power at the PU receiver, $L(d)$ is the total path loss at a distance d from the PU transmitter, and Γ is the Signal to Interference (SIR) threshold at the PU receiver. For avoiding any harmful interference to the PU receiver, the SU transmitter should be able to observe a signal from the PU transmitter within the range of $R + D$ which ensures the protection of the SU receiver, even if it is located on the edge of its service area. For instance, when an active PU transmitter is present, but is at a far distance from the SU, the interference to the PU receiver will not be harmful and such a case should be treated as white space by definition [2].

4.4 Classification of Sensing Techniques

The spectrum sensing techniques can be classified on the basis of signal processing techniques, signal bandwidth, cooperation among SUs, and number of radio frequency (RF) chains as illustrated in Figure 4.3.

Cyclostationary feature detection, matched filter detection, energy detection, eigenvalue-based detection, and a few other sensing techniques are introduced in the following section.

4.4.1 Matched Filter Detection

This method has been established as the optimal detector for the detection of a PU signal, where the characteristics of the signal transmitted by the PU are well known, as it magnifies

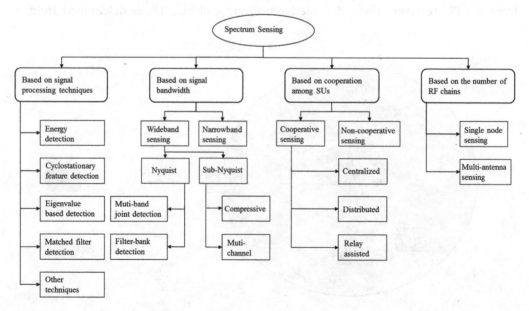

FIGURE 4.3
Classification of spectrum sensing techniques.

the Signal to Noise Ratio (SNR) of the received signal [3–5]. It has the advantage of taking less time to achieve the desired detection performance, such as low P_{md} and P_f. The matched filter detection method actually demodulates a PU signal, thus it needs a priori information of the signal of a PU at both physical (PHY) and medium access control (MAC) layers, for example, pulse shaping, modulation type, packet format, order, and so on. CR has to pre-store this information, and it has to provide coherency with the PU signal by synchronization and channel equalization [5]. However, such information is not readily available to the SU making the use of this detector difficult. In addition to this, a significant drawback is that the SU has to use a dedicated detector for each PU signal class [6].

4.4.2 Cyclostationary Feature Detection

This is another spectrum sensing algorithm for detecting the PU signals by using the cyclostationary characteristics of a received signal [7,8,9–12]. The cyclostationary features are induced by the periodicity in the statistics of the PU signal, such as mean or autocorrelation. Sometimes, periodicity may be induced deliberately to aid spectrum sensing [13–16]. In place of the Power Spectrum Density (PSD), the cyclic correlation function may also be used for differentiating noise from the PU signal. Generally, the noise signal is Wide Sense Stationary (WSS) without correlation while the signals are cyclostationary with spectral correlation because of redundancies in the signal properties. The Cyclic Spectral Density (CSD) of the received signal may be calculated as [17].

$$S(f, \alpha) = \sum_{\tau=-\infty}^{\infty} R_y^\alpha(\tau)\, e^{-j2\pi f t} \tag{4.7}$$

where

$$R_y^\alpha(\tau) = E\big[y(n + \tau)y(n - \tau)\, e^{j2\pi\alpha n}\big] \tag{4.8}$$

is the Cyclic Autocorrelation Function (CAF) and α is the cyclic frequency. The peak output is obtained from the CSD when the cyclic frequency is the same as one of the fundamental frequencies of the PU signal.

The Orthogonal Frequency Division Multiplexing (OFDM) signal may be reformed prior to transmission to generate some kind of periodicity at certain frequencies [13–16]. The periodicity generated can be used for the classification of signals. Hardware implementation of the cyclostationary feature detection has been provided in [18]. Therefore, cyclostationary feature detection can perform better than the Energy Detection (ED) scheme [19] but requires a perfect awareness of the delay lag and cyclic frequency. The implementation complexity of this method increases by N^2 complex multiplications as required to calculate the cross-correlation of the N point Fast Fourier Transform (FFT) outputs whereas Energy Detection (ED) has N points complexity.

4.4.3 Energy Detection

Energy detection is extensively utilized as a spectrum-sensing algorithm owing to its simple implementation and less computational complexity [5,7,20–32]. In addition, it is more generally relative to other methods, as this method does not need any prior information of the PU signal. In this, the presence or absence of a PU signal is determined by analyzing the

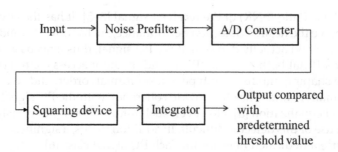

FIGURE 4.4
Block diagram of energy detector.

output of the energy detector to a predetermined threshold. The block diagram for the ED scheme is shown in Figure 4.4. The signal to be detected is crossed through a noise pre-filter to restrict the adjacent bandwidth signals and noise. The output of the filter is fed to an Analog to Digital Converter (ADC), which converts the signal from the analog domain to the digital domain. Thereafter, the digital signal is passed through a squaring device and then to an integrator. The output from the integrator is an estimate of the energy contained in the signal [33].

The energy estimated is equated to a predetermined threshold to decide between the two hypotheses (H_0 or H_1). The output of the detector is represented by test statistics X given as

$$X = \frac{1}{N} \sum_{n=1}^{N} |y(n)|^2 \tag{4.9}$$

where $y(n)$ is the received signal and N is the number of samples used for detection. The challenges with ED based sensing include the setting of the appropriate threshold, failure to distinguish interference from the PU signal, estimation of noise variance, and bad performance in low SNR regions. In addition, ED based sensing suffers a problem in detecting spread spectrum signals [5,28].

The threshold used in ED based spectrum sensing relies on the noise variance, but a little fault in the estimation of the noise can lead to a momentous performance loss [34]. The problem is addressed in [35], where noise power is estimated dynamically by detaching the signal and noise subspaces with an algorithm called multiple signal classification (MUSIC). Then, estimated noise power is used to determine the threshold for a constant value of P_f. Therefore, the setting of a threshold plays a very important part in the sensing performance of ED based sensing. Literature works on the optimization of the threshold for ED based schemes have been covered in [36–40].

To meet the necessary constraint of PU protection, which is to keep a watch on the probability of any misdetections (say 0.1), the threshold is usually kept low, which in turn will increase the P_f thus leading to a decrease in the chances of leveraging spectrum holes. Similarly, to meet the constraint of the P_f, the threshold is kept high, which will increase the probability of misdetections, thus causing interference to PUs. Further, spectrum sensing is usually performed repeatedly to investigate the absence/presence of any possible PU activity. Assuming that spectrum sensing done by an SU is perfect (i.e., 100% P_d and 0% P_f), there still are chances that a PU can appear in between two sensing epochs and may suffer interference from the SU transmission. Moreover, in an imperfect sensing case when there is a misdetection, the PU may disappear suddenly in between two sensing epochs and will not result in interference to the SU. This sudden appearance and disappearance of a PU affects the effective utilization of the spectrum. The above-mentioned problems have been addressed in [41] where a new objective function, spectrum utilization, has been formulated. The optimization of a threshold in sensing techniques is still an open research problem for the successful implementation of cognitive radio networks.

4.4.4 Eigenvalue-Based Sensing

This method of detection is established based on the decomposition of eigenvalues of the covariance matrix of the received signal. The SU needs to gather the received samples in two dimensions, one dimension being time and the other can be either the number of multiple antennas, branches or the number of cooperating nodes in Cooperative Spectrum Sensing (CSS). A single SU can also employ this technique separately assuming it uses the sampling on the segment of the received signal or has multiple antennas.

Different eigenvalue-based algorithms such as Maximum Eigenvalue (ME) 0, Maximum to Minimum Eigenvalue (MME), Energy to Minimum Eigenvalue (EME) [43], Scaled Largest Eigenvalue (SLE) [44], Signal Condition Number (SCN) [45], and so on are utilized as the test statistics to perform sensing. Many other eigenvalue-based algorithms are accessible in the literature based on the test statistics required [46,47,48,49,50,51]. From the literature, it has been noticed that the performance of eigenvalue-based algorithms have been analyzed for different kinds of PU signals, namely wireless microphone signals [42], Independent and Identical Distribution (IID) Gaussian signals [42,45], captured digital television (DTV) signals [43], OFDM signals [47], and Binary Phase Shift Keying (BPSK) modulated signals [48]. In view of this, the performance of various eigenvalue-based algorithms for the disparate class of PU signals has been analyzed in [52]. From the analysis, it has been observed that eigenvalue-based algorithms work only when the PU signal has a correlation among the samples of the signals.

4.4.5 Other Sensing Techniques

Other spectrum sensing techniques include multi-taper spectral estimation, Hough transform, wavelet detection, autocorrelation-based detection, covariance-based detection, moment-based detection, Max-Min SNR based detection, and so on. The multi-taper spectrum estimation is similar to the maximum likelihood power spectral density estimator and is approximately optimal for wideband signals [53]. The complexity of the algorithm is less than that of the maximum likelihood detector, but it is computationally more critical. The random Hough transform of the received signal may be used for the detection of any form of signal having a periodic pattern [54]. The wavelet detection is introduced in [55] for spectrum sensing in wideband channels. In this, wavelets are utilized for detecting the edges corresponding to changes from an engaged band to a vacant band and vice versa. The method recommended in [55] was enhanced in [56] by utilizing sub-Nyquist sampling for developing a more realistic sensing algorithm. Assuming the spectrum of the signal to be sparse, sub-Nyquist sampling can be used for coarse sensing. In [57,58], an analog implementation of the wavelet method is recommended for coarse sensing, which enables real time operation and low power consumption.

Autocorrelation based detectors for detecting the presence of PU signals are discussed in [59–61]. The advantage of this method is its ability to differentiate between noise and signal spectrum over the sensing bandwidth. Generally, signals have high correlation due to the existence of RF channel guard bands and utilization of practical modulation schemes.

Assuming transmitted signals of PU as BPSK, Quadrature Phase Shift Keying (QPSK) or M-ary Quadrature Amplitude Modulation (QAM) or continuous uniformly distributed random variables, where noise is assumed to be IID circularly symmetric complex Gaussian random variables all having unknown variance, the ratio of the fourth and second moments is used as the test statistics in [62,63]. An analytical expression for the P_d and P_f are also provided. In [64], a max-min SNR based signal detection technique is proposed, which exploits the characteristics of the pulse shaping filter of the primary transmitter. In this, the received signal is oversampled and then a linear combiner is used to combine the oversampled signal. The resulting combined signal has two components having distinct SNR values. Thereafter, the ratio of the energy of the signal related to the maximum and minimum SNR values is used as the test statistics, and expressions for the P_d and P_f are derived mathematically for the Additive White Gaussian Noise (AWGN) channel.

4.5 Cooperative Spectrum Sensing

In CSS, reports from distantly located SUs are integrated at the fusion center to resolve between the two hypotheses. In the literature of Cognitive Radio Networks (CRNs) [65–75], cooperation among SUs offers a solution to the problems of shadowing, fading, and noise uncertainty. It appreciably decreases both the P_m and P_f. In addition to this, cooperation decreases the sensing time (or duration), and the hidden node problem can be addressed. The idea behind CSS is to improve the performance by utilizing the geographical variance of differently spaced SUs. It has been proved analytically and through simulation that cooperative sensing provides a significant performance improvement as compared to local sensing. The improvement in the sensing performance because of this geographical diversity is known as cooperative gain. In CSS, there are basically three steps: first, the sensing is performed by each CR separately, second, the sensing results are reported to the Fusion Center (FC) via a control channel, and third, the reported results are combined to make a global decision and the final decision is reported back to every CR. In CSS architectures, the control channel used may be realized through distinct approaches including a dedicated control channel or an Industrial, Scientific, and Medical (ISM) band [76]. Other methodologies for control channel implementation have been mentioned in [77,78].

4.5.1 Cooperation Models

Depending on how the SUs share their sensing results, several architectures have been proposed in the literature [65,79]. Centralized and distributed sensing are commonly used and are discussed below.

4.5.1.1 Centralized Sensing

In centralized CSS, all the SUs send their sensing information directly to a central entity called fusion centre (FC). The FC then combines all the sensing information received from multiple SUs and determines a final opinion regarding the presence/absence of a PU. The FC then broadcasts that global decision to different CRs or directly governs the traffic of CRs. This architecture is also known as parallel fusion architecture as illustrated in Figure 4.5.

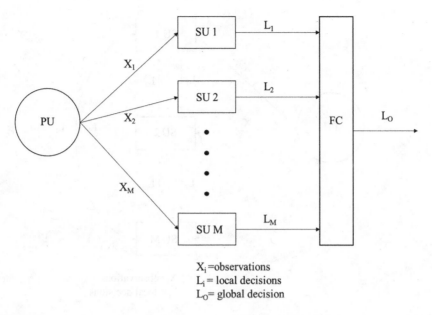

X$_i$=observations
L$_i$ = local decisions
L$_O$= global decision

FIGURE 4.5
Centralized sensing.

4.5.1.2 Distributed Sensing

In this type of architecture, CRs share information and then reach a central judgement about the presence/absence of PU by iterations. A distributed algorithm is used by every SU for sharing the sensing information to different SUs. Then the SU combines the received sensing information with its own sensing results to reach a global decision about the presence/absence of a PU as per some condition. If the condition is not satisfied, the procedure is repeated until the final decision is reached. This is more advantageous as compared to centralized sensing, as there is no need for any backbone infrastructure. Distributed sensing (or decentralized sensing) is illustrated in Figure 4.6.

4.5.2 Fusion Schemes

In CSS, fusion schemes refer to the process of combining the local sensing results from multiple SUs. Depending on the type of data shared by SUs, fusion schemes can be classified as soft or hard fusion schemes as discussed below.

4.5.2.1 Soft Decision Fusion

In soft (or data) fusion schemes, each SU forwards the explicit test statistics to the fusion center. These received tests statistics are combined at the FC by some prevailing receiver diversity techniques like Equal Gain Combining (EGC) and Maximum Ratio Combining (MRC). The MRC technique is considered to be the optimal combining strategy for achieving the highest output SNR, under the condition that channel state information between the PU and SU is perfectly known. The schemes which uses soft decision fusion achieve improved performance in comparison to hard fusion schemes but require a large cooperation overhead as a huge number of bits need to be directed to the FC for sending exact

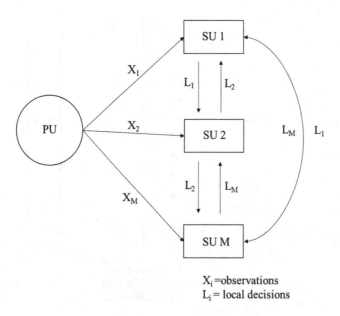

X_i = observations
L_i = local decisions

FIGURE 4.6
Distributed sensing.

test statistics. In [66–69], different methodologies for cooperation among SUs have been discussed.

4.5.2.2 Hard Decision Fusion

In this scheme, each SU makes a decision locally and forwards only a one-bit opinion to the FC, that is, bit '1' for the presence of the PU and bit '0' for the absence of the PU. The main advantage of this scheme is the reduction in the number of bits needed to be sent to the FC [70,71]. These one-bit decisions are combined at the FC by applying some logical fusion rules. The frequently utilized fusion rules includes AND, OR, and MAJORITY rule, which are particular cases of the common K-out-of-M rule. These fusion rules are outlined as follows [72]:

K-out-of-M rule: In this rule, the FC makes the decision in the favor of the presence of a PU, if and only if K or more than K SUs out of a total of M cooperating SUs report the presence of the PU. Therefore, in this rule, hypothesis H_1 is decided if K or more than K SUs make the decision in favor of hypothesis H_1. If the results received from the SUs are assumed to be separate, then cooperative probability of detection (Q_d) and false alarm (Q_f) at the FC are given as:

$$Q_d = \sum_{i=K}^{M} \binom{M}{i} P_{di}^i (1 - P_{di})^{M-i} \tag{4.10}$$

$$Q_f = \sum_{i=K}^{M} \binom{M}{i} P_{fi}^i (1 - P_{fi})^{M-i} \tag{4.11}$$

where P_{di} and P_{fi} represent the detection and false alarm probabilities of the ith user, respectively. In Equations 4.11 and 4.12, if K is equal to or greater than $M/2$, then the rule is said to be a *Half Voting* or *MAJORITY Rule*.

OR rule: In this rule of fusion, FC will decide in favor of hypothesis H_1 if any one of the SUs makes the decision in favor of hypothesis H_1, that is, setting $K = 1$ in Equations 4.11 and 4.12. This rule minimizes the possibility of SUs creating interference to the PUs. If the results of all the SUs are considered as separate, then the expressions for Q_d and Q_f under this rule will be given as:

$$Q_{dOR} = 1 - \prod_{i=1}^{M} (1 - P_{di}) \tag{4.12}$$

$$Q_{fOR} = 1 - \prod_{i=1}^{M} (1 - P_{fi}) \tag{4.13}$$

AND Rule: In the AND fusion rule, FC claims the presence of PU only if all the SUs participating in the cooperation report the presence of PU, that is, $K = M$ in Equations 4.11 and 4.12. This rule of fusion will result in a decrease in the probabilities of both detection and false alarm. This will surely boost the prospects of improving spectrum utilization, but concurrently, the risk of interference to the PU will also increase. Under the same assumption of independent decisions from all the SUs, Q_f for this AND rule will be given as:

$$Q_{dAND} = \prod_{i=1}^{M} P_{di} \tag{4.14}$$

$$Q_{fAND} = \prod_{i=1}^{M} P_{fi} \tag{4.15}$$

The sensing performance of soft fusion schemes is always superior to that of the hard fusion schemes, but simultaneously the bandwidth need of the control channel also increases. An infinite number of bits per SU are required to be directed to the FC in soft fusion schemes as compared to only one-bit per SU in hard fusion schemes. Thus, there exists a fundamental trade-off between bandwidth cost of the control channel and sensing performance, which has been improved in [80].

4.5.3 Double Threshold-Based CSS

The CSS, where each SU uses a double threshold-based ED method, was introduced in the literature to boost the accuracy of the sensing results in low SNR regions [81–84]. In this scheme, each SU uses a double threshold instead of the conventional single threshold. The SU reaches a decision for the presence or absence of a PU only if the observed energy lies above the upper threshold or below the lower threshold, respectively. If the observed energy lies in between the two threshold values, then SU does not reach a decision. If in this case the observed energy of all the SUs lies in between two threshold values, then FC will not receive any decision from any SU, and this problem is known as a sensing failure problem which has been addressed in [85].

4.6 Conclusion

In this chapter, a brief review of the literature related to spectrum sensing is provided. It covers both the cooperative and non-cooperative aspects of spectrum sensing. The literature survey presented in this chapter enables us to identify the issues and challenges related to the existing algorithms. It is established that in spite of a number of good spectrum sensing algorithms, sensing in low SNR regions still needs to be improved. Further, there is an imperative need to reinvestigate the existing spectrum sensing algorithms and improve them.

Acknowledgments

We thank our parents for their support and motivation.

References

1. A. Ghasemi and E. S. Sousa, "Spectrum Sensing in Cognitive Radio Networks: Requirements, Challenges and Design Trade-Offs," *IEEE Communications Magazine*, vol. 46, no. 4, pp. 32–39, April 2008.
2. L. Khalid, "Efficient Techniques for Cooperative Spectrum Sensing in Cognitive Radio Networks," PhD dissertation, University of Toronto, 2008.
3. R. Tandra and A. Sahai, "Fundamental Limits on Detection in Low SNR Under Noise Uncertainty," *International Conference on Wireless Networks, Communications and Mobile Computing*, pp. 464–469, 2005.
4. J. Proakis, *Digital Communications*, Mc Graw Hill, 2008.
5. D. Cabric, S. M. Mishra, and R. W. Brodersen, "Implementation Issues in Spectrum Sensing for Cognitive Radios," *Proceedings Asilomar Conference on Signals, Systems and Computers*, pp. 772–776, November 2004.
6. H. Arslan, *Cognitive Radio, Software Defined Radio, and Adaptive Wireless Systems*, Springer, Netherlands, 2007.
7. T. Yucek and H. Arslan, "A Survey of Spectrum Sensing Algorithms for Cognitive Radio Applications," *IEEE Communication Surveys & Tutorials*, vol. 11, no. 1, pp. 116–130, 2009.
8. S. K. Sharma, T. E. Bogale, S. Chatzinotas, B. Ottersten, L. B. Le and X. Wang, "Cognitive Radio Techniques Under Practical Imperfections: A Survey," *IEEE Communications Surveys & Tutorials*, vol. 17, no. 4, pp. 1858–1884, Fourthquarter 2015.
9. N. Khambekar, L. Dong and V. Chaudhary, "Utilizing OFDM Guard Interval for Spectrum Sensing," *IEEE Wireless Communications and Networking Conference*, Kowloon, pp. 38–42, 2007.
10. M. Oner and F. Jondral, "Cyclostationarity-Based Methods for the Extraction of the Channel Allocation Information in a Spectrum Pooling System," *IEEE Radio and Wireless Conference*, pp. 279–282, 2004.
11. J. Lunden, V. Koivunen, A. Huttunen and H. V. Poor, "Spectrum Sensing in Cognitive Radios Based on Multiple Cyclic Frequencies," *2nd International Conference on Cognitive Radio Oriented Wireless Networks and Communications*, Orlando, FL, USA, pp. 37–43, 2007.
12. K. Kim, I. A. Akbar, K. K. Bae, J. S. Um, C. M. Spooner and J. H. Reed, "Cyclostationary Approaches to Signal Detection and Classification in Cognitive Radio," *2nd IEEE International Symposium on New Frontiers in Dynamic Spectrum Access Networks*, Dublin, pp. 212–215, 2007.

13. K. Maeda, A. Benjebbour, T. Asai, T. Furuno and T. Ohya, "Recognition among OFDM-Based Systems Utilizing Cyclostationarity-Inducing Transmission," *2nd IEEE International Symposium on New Frontiers in Dynamic Spectrum Access Networks*, Dublin, pp. 516–523, 2007.

14. P. D. Sutton, K. E. Nolan and L. E. Doyle, "Cyclostationary Signatures for Rendezvous in OFDM-Based Dynamic Spectrum Access Networks," *2nd IEEE International Symposium on New Frontiers in Dynamic Spectrum Access Networks*, Dublin, pp. 220–231, 2007.

15. P. D. Sutton, J. Lotze, K. E. Nolan and L. E. Doyle, "Cyclostationary Signature Detection in Multipath Rayleigh Fading Environments," *2nd International Conference on Cognitive Radio Oriented Wireless Networks and Communications*, Orlando, FL, USA, pp. 408–413, 2007.

16. M. K. Tsatsanis and G. B. Giannakis, "Transmitter Induced Cyclostationarity for Blind Channel Equalization," *IEEE Transactions on Signal Processing*, vol. 45, no. 7, pp. 1785–1794, July 1997.

17. W. A. Gardner, "Exploitation of Spectral Redundancy in Cyclostationary Signals," *IEEE Signal Processing Magazine*, vol. 8, no. 2, pp. 14–36, April 1991.

18. A. Tkachenko, D. Cabric and R. W. Brodersen, "Cyclostationary Feature Detector Experiments Using Reconfigurable BEE2," *2nd IEEE International Symposium on New Frontiers in Dynamic Spectrum Access Networks*, Dublin, pp. 216–219, 2007.

19. D. Cabric and R. W. Brodersen, "Physical Layer Design Issues Unique to Cognitive Radio Systems," *IEEE 16th International Symposium on Personal, Indoor and Mobile Radio Communications*, Berlin, vol. 2, pp. 759–763, 2005.

20. N. Sai Shankar, C. Cordeiro and K. Challapali, "Spectrum Agile Radios: Utilization and Sensing Architectures," *First IEEE International Symposium on New Frontiers in Dynamic Spectrum Access Networks*, Baltimore, MD, USA, pp. 160–169, 2005.

21. G. Ganesan and Ye Li, "Agility Improvement Through Cooperative Diversity in Cognitive Radio," *IEEE Global Telecommunications Conference*, St. Louis, MO, 2005.

22. G. Ganesan and Y. Li, "Cooperative Spectrum Sensing in Cognitive Radio Networks," *First IEEE International Symposium on New Frontiers in Dynamic Spectrum Access Networks*, Baltimore, MD, USA, pp. 137–143, 2005.

23. A. Ghasemi and E. S. Sousa, "Optimization of Spectrum Sensing for Opportunistic Spectrum Access in Cognitive Radio Networks," *4th IEEE Consumer Communications and Networking Conference*, Las Vegas, NV, pp. 1022–1026, 2007.

24. F. F. Digham, M. S. Alouini and M. K. Simon, "On the Energy Detection of Unknown Signals Over Fading Channels," *IEEE International Conference on Communications (ICC)*, vol. 5, pp. 3575–3579, 2003.

25. P. Qihang, Z. Kun, W. Jun and L. Shaoqian, "A Distributed Spectrum Sensing Scheme Based on Credibility and Evidence Theory in Cognitive Radio Context," *IEEE 17th International Symposium on Personal, Indoor and Mobile Radio Communications*, Helsinki, pp. 1–5, 2006.

26. J. Lehtomaki, "Analysis of Energy Based Signal Detection," PhD dissertation, University of Oulu, Finland, December 2005.

27. A. Sahai, R. Tandra, S. B. Mishra and N. Hoven, "Fundamental Design Tradeoffs in Cognitive Radio Systems," *Proceedings of the First International Workshop on Technology and Policy for Accessing Spectrum*, 2006.

28. T. Yucek and H. Arslan, "Spectrum Characterization for Opportunistic Cognitive Radio Systems," *IEEE Military Communications Conference*, Washington, DC, pp. 1–6, 2006.

29. X. Liu and S. Shankar, "Sensing-Based Opportunistic Channel Access," *Mobile Networks and Applications*, vol. 11, no. 4, pp. 577–591, 2006.

30. K. Kim, Y. Xin and S. Rangarajan, "Energy Detection Based Spectrum Sensing for Cognitive Radio: An Experimental Study," *IEEE Global Telecommunications Conference*, Miami, FL, pp. 1–5, 2010.

31. A. Muller, J. Coon and R. Piechocki, "Diversity Analysis for Energy Detection-Based Spectrum Sensing," *IET Communications*, vol. 6, no. 7, pp. 759–764, May 2012.

32. I. E. Atawi, O. S. Badarneh, M. S. Aloqlah and R. Mesleh, "Energy-Detection Based Spectrum-Sensing in Cognitive Radio Networks Over Multipath/Shadowed Fading Channels," *Wireless Telecommunications Symposium*, New York, NY, pp. 1–6, 2015.

33. H. Urkowitz, "Energy Detection of Unknown Deterministic Signals," *Proceedings of the IEEE*, vol. 55, no. 4, pp. 523–531, April 1967.

34. A. Sahai, N. Hoven, and R. Tandra, "Some Fundamental Limits on Cognitive Radio," *Proceedings of the Allerton Conference on Control, Communications, and Computation*, Monticello, Illinois, pp. 1662–1671, October 2004.

35. M. P. Olivieri, G. Barnett, A. Lackpour, A. Davis and Phuong Ngo, "A Scalable Dynamic Spectrum Allocation System with Interference Mitigation for Teams of Spectrally Agile Software Defined Radios," *First IEEE International Symposium on New Frontiers in Dynamic Spectrum Access Networks*, Baltimore, MD, USA, pp. 170–179, 2005.

36. Z. Ye, G. Memik and J. Grosspietsch, "Energy Detection Using Estimated Noise Variance for Spectrum Sensing in Cognitive Radio Networks," *IEEE Wireless Communications and Networking Conference*, Las Vegas, NV, pp. 711–716, 2008.

37. P. R. Nair, A. P. Vinod and A. K. Krishna, "An Adaptive Threshold Based Energy Detector for Spectrum Sensing in Cognitive Radios at low SNR," *IEEE International Conference on Communication Systems*, pp. 574–578, November 17–19, 2010.

38. L. Luo and S. Roy, "Efficient Spectrum Sensing for Cognitive Radio Networks via Joint Optimization of Sensing Threshold and Duration," *IEEE Transactions on Communications*, vol. 60, no. 10, pp. 2851–2860, October 2012.

39. N. Wang, Y. Gao and X. Zhang, "Adaptive Spectrum Sensing Algorithm Under Different Primary User Utilizations," *IEEE Communications Letters*, vol. 17, no. 9, pp. 1838–1841, September 2013.

40. L. K. Mathew, S. Sharma and P. Verma, "An Adaptive Algorithm for Energy Detection in Cognitive Radio Networks," *Second International Conference on Advances in Computing and Communication Engineering*, pp. 104–107, May 1–2, 2015.

41. P. Verma and B. Singh, "Joint Optimization of Sensing Duration and Detection Threshold for Maximizing the Spectrum utilization," *Digital Signal Processing*, vol. 74, pp. 94–101, 2018.

42. Y. Zeng, C. L. Koh and Y. C. Liang, "Maximum Eigenvalue Detection: Theory and Application," *IEEE International Conference on Communications*, Beijing, pp. 4160–4164, 2008.

43. Y. Zeng and Y. C. Liang, "Eigenvalue-Based Spectrum Sensing Algorithms for Cognitive Radio," *IEEE Transactions on Communications*, vol. 57, no. 6, pp. 1784–1793, June 2009.

44. L. Wei and O. Tirkkonen, "Analysis of Scaled Largest Eigenvalue Based Detection for Spectrum Sensing," *IEEE International Conference on Communications*, Kyoto, pp. 1–5, 2011.

45. S. K. Sharma, S. Chatzinotas and B. Ottersten, "Eigenvalue-Based Sensing and SNR Estimation for Cognitive Radio in Presence of Noise Correlation," *IEEE Transactions on Vehicular Technology*, vol. 62, no. 8, pp. 3671–3684, October 2013.

46. L. S. Cardoso, M. Debbah, P. Bianchi and J. Najim, "Cooperative Spectrum Sensing Using Random Matrix Theory," *3rd International Symposium on Wireless Pervasive Computing*, Santorini, pp. 334–338, 2008.

47. L. Wei and O. Tirkkonen, "Cooperative Spectrum Sensing of OFDM Signals Using Largest Eeigenvalue Distributions," *IEEE 20th International Symposium on Personal, Indoor and Mobile Radio Communications*, Tokyo, pp. 2295–2299, 2009.

48. A. Kortun, T. Ratnarajah, M. Sellathurai, C. Zhong and C. B. Papadias, "On the Performance of Eigenvalue-Based Cooperative Spectrum Sensing for Cognitive Radio," *IEEE Journal of Selected Topics in Signal Processing*, vol. 5, no. 1, pp. 49–55, February 2011.

49. W. Zhang, G. Abreu, M. Inamori and Y. Sanada, "Spectrum Sensing Algorithms via Finite Random Matrices," *IEEE Transactions on Communications*, vol. 60, no. 1, pp. 164–175, January 2012.

50. L. Wei and O. Tirkkonen, "Spectrum Sensing in the Presence of Multiple Primary Users," *IEEE Transactions on Communications*, vol. 60, no. 5, pp. 1268–1277, May 2012.

51. S. K. Sharma, S. Chatzinotas and B. Ottersten, "Maximum Eigenvalue Detection for Spectrum Sensing Under Correlated Noise," *IEEE International Conference on Acoustics, Speech and Signal Processing*, Florence, pp. 7268–7272, 2014.

52. P. Verma and B. Singh, "Performance Analysis of Various Eigenvalue-Based Spectrum Sensing Algorithms for Different Types of Primary User Signals," *Advances in Electronics, Communication and Computing*, pp. 389–397, 2018.

53. S. Haykin, "Cognitive Radio: Brain-Empowered Wireless Communications," *IEEE Journal on Selected Areas in Communication*, vol. 23, no. 2, pp. 201–220, February 2005.
54. K. Challapali, S. Mangold, and Z. Zhong, "Spectrum Agile Radio: Detecting Spectrum Opportunities," *Proceedings of International Symposium on Advanced Radio Technologies*, Boulder, Colorado, USA, March 2004.
55. Z. Tian and G. B. Giannakis, "A Wavelet Approach to Wideband Spectrum Sensing for Cognitive Radios," *1st International Conference on Cognitive Radio Oriented Wireless Networks and Communications*, Mykonos Island, pp. 1–5, 2006.
56. Z. Tian and G. B. Giannakis, "Compressed Sensing for Wideband Cognitive Radios," *IEEE International Conference on Acoustics, Speech and Signal Processing*, Honolulu, HI, pp. 1357–1360, 2007.
57. Y. Youn, H. Jeon, J. H. Choi and H. Lee, "Fast spectrum sensing algorithm for 802.22 WRAN Systems," *International Symposium on Communications and Information Technologies*, Bangkok, pp. 960–964, 2006.
58. Y. Hur et al., "A Cognitive Radio (CR) Testbed System Employing a Wideband Multi-Resolution Spectrum Sensing (MRSS) Technique," *IEEE Vehicular Technology Conference*, Montreal, Que., pp. 1–5, 2006.
59. R. K. Sharma and J. W. Wallace, "Improved Spectrum Sensing by Utilizing Signal Autocorrelation," *IEEE 69th Vehicular Technology Conference*, Barcelona, pp. 1–5, 2009.
60. R. K. Sharma and J. W. Wallace, "Improved Autocorrelation-Based Sensing Using Correlation Distribution Information," *International ITG Workshop on Smart Antennas*, Bremen, pp. 335–341, 2010.
61. M. Naraghi-Pour and T. Ikuma, "Autocorrelation-Based Spectrum Sensing for Cognitive Radios," *IEEE Transactions on Vehicular Technology*, vol. 59, no. 2, pp. 718–733, February 2010.
62. T. E. Bogale and L. Vandendorpe, "Moment Based Spectrum Sensing Algorithm for Cognitive Radio Networks with Noise Variance Uncertainty," *47th Annual Conference on Information Sciences and Systems*, Baltimore, MD, pp. 1–5, 2013.
63. M. R. Morelande and A. M. Zoubir, "Detection of Phase Modulated Signals in Additive Noise," *IEEE Signal Processing Letters*, vol. 8, no. 7, pp. 199–202, July 2001.
64. T. E. Bogale and L. Vandendorpe, "Max-Min SNR Signal Energy Based Spectrum Sensing Algorithms for Cognitive Radio Networks with Noise Variance Uncertainty," *IEEE Transactions on Wireless Communications*, vol. 13, no. 1, pp. 280–290, January 2014.
65. I. F. Akyildiz, B. F. Lo and R. Balakrishnan, "Cooperative Spectrum Sensing in Cognitive Radio Networks: A Survey," *Physical Communication*, vol. 4, no. 1, pp. 40–62, 2011.
66. E. Visotsky, S. Kuffner and R. Peterson, "On Collaborative Detection of TV Transmissions in Support of Dynamic Spectrum Sharing," *First IEEE International Symposium on New Frontiers in Dynamic Spectrum Access Networks*, Baltimore, MD, USA, pp. 338–345, 2005.
67. J. Ma and Y. G. Li, "Soft Combination and Detection for Cooperative Spectrum Sensing in Cognitive Radio Networks," *IEEE Global Telecommunications Conference*, Washington, DC, pp. 3139–3143, 2007.
68. Z. Quan, S. Cui and A. H. Sayed, "Optimal Linear Cooperation for Spectrum Sensing in Cognitive Radio Networks," *IEEE Journal of Selected Topics in Signal Processing*, vol. 2, no. 1, pp. 28–40, February 2008.
69. Y. Yan, A. Li and H. Kayama, "Study on Soft Decision Based Cooperative Sensing in Cognitive Radio Network," *IEEE 70th Vehicular Technology Conference Fall*, Anchorage, AK, pp. 1–5, 2009.
70. A. Ghasemi and E. S. Sousa, "Collaborative Spectrum Sensing for Opportunistic Access in Fading Environments," *First IEEE International Symposium on New Frontiers in Dynamic Spectrum Access Networks*, Baltimore, MD, USA, pp. 131–136, 2005.
71. S. M. Mishra, A. Sahai and R. W. Brodersen, "Cooperative Sensing among Cognitive Radios," *IEEE International Conference on Communications*, Istanbul, pp. 1658–1663, 2006.
72. E. Hossain and V. Bhargava, *Cognitive Wireless Communication Networks*, Springer, 2007.

73. A. S. Cacciapuoti, I. F. Akyildiz and L. Paura, "Correlation-Aware User Selection for Cooperative Spectrum Sensing in Cognitive Radio Ad Hoc Networks," *IEEE Journal on Selected Areas in Communications*, vol. 30, no. 2, pp. 297–306, February 2012.

74. S. Xie, Y. Liu, Y. Zhang and R. Yu, "A Parallel Cooperative Spectrum Sensing in Cognitive Radio Networks," *IEEE Transactions on Vehicular Technology*, vol. 59, no. 8, pp. 4079–4092, October 2010.

75. Y. Liu, S. Xie, R. Yu, Y. Zhang and C. Yuen, "An Efficient MAC Protocol With Selective Grouping and Cooperative Sensing in Cognitive Radio Networks," *IEEE Transactions on Vehicular Technology*, vol. 62, no. 8, pp. 3928–3941, October 2013.

76. D. Cabric, S. M. Mishra, D. Willkomm, R. Brodersen and A. Wolisz, "A Cognitive Radio Approach for Usage of Virtual Unlicensed Spectrum," *Proceedings of 14th IST Mobile wireless Communications Summit*, pp. 1–4, 2005.

77. M. M. Buddhikot, P. Kolodzy, S. Miller, K. Ryan and J. Evans, "DIMSUMnet: New Directions in Wireless Networking Using Coordinated Dynamic Spectrum," *Sixth IEEE International Symposium on a World of Wireless Mobile and Multimedia Networks*, pp. 78–85, 2005.

78. J. Perez-Romero, O. Sallent, R. Agusti and L. Giupponi, "A Novel on-Demand Cognitive Pilot Channel Enabling Dynamic Spectrum Allocation," *2nd IEEE International Symposium on New Frontiers in Dynamic Spectrum Access Networks*, Dublin, pp. 46–54, 2007.

79. I. F. Akyildiz, W. Y. Lee, M. C. Vuran and S. Mohanty, "NeXt Generation/Dynamic Spectrum Access/Cognitive Radio Wireless Networks: A Survey," *Computer Networks*, vol. 50, no. 13, pp. 2127–2159, September 2006.

80. P. Verma and B. Singh, "On the Decision Fusion for Cooperative Spectrum Sensing in Cognitive Radio Networks," *Wireless Networks*, vol. 23, no. 7, pp. 2253–2262, 2017.

81. C. H. Sun, W. Zhang and K. Ben Letaief, "Cooperative Spectrum Sensing for Cognitive Radios Under Bandwidth Constraints," *IEEE Conference on Wireless Communications and Networking*, pp. 1–5, March 2007.

82. J. Zhu, Z. Xu, F. Wang, B. Huang and B. Zhang, "Double Threshold Energy Detection of Cooperative Spectrum Sensing in Cognitive Radio" *IEEE International Conference on Cognitive Radio Oriented Wireless Networks and Communication*, pp. 1–5, 2008.

83. J. Wu, T. Luo, J. Li and G. Yue, "A Cooperative Double-threshold Energy Detection Algorithm in Cognitive Radio Systems" *IEEE International Conference on Wireless Communication, Networking & Mobile Computing*, pp. 1–4, 2009.

84. P. Verma and B. Singh, "Simulation Study of Double Threshold Energy Detection Method for Cognitive Radios," *2015 2nd International Conference on Signal Processing and Integrated Networks (SPIN)*, Noida, 2015, pp. 232–236.

85. P. Verma and B. Singh, "Overcoming Sensing Failure Problem in Double Threshold Based Cooperative Spectrum Sensing," *Optik—International Journal for Light and Electron Optics*, vol. 127, no. 10, pp. 4200–4204, May 2016.

Part III

Advanced Wireless Sensing Techniques

5

Efficient Sensing Schemes for Cognitive Radio

G. Nagarajan and T. Perarasi

CONTENTS

5.1 Introduction

This chapter focuses on the basics and advancements of spectrum sensing techniques. It provides a wide knowledge on the functions of classifications, techniques, and advancements involved in sensing in recent wireless technology. Due to the deployment of the latest technologies and the need for extended data rates developed a thrust in sensing. Various techniques are adopted to sense the spectrum and to share the resources effectively without any loss in the data rates. This chapter also covers the application of sensing which is known as green sensing.

5.2 Functions of Cognitive Radio

Every node in a Cognitive Radio Network should sense the channel to determine the vacant portion of the spectrum. A "spectrum hole" is a sub band of the spectrum that is not exploited in a particular area for a prescribed duration. Spectrum sensing is the process of locating and verifying spectrum holes.

The radio link properties of sensing are the broadcast power, interference, radio functioning environment, and so on. Sensing improves spectrum utility. The major objectives of a cognitive radio network include [1]:

1. To afford reliable communication for all users in the network without causing interference to the primary user;
2. To enable competent exploitation of the spectrum in a nondiscriminatory way.

The aim of the cognitive radio (CR) technology is to take advantage of the maximum efficient spectrum and to improve its utilization by using Dynamic Spectrum Access (DSA) techniques. The channel of licensed users can be effectively accessed for higher spectral efficiency with spectrum management techniques. In order to achieve this goal, the cognitive radio users (CRU) in the Cognitive Radio Network must the Dynamic Spectrum Management Framework (DSMF), which consists of spectrum sensing, spectrum decision, spectrum sharing, spectrum mobility, and spectrum management.

A spectrum hole is a band of a frequency assigned to the primary user as shown in Figure 5.1. In the absence of signaling among the primary and secondary users, a spectrum hole is identified by sensing used data bases, a beaconing technique or a combination of both. The major function of this network is to find spectrum holes and utilize them with less interference to the primary user (PU).

Spectrum sensing is a method to determine radio channel characteristics. The available spectrum characteristics include power of broadcast, noise, and its operating environment in time, frequency, and space domains, and the code [2]. It is a process to identify available spectrum bands for use.

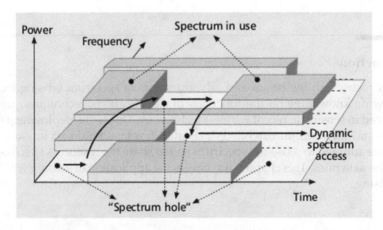

FIGURE 5.1
Dynamic spectrum access technique.

Spectrum decision is the capability of cognitive radio to select the best spectrum band to satisfy the cognitive user without causing any harm to the licensed or primary user. CR ought to be applicable for several antennas and should nullify meddling, increase ability or extend the transmission range [3].

Spectrum sharing avoids collisions between the nodes. Opportunistic Spectrum Access (OSA) helps in effective sharing of power for a greater Signal to Noise Ratio (SNR), channel allocation, and mitigating interference power to the PU.

Spectrum mobility is the process of allocating spectrum bands on the PU's licensed range. The secondary user (SU) must not be allowed to interfere with the PU. At the time of primary user arrival, the cognitive radio user must back off as soon as possible. Spectrum management is the process of capturing the best available spectrum to meet user communication requirements. Cognitive radios select the spectrum that meets a higher quality of service [4]. The functions include a combination of spectrum analysis and spectrum decision.

5.3 Types of Spectrum Sensing

Spectrum sensing is the ability of a device to successfully monitor the surrounding environment to extract information from its surroundings by using its radio. It upgrades the utilization of the available bands. In cooperative spectrum sensing, a signal is detected based on a fusion center decision, hence it overcomes the hidden terminal problems. In nonoperative spectrum sensing, signal detection stays centered on local decisions made thru SUs.

1. In-band sensing a long and repeated errors to sense the spectrum and
2. Out-of-band sensing-how quickly the CR finds its spectrum

An issue that arises in sensing is the need to use exact sensing techniques and transmission times. Maximum spectrum usage and interference avoidance are required in sensing. This type of sensing periodically determines where manipulators are in the transmission period and then in the sensing interval. Sensing time and accuracy are proportional.

The main advantage of spectrum sensing is to recognize more spectrum availability short of probing through the key networks. CR users are meticulously harmonized by recognizing a checker which includes two main issues:

1. In-band sensing-sensing the duration and frequency of usage, and
2. Out-of-band sensing-predicting the available band.

5.3.1 In-band Sensing Control

This method deals with chances of possible utility and also the cancellation of noise. This adopts a periodic nature where users access the spectrum during the transmission and observation periods. For a higher sensing time, the accuracy increases which reduces the noises. For further variations in time, the amount of time available to the CR to transmit the content decreases and vice versa, which leads to the selection of users in sensing.

Optimization of sensing is discussed in [5] and [6]. In [7], the false alarm probability is not taken into account to improve the efficiency of a channel with available detection probability. Reference 8 explains the use of a multiple spectrum environment to boost the throughput of a CR. References 3 and 9 depend on transmission times. In [11], throughput is maximized with a packet collision probability under a certain threshold. The false alarm probability for calculation of throughput is not considered in [12]. Multiple heterogeneous networks are analyzed in [13]. Issues of sensing are explained based on sensing and transmission times. Both times are considered to increase efficiency with minimum interference in [14].

5.3.2 Out-of-band Sensing Control

The performance of Cognitive Radio Ad Hoc Networks (CRAHNs) can be determined by the new band. A coordination scheme is required so that sensing can discover a new user and minimize delay which leads to a reduction in switching time. Proper selection of sensing reduces the discovery time in out-of-band sensing schemes. An n-step serial search is proposed which projects onto channel models [15]. Transmission time and searching sequence are optimized by suppressing delay and superposing the spectrum as in [16,17].

For CR users to sense more bands, better range has to be detected at the cost of search time. In [18], to increase capacity with bands, an optimal stopping time is determined.

5.3.3 Cooperation

In cognitive radio ad hoc networks (CRAHNs), spectrum is allocated based on local observation. The observation range is smaller than its transmitting limit. Receiver uncertainty arises due to the unused portion of the band and transmission limits [19]. For the case where CR receivers are weak with lower SNR because of fading or shadowing, PUs cannot be detected. This is mitigated by CRAHN in [20]. A cluster is created to share local information [21] where both router and clients are supported. No central entity is present in CRAHNs, thus cooperation is implemented distributively.

A link between the PU and SU exists by sharing information promptly for evacuating the spectrum when necessary. To achieve this, a control channel is required. Asynchronous sensing and time scheduling make it very difficult to exchange information among neighbors. This creates a problem in CRAHNs which is alleviated by spectrum decision, spectrum sharing, and mobility.

A protocol is framed in [22] that uses a spreading code for transmission with tolerable interference among users. A flooding-based routing scheme is essential. An optimal cooperative sensing is proposed which uses local test statistics of information, that is, if the CR has a high SNR and uses a real hypothesis, a weighting coefficient is used. The coefficient value is small for a deep fading channel. Cooperative detection is accurate [23,24]. Fading and shadowing effects are considered with this method.

More than one radio (node) is needed in order for them to cooperate with each other. Each node collects data for the detection of a PU. Collected data is formulated in the fusion center and a final decision is made as portrayed in Figure 5.2.

The inception "n" is an integer, representing the "n-out-of-K" voting rule. For values of $n = 1$, an OR rule is applied. The AND rule is applied when $n = k$. Distances between the elements are small compared to the spacing between the transmitter and receiver thus creating identical path losses.

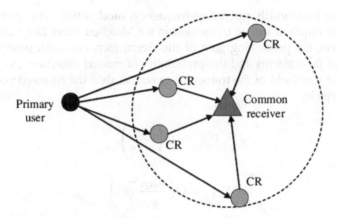

FIGURE 5.2
Cooperative spectrum sensing.

5.3.4 Noncooperative Sensing

With this method, each node makes its own decision without any central entity being pre-loaded. This process does not need a fusion center and will not need any center for transmitting the information to nearby nodes. This scheme is an independent one.

5.4 Conventional Spectrum Sensing Techniques

All critical challenges in a network need to be considered when designing a spectrum sensing method. First, CR finds it difficult to identify primary signals. Second, CR has to detect signaling at low SNR and detection probabilities. Several spectrum sensing schemes, such as matched-filter detection, cyclostationary detection, and energy detection have been presented.

5.4.1 Matched Filter Detection

In matched filter detection, *a priori* knowledge of primary signals is required. Then the yield of the matched filter is sampled and compared with the threshold. This method of detection maximizes the output SNR for a given input signal as shown in Figure 5.3. This is a prime method for detecting a PU when the dispersed signal is known. Even in the presence of additive white stochastic noise, a maximum value of SNR is achieved. Knowledge about

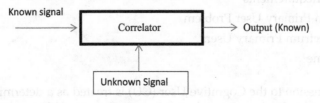

FIGURE 5.3
Matched filter detector.

the PU, including bandwidth, operating frequency, modulation type, pulse shaping, and frame format, are required before transmission for Matched Filter Detector (MFD). Due to coherent detection, the processing gain of the signal increases with time which increases the probability of false alarms and the probability of missed detections.

Let γ_{MFD} be the threshold of the transmitting signal, then the received power of the path loss model is given by

$$P_{\frac{fa}{\gamma_{\mathrm{MFD}}}} = Q\left(\frac{\gamma_{\mathrm{MFD}}}{\sigma_n\sqrt{E}}\right) \tag{5.1}$$

$$P_{\frac{d}{\gamma_{\mathrm{MFD}}}} = Q\left(\frac{\gamma_{\mathrm{MFD}} - E}{\sigma_n\sqrt{E}}\right) \tag{5.2}$$

The hypothesis model of analysis is carried in the transmitter. This model helps in distinguishing used and unused bands from the Primary User (PU). A filter that increases the SNR even in the presence of noise is a matched filter. Figure 5.3 shows that the PU signal $s(t)$ and the received signal $r(t)$ are in correlation with T symbol duration. Then the output is sampled. Let Y be the sampled value which is higher than the threshold. This is an optimal detector method which needs "O" samples to achieve better detection [25]. This helps to synchronize the users. The behavior of the matched filter is predicted from the value of synchronization.

If the CR uses a separate filtering unit for each PU, the cost and complexity increase which is not practically possible [26]. In practice, the PU sends a pilot signal along with data which necessitates energy and feature detecting, which are common methods in CRAHNs.

xG user is discussed in [27] and explains the advantage of the matched filter which is that it needs less time to have increased processing gain with known basic information. The performance of the filter depends on the information provided to it. If the power of noise is explained to the receiver, an energy detector is preferred [28].

The major drawback of this detector is that the detector requires a dedicated sensing receiver for all primary users. Prior knowledge of the transmitter is required for MFD which increases power consumption.

5.4.2 Energy Detection Method

For noise to be Gaussian and for known data, a matched filter is preferred [29]. For an unknown signal, it is analyzed as a function of random processes. An energy detector is preferred for this topology; it measures the energy over a particular time. Energy detection is preferred due to its low complexity. There are some challenges which need to be solved for efficient spectrum sensing which include:

1. Hardware Requirements
2. The Hidden Primary User Problem
3. Spread Spectrum Primary Users
4. Sensing Time

The PU transmission to the Cognitive User (CU) is treated as a deterministic signal with unknown parameters. In such situations, an Energy Detector (ED) is an appropriate mechanism while considering the security threats faced by PUs and exposing information to CUs.

Without obtaining unwanted and unauthorized information, the ED deals with the energy content of the received signal over a period of time. Since only the energy of the waveform is considered rather than its shape or other terminologies, this technique is simple in structure and can be applied to detect any form of deterministic signal of any overlaying technologies and ultra-wide band systems. However, to meet a specific detection probability, samples are required. Hence, ED is more advantageous for detecting a signal with a known power.

In this method, the received signal is equated with the brink to plump whether the PU signal is present. Figure 5.4 shows the structure of an ED which is comprised of a square law device followed by a finite time integrator. The output of the integrator is the energy of the $y(t)$ over the finite time T.

There are two possibilities for the received signal. The first one is the noise alone and the other one is a signal with noise. This signal is modeled as a deterministic signal with unknown parameters. The receiver must resolve the presence of this unknown deterministic signal based on the output of the integrator [30,31].

A binary hypothesis test is preferred. During the idle condition, the received signal is only noise and under a busy scenario, the received signal is the combination of both the signal and noise. This yields the following mathematical representation:

$$H_0: y_1(k) = w_1(k) \tag{5.3}$$

$$H_1: y_1(k) = s(k) + w_1(k) \tag{5.4}$$

for $k = 1, 2, 3, \ldots, n$, $n =$ the number of received samples, $w(k) =$ represents ambient noise, and $s(k) =$ represents the PU signal.

At the common receiver, all single bit decisions are fused together according to a logic rule

$$Y = \sum_{i=1}^{K} D_i \begin{cases} \geq n, & H_1 \\ < n, & H_0 \end{cases} \tag{5.5}$$

where H_0 and H_1 denote the inferences from the common receiver [32].

An optimal method to detect a signal even if the noise power is known is to use an ED. The CR detects the information based on the received energy. The ED needs $1/\text{SNR}$ samples for the probability of detection. ED has a longer detection time for weak signals in the range of 10 to 40 Db. The amount of energy detected depends on the SNR. A minimum value of SNR is called the SNR wall [33].

Unlike the matched filter method, an ED does not require any knowledge of the signal. It uses a received signal strength indicator (RSSI) to determine whether a channel is idle or not. This method produces an output for a higher threshold level. Spectrum agile devices are not suited for ED methodology [34].

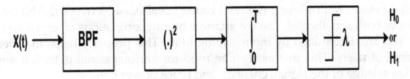

FIGURE 5.4
Energy detection method.

This method does not require prior knowledge of the primary user, but it does require an idea of the sensing time to achieve the desired probabilities of detections and false alarms. Limitations occur due to noise uncertainty and background interference.

For a received signal greater than threshold, the power is known and power outside the allocated band is not known. A periodogram method is used for power calculation in the CR and is expressed as

$$P_{\frac{fa}{\gamma_{ED}}} = Q\left(\frac{\gamma_{ED}}{2}, Z\right) \tag{5.6}$$

where, γ_{ED} = threshold energy level in the ED and Z = allocated band region.

$$P_{\frac{d}{\gamma_{ED}}} = Qx^2\left(\gamma_{ED}, Z, \frac{P}{2\sigma w^2}\right) \tag{5.7}$$

The major drawback of this detection method is that the detector takes a longer time to achieve a high probability of detection and this method is not applicable for partitioning the licensed and unlicensed regions.

5.4.3 Cyclostationary Energy Detection

The periodicity nature of PUs is utilized in cyclostationary feature detection. It is robust to noise uncertainties and a low SNR. It has a high computational complexity and long sensing time.

If X is a zero mean continuous signal then its autocorrelation function is given by

$$R_{XX}(t, \tau) = e[x(t), x^*(t, \tau)] \tag{5.8}$$

The probability of false alarm and probability of detection for CSD are given by

$$P_{\frac{fa}{\gamma_{csd}}} = (1 - \gamma_{CSD})^{(Z-1)} \tag{5.9}$$

$$P_{\frac{d}{\gamma_{CSD}}} = 1 - P_{CDF}(\gamma_{CDF/Z\lambda/\sigma^2}) \tag{5.10}$$

Parameters such as pilot signals, cyclic prefixes, symbol rate, spreading codes or modulation types from local observations help in the detection of a PU by this method. The periodic nature of the signal helps in spectral correlation functions like ED, where $r(t)$ is convolved with the signal over T to detect the PU [35].

The advantage of the feature detection is its robustness to uncertainty in noise power. Synchronization is not maintained which creates complexity in computation and requires a minimum sensing time [36]. A neural network is proposed for detection in [37]. Feature detection extends the detection of Gaussian Minimum Shift Keying (GMSK) in Orthogonal Frequency Division Multiplexing (OFDM) based Local Area Network (LAN) by the cyclic signatures of both signals [38]. The covariances or autocorrelations of signal and noise are different and are determined by the receiving filter. This property helps in differentiating the presence of users. This method can be used for various signal detection applications without knowledge of the signal, channel, and noise power [39].

This method is applicable for military applications to detect weak signals. Due to the operations of sampling, scanning, and modulation, the cyclostationary method is preferred.

This considers both shadowing and fading effects which are difficult to identify with unused bands and deep fades [40]. Due to the periodic nature, noise and modulated signals are differentiated. Thus, the cyclostationary method is preferred [41]. But this method is complex and requires a long time.

The features of the received signal are extracted using cyclic spectral analysis and are represented by a spectral coherent and correlation density function. This method is not suitable for stationary noise. Even a signal with a low strength (SNR) can be easily detected. Thus, ED is preferred due to its lower complexity [42].

5.5 Efficient Schemes

In spectrum sensing, sensing results are verified by hypothesis testing to detect PUs. The hypothesis testing schemes that are used in spectrum sensing are introduced in this section. Composite hypothesis testing methods such as the generalized likelihood ratio test (GLRT) and sequential testing methods such as the sequential probability ratio test (SPRT) are also discussed.

5.5.1 Binary Hypothesis Testing

The Neyman Pearson (NP) test and the Bayes test are the two basic hypothesis testing methods. In NP, the detection probability P_d is maximized for $P_f \leq \alpha$, where α is the maximum false alarm probability. The NP test is equivalent to the likelihood ratio test (LRT) depending on signal detection. An NP-based LRT is used at the fusion center in cooperative sensing.

As a result, the optimal test at the Fusion Center (FC) in cooperative sensing is the NP-based LRT if conditional independence is assumed. Thus, the detector (local sensing) or the FC (cooperative sensing) declares the presence or absence of a PU. The risk to be minimized in the Bayes test is the sum of probabilities of two incorrect detection cases (false alarm and misdetection) and two correct detection cases. With knowledge of *a priori* probabilities $P(H_i)$, the LRT of a Bayes test can be represented. Thus, FC can minimize the Bayes risk by declaring H_1 if $\Lambda(y) > \lambda$ and declaring H_0 otherwise.

5.5.2 Composite Hypothesis Testing

The test that calculates the unknown parameters in a probability distribution function is composite testing. GLRT is robust and implementation is easy. GLRT for multiple frequencies is explained in [43]. In [44], the Rao test and the locally most powerful (LMP) test are proposed for detecting weak PU signals at the FC. The Rao test is equivalent to GLRT and does not require Maximum Likelihood Estimate (MLE). A composite hypothesis testing approach is proposed in [45] for cooperative sensing.

The linear test statistics are derived for an unknown PU and channels' statistics scenarios. When channel statistics are known, the test statistics of the LMP detector are also derived. This method provides robustness to the uncertainties in PU signals and channel gains and its performance is comparable to the optimal NP-based LRT.

5.5.3 Sequential Testing

In general, the number of samples and the sensing time are fixed. With the help of sensing time, a sample can be utilized. Wald developed SPRT [46] to minimize the sensing time subject to detection performance. If the likelihood ratio is superior to λ_1, the detector decides on H_1, while if it is smaller than λ_0, it decides on H_0. At an intermediate level, currently available information is not sufficient to achieve the final decision. In this case, the process is repeated until the next decision is reached. SPRT is applied for detection at the FC in cooperative sensing.

The main advantage of SPRT is that it requires fewer samples on average to attain the same detection performance. It is optimal in minimizing the average number of independent samples and average sensing time. The disadvantage includes the cost for obtaining samples.

It is difficult for the SUs to differentiate the PU signals from other pre-existing SU transmitter signals. Therefore, all are treated as one received signal, $s(t)$. The received signal at the SU, $x(t)$, can be expressed as

$$x(t) = \begin{cases} n(t) & H_0 \\ S(t) + n(t) & H_1 \end{cases} \tag{5.11}$$

where, $n(t)$ = Additive white Gaussian noise (AWGN), H_0 = Hypotheses of the absence of PU signals, and H_1 = Hypotheses of the presence of the PU signals.

The objective for spectrum sensing is to decide between H_0 and H_1 based on the observation $x(t)$. If a primary signal is absent, Y_j follows a central chi-square distribution with M degrees of freedom. Otherwise, Y_j follows a non-central chi-square distribution with M degrees of freedom and a non-centrality parameter $\lambda = M\gamma j$,

$$Y_j = \begin{cases} X_M^2 & H_0 \\ X_M^2(\lambda_j) & H_1 \end{cases} \tag{5.12}$$

5.5.4 Fusion Rules

A cognitive device works on shared data between users. There are two types of decisions. They require both soft and hard decisions. Under missed conditions, the decision soft outperforms the hard decision. For a large number of users, hard decision performs better than soft decision [10]. The Chair-Varshney rule is based on a log-likelihoodratio test. The performance of equal gain combining (EGC), selection combining (SC), and switch and stay combining (SSC) are investigated for an ED under Rayleigh fading. The EGC method has a magnitude of the second order while SC and SSC have one order of magnitude gain. When hard decisions are used AND, OR or M-out-of-Nmethods can be used for combining information. In the AND-rule, the decision is maximum while in OR, the decision is minimum. For M-out-of-N rule, the decisions are equal to the number of values.

5.6 Simulation Results Justifying the Sensing Functions

Spectral density shows the occupancy of a spectrum by various users. If prime users are not currently using the spectrum, then it can be occupied by the secondary users. Figure 5.5 shows the spectral density of a transmitted signal. The reference low frequency signal is considered to be the PU as shown in Figure 5.6.

Figure 5.7 demonstrates the allocation of users to free bands in a network. The linkage continuously monitors the availability of signals once the PU leaves the network. Then the SU uses the created hole with minimum interference to the PU.

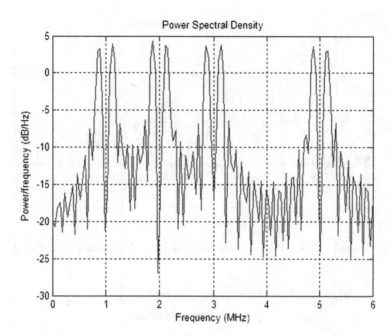

FIGURE 5.5
Power spectral density of primary user in the network.

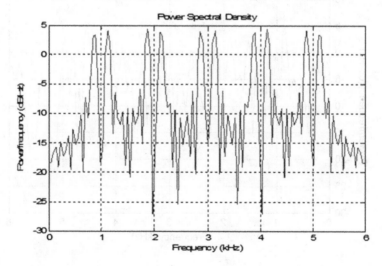

FIGURE 5.6
Existence of users in the network.

Figure 5.8 shows the addition of noise to the existing Cognitive Radio Network (CRN). This noise either attenuates the signal or amplifies the signal depending on the existence or nonappearance of the signal. Depending on the value of normalization, spectra are allocated as shown and explained in Table 5.1. As the power consumption is changed with the available network, this type of sensing is called green sensing.

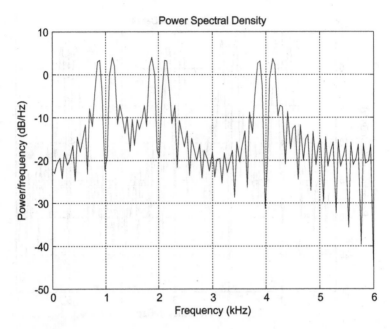

FIGURE 5.7
Sensing of users in the network.

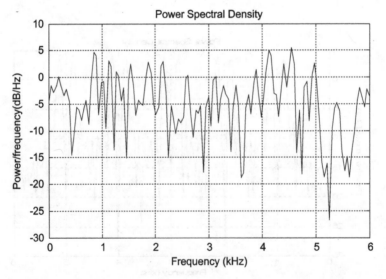

FIGURE 5.8
Signal spectrum with additive noise.

5.7 Conclusion and Future Enhancements

In this chapter, several spectrum sensing techniques have been discussed. There are a number of sensing techniques, but the three that are mainly used are matched filter, ED, and cyclostationary features based detection techniques. Each sensing technique has its own

TABLE 5.1

Simulation Terms Used for Spectrum Allocation and Sensing

Does primary user enter Y/N: Y
Does second primary user enter Y/N: Y
Does third primary user enter Y/N: N
Does fourth primary user enter Y/N: Y
Does fifth primary user enter Y/N: N
Does secondary user enter the network Y/N: Y
Assigned to User 1 as it was not present.
Do u want to add noise: Y
Enter the SNR in dB:.1
Adding noise
User 1 is present. User 2 is present.
User 3 is present. User 4 is present.
User 5 is present.
Do you want to attenuate the signals? [Y/N]: Y
Enter the percentage to attenuate the signal: 10
Attenuating

advantages and disadvantages. Among the functions of sensing, various detection methods are considered and it has been shown that, in general, ED is a suitable method. The hypothesis test rule and voting rule are applied for the sensing mechanism to calculate the spectral density. Power consumption in the network is considered for analysis. Since power is saved in the allotted region, this sensing scheme is called green sensing in cognitive radio. It has been proven to allow only minimum interference to the PU.

Acknowledgments

We thank our parents, spouses, children, and students for their support and motivation.

References

1. Yucek, T. and Arslan, H., "A survey of spectrum sensing algorithms for cognitive radio applications," *IEEE Communications On Surveys & Tutorials*, vol. 11, no. 1, pp. 116–130, First Quarter 2009.
2. Tragos, E.Z., Zeadally, S., Alexandros G.F. and Siris, V.A., "Spectrum assignment in cognitive radio networks," *IEEE Communication Survey & Tutorials*, vol. 15, no. 3, pp. 1108–1135, 2013.
3. Jang, J., Sun, H., Baglee, D. and Vincent Poor, H., "Achieving autonomous compressive spectrum sensing for cognitive radios," *IEEE Transactions on Vehicular Technology*, vol. 65, no. 3, February 2015.
4. Abdi, Y. and Ristaniemi, T., "Joint local quantization and linear cooperation in spectrum sensing for cognitive radio networks," *IEEE Transactions on Signal Processing*, vol. 62, no. 17, pp. 4349–4362, September 2014.
5. Akyildiz, I.F., Brandon, F.Lo and Balakrishnan, R., "Cooperative spectrum sensing in cognitive radio networks: A survey," *Physical Communication*, vol. 4, pp. 40–62, 2011.

6. Evic, N.V., Akyildiz, I.F. and Perez-Romero, J., "Dynamic cooperator selection in cognitive radio networks," *Ad hoc Networks*, vol. 10, pp. 789–802, 2012.

7. Letaief, K.B. and Zhang, W., "Cooperative communications for cognitive radio networks," *IEEE International Conference on Cognitive Radio Oriented Wireless*, pp. 878–893, 2009.

8. Quan, Z., Xui, S., Sayed, A. and Poor, H., "Optimal multiband joint detection for spectrum sensing in cognitive radio networks," *IEEE Transactions on Signal Processing*, vol. 57, no. 3, pp. 1128–1140, March 2009.

9. Sharma, S.K., Lagunas, E., Chatzinotas, S. and Ottersten, B., "Application of compressive sensing in cognitive radio communications: A survey," *IEEE Communications Surveys Tutorials*, vol. 18, no. 3, pp. 1838–1860, third quarter 2016.

10. Maleki, S., and Leus, G., "Censored truncated sequential spectrum sensing for cognitive radio networks," *IEEE Journal on Selected Areas in Communications*, vol. 31, no. 3, pp. 364–378, March 2013.

11. Wang, Y.G., Liu, Z., Yang, L. and Jiang, W.L., "Generalized compressive detection of stochastic signals using neyman pearson theorem," *Signal, Image and Video Processing*, pp. 1–10, 2014.

12. Daniel Tyson, "Optus joins the 700 MHz test party – announces test sites in Darwin and Perth," *AUSDROID*, July 2014.

13. Kailkhura, B., Nadendla, V.S.S. and Varshney, P.K., "Distributed inference in the presence of eavesdroppers: A survey," *IEEE Communications Magazine*, vol. 53, no. 6, pp. 40–46, June 2015.

14. Elkashlan, M., Wang, L., Duong, T.Q., Karagiannidis, G.K. and Nallanathan, A., "On the security of cognitive radio networks," *IEEE Transactions on Vehicular Technology*, vol. 64, no. 8, pp. 3790–3795, August 2015.

15. Guizani, M., Khalfi, B., Ghorbel, M.B. and Hamdaoui, B., "Largescale cognitive cellular systems: Resource management overview," *IEEE Communications Magazine*, vol. 53, no. 5, pp. 44–51, 2015.

16. Naeem, M., Anpalagn, A. and Jaseemuddin, M., "Resource allocation techniques in cooperative cognitive radio network," *IEEE Communications on Survey & Tutorial*, vol. 16, no. 2, pp. 729–744, 2014.

17. Wang, L., Sheng, M. and Zhang, Y., "Robust energy efficiency maximization in cognitive radio networks: The worst-case optimization approach," *IEEE Transactions on Communication*, vol. 63, no. 1, pp. 51–65, 2015.

18. Chaudhari, S., Lunden, J., Koivunen, V. and Poor, H.V., "Cooperative sensing with imperfect reporting channels: Hard decisions or soft decisions," *IEEE Transactions on Signal Processing*, vol. 60, no. 1, pp. 18–28, January 2012.

19. Chaudhari, S., Lundén, J., Koivunen, V. and Poor, H.V., "BEP walls for cooperative sensing in cognitive radios using K-out-of-N fusion rules," *Signal Processing*, vol. 93, no. 7, pp. 1900–1908, July 2013.

20. Abdi, Y. and Ristaniemi, T., "Joint local quantization and linear cooperation in spectrum sensing for cognitive radio networks," *IEEE Transactions on Signal Processing*, vol. 62, no. 17, pp. 4349–4362, September 2014.

21. Lopez-Benitez, M. and Casadevall, F., "Signal uncertainty in spectrum sensing for cognitive radio," *IEEE Transactions on Communication*, vol. 61, no. 4, pp. 1231–1241, April 2013.

22. Sofotasios, P., Rebeiz, E., Zhang, L., Tsiftsis, T., Cabric, D. and Freear, S., "Energy detection based spectrum sensing over k-μ and k-μ extreme fading channels," *IEEE Transactions On Vehicular Technology*, vol. 62, no. 3, pp. 1031–1040, March 2013.

23. Cai, Y., Mo, Y., Ota, K., Luo, C., Dong, M. and Yang, L.T., "Optimal data fusion of collaborative spectrum sensing under attack in cognitive radio networks," *IEEE Network*, vol. 28, no. 1, pp. 17–23, January 2014.

24. Marcum, J., "A statistical theory of target detection by pulsed radar," pp. 1–58, July 1948.

25. Maleki, S., Chepuri, S.P. and Leus, G., "Optimization of hard fusion based spectrum sensing for energy-constrained cognitive radio networks," *Physical Communications*, vol. 9, pp. 193–198, 2013.

26. Bagwari A. and Tomar, G.S., "Adaptive double-threshold based energy detector for spectrum sensing in cognitive radio networks," *International Journal of Electronics Letters*, pp. 178–181, 2013.

27. Tse, D. and Viswanath, P.: *"Fundamentals of Wireless Communication"* Cambridge University Press, Ch. 3–4, pp. 64–180, September 2004.

28. Neumark S.: *"Solution of Cubic and Quartic Equations,"* Elsevier, 1st edition, ch. 2, pp. 5–12, 1965.

29. Mishra, S.M., Sahai, A. and Brodersen, R.W., "Cooperative sensing among cognitive radios," *IEEE International Conference on Communications*, vol. 4, pp. 1658–1663, June 2006.

30. Cabric, D., Mishra, S. and Brodersen, R., "Implementation issues in spectrum sensing for cognitive radios," *IEEE Journal on Selected Areas Communicatiions*, vol. 1, no. 11, pp. 772–776, November 2004.

31. Zou, Y., Yu-Dong and Zheng, Y.B., "Spectrum Sensing and Data Transmission Tradeoff in Cognitive Radio Networks," *IEEE 19th Annual Wireless and Optical Communications Conference*, 10.1109/WOCC.2010.5510601, pp. 1–5, 2010.

32. Yin, S., Qu, Z. and Li, S., "Achievable throughput optimization in energy harvesting cognitive radio systems," *IEEE Journal on Selected Areas on Communication*, vol. 33, no. 3, pp. 407–422, March 2015.

33. Wang, W. and Zhang, Q., "Privacy-preserving collaborative spectrum sensing with multiple service providers," *IEEE Transactions on Wireless Communications*, vol. 14, no. 2, pp. 1011–1019, 2015.

34. Chen, Y., "Analytical performance of collaborative spectrum sensing using censored energy detection," *IEEE Transactions on Wireless Communications*, vol. 9, no. 12, pp. 3856–3865, December 2010.

35. Khafagy, M.G., Ismail, A., Alouini, M.S. and Aıssa, S., "Efficient cooperative protocols for full duplex relaying over nakagami-fading channels," *IEEE Transactions on Wireless Communications*, vol. 14, no. 6, pp. 3456–3470, June 2015.

36. Maleki, S. and Leus, G., "Censored truncated sequential spectrum sensing for cognitive radio networks," *IEEE Journal on Selected Areas on Communications*, vol. 31, no. 3, pp. 364–378, March 2013.

37. Maleki, S., Leus, G., Chatzinotas, S. and Ottersten, B., "On energy-efficient distributed spectrum sensing with combined censoring and sleeping," *IEEE Transactions on Wireless Communications*, vol. PP, no. 99, pp. 1–1, 2015.

38. Najimi, M., Ebrahimzadeh, A., Andargoli, S. and Fallahi, A., "A novel sensing nodes and decision node selection method for energy efficiency of cooperative spectrum sensing in cognitive sensor networks," *IEEE Journal On Sensors*, vol. 13, no. 5, pp. 1610–1621, May 2013.

39. Monemian, M. and Mahdavi, M., "Analysis of a new energy-based sensor selection method for cooperative spectrum sensing in cognitive radio networks," *IEEE Journal on Sensors*, vol. 14, no. 9, pp. 3021–3032, September 2014.

40. Chepuri, S. and Leus, G., "Sparse sensing for distributed detection," *IEEE Transactions on Signal Processing*, vol. 11, no. 9, pp. 1–15, 2015.

41. Liu, X., Evans, B. and Moessner, K., "Energy-efficient sensor scheduling algorithm in cognitive radio networks employing heterogeneous sensors," *IEEE Transactions on Vehicular Technology*, vol. 64, no. 3, pp. 1243–1249, March 2015.

42. Sutton, P.D., Nolan, K.E. and Doyle, L.E., "Cyclostationary signatures in practical cognitive radio applications," *IEEE Journal On Selected Areas On Communications*, vol. 26, no. 1, pp. 13–24, January 2008.

43. Poor, H.V., *"An Introduction to Signal Detection and Estimation,"* Berlin Heidelberg: Springer-Verlag, pp. 1–13, 1994.

44. Chatziantoniou, E., Allen, B. and Velisavljevic, V., "Threshold optimization for energy detection-based spectrum sensing over hyper-rayleigh fading channels," *IEEE Communications Letters*, vol. 11, no. 6, pp. 1–4, March 2015.

45. Guo, C., Chen, S., Feng, C. and Zeng, Z., "Correlation-statistics-based spectrum sensing exploiting energy and polarization for dual-polarized cognitive radios," *IEEE Transactions on Wireless Communications*, vol. 14, no. 3, pp. 1533–1554, March 2015.

46. Han, W., Huang, C., Li, J., Li, Z. and Cui, S., "Correlation-based spectrum sensing with oversampling in cognitive radio," *IEEE Journal on Selected Areas in Communications*, vol. 33, no. 5, pp. 788–802, May 2015.

6

New Spectrum Sensing Technique for Advanced Wireless Networks

Ashish Bagwari, Jyotshana Bagwari, Geetam Singh Tomar, and Robin Singh Bhadoria

CONTENTS

6.1 Introduction

At present, the wireless communication network (WCN) is using fixed spectrum allocation (FSA) schemes. In FSA, only those users who have a fixed licensed spectrum, known as licensed users, can communicate with each other. The numbers of licensed users are increasing day by day which is the problem associated with FSA. There are limited bands of frequencies for mobile users, and future communication problems will arise due to the need for additional bandwidth. To resolve this critical problem, an effective scheme for a wireless communication network is Dynamic Spectrum Allocation (DSA). Cognitive radio network (CRN) is an advanced wireless technology which uses the DSA scheme and makes use of the FSA scheme in an effective way. CRN can sense channel usage and is regulated under the wireless regional area networks (WRAN) of Institute of Electrical and Electronics Engineers (IEEE) 802.22 standard. It consists of a licensed user which is also known as the primary user (PU), and an unlicensed user which is known as the secondary user (SU) or Cognitive Radio (CR). CRN uses the PU frequency band between the CR users for communication when the primary user is not using the licensed band. There are three basic methods for detecting the PU signal by the CR's; the matched filter detection method, energy detection method, and cyclostationary feature detection method [1,2]. Different methods have been proposed to improve these Spectrum Sensing (SS) techniques. In CRN, there are some limitations such as a spectrum sensing failure problem, security, and long sensing time. To resolve such issues, we have proposed a new spectrum sensing technique known as an advanced-two-phase detectors' scheme where we sense the PU signal under low SNR, which mitigates the sensing failure problem and has a quick sensing time.

6.2 Challenges in CRN

CRN follows IEEE 802.22 standards which are associated with WRAN (wireless regional area networks). In CRN, there are various challenges related to spectrum sensing such as

1. Spectrum Sensing Failure Problem.
2. Spectrum Sensing Time.
3. Fading and Shadowing Problem.
4. Security.

In this chapter, we devise a spectrum sensing technique which is helpful for resolving critical sensing issues.

6.3 Related Works

6.3.1 Energy Detector and Cyclostationary (ED and Cyclo) Detection Scheme

In the present wireless communication network, there is a perceived scarcity of radio spectrum, with most of the total band width remaining unused [3,4]. Thus, cognitive radios have worked in this area to improve spectrum utilization with what is a valuable promising solution. A cognitive radio network identifies the unused licensed frequency bands and utilizes these bands effectively by allowing secondary users while avoiding interference with the licensed PU. Detection of empty or free channels in a licensed spectrum is a challenging task in CRN. CRNs follow two main rules, (i) spectrum sensing should be accurate to identify the presence or absence of primary user signals and (ii) the sensing of multiple licensed radio channels has to be performed as quickly as possible. In [5,6], the authors proposed an energy detector while in [7,8], the authors introduced cyclostationary detectors to sense licensed signals. An energy detector is a simple detector, but its performance is not robust and it cannot detect a signal at a low SNR. On the other side, the cyclostationary detection method detects a signal at a low SNR, but is computationally more complex, requires prior information of the primary user, and requires a longer sensing time. In the following, several authors have discussed the two stages of energy detection [5,9] and cyclostationary detection [1,10] in the framework of two-stage sensing. Few researchers have done work on wide-band spectrum sensing in cognitive radio networks. As in [11], a two-stage detection method was proposed with different sensing bandwidths, where both stages were based on energy detection. The proposed detection method did not perform well under low SNR due to the presence of energy detectors. Further, in [3], a two-stage spectrum sensing method has been proposed by the authors which deals with the above issues. The two-stage sensing scheme considers an energy detector and cyclostationary detector, where the authors assumed that the total numbers of channels are L, and the channels are sensed serially by secondary users. The first stage is known as a coarse sensing stage and carries an energy detector to note the spectrum sensing decision. If the energy of a detected signal is equal to or greater than a certain threshold, the channel is considered occupied. The second stage detector, known as the fine sensing stage, carries a cyclostationary detector which will then try to identify the licensed frequency band. If the decision metric in the second stage is above a certain threshold, the channel is considered to be occupied. Otherwise, it is declared to be free and available for cognitive radio users. The authors examined the proposed two-stage detector's performance in relation to the probability of a detection alarm, the probability of false alarm, and the sensing time.

6.3.1.1 Limitations

The two-stage detection scheme [3] enhances the detection performance. To produce a better sensing performance, this method consists of two detectors; An energy detector in first stage and a cyclostationary detector in the second stage, but it requires a longer sensing time and is computationally more complex.

6.3.2 Adaptive Spectrum Sensing

The demand for radio spectrum is increasing significantly due to the increase in the number of customers in wireless network services [12]. The trend of new wireless communication devices and applications is expected to continue in the coming years, which will increase the demand for more frequency bands. The traditional fixed spectrum allocation policy is a serious obstacle in the development or innovation of such new technologies. In 2008, the Federal Communication Commission (FCC) made a rule which permitted unlicensed fixed and portable devices in urban and rural regions to use unallocated bands [4]. Cognitive Radio is a key technology based on a dynamic spectrum allocation scheme that helps to mitigate the scarcity of the frequency bands. The most crucial job of cognitive radio is to detect a primary user signal or sense a licensed frequency band. Once a licensed spectrum band is identified, cognitive radio users utilize this vacant band, and the vacant band is known as white space or a spectrum hole. The technique of sensing a licensed signal in the radio environment is called spectrum sensing [13,14]. The spectrum sensing technique is concerned with two things: first, the primary users should not be disturbed by cognitive radio users during communication, and second, white space should be sensed well-manners for required throughput and quality of service (QoS) [15].

The adaptive spectrum sensing detector carries an estimating signal-to-noise ratio device, energy detector, and a one-order cyclostationary detector for spectrum sensing. This device carries two detectors and assumes N numbers of channel to be sensed by CR users. Once cognitive radio senses the channel, it acquires the signal and passes it to the estimating SNR device to estimate the SNR of the sensed channel [10,16,17]. Therefore, based on an estimated SNR value and the desired threshold, the system will choose one of the appropriate detectors out of two for signal detection, that is, either the energy detector or the one-order cyclostationary detector. After studying most of the research papers, we can conclude that the energy detector does not perform well at very low SNR. That is why this approach is used with a one-order cyclostationary detector under low SNR. However, for a high SNR, it uses the energy detector to detect the licensed channels.

6.3.2.1 Limitations

The adaptive spectrum sensing technique in [12] presents a new plan. In this, one of the stages of the detection technique is running at a time based on the estimated SNR [18]. It does not consider the failure problem of spectrum sensing though it does reduce the mean sensing time [19].

6.3.3 Adaptive Sensing Technique Using Energy Detector Scheme

Adaptive sensing technique using energy detector (EDT-ASS-2015). The impairment of the further deployment of services and coverage is due to the scarcity of the available spectrum for wireless communication [20]. A new strategy has been proposed by the authors to detect white spaces in the radio spectrum. With this method, the nodes of cognitive radio (CR) networks perform spectrum sensing based on energy detection in a cooperative way. Thus, the authors use a cost-function that contains all the information about the presence or absence of primary users and that depends upon a single parameter. Based on this parameter, the detection of white spaces has significantly improved the deflection coefficient associated with the detector in comparison to other state-of-the-art algorithms.

An effective and strong ED-based technique is proposed which performs the SS process on an adaptive parameter instead of a soft-combiner of energy estimates. The problem of the mean square error (MSE) minimization of a new cost-function has been solved by using the least mean squares (LMS) algorithm. The cost-function performs both single-node and weighted cooperative SS by an adaptive test statistic which depends on pre-processed inputs and the desired signal is chosen to improve the well-known deflection coefficient [21,22] of the test statistic. Therefore, this method remarkably increases the deflection coefficient in comparison to that achieved by conventional ED methods. Furthermore, a new weighting proposal is presented instead of determining the algorithm with various weighting strategies from the literature [23,24].

6.3.3.1 Limitations

In [20], using an energy detector (EDT-ASS-2015), the authors presented an adaptive sensing technique. Discussion on the cost-function and conclusions about the PU's absence or presence was provided by the authors, but they did not consider the sensing failure problem [19].

6.3.4 Energy Detector and Energy Detector with Adaptive Threshold (ED and ED-ADT) Detection Scheme

Advanced wireless networks deal with bandwidth crisis problems by minimizing the sensing failure problem. Spectrum sensing senses the vacant band for mobile users to minimize the bandwidth limitations problem [25]. To detect PU frequency bands, there are various sensing techniques available [1,2]. In this section, the authors proposed ED and ED-ADT sensing techniques, where the proposed system model consists of two detectors. The first stage uses a single threshold energy detector, and the second stage uses an adaptive double-threshold (ED-ADT) energy detector scheme. The authors used an ADT scheme in the first stage which takes somewhat more time to sense the PU signal. The ED takes less time to detect the PU signal. But under the spectrum sensing failure problem, ED does not perform well, which is why the authors have used ADT-based ED in the second stage.

6.3.4.1 Limitations

The ED and ED-ADT detection schemes focused on the problem of failure over sensing. The authors divided a confused region into four equal parts which mitigates the sensing failure problem but requires somewhat more sensing time. The proposed advanced-two-phase detectors (TPD) scheme is a modern version of ED and ED-ADT detector-2015 [25] and gives better results which are discussed in the analysis section.

6.4 Proposed Scheme

6.4.1 Advanced-Two-Phase Detectors

An hypothesis test is used for the detection of a primary user signal. There are two types of hypothesis testing. The first one is H_1 (alternate hypothesis) which considers the presence of the PU signal. $r(n)$ is the received signal and can be written as [1]

$$r(n) = x(n) \times h(n) + \omega(n), \quad H_1 \tag{6.1}$$

The second one is H_0 (null hypothesis) which considers the absence of the PU signal. $r(n)$ can be represented as

$$r(n) = \omega(n), \quad H_0 \tag{6.2}$$

In Equations 6.1 and 6.2, CR users sense the $r(n)$ signal. The primary user's signal is $x(n)$, the gain of the channel is $h(n)$, additive white Gaussian noise having zero mean is represented as $w(n)$, σ_ω^2 is noise variance, and n is the number of samples, that is, $n = 1, 2, \ldots N$.

Figure 6.1 illustrates the flow chart of advanced-two-phase detectors. There are two phases, where the first phase consists of a single adaptive threshold (ED-SAT) energy detector, and the second phase has two adaptive thresholds (ED-TAT) energy detectors. In the given figure, the first phase ED-SAT finds the PU signal, determines signal energy (E), and compares it with a pre-defined threshold (λ_1). If the signal energy is equal to or greater than a certain threshold, the detector confirms that the PU signal is present, otherwise, the second phase detector ED-TAT will repeat the same process. The second phase detector performs the detection operation on three levels; the first is above a pre-determined

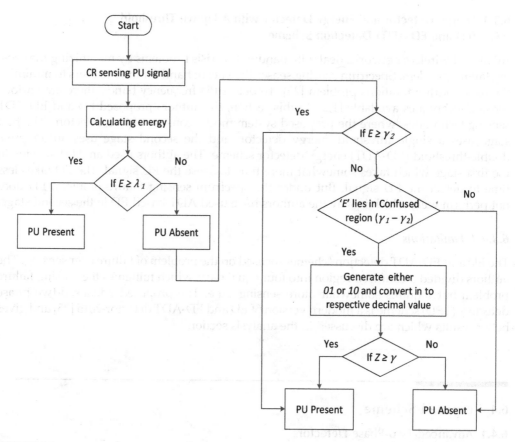

FIGURE 6.1
Flow chart of advanced-two-phase detectors.

threshold (γ_2), the second is below a pre-determined threshold (γ_1), and the third is between the pre-determined thresholds (γ_1) & (γ_2).

Considering all cases and their outcomes:

First Case: The detector confirms the presence of the PU signal when the signal energy (E) is equal to or greater than the pre-determined threshold (γ_2).

Second Case: The signal energy (E) is below the pre-determined threshold (γ_1), then the detector confirms the absence of the PU signal.

Third Case: The signal energy (E) is between pre-determined thresholds (γ_1) & (γ_2). This condition is known as a confused region and is a phenomenon of the sensing failure problem. To resolve this issue, there are two adaptive threshold concepts as discussed in Section 6.2. Finally, the output (Z) compares with a pre-determined threshold (γ), and gives the final decision as shown in Figure 6.1.

- Detection probability of advanced-two-phase detectors can be defined as

$$P_D^{\text{Advanced}-\text{TPD}} = P_r \times P_d^{\text{ED}-\text{SAT}} + (1 - P_r) \times P_d^{\text{ED}-\text{TAT}} \tag{6.3}$$

$$P_D^{\text{Advanced}-\text{TPD}} = P_r\left(P_d^{\text{ED}-\text{SAT}} - P_d^{\text{ED}-\text{TAT}}\right) + P_d^{\text{ED}-\text{TAT}} \tag{6.4}$$

- Errors rate of advanced-two-phase detectors can be defined as

$$P_e^{\text{Advanced}-\text{TPD}} = P_F^{\text{Advanced}-\text{TPD}} + \left(1 - P_D^{\text{Advanced}-\text{TPD}}\right) \tag{6.5}$$

$$P_e^{\text{Advanced}-\text{TPD}} = 1 + P_r\left(P_f^{\text{ED-SAT}} - P_f^{\text{ED-TAT}} - P_d^{\text{ED-SAT}} + P_d^{\text{ED-TAT}}\right)$$
$$+ \left(P_f^{\text{ED-TAT}} - P_d^{\text{ED-TAT}}\right) \tag{6.6}$$

where $P_d^{\text{ED-SAT}}$ and $P_d^{\text{ED-TAT}}$ are the detection probabilities of the ED-SAT and ED-TAT detectors, respectively, and the false alarm probabilities of the ED-SAT and ED-TAT detectors are $P_f^{\text{ED-SAT}}$ and $P_f^{\text{ED-TAT}}$, respectively. P_r denotes the probability factor, which ranges from $0 \le P_r \le 1$. The probability factor depends on the SNR of the channels to be detected. If $P_r < 0.5$, the channel is very noisy and vice-versa, which shows the channel is less noisy.

6.4.1.1 First Phase: Energy Detector with Single Adaptive Threshold (ED-SAT)

The most commonly used detector by researchers to detect PU signals is an energy detector. Figure 6.2 represents the conventional ED in which the PU signal is given as an input to a band pass filter (BPF) and then after filtration it passes to the ADC. ADC stands for the analog to digital converter which converts an analog signal to a digital signal and also provides binary bit patterns. These binary bit patterns are given to a square law device (SLD), which evaluates the energy of the received input signals. Then, the output of the SLD is received by an integrator which integrates at a T interval. The final decision is made by a decision-making device (DMD) against the incoming input signal to confirm whether the PU is present or absent with the help of a single threshold value.

6.4.1.1.1 Expression of Single Adaptive Threshold

The expression of single adaptive threshold (λ_1) is written as [5]

$$\lambda_1 = \left[N \times \sigma_\omega^2 \left\{Q^{-1}\left(\overline{P_f}\right) \times \sqrt{\frac{2}{N}} + 1\right\}\right] \tag{6.7}$$

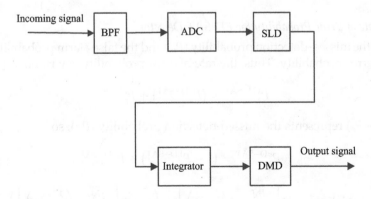

FIGURE 6.2
Energy detector with single adaptive threshold (ED-SAT).

Here, N represents the number of samples, P_f is the false alarm probability, $Q^{-1}()$ denotes the inverse-Q-function, and σ_ω^2 represents the noise variance. Upon analyzing Equation 6.7, we find that the threshold (λ_1) is directly proportional to noise variance (σ_ω^2) and noise variance depends on the noise signal. The noise signal is random in nature and change w.r.t. time. Due to this, the noise variance (σ_ω^2) varies and then the threshold (λ_1) also changes. The threshold is adaptive in nature, hence, at every time instant, its value changes.

$$E = \frac{1}{N} \sum_{n=1}^{N} |r(n)|^2 \qquad (6.8)$$

In Equation 6.8, N is total number of samples, $r(n)$ represents the received signals, and E is the observed energy of $r(n)$. Now, the local decision of the ED-SAT detector can be written as

$$ED - SAT|_{o/p} = \begin{cases} E < \lambda_1, & H_0 \\ E \geq \lambda_1, & H_1 \end{cases} \qquad (6.9)$$

6.4.1.1.2 Detection Probability for ED-SAT Detector

The expression for detection probability can be written as [12]

$$P_d^{ED-SAT} = Q\left[\sqrt{\frac{N}{2}} \times \left(\frac{\lambda'}{N} - 1\right)\right] \qquad (6.10)$$

In Equation 6.10, N is the number of samples, $Q()$ represents the Gaussian tail probability Q-function, and λ' is defined as $\lambda' = (\lambda_1/(\sigma_x^2 + \sigma_\omega^2))$, where λ_1 represents a single adaptive threshold, σ_x^2 denotes the PU signal variance, and σ_ω^2 is noise variance.

6.4.1.1.3 False Alarm Probability for ED-SAT Detector

The expression for the false alarm probability can be written as [12]

$$P_f^{ED-SAT} = Q\left[\sqrt{\frac{N}{2}} \times \left(\frac{\lambda''}{N} - 1\right)\right] \qquad (6.11)$$

In Equation 6.11, N represents the number of samples and λ'' is defined as $\lambda'' = (\lambda_1/(\sigma_\omega^2))$.

6.4.1.1.4 Rate of Error Probability for ED-SAT Detector

The sum of the missed-detection probability (P_m) and the false alarm probability (P_f) is called the rate of error probability. Thus, the rate of error probability is written as [25,27]

$$P_e^{ED-SAT} = \left(P_m^{ED-SAT}\right) + P_f^{ED-SAT} \qquad (6.12)$$

Here, $(1 - P_d)$ represents the missed-detection probability (P_m), so

$$P_e^{ED-SAT} = \left(1 - P_d^{ED-SAT}\right) + P_f^{ED-SAT} \qquad (6.13)$$

$$P_e^{ED-SAT} = Q\left[\sqrt{\frac{N}{2}} \times \left(\frac{\lambda''}{N} - 1\right)\right] + \left(1 - Q\left[\sqrt{\frac{N}{2}} \times \left(\frac{\lambda'}{N} - 1\right)\right]\right) \qquad (6.14)$$

6.4.2 Energy Detector with two Adaptive Thresholds (ED-TAT)

It is difficult in CRN for a detector to find the correct signal when the PU signal and noise superimpose on each other. This process is referred to as a sensing failure problem and the overlapped area is known as the confused region, which is discussed in [19]. The advanced-TPD sensing scheme is an effective solution to overcome this problem.

Generally, CRN consists of three sections. In the first section, only a noise signal exists which is denoted by H_0. In the second section, only the PU signal exists which is denoted by H_1, and the third section is the *confused region* which is the combination of noise and the PU signal. Figure 6.3a represents the case for C-ED where authors assume that the confused region is zero or null and simply divide all the sections into two parts using the single threshold (γ) concept. If the observed energy is greater than or equal to γ, then H_1, and if the observed energy is less than γ, then H_0. In Figure 6.3b, we have considered the confused region (between γ_1 and γ_2) and divided it into two parts, that is, between $\gamma_1 - \gamma$ and $\gamma - \gamma_2$. Now, the entire four sections of Figure 6.3b (H_0, H_1, and the confused region) are defined as below the γ_1 and above the γ_2, which comes under the upper part (UP) of the detector, while the confused region, that is, between $\gamma_1 - \gamma$ and $\gamma - \gamma_2$, is the lower part (LP). Therefore, the detector output can be represented as

$$ED - TAT|_{o/p} = UP + LP = Z \tag{6.15}$$

If the observed energy for the pre-defined threshold is γ_1, it shows H_0, and shows H_1 if the observed energy is greater than or equal to the pre-defined threshold γ_2. But for the confused

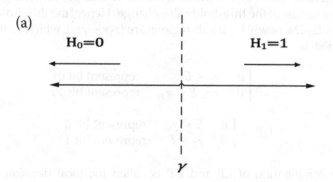

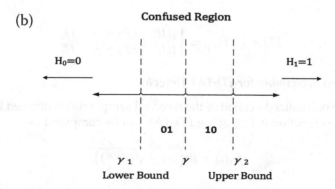

FIGURE 6.3
(a) Single threshold detection scheme, (b) Double threshold detection scheme.

region, if the observed energy lies between $(\gamma_1 - \gamma)$, it shows 01 and further converts the binary di-bits into a decimal number, that is, 1. Similarly, if the observed energy lies between $(\gamma - \gamma_2)$, it shows 10 and its decimal value is 2. Now the pre-defined threshold (γ) can be computed as [5]

$$\gamma = \left[\left(\frac{N}{\sigma_\omega^2} \right) \times \left\{ Q^{-1}\left(\overline{P_f}\right) \times \sqrt{\frac{2}{N}} + 1 \right\} \right] \qquad (6.16)$$

The values of the lower threshold (γ_1) and the upper threshold (γ_2) depend on noise variance, so the minimum noise variance shows the lower threshold and the maximum noise variance shows the upper threshold. The lower threshold (γ_1) and upper threshold (γ_2) can be estimated as

$$\gamma_1 = \left[\left(\frac{N}{\rho \times \sigma_\omega^2} \right) \times \left\{ Q^{-1}\left(\overline{P_f}\right) \times \sqrt{\frac{2}{N}} + 1 \right\} \right] \qquad (6.17)$$

$$\gamma_2 = \left[\left(N \times \rho \times \sigma_\omega^2 \right) \times \left\{ Q^{-1}\left(\overline{P_f}\right) \times \sqrt{\frac{2}{N}} + 1 \right\} \right] \qquad (6.18)$$

Equations 6.17 and 6.18 show the mathematical expression of the lower threshold (γ_1) and upper threshold (γ_2), respectively. Consider the above equations, that is, Equations 6.17 and 6.18. In both equations, the values of the thresholds (γ_1 & γ_2) depend on noise variance (σ_ω^2), and noise variance is variable as its value changes according to the noise signal. Therefore, the values of the thresholds also change. Hence, the thresholds are known as adaptive thresholds. The newly built sub-regions are ($\gamma_1\gamma - \gamma\gamma_2$), which comes under the LP and can be selected as

$$LP = \begin{cases} \text{if} \quad \gamma_1 \leq E < \gamma, & \text{represent bit 01} \\ \text{if} \quad \gamma \leq E < \gamma_2, & \text{represent bit 10} \end{cases} \qquad (6.19)$$

$$UP = \begin{cases} \text{if} \quad E < \gamma_1, & \text{represent bit 0} \\ \text{if} \quad \gamma_2 \leq E, & \text{represent bit 1} \end{cases} \qquad (6.20)$$

Therefore, the combination of LP and UP is called the local decision of the ED-TAT detector [25]

$$ED - TAT|_{o/p} = \begin{cases} (UP + LP) < \gamma, & H_0 \\ (UP + LP) \geq \gamma, & H_1 \end{cases}. \qquad (6.21)$$

6.4.2.1 Detection Probability for ED-TAT Detector

Assume that the normalized version of the received sample $r(n)$ is denoted by r_i. The cumulative distribution function (CDF) of the ED-TAT can be computed as

$$f_{Zi}(z) = Pr\left(|r_i| \leq \sqrt{(z^{(2/a)})} \right) \qquad (6.22)$$

where $r(n)$ is a zero-mean primary signal with an average power σ_r^2 that does not depend on complex Gaussian noise $w_i(n)$, a is an arbitrary constant having a value of two, and h_i

is the Rayleigh faded channel which is independent of Gaussian noise. Hence, $|h_i|$ is Rayleigh distributed with variance $\sigma_h^2/2$. Therefore, the ED-TAT detector's PDF for H_j (where $j = 0, 1$) is given as

$$f_{Z_i|H_j}(z) = \left[\frac{2 \times z^{(2/a)}}{(z \times a)}\right] \times f_{|r_i|^2|H_j}(z^{(2/a)}) \tag{6.23}$$

where $f_{|r_i|^2|H_1}$ is exponentially distributed as follows

$$f_{|r_i|^2|H_1}(z) = \left[(1+S)^{-1}\right] \times \exp[-z \times (1+S)^{-1}], \quad z \geq 0 \tag{6.24}$$

Note that $S = (\sigma_h^2 \times \sigma_x^2)/\sigma_w^2$ is the average SNR of the sensing channel. Using Equations 6.23 and 6.24, we have

$$f_{Z_i|H_1}(z) = \left[\frac{2 \times z^{(2/a)} \times (1+S)^{-1}}{(z \times a)}\right] \times \exp[-z^{(2/a)} \times (1+S)^{-1}], \quad z \geq 0 \tag{6.25}$$

For ED-TAT, the detection probability can be calculated as

$$P_d^{\text{ED-TAT}} = \int_{\gamma}^{+\infty} f_{Z_i|H_1}(z)\, dz \tag{6.26}$$

$$P_d^{\text{ED-TAT}} = \int_{\gamma}^{+\infty} \left[\frac{2 \times z^{(2/a)}}{(z \times a) \times (1+S)}\right] \times \exp\left[-\frac{z^{(2/a)}}{(1+S)}\right] dz \tag{6.27}$$

$$P_d^{\text{ED-TAT}} = \exp\left[-\frac{\{(\gamma)^{(1/a)}\}^2}{(1+S)}\right] \tag{6.28}$$

6.4.2.2 False Alarm Probability for ED-TAT Detector

Considering Equation 6.29, $f_{|r_i|^2|H_0}$ is exponentially written as

$$f_{|r_i|^2|H_0}(z) = \exp[-z], \quad z \geq 0 \tag{6.29}$$

Using Equations 6.29 and 6.23, we have

$$f_{Z_i|H_0}(z) = \left[\frac{2 \times z^{(2/a)}}{(z \times a)}\right] \times \exp(z^{(2/a)}), \quad z \geq 0 \tag{6.30}$$

The calculation for the false alarm probability for ED-TAT is

$$P_f^{\text{ED-TAT}} = \int_{\gamma}^{+\infty} f_{Z_i|H_o}(z)\, dz \tag{6.31}$$

$$P_f^{\text{ED-TAT}} = \int\limits_{\gamma}^{+\infty} \left[\frac{2 \times z^{(2/a)}}{(z \times a)}\right] \times \exp\left(z^{(2/a)}\right) dz \tag{6.32}$$

$$P_f^{\text{ED-TAT}} = \exp\left[-\left\{(\gamma)^{(1/a)}\right\}^2\right] \tag{6.33}$$

6.4.2.3 Total Error Probability for ED-TAT Detector

The dependency of the total error rate on the false alarm probability (P_f) and the misdetection probability (P_m) according to IEEE 802.22 is

$$P_e^{\text{ED-TAT}} = P_f^{\text{ED-TAT}} + \left(1 - P_d^{\text{ED-TAT}}\right) \tag{6.34}$$

Substituting the value of $P_d^{\text{ED-TAT}}$ from Equation 6.28 and $P_f^{\text{ED-TAT}}$ from Equations 6.33 and 6.34, we get

$$P_e^{\text{ED-TAT}} = 1 + \exp\left[-\left\{(\gamma)^{(1/a)}\right\}^2\right] - \exp\left[-\frac{\left\{(\gamma)^{1/a}\right\}^2}{(1+S)}\right] \tag{6.35}$$

where $(1 - P_d^{\text{ED-TAT}})$ shows the misdetection probability $(P_m^{\text{ED-TAT}})$.

6.4.3 Total Sensing Time of Advanced-two-Phase Detectors

The total time taken by CR users to detect a licensed frequency band is the spectrum sensing time. It can be calculated as

$$T_{\text{Advanced-TPD}} = T_{\text{ED-SAT}} + T_{\text{ED-TAT}} \tag{6.36}$$

In Equation 6.36, $T_{\text{Advanced-TPD}}$ represents the total time taken by the advanced-two-phase detector for SS time. The ED-SAT and ED-TAT detector's observation times are $T_{\text{ED-SAT}}$ and $T_{\text{ED-TAT}}$, respectively. Figure 6.1 shows the cascaded placement of ED-SAT and ED-TAT. The sensing time for the ED-SAT detector can then be computed as

$$T_{\text{ED-SAT}} = C \times P_r \times S_1 \tag{6.37}$$

In Equation 6.37, S_1 denotes the mean sensing time for each channel and C denotes the number of sensed channels.

$$\text{where} \quad S_1 = \frac{1}{2} \times \left(\frac{M_{\text{ED-SAT}}}{B}\right) \tag{6.38}$$

$M_{\text{ED-SAT}}$ is the number of samples and B represents the channel bandwidth. Similarly, the sensing time for ED-TAT is represented as

$$T_{\text{ED-TAT}} = C \times (1 - P_r) \times S_2 \tag{6.39}$$

In Equation 6.39, S_2 represents the mean sensing time for each channel, $(1-P_r)$ is the probability factor that a channel will be reported to the ED-TAT detector, and C denotes the number of sensed channels.

$$\text{where} \quad S_2 = \frac{1}{2} \times \left(\frac{M_{\text{ED-TAT}}}{B} \right) \tag{6.40}$$

$M_{\text{ED-TAT}}$ is the number of samples and B represents the channel bandwidth.

Thus, by substituting Equations 1.37, and 1.39 into Equation 6.36, the total sensing time can be calculated as

$$T_{\text{Advanced-TPD}} = C \times P_r \times S_1 + C \times (1 - P_r) \times S_2 \tag{6.41}$$

$$T_{\text{Advanced-TPD}} = C \times \left[P_r \times S_1 + (1 - P_r) \times S_2 \right] \tag{6.42}$$

Equation 6.42 shows the observation or sensing time for advanced-TPD.

- *Simulation model.* Using MATLAB, a simulation environment is created. The steps for stimulation are described as:

  1. Generate quadrature phase shift keying (QPSK) modulated signal $x(n)$.
  2. Pass input $x(n)$ Rayleigh signal through a noisy channel, having channel gain (h), and noise is AWGN (additive white Gaussian noise) which is denoted by $\omega(n)$ having zero mean, that is, $\omega(n) \sim N(0, \sigma_\omega^2)$, and σ_ω^2 is noise variance according to Equation 6.1.
  3. CR users receive signal $r(n)$ which is defined as $\omega(n)$ under the null hypothesis and $x(n)*h + \omega(n)$ under the alternate hypothesis.
  4. Evaluate thresholds $\lambda_1, \gamma, \gamma_1,$ and γ_2 from Equations 6.7, 6.16–6.18 for a fixed probability of false alarm $P_f = 0.1$.
  5. Find the test statistics (E) from Equation 6.8.
  6. Do the comparison of E with thresholds λ_1 and γ_2 of step 4 to claim hypothesis H_0 (0 bit) or H_1 (1 bit) according to Equations 6.9 and 6.20, respectively.
  7. Calculate Z from Equation 6.15 and compare with threshold γ to claim hypothesis H_0 (0 bit) or H_1 (1 bit) according to Equation 6.21 to maintain a fixed probability of false alarm $P_f = 0.1$.
  8. Repeat steps 1-7 approximately 1000 times to find the detection probability versus SNR under the constraints that the false alarm probability is set at 0.1.

6.5 Numerical Results and Analysis for Advanced-two-Phase Detectors Scheme

In this model, we have to check the systems using a QPSK modulation scheme and wireless channel. Here, the proposed advanced-two-phase detector's spectrum sensing technique is compared with ED and cyclo detector-2010 [3], adaptive spectrum sensing-2012 [12], energy detection technique for adaptive spectrum sensing-2015 (EDT-ASS-2015) [20], and

TABLE 6.1

Parameter Values for Simulation

Parameter	Value
Signal type	QPSK
Channel (between primary users and cognitive radio users)	Rayleigh
Number of samples (N)	1000
Threshold (λ_1)	1.7
Threshold (γ)	1.15
Threshold (γ_1)	0.9
Threshold (γ_2)	1.4
Range of signal-to-noise ratio	−20–0 dB
Probability of false alarm for each detection scheme	0.1
Software	MATLAB® 2012a

ED and ED-ADT detector-2015 [25]. The parameters which are used for simulation are given in Table 6.1.

In Figure 6.4, we used an advanced-TPD technique for 1000 samples and to achieve a false alarm probability of 0.1 which sets the threshold for the system. In the simulation environment, the values of λ_1, γ_2, γ_1, and γ_2 change at every iteration. But in this case, we have chosen $\lambda_1 = 1.7$, $\gamma_1 = 0.9$, $\gamma_2 = 1.4$ and $\gamma = 1.15$ as trade-off values.

We have made a detection performance comparison in a simulation environment between the proposed advanced-TPD, ED and the cyclo detector-2010, adaptive spectrum sensing-2012, energy detection technique for adaptive spectrum sensing-2015 (EDT-ASS-2015), and ED and ED-ADT detector-2015 scheme. The analysis in Figure 6.4 shows that the advanced-TPD technique outperforms ED and cyclo detector-2010, adaptive spectrum

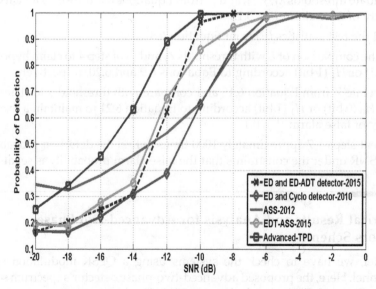

FIGURE 6.4

Detection probability with respect to SNR values at $P_f = 0.1$.

sensing-2012, energy detection technique for adaptive spectrum sensing-2015 (EDT-ASS-2015), and ED and ED-ADT detector-2015 by 34.4%, 33.9%, 13.4%, and 2.9% at −10 dB SNR in terms of detection probability, respectively. The detection probability value of 0.9 is acceptable according to IEEE 802.22 if the false alarm probability is set at 0.1. Thus, the advanced-TPD scheme can detect a PU signal at approximately −12.0 dB SNR.

Figure 6.5 represents the performance of the proposed advanced-TPD using the same parameters in terms of Total Error Probability. Figure 6.5 shows that the proposed advanced-TPD scheme has a minimum error rate that is 0.1 at−8 dB SNR as compared to the other four schemes.

The behavior of P_d with respect to P_f is shown by the Receiver Operating Characteristics (ROC) curve [28]. The detection probability value should be large at a minimum value of P_f according to IEEE 802.22. We will perform a simulation utilizing the QPSK modulation scheme in the next step of the simulations given in Figure 6.6. First, we will investigate how the detection probability changes with respect to the false alarm probability.

Thus, we estimated our simulations for different false alarm probabilities when SNR is −6, −8, −10, −12, & −14 dB, and 1000 samples are applied into the advanced-TPD. The given figure shows a lowering of the false alarm probability more than that of the detection probability. Then we decide to keep our simulations for $P_f = 0.1$ and at an SNR −10 dB, the value of detection probability is close to 0.9, that is, 0.9950, which is acceptable for licensed signal detection as per IEEE 802.22 norms [26].

The relationship of spectrum sensing time with respect to SNR is shown in Figure 6.7. The time taken by CR users to detect PU spectrum bands for spectrum sensing should be as small as possible, as suggested by IEEE 802.22. From Figure 6.7, the conclusion can be drawn that as SNR increases, the spectrum sensing time decreases. Therefore, they are inversely proportional. Equation 6.42 is used for plotting the graph between spectrum sensing time and SNR. The values of parameters used in this are defined in Table 6.1.

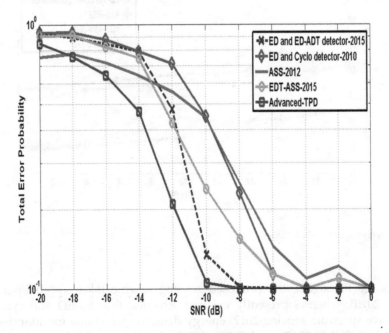

FIGURE 6.5
Probability of error with respect to SNR values.

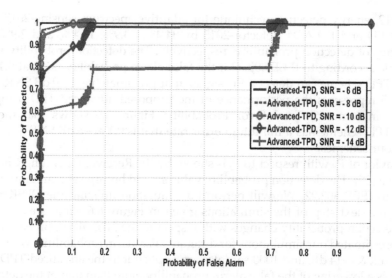

FIGURE 6.6
ROC Curves for advanced-TPD under different SNR values.

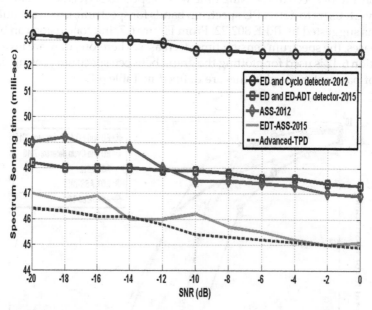

FIGURE 6.7
Sensing Time with respect to SNR values.

To detect the PU signal, the proposed sensing scheme takes approximately 46.4 ms at SNR = −20 dB, whereas presently existing schemes, that is, ED and cyclo detector-2010, adaptive spectrum sensing-2012, energy detection technique for adaptive spectrum sensing-2015 (EDT-ASS-2015), and ED and ED-ADT detector-2015, require around 53.2, 49.0, 47.0 , and 48.2 ms, respectively.

6.6 Conclusion and Future Work

In this chapter, a new spectrum sensing technique for advanced wireless networks has been suggested. This scheme reduces the error rate and sensing time and also enhances detection performance. Simulation results confirm that the proposed advanced-TPD scheme outperforms other existing schemes at a low SNR. This scheme produces a lower detection time than the ED and cyclo detector-2010, adaptive spectrum sensing-2012, EDT-ASS-2015, and ED and ED-ADT detector-2015 schemes in the order of 6.8, 2.6, 0.6, and 1.8 ms at −20 dB SNR, respectively.

Acknowledgments

We thank our parents for their support and motivation, for without their blessings and God's grace this chapter would not be possible. This work is dedicated to Anushka Gaur and Anshul Semwal, for their true and valuable love.

References

1. A. Bagwari and B. Singh, "Comparative performance evaluation of spectrum sensing techniques for conitive radio networks," *Fourth IEEE International Conference on Computational Intelligence and Communication Networks (CICN- 2012)*, vol. 1, pp. 98–105, 2012.
2. X. Xing, T. Jing, W. Cheng, Y. Huo, and X. Cheng, "Spectrum prediction in cognitive radio networks," *IEEE Wireless Communications*, vol. 20, no. 2, pp. 90–96, April 2013.
3. S. Maleki, A. Pandharipande, and G. Leus, "Two-stage spectrum sensing for cognitive radios," *IEEE Conference on Acoustics Speech and Signal Processing (ICASSP)*, pp. 2946–2949, 2010.
4. Federal Communications Commission-Second Report and Order and Memorandum Opinion and Order, "Unlicensed operation in the TV broadcast bands," FCC 08-260, November 2008.
5. R. Tandra and A. Sahai, "SNR walls for signal detection," *IEEE Journal of Selected Topic In Sig. Proceedings*, vol. 2, no. 1, pp. 4–16, February 2008.
6. D. Teguig, B. Scheers, and V. Le Nir, "Data Fusion Schemes for Cooperative Spectrum Sensing in Cognitive Radio Networks," *IEEE Transactions on Wireless Communications*, vol. 7, no. 4, pp. 1326–1337, 2008.
7. J. Lunden, V. Koivunen, A. Huttunen, and H. V. Poor, "Spectrum sensing in cognitive radios based on multiple cyclic frequencies," *IEEE Proceedings on CrownCom.*, Orlando, FL, USA, pp. 37–43, August 2007.
8. P. D. Sutton, K. E. Nolan, and L. E. Doyle, "Cyclostationary signatures in practical cognitive radio applications," *IEEE Journal on Selected Areas in Communications*, Vol. 26, pp. 13–24, January 2008.
9. D. Cabric, A. Tkachenko, and R. W. Brodersen, "Spectrum sensing measurements of pilot, energy, and collaborative detection," *IEEE MILCOM*, pp. 1–2, October 2006.
10. S. K. Sharma, S. Chatzinotas, and B. Ottersten, "Eigenvalue based SNR estimation for cognitive radio in presence of channel correlation," *2013 IEEE Global Communications Conference (GLOBECOM)*, Atlanta, GA, USA, pp. 1107–1112, December 2013.

11. L. Luo, N. M. Neihart, S. Roy, and D. J. Allstot, "A two-stage sensing technique for dynamic spectrum access," *IEEE Transactions on Wireless Communications*, vol. 8, pp. 3028–3037, June 2009.

12. W. Ejaz, N. ul Hasan, and H. S. Kim, "SNR-based adaptive spectrum sensing for cognitive radio networks," *International Journal of Innovative Computing, Information and Control*, vol. 8, no. 9, pp. 6095–6105, 2012.

13. T. Yücek and H. Arslan, "A Survey of Spectrum Sensing Algorithms for Cognitive Radio Applications," *IEEE Communications Survey & Tutorials*, vol. 11, no. 1, pp. 116–130, First Quarter 2009.

14. J. Ma, G. Li, and B. H. Juang, "Signal processing in cognitive radio," *Proceedings of the IEEE*, vol. 97, no. 5, pp. 805–823, 2009.

15. S. Haykin, "Cognitive radio: brain-empowered wireless communications," *IEEE Journal on Selected Areas in Communications*, vol. 23, no. 2, pp. 201–220, 2005.

16. S. Dan and G. Lindong, "A novel blind SNR estimator based on the modified PASTd algorithm for IF signals," *Proceedings of International Conference on Systems and Networks Communications*, Tahiti, pp. 45–48, November 2006.

17. J. Hua, L. Meng, Z. Xu, and G. Li, "An adaptive signal-to-noise ratio estimator in mobile communication channels," *Digital Signal Processing*, vol. 20, no. 3, pp. 692–698, 2010.

18. J. Vartiainen, H. Saarnisaari, J. J. Lehtomaki, and M. Juntti, "A blind signal localization and SNR estimation method," *Proceedings of IEEE Military Communication Conference*, Washington, DC, USA, pp. 1–7, October 2006.

19. S.-Q. Liu, B.-J. Hu, and X.-Y. Wang, "Hierarchical cooperative spectrum sensing based on double thresholds energy detection," *IEEE Communications Letters*, vol. 16, no. 7, pp. 1096–1099, July 2012.

20. I. Sobron, P. S. R. Diniz, W. A. Martins, and M. Velez, "Energy detection technique for adaptive spectrum sensing," *IEEE Transactions on Communications*, vol. 63, no. 3, pp. 617–627, March 2015.

21. Z. Quan, S. Cui, and A. H. Sayed, "Optimal linear cooperation for spectrum sensing in cognitive radio networks," *IEEE Journal on Selected Topics Signal Process*, vol. 2, no. 1, pp. 28–40, February 2008.

22. J. Unnikrishnan and V. Veeravalli, "Cooperative sensing for primary detection in cognitive radio," *IEEE Journal on Selected Topics Signal Process*, vol. 2, no. 1, pp. 18–27, February 2008.

23. V. Blondel, J. Hendrickx, A. Olshevsky, and J. Tsitsiklis, "Convergence in multiagent coordination, consensus, flocking," *Proceedings of 44th IEEE CDCECC*, Seville, Spain, pp. 2996–3000, December 2005.

24. F. S. Cattivelli and A. H. Sayed, "Diffusion LMS strategies for distributed estimation," *Signal Processing, IEEE Transactions*, vol. 58, no. 3, pp. 1035–1048, March 2010.

25. A. Bagwari, J. Kanti, G. S. Tomar, and A. Samarah, "Reliable spectrum sensing scheme based on dual detector with double-threshold for IEEE 802.22 WRAN," *Journal of High Speed Networks*, IOS Press, vol. 21, no. 3, pp. 205–220, August 7, 2015.

26. T. Do and B. L. Mark, "Improving spectrum sensing performance by exploiting multiuser diversity," *Foundation of Cognitive Radio Systems*, Prof. S. Cheng (Ed.), IEEE, Los Angeles, USA, pp. 119–140, March 2012.

27. A. Bagwari and G. S. Tomar, "Adaptive double-threshold based energy detector for spectrum sensing in cognitive radio networks," *International Journal of Electronics Letters (IJEL)—Taylor & Francis Group*, vol. 1, no. 1, pp. 24–32, April 4, 2013.

28. Z. Ling-Ling, H. Jian-Guo, and T. Cheng-Kai, "Novel energy detection scheme in cognitive radio," *IEEE Conference on Signal Processing, Communications and Computing (ICSPCC)*, China, pp. 1–4, September 2011.

7

Compressive Sensing in the Multiple Antenna Regime

G. Nagarajan and S. Arunmozhi

CONTENTS

7.1 Introduction

Advances in wireless communication technology have been very rapid in the recent decade. The requirements for a huge bandwidth and high data rate for satisfying end users are growing very quickly. Modern wireless technology has included the collection of data through sensors. Such wireless sensor networks (WSN) are widely used in various fields to collect data like position, temperature, pressure, and so on. In networks like the WSNs, we are in need of communication to a limited number of users, that is, not all users are in communication at any point of time. This paves the way for the development of the compressed sensing (CS) requirement. If the transmitted data vector is considerably smaller than the original data to be transmitted, there arises the issue of recovery from the sparse vector set. Compressed sensing algorithms are able to do this efficiently [1,2]. In the analysis, a single antenna system is considered for transmitting the analog signal and the base station exploits the channel state information (CSI) of all the nodes when adapting the CS decoding technique. The CSI estimation requires a large amount of data from various resources. The use of CS for the CSI estimation has opened an area of exploration for using compression in other estimations where partial data requirements can make the system perform normally [3]. When there is a requirement for CSI estimations from many sources, the need for multiple signals from many antennas could favor the estimations. In a multiple antenna environment, this CS could perform well by estimating the CSI with the partial data available at any point in time [4]. When greater numbers of transmitting antennas are used at the base station and nodes, there is significant improvement in the bit error rate (BER) and delay performance. There is a requirement for CSI estimation in cellular systems that operate in frequency division duplex (FDD) mode. The CSI estimation in such systems is a tedious task. In such a scenario, a CS technique plays a vital role. The implementation of multiple input and multiple output (MIMO) schemes for wireless communication advancement is not without issues, including [4,5]:

- Received power
- Total interference power
- Signal-to-interference-plus noise ratio (SINR)
- Signal processing complexity
- Handover between base stations
- Information theoretic issues of millimetre-Wave (mmWave) massive MIMO
- Hardware requirements

Inspite of the challenges, the CSI of a system has to be estimated under the various conditions of wireless channels. The field of digital signal processing has seen an enormous growth in recent years providing an avenue for mitigating some of the problems in the wireless environment. To be specific, the CS proposed in the past decade alleviates the bottleneck of using the sparse structure of the measured frequency spectrum. For example, the costly issue of requiring more hardware is best addressed by the implantation of a spectrum sensing approach based on CS. A low speed analog to information converter (AIC) is employed in CS-based detection which eliminates the conventional high-speed Nyquist analog to digital convertor (ADC).

The low speed AIC basically operates on the information rate of the captured signal, while the old ADC works on the symbol rate. A practical realization of the low rate AIC is elucidated in [6], where the analog signal is multiplied by a pseudo-random maximal length Pseudo-random Noise (PN) sequence of {1,−1}. The major advantage of utilizing the PN sequence is that it has a higher rate of change than the Nyquist rate. Initially, the received signal is augmented and then sampled at its information rate using low-speed ADC. The system has some setbacks as it is subject to model mismatches and nonlinearity which are inherent in pseudo random generators, multipliers, and integrators. The problem of spectrum sensing reaches another dimension in a multiple antenna-based cognitive radio (CR) environment, paving the way for yet another challenge. The researchers in [7] have shown that the optimal multiple antenna spectrum sensing detection not only requires information on the channel gains, but also the noise variance and primary user signal variance along with highly correlated data sets for the sake of applying CS. The technological and innovational progress of the CR techniques has seen a tremendous evolution. In the case of wideband CR networks, spectrum sensing still remains a challenging issue, and so far, the developments have not met the problems.

In this chapter, some of the investigations of CS approaches for the sake of reducing the errors that may be caused due to the data loss in a multiple antenna scenario are addressed. The error is reduced considerably by means of efficient compression which significantly reduces the amount of data sent from source to destination and from destination to source. Thus, the use of CS techniques supports a reduction in the overhead data.

The remainder of this chapter is organized as follows: First, an overview of CS requirements for the future wireless network is illustrated, followed by the introduction of the CS effect for a massive MIMO scheme. Then a spatially modulated (SM-MIMO) improvement with the help of compressive collaborative spectrum sensing is presented. Finally, an overview on the usage of selecting compressed principal components applicable for multiple antennas is presented.

7.2 Compressive Sensing for the Future Wireless Networks

The opportunities and challenges of applying CS techniques to the future wireless networks such as 5G solutions with multiple antennas and exploiting the multifold sparsity inherent in them can be implemented in a number of ways:

- The signal detection complexity can be reduced by channel impulse response (CIR)-sparsity in the context of massive MIMO systems. This helps in both reducing the channel-sounding overhead required for reliable channel estimation, as well as the spatial modulation (SM)-based signal sparsity inherent in massive SM-MIMO. The codeword sparsity of non-orthogonal multiple access (NOMA) is also used.

- The hardware cost as well as power consumption can be reduced with the exploitation of sparse spectrum occupation with the integration of CR techniques and the sparsity of the ultra-wide band (UWB) signal.

- To improve the transmit-recording performance, the CIR sparsity can be adopted in the mmWave communications. This also reduces the CIR estimation overhead.

- The inherent property of the sparsity used in the interfering base stations (BSs) and of the traffic load in ultra-dense networks (UDN) can be capitalized on in the reduction of the overheads required for inter-cell-interference (ICI) mitigation. This can also be utilized for coordinated multiple points (CoMP), transmission/reception for large-scale random access, and for traffic prediction.

The capacity of the next generation schemes can be increased with a system that relies on [8]:

- Obtaining an improved spectral efficiency for a larger number of channels by using techniques such as spatial-multiplexing MIMO;

- An increased transmission bandwidth including spectrum sharing and extension; and

- Better spectrum reuse relying on more cells per area for improving the area-spectral-efficiency (ASE).

The discussion above is elaborated below [9]:

- Increased spectral efficiency can be achieved. It is a known fact that the massive multi-antenna aided spatial-multiplexing techniques can substantially increase the system capacity. The channel estimation in massive MIMO and the signal

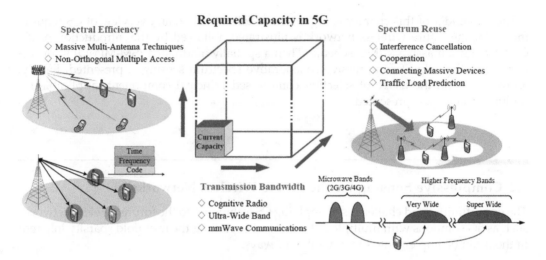

FIGURE 7.1
Requirements for future 5G wireless network. (Courtesy of Gao Hen et al. "Compressive sensing techniques for next-generation wireless communications." *arXiv preprint arXiv:1709.01757*, 2017. [18].)

　　detection of massive SM-MIMO remains a challenging issue. Second, NOMA techniques are theoretically capable of supporting more users than conventional orthogonal multiple access (OMA) under the limitation of radio resources, but the optimal design of sparse code words capable of approaching the NOMA capacity has many open challenges.

- Larger transmission bandwidth may be obtained employing both CR and UWB techniques. Both of these techniques can coexist with licensed services under the roof of spectrum sharing, using the sub-Nyquist sampling as a measure of compression. Yet another promising technology is the mmWave communication, which is capable of facilitating high data rates with its wider bandwidth. However, there is the problem of limited availability of the hardware resources at a low cost and because of its high path-loss, the challenge is greater in the channel estimation and transmitting precoding in mmWave systems than those in the existing cellular systems (Figure 7.1).

- The use of small cells leads to better spectrum reuse realization. Small cells implementation improves the ASE as expressed in bits/s/Hz/km^2. However, there are open research issues in the realization of the interference mitigation, CoMP transmission/reception, and massive random access. These topics possess many possibilities for sparsity implementation.

7.3　Compressive Sensing for Massive MIMO

The availability of accurate CSI is mandatory for reaping the utmost benefits of a system that uses massive antenna arrays at the transmitter to improve the transmission diversity. The BS along with the downlink precoding also performs a beam forming technique with a large scale antenna array to achieve a very high array gain. The BS works hard to acquire the nitty gritty downlink CSI by just estimating the subtle elements of the uplink pilot symbols transmitted from the user equipment. The complexity is further increased by the addition of the CSI at the transmitter side becomes greater in the case of massive MIMO schemes to form a closed-loop beam forming. Thus there arises a strong demand for the CSI acquisition mechanism design, particularly for massive MIMO communication systems operating in an FDD mode.

In recent developments, such as the Long Term Evolution Advanced (LTE-A) and the modern cellular systems, there is a dedicated feedback mechanism to facilitate downlink MIMO precoding. A dedicated uplink is used by the end user's equipment to send the measured downlink channel information to its BS as a feedback mechanism. In the conventional time division duplex (TDD) systems, there is a reciprocity-based CSI acquisition. The CSI derived in the case of the FDD system by the user's equipment is more accurate than that of the TDD model. This is possible because of its ability to capture the impact of downlink interferences. The concept of "codebook" is addressed here in FDD systems, which provides the CSI feedback with the help of quantizing the amplitude and phase response of a predefined set of vectors. These codebooks give an efficient feedback by means of giving only a limited number of bits representating one codebook entry. For example, in representing the MIMO channel matrix, instead of all the values in the matrix, eigen vectors can be used which reduces the information to be transmitted. In the Third Generation Partnership Program (3GPP) LTE specifications, the CSI components are called the precoding matrix indicator (PMI). Such a codebook approach where there is a limited feedback significantly reduces the required radio resources for transmitting the CSI information and provides a more tangible solution.

The recent developments like the massive MIMO obviously have a huge amount of information as the numbers of antennas are very large. As a consequence, the size of the codebook needs to be extensively expanded so that the fine-grain spatial channel structures are effectively communicated. In scenarios where the requirement for the radio resource dedicated for sending the CSI feedback remains unchanged, the feedback reliability is greatly affected by the size of the codebook as it is transmitted at a reduced coding rate. Such a scenario has resulted in much research on providing CSI feedback for massive MIMO systems. For instance, in [9], the authors have proposed a novel codebook design technique for massive MIMO. The authors have illustrated that a low-complex encoding method has more scalability than the conventional look-up table methodology. More alternatives are available in the literature.

7.3.1 Compressive Sensing-Based Channel Feedback

In recent years, the fields of image processing and pattern recognition have come across an efficient and novel mathematical tool known as CS (or compressive sampling) to produce effective outcomes with the help of limited data [10]. Intensive research is in progress in the use of CS which provides an insight into reconstructing the signals via optimization with fewer samples than that required by the traditional Shannon-Nyquist sampling theorem. This is applicable for the signals that are sparse in a certain domain. In scenarios which demand more amount of sparse representation of signals, the CS kind of technique helps to improve the performance. For large antenna arrays such as those in massive MIMO systems, there is a limitation in antenna spacing due to equipment form factors. In today's infrastructure nodes, BSs of small cells, remote radio heads with restricted physical sizes, and other small handheld devices are placed within limited spaces. To support the massive MIMO features on these space-constrained devices, a very compact antenna array is required. Due to the limitation in space, there is a strong spatial correlation in the MIMO spatial channel matrix entries [11] which may lead to a need for sparse representation in a domain other than space. Therefore, compressing the channel response by applying CS techniques effectively reduces the required feedback overhead for CSI reporting. Some of the CS techniques and their algorithms for sparse signal compressions and recovery are presented as follows.

7.3.2 Algorithmic Framework of Compressive Sensing

In the recovery of sparse signals from a set of small measurements which are random from the original signal, the application of CS finds its niche. The compression of the sparse signals has to be done in an efficient manner. To understand the algorithmic procedures of CS, an $N \times 1$ sparse signal vector denoted as x is considered. Here, only $K \ll N$ elements of x have nonzero values, whereas the remaining $N - K$ entries of x are zero. By using the random projections, the CS encoding captures the K values which are not zero. This is done by compressing the signal into $M \ll N$ units of measurements. Specifically, the sparse signal "x" with dimension $N \times 1$ can be compressed into an $M \times 1$ vector which is denoted by "y" as shown in Equation 7.1.

$$y = \Phi x \tag{7.1}$$

where Φ is a matrix with dimension $M \times N$ having random entries that are independent and identically distributed (i.i.d.). The random entries follow distributions such as Bernoulli or Gaussian. As the assumption is $M \ll N$, Equation 7.1 is an underdetermined linear system (here, only a few equations are available for determining the unknowns). Such underdetermined systems will have an infinite number of solutions while solving for "x" from "y." The estimation of "x" becomes very difficult and sometimes impossible. The optimization procedure used by the concept of CS has paved the way for recovering "x" from "y" with a very high probability. The signal vector denoted by "x" has sparse samples as it is incoherently sampled (through Φ).

There is a possibility that in many of the practical scenarios, the target signal "x" ($N \times 1$) does not necessarily have any sparsity. In such a scenario, CS becomes an unfeasible approach. In such cases, if there is a possibility that the correlation among the signal samples "x" has a higher value, then the sparse representation is feasible by applying a certain sparsifying transformation such as:

$$S = \Psi x \tag{7.2}$$

where S is a vector with dimension $N \times 1$ representing "x" in a transformed domain, and the transformation basis function with dimension $N \times N$ is denoted by Ψ which sparsifies "x." Discrete Fourier transform (DFT) and discrete cosine transforms (DCT) are commonly used typical examples of Ψ, and it is a known fact that these transformations are usually orthogonal. Due to this property, we can reverse the transformation in a simple way.

$$x = \Psi^T S \tag{7.3}$$

the use of compressive sensing blindly encodes S from y by means of random projection and hence the overhead is reduced.

$$y = \Phi x = \Phi \Psi^T S \tag{7.4}$$

The process of effectively reconstructing the vectors "*x*" from "*y*" can be termed as an optimization process.

7.3.3 CSI Feedback Schemes Using Compressive Sensing

In a point to point application of a wireless system with massive MIMO, it is assumed that there are $N_t \gg 1$ transmitter antennas at the BS and $N_r \geq 1$ receiver antennas at the user's equipment. The downlink signal can be given by

$$r = Hd + n \tag{7.5}$$

where d with size $N_t \times 1$ denotes the transmitter signal vector and r with dimension $N_r \times 1$ gives the receiver signal vector, respectively. H is an $N_r \times N_t$ MIMO channel matrix representing a flat-fading channel model entry. The additive Gaussian white noise is denoted by n which is an $N_r \times 1$ vector. Usually, with the help of the downlink pilot signals, it is assumed that the channel coefficients are perfectly estimated at the user end. But the BS has to acquire at least a partial amount of information though full information is required about the estimated channel status. This is required for adaptively configuring the physical layer parameters such as MIMO precoder weights. In [12], the authors have used the Hermitian conjugate or pseudo-inverse of the MIMO matrix H to perform operations like beam forming and zero-forcing beam forming. Another approach is to apply the singular value decomposition (SVD) for extracting the beam forming vector from H which is done with the help of a principal singular vector of H.

The process of acquiring the feedback of H over a massive MIMO system that uses the FDD scheme becomes tire some work. In cellular communication systems, the channel response H uses a vector/matrix quantization approach for the purpose of quantizing by a predefined codebook with finite entries. The user equipment then sends a codebook entry index as feedback to the transmitter. The size of the codebook now depends on the number of transmitter antennas in the massive MIMO which has to be expanded to properly capture H. To put it another way, the overhead in transmitting the CSI as feedback increases considerably, which is not recommended as the radio resource usage is not justified. Random projection is a technique used to reduce the dimension of H. Such random projection is used in CS techniques and could compress the required feedback payload. For ease of operation, the real and imaginary parts of the MIMO channel matrix H are analyzed separately. The notation $\bar{H}$ is used to represent either the real part or the imaginary part of H. Before proceeding further, the target signal $\bar{H}$ is first vectorized into a suitable dimension of $(N_r \times N_t) \times 1$:

$$r = vec(\bar{H}) \tag{7.6}$$

To compress h, random projection is used,

$$y = \Phi h \tag{7.7}$$

The basis function Φ is a matrix of dimension $M \times (N_r \times N_t)$ where the entries are independent random entries. Usually, the value of M is smaller than $(N_r \times N_t)$. The channel h undergoes a compression and is encoded as a vector y which will be an $M \times 1$ vector. The load in the feedback is reduced due to the projection and the compression ratio and is given as $\eta = M/(N_r \times N_t)$. In the analysis of the massive MIMO scheme as discussed earlier, there is a spatial demand and hence sparse data availability becomes a problem where the projection schemes are of the utmost importance to improve the performance of the overall system.

The CS theory also proposes an added advantage in recovering the channel information accurately from "y" even if the value of M is likely to be much smaller than ($N_r \times N_t$). As a result, the possibility of a low compression ratio with an efficient CSI feedback scheme is promising. The determination of the sparsifying transformation matrix Ψ and the elements of Φ are done offline. The values of Ψ as well as the contents of Φ based on pre-configurations are well known to the BS and user equipment. This favors the optimization procedures at the BS. The h in the transmitter, which is available in other transforms, can be recovered by using an inverse sparsifying transformation on S, given by:

$$h = \Psi^T S \tag{7.8}$$

The CS is a promising technique for the massive MIMO CSI estimation. The system has a bottleneck in choosing a proper sparsifying basis function, which is discussed in the following section.

7.3.4 The Sparsifying Basis Function

The best recovery is done only when the selection of the sparsifying basis, Ψ, is good. The constraint in selecting a sparsifying basis is the given compression ratio. The choice of the basis function must satisfy the provision of a sparser representation (fewer nonzero elements in S) of "h." The best basis function will achieve a good signal recovery with elevated accuracy. The commonly used bases in the literature are the two-dimensional discrete cosine transformation (2D-DCT) and Karhunen-Loeve transformation (KLT). In the field of digital image processing, image compression uses the 2D-DCT, as the technique exploits the spatial correlation among the pixels to reduce the dimensions of the image. A similar kind of spatial reduction is required in the massive MIMO environment. In massive MIMO systems, the idea is that either real or imaginary MIMO channel matrix $\bar{H}$ elements might be strongly correlated in at least one of the dimensions because of the small antenna spacing present at the transmitter side. Hence, the spatial correlation can be utilized here, as is done in image processing, by applying the 2D-DCT transformation. The sparsifying basis realizes a sparse representation of $\bar{H}$ in the spatial frequency domain with the advantage of correlation structures. The process of obtaining a 2D-DCT over the real or imaginary term $\bar{H}$ is shown as $C_N^T \hat{H} C_N$. The dimension of C_L is an $L \times L$ DCT matrix and the sparse representation of h can be expressed as

$$S = \left(C_{N_t} \otimes C_{N_R}\right)^T vec(\hat{H}) = \left(C_{N_t} \otimes C_{N_R}\right)^T h \tag{7.9}$$

The Kronecker product is denoted by the symbol $\otimes$. Then the sparsifying basis Ψ associated with 2D-DCT is given as (Figure 7.2);

$$\Psi_{2D-DCT} = \left(C_{N_t} \otimes C_{N_R}\right)^T \tag{7.10}$$

The correlation structure of h is the vital factor in deciding the sparsity that 2D-DCT can achieve. The other transform KLT is also capable of providing the optimal sparse representation. KLT exploits only one nonzero element ($K = 1$) regardless of the correlation structure, as given in [13]. The beauty of the KLT basis is that it guarantees accurate channel recovery even if only a few measurements are available.

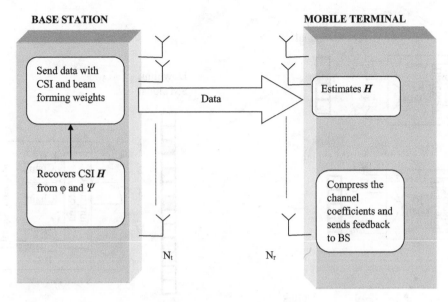

FIGURE 7.2
CSI feedback based on compressive sensing.

The CS approach in this section provides a potential way to reduce the payload required for the CSI feedback in massive MIMO systems. To meet our sparse representation of the channel, there is a need for high spatial correlation among the antennas. Such an assumption in practical systems becomes invalid, mostly when the carrier frequency is increased to mmWave ranges.

7.4 SM-Massive MIMO

In massive MIMO systems, each antenna requires a dedicated radio frequency (RF) chain. This will substantially increase the power consumption of RF circuits and the number of antennas in the BS becomes larger. To address this issue, a much smaller number of RF chains and antennas is activated for transmission as shown in Figure 7.3. The BS of massive SM-MIMO, by employing hundreds of antennas, uses only smaller chains at any point in time. Explicitly, only a small fraction of the antennas is selected for the transmission of classic modulated signals in each time slot. The three dimensional (3D) constellation diagram and the spatial constellation are exploited for the SM-MIMO systems. Moreover, massive SM-MIMO can also be used in the uplink [14], where multiple users are equipped with a single RF chain, but multiple antennas can simultaneously transmit their SM signals to the BS. The use of spatial modulation greatly increases the uplink throughput, although at the cost of having no transmitting diversity gain. The diversity gain problem can be mitigated by activating a limited number of the antennas. The problem of signal detection and channel estimation becomes undetermined as the number of transmitting antennas is higher than the number of activated receiving antennas.

The optimal maximum likelihood or near-optimal sphere decoding algorithms that can be used suffer from a potentially excessive complexity. The conventional low-complexity linear

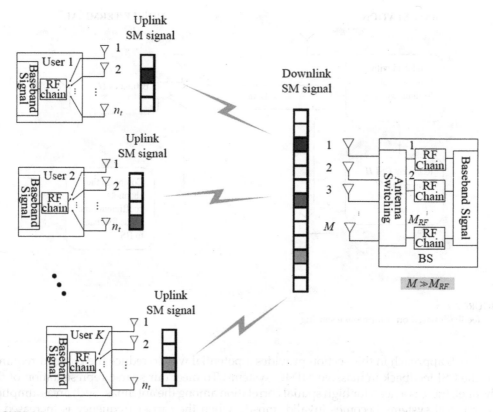

FIGURE 7.3

The SM signals in massive SM-MIMO systems are sparse. (Courtesy of Gao Hen et al. "Compressive sensing techniques for next-generation wireless communications." *arXiv preprint arXiv:1709.01757, 2017. [18].*)

algorithms, such as the linear minimum mean square error (LMMSE) algorithm, also suffer from the obvious performance loss inflicted by under-determined rank-deficient systems. Fortunately, in the downlink of massive SM-MIMO, since only a fraction of the transmitting antennas is active in each time slot, the downlink SM signals are sparse in the signal domain. This gives way for the use of a standard CSmodel for developing SM signal detection. Moreover, it is observed in Figure 7.3 that for the uplink of massive SM-MIMO, each user's uplink SM signal also exhibits sparsity, thus the aggregated SM signal incorporating all of the multiple users' uplink SM signals exhibits sparsity. To further explore the intrinsic sparsity of massive SM-MIMO channels and the methodology to exploit the estimated CSI associated with the active antennas for the purpose of reconstructing the complete CSI is a challenging problem which requires further investigations.

7.5 Principal Components for Multiple Antennas

In a CR system, wide research has been carried out on a newly emerging technology called spectrum sensing. Over a decade of extensive research has been conducted in wireless networks to design a CR application having accurate and robust signal detection methods. The spectrum sensing approach can be broadly classified into two types. In the first approach, for efficient detection of the signal, knowledge of the channel and the signal properties of licensed users are studied. Some of the detection methods are waveform-based sensing, cyclostationary detection, and detection using matched filters [15]. The technique used in the second approach is commonly referred to as a blind signal detector. It includes some of the sensing techniques such as covariance-based, energy detection, and wavelet-based detection methods.

This approach need not obtain the primitive information of the channel used and its characteristics. In the first approach, the detected signal has a high accuracy compared to the second approach, but is utilized for wireless signals of a specific type. There is also a need for a complex detection technique in the first approach, while the second approach can be utilized for most signals and does not require a complex estimation. This leads to a better choice for a wireless environment having a heterogeneous network.

In recent years, the blind signal detection technique has provoked much research interest due to its wide scope of applications and its flexibility. Out of all the detection techniques available, the simplest one is the energy detection technique, however, it demands the exact setting of the detection threshold with the knowledge of noise variance.

However, in practice, exact detection of noise variance is not possible because it is influenced by factors such as radio interference, humidity, environment temperature, and device aging. These factors have a major influence on noise variance which greatly affects the performance of the exact detection (ED) [16]. Thus, it cannot be implemented in real systems because of its unreliability. Therefore, in order to avoid these problems, a blind signal detection technique that operates on principal component analysis (PCA) is used to obtain an optimal solution. This PCA approach provides a better performance when it is compared with other algorithms such as Covariance Based Algorithm (CBD) and so on. By further improving the algorithm for environments having multiple antennas, a good performance can be obtained.

7.5.1 PCA Algorithm

The main application of PCA, which is a multivariate analysis technique, is the dimensionality reduction for a given data set which has a large number of interrelated variables. The objective of the PCA is to retain the variations present in a given data set as much as possible, which is proven in [17]. The dimensionality reduction of PCA is obtained by a linear transformation to a different set of variables. The uncorrelated principal components (PCs) are ordered such that most of the variations of any given original data set are present in the first few PCs. Thus, the last portion of the PCs is not significant or has some redundant information which is not of importance and can be ignored if necessary.

The most widely used eigen value decomposition of a positive semi-definite symmetric matrix is used in the PC estimation. This is otherwise called the covariance matrix. Consider complex baseband signals whose samples are received from each antenna source. The samples are initially decomposed into their constituent I and Q components and can be shown as,

$$x(n) = [x_{1I}, x_{1Q}, x_{2I}, x_{2Q}, \ldots]^T \tag{7.11}$$

The general assumption is that the decomposed complex baseband samples in any column vector correspond to the same time instant. The correlation of the data set is increased when the samples are received from multiple antennas or different sources. In the case of massive MIMO types of schemes, this correlation is very high and PCA has great opportunities for applications in such systems. Let there be S complex samples used for making a single sensing decision from a $2K$ (K is the number of receiver antennas) dimensional data set. The matrix for the mentioned case is illustrated as:

$$X = [x(n), x(n-1), \ldots x(n-M+1)] \tag{7.12}$$

here, $M = S/K$. A sample covariance matrix of the data matrix is given below:

$$\hat{R}(M) = \frac{1}{M} \sum_{n=1}^{M} x(n)x^T(n) \tag{7.13}$$

The signal $x(n)$ is assumed to be a zero-mean vector. Let the eigen values be ordered in the fashion $\lambda_1 \geq \lambda_2 \ldots \geq \lambda_{2K}$ by their characteristic roots such that the following condition is met.

$$|\hat{R}(M) - \lambda I| = 0 \tag{7.14}$$

where I is an identity matrix with a dimension of $\hat{R}(M)$. Now, $\gamma_1, \gamma_2, \ldots \gamma_{2K}$ are the normalized eigen vectors (characteristic vectors) of the eigen vectors satisfying $\hat{R}(M)$ then,

$$\hat{R}(M)\gamma_i = \lambda_i \gamma_i \tag{7.15}$$

$$\gamma_i^T \gamma_i = \delta_{ij} \tag{7.16}$$

where δ_{ij} is a Kronecker delta. The k most significant eigen vectors compose a feature matrix denoted as F with $2K \geq k \geq 1$; where

$$F = [\gamma_1, \ldots, \gamma_k] \tag{7.17}$$

The k most significant eigen vectors correspond to the k highest ordered eigen values. The conversion of an original data set into its corresponding PC is given by Equation 7.18.

$$p_i = F^T x_i \tag{7.18}$$

The PC provides an orthogonal linear transformation of the original data set. As mentioned earlier, it is a known fact that only the first few (k) principal components account for the maximum variation of the data. Hence the remaining PC can be ignored if not needed. The choice of the first k principal components is still an open issue. There is no universally accepted method for choosing k, rather it depends more upon the specific problem. Several procedures have been suggested to determine k. Thus, PCA helps the compression in a multiple antenna system like massive MIMO which have highly correlated data sets.

7.6 Conclusion

In this chapter, a CS scheme is discussed with examples of multiple antenna models. The use of CS has reduced the overhead of CSI feedback by sparsifying the statistics and transmits them at a reduced rate. In environments with much spatial correlation, the use of CS is of great advantage. Multiple antenna systems, which are promising for the future wireless networks, perform well with sparse data usage. The CS algorithms may improve the performances of the existing massive MIMO systems. A novel method of blind signal detection which operates on the basis of PCA has been presented. This PC analysis using only a few necessary components may help a multiple antenna system and researchers are intrigued by the technology.

References

1. Karnouskos, Stamatis, Orestis Terzidis, and Panagiotis Karnouskos. "An advanced metering infrastructure for future energy networks." In *New Technologies, Mobility And Security (NTMS) Conference*, pp. 597–606, 2007.

2. Applebaum, Lorne, Waheed U. Bajwa, Marco F. Duarte, and Robert Calderbank. "Multiuser detection in asynchronous on-off random access channels using lasso." In *IEEE 2010 48th Annual Allerton Conference on Communication, Control, and Computing (Allerton)*, pp. 130–137, 2010.

3. Li, Husheng, Rukun Mao, Lifeng Lai, and Robert C. Qiu. "Compressed meter reading for delay-sensitive and secure load report in smart grid." In *IEEE 2010 First IEEE International Conference on Smart Grid Communications (SmartGridComm)*, pp. 114–119, 2010.

4. Louie, Raymond H.Y., Wibowo Hardjawana, Yonghui Li, and Branka Vucetic. "Distributed multiple-access for wireless communications: Compressed sensing with multiple antennas." In *IEEE Global Communications Conference (GLOBECOM)*, pp. 3622–3627, 2012.

5. Feng, Daquan, Chenzi Jiang, Gubong Lim, Leonard J. Cimini, Gang Feng, and Geoffrey Ye Li. "A survey of energy-efficient wireless communications." *IEEE Communications Surveys & Tutorials*, vol. 15, no. 1, pp. 167–178, 2013.

6. Chen, Xi, Zhuizhuan Yu, Sebastian Hoyos, Brian M. Sadler, and Jose Silva-Martinez. "A sub-Nyquist rate sampling receiver exploiting compressive sensing." *IEEE Transactions On Circuits And Systems I: Regular Papers*, vol. 58, no. 3, pp. 507–520, 2011.

7. Ramirez, David, Gonzalo Vazquez-Vilar, Roberto Lopez-Valcarce, Javier Via, Ignacio Santamaria, "Detection of rank- P signals in cognitive radio networks with uncalibrated multiple antennas."*IEEE Transactions on Signal Processing*, vol. 59, pp. 3764–3774, 2011.

8. Bogale, Tadilo Endeshaw, and Long Bao Le. "Massive MIMO and mmWave for 5G wireless HetNet: Potential benefits and challenges." *IEEE Vehicular Technology Magazine*, vol. 11, no. 1, pp. 64–75, 2016.

9. Rusek, Fredrik, Daniel Persson, Buon Kiong Lau, Erik G. Larsson, Thomas L. Marzetta, Ove Edfors, and Fredrik Tufvesson. "Scaling up MIMO: Opportunities and challenges with very large arrays." *IEEE Signal Processing Magazine*, vol. 30, no. 1, pp. 40–60, 2013.

10. Wei, Lili, Rose Qingyang Hu, Yi Qian, and Geng Wu. "Key elements to enable millimeter wave communications for 5G wireless systems." *IEEE Wireless Communications*, vol. 21, no. 6, pp. 136–143, 2014.

11. Hur, Sooyoung, Taejoon Kim, David J. Love, James V. Krogmeier, Timothy A. Thomas, and Amitava Ghosh. "Millimeter wave beamforming for wireless backhaul and access in small cell networks." *IEEE Trans. Communications*, vol. 61, no. 10, pp. 4391–4403, 2013.

12. Yang, Hong, and Thomas L. Marzetta. "Performance of conjugate and zero-forcing beamforming in large-scale antenna systems." *IEEE Journal on Selected Areas in Communications*, vol. 31, no. 2, pp. 172–179, 2013.

13. Fowler, James E. "Compressive-projection principal component analysis." *IEEE Transactions on Image Processing*, vol. 18, no. 10, pp. 2230–2242, 2009.

14. Gao, Zhen, Linglong Dai, Zhaocheng Wang, Sheng Chen, and Lajos Hanzo. "Compressive-sensing-based multiuser detector for the large-scale SM-MIMO uplink." *IEEE Transactions on Vehicular Technology*, vol. 65, no. 10, pp. 8725–8730, October 2016.
15. Yucek, Tevfik, and Huseyin Arslan. "A survey of spectrum sensing algorithms for cognitive radio applications." *IEEE Communications Surveys & Tutorials*, vol.11, no. 1, pp. 116–130, 2009.
16. Hoven, Niels, Rahul Tandra, and Anant Sahai. "Some fundamental limits on cognitive radio." *Wireless Foundations EECS*, University of California, Berkeley, 2005.
17. Jolliffe. I. T., "Principal component analysis and factor analysis." In *Principal Component Analysis*. Springer, New York, pp. 115–128, 1986.
18. Gao, Hen, Linglong Dai, Shuangfeng Han, Zhaocheng Wang, and Lajos Hanzo. "Compressive sensing techniques for next-generation wireless communications." *arXiv preprint arXiv:1709.-01757*, 2017.

8

Multiple Antennas Based Collaborative Spectrum Sensing Techniques

G. Nagarajan and T. Perarasi

CONTENTS

8.1 Introduction

Cognitive Radio is the effective utilization of spectrum based on criteria such as the time, transmitted wave, and frequency. Increased numbers of users in the wireless world have paved the way for the deployment of spectral efficiency which is easily achieved by the concept of cognitive radio (CR). CR provides better bandwidth efficiency in spectrum utility [1].

The objective of this chapter is to provide readers with an overview of the advancements in antenna techniques. This will also help them to understand the concepts of antenna, algorithms involved in designs, and structure implementations. The thrust of the next generation mobile, afford the development in the technologies. This now acts as a bridge between the spectrum brokers and the technologists. This chapter delivers an overview of the state of research and investigations into smart antennas and their potential utility in commercial mobile radio networks [2]. Antennas embodying these techniques are generally referred to as smart antennas because their characteristics are adapted to the signal regime in which they are situated. Although some authors distinguish between smart, intelligent, and adaptive antennas, the terms are effectively synonymous.

The adoption of smart antenna techniques has been seen by many investigators as capable of offering significant advantages in terms of improved coverage, increased network capacity, and enhanced use of spectral resources, yet to date they have not been applied commercially in mobile radio systems [3].

The antennas used are not smart antennas, but the systems are smart. A smart antenna system combines an antenna array with digital signal-processing to transmit and receive in an adaptive and sensitive manner. This provides a system that can automatically change the directionality of its radiation patterns in response to its signal environment [4–9].

8.2 Antenna Systems

An antenna is a transducer that transfers energy from one form to another. This system has its own preferred direction for both transmission and reception. A brute force method adds new transmitter sites and antenna towers to split or sectorize cells [10–13]. A 360^δ area is split into three 120° subdivisions. An omni directional antenna provides a high gain. Sectoring of an antenna produces more gain as a function of azimuth. Gain with respect to the antenna is referred as an antenna gain and not as processing gain. Sectoring provides access to many channels. While sector antennas reproduce use of channels, they do not overwhelm the major disadvantages of standard omni directional antenna broadcast such as co channel interference.

To formulate an antenna to be more intelligent, its physical size is varied by adding elements. An antenna system is designed to shift signals before transmission. A phased array antenna is the basic antenna designed to do this.

8.2.1 Sectorized Systems

Sectorized systems divide the region into various sectors using directional antennas from the base station. Each sector forms a cell as shown in Figure 8.1. Frequency reuse increases coverage and also suppresses interference across the cell. In practice, six sectors are used. A base station is designed to cover the entire region.

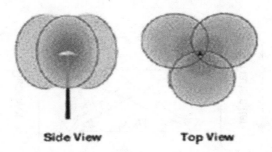

FIGURE 8.1
Sectorized antenna and coverage patterns.

8.2.2 Diversity Systems

The diversity system integrates two antenna elements at the base station with a space diversity to increase signals at the receiver by nullifying multipath effects. The strength at the receiver can be improved using diversity with the method listed below:

1. *Switched diversity*: Let an antenna be assumed at a particular locality for a stipulated duration. Continuous switching between antennas occurs to improve the output at the receiver. Gain does not increase since only one antenna is used at a time.

2. *Combined diversity*: Multipath phase errors are corrected and the powers of signals are combined to improve gain. Maximal ratio combining (MRC) helps in improving energy at the receiver.

Switching between the elements is done using a diversity antenna that introduces multipath fading with no uplink gain attainment. Extraction of the strongest signal from a set is not possible when there is interference. This results in interference during reception. This paves way to the tremendous growth in antenna systems that intelligently improve the operation of diversity.

8.3 MIMO

There are two main categories of multiple antennas: diversity and spatial multiplexing techniques. Diversity helps in attaining the signal in or to transmit the same from multiple antennas which result in increase of reliability. The basic principle is that it converts a Rayleigh faded signal into a more stable additive white gaussian noise (AWGN).

A spatial multiplexing technique increases the transmission speed by the use of multiple data streams from multiple antennas. The transmission speed is less than the capacity of the multi input and multi output (MIMO) channel [14–15]. The maximum speed is equal to the capacity of the MIMO channel. $N_R \times N_T$ with multiple transmitters are depicted as in Figure 8.2.

Figure 8.3 shows a single base station serving as a node for multiple mobile nodes. Three nodes out of the given four nodes are considered in the time, frequency, and spatial streams.

Let N_B be the base station and N_M be the antennas. "K" is the independent users. Let $(K \cdot N_M) \times N_B$ be the channels for downlink and $N_B \times (K \cdot N_M)$ be the uplink channels.

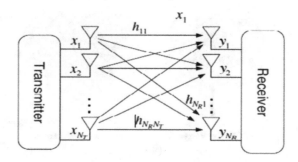

FIGURE 8.2
$N_R \times N_T$ MIMO system.

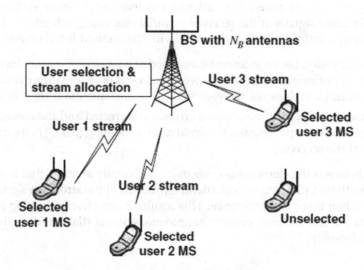

FIGURE 8.3
Multi user MIMO communication system, $K = 4$.

Under a multi user system, many to one transmission occurs in uplink and one to many occurs in the downlink. This generally boosts the degrees of freedom with multiple antennas. Under MIMO, downlink channels are broadcast channels (BC) and uplink channels are called multiple access channels. As all channels are available to all users, $(K \cdot N_M) \times N_B$ uplink occurs [16–19].

8.3.1 MIMO-OFDM Conjunction

The problems that arises in the wireless links are speed, range, and reliability. All these are interrelated. Higher speeds are attained at the cost of other parameters and vice versa. A technique that provides and supports all the parameters in one package is orthogonal frequency division multiplexing (OFDM)-MIMO.

The process of OFDM is to divide the spectrum band into multiple, smaller sub signals without interference. MIMO has the capacity to link many smaller antennas as a single unit. OFDM is used to mitigate the multipath effect and MIMO provides efficient utility of the bandwidth. OFDM with MIMO increases coverage, reliability, and the data rate by hundreds of megabits. In the spatial domain, the capacity of MIMO is large and OFDM works effectively in the time domain, thus eliminating the effect of Inter Symbol Interference (ISI) [20–21]. OFDM generates a time varying channel whereas MIMO has increased the capacity of transmitting the signals with an array of antennas. MIMO has the advantage of multipath propagation.

8.4 Smart Antennas

Multiple antennas with innovative signal processing techniques have been used for years. Smart antennas are used in defense and are not commercialized with reduction in cost digital signal processors digital signal processors (DSPs) and application specific IC (ASICs) with software makes intelligent antenna into the mobile world. Smart antennas provide great coverage, minimum interference, and improvements in the capacity.

8.4.1 Working of Smart Antenna Systems

Switched beam and adaptive arrays use a base station in beam forming and reject noise the outside main lobe [22]. Spatial division multiple access (SDMA) services are advanced processing techniques that, in effect, locate and track fixed or mobile terminals. These adaptively steer toward users and away from interferers. This creates interference suppression, frequency reuse levels of interference suppression.

Figure 8.4 explains the use of algorithms and hardware to get a main beam with the suppression of interference. It uses channel allocation in real time. Traditional beam forming and beam steering techniques steer the a direction of the transmission toward a user. Spatial processing maximizes the use of multiple antennas.

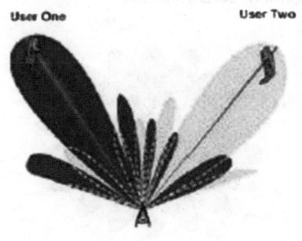

FIGURE 8.4

Fully adaptive spatial processing, supporting two users on the same conventional channel simultaneously in the same cell.

8.5 Types of Smart Antenna Systems

Smart antenna system technology includes intelligent antennas, phased arrays, SDMA, spatial processing, digital beam forming, adaptive antenna systems, and other techniques. The finite values of elements have predefined patterns or sectors. The following are distinctions between the two major categories of smart antennas regarding the choices for transmitting.

    i. *Switched beam*: These are a finite number of fixed, predefined patterns or combining strategies (sectors).

    ii. *Adaptive array*: This structure has an infinite number of patterns that may be adjusted in real scenarios.

8.5.1 Switched Beam Antennas

These antennas form multiple fixed beams with better sensitivity in a prescribed direction as in Figure 8.5. The directional pattern can be shaped by the metal's properties and physical design. These antennas combine the output to form sectorization rather than a single element.

8.5.2 Adaptive Array Antennas

An adaptive antenna is an advanced smart antenna. With the help of a signal processing algorithm, this antenna helps to locate and track types of signals so as to minimize interference and to maximize the received signal strength. This structure provides gain, tracking, and reduces noise. The dual purposes of a smart antenna are to improve signal quality during transmission and improve capacity by frequency reuse [23].

Smart antennas are more complex than base station transceivers. An antenna array uses a separate transceiver for each element. Antenna beam forming is intensive but Smart antenna are implemented with DSP that increases the cost. A linear array of 10 elements spaced a half wavelength apart operated at 2 GHz is 70 cm wide.

FIGURE 8.5
Switched beam system coverage pattern.

8.6 Smart Antennas in a WiMAX System

Worldwide interoperability for microwave access (WiMAX) contains two types of antennas. One is for base stations and the other is for terminals. Adaptive antennas and MIMO are at the base station. Mobility for end users are at other terminals. Figure 8.6 shows terminals in different localities.

The major problem in the mobile world is coverage of space including dead spots. The data rate for internet, audio, and video information is not sufficient. There are two methods to increase the speed of data transmission.

(a) Improvement in efficiency with a reduction in quality due to a weak signal at the receiver. This decreases the bandwidth due to the consumption of error correcting codes.

(b) Improvement occurs by increasing transmitter power or receiver sensitivity. A power amplifier is used at the transmitter and a low noise amplifier is used at the receiver. Usage of such amplifiers increases the cost. A carefully designed antenna transfers most of the power in a particular direction rather than in all directions. A dipole or patch antenna radiates energy in the horizontal plane with an omni directional radiation pattern.

WiMAX increases the coverage area. With usage of adaptive arrays at both the base station and terminal, spectral efficiency varies from 3 to 10 times. For a cell area of 0.8 bits/s/Hz/mi, the gain is 2.5 bit/sec/Hz. Antenna arrays with modulators and digital signal processors improve the coverage area, channel capacity, and throughput [24–26].

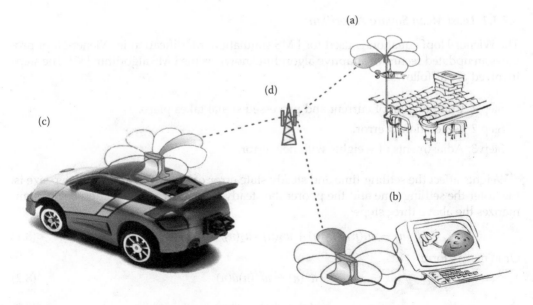

FIGURE 8.6
WIMAX user terminal antenna system basic antenna types. (a) Fixed terminal outdoor antenna. (b) Fixed terminal indoor antenna. (c) Mobile terminal antenna. (d) Base station antenna.

8.7 Smart Antenna: Its Algorithms and Implementation

"Smart Antenna" refers to an antenna array terminating in a signal processor which adjusts its own beam pattern to minimize interfering signals. A decision is made about which beam is sent at a point in time based on the requirements of the system. Beam forming allows steering the beam in a certain direction [27]. A phased array has a fixed beam toward the desired signal. The other category is an array of multiple antenna elements. The received signals are combined to maximize the desired signal-to-interference plus noise power ratio [28–30].

Array patterns are adjusted by Sample Matrix Inversion (SMI). The number of interferers and their positions remain constant due to nulling the loss by LMS and SMI. The null of SMI is greater than the SMI. The weighting factors of LMS and SMI algorithms give superior flexibility and control. Two methods are involved, namely block adaptive and sample-by-sample methods. Block implementation of the adaptive beam-former uses a block of data to estimate the beam-forming weight vector and is known as SMI. The sample-by-sample methods used are least mean square (LMS) algorithm, constant modulus algorithm (CMA), least square CMA, and recursive least square (RLS) algorithm [31–32].

8.7.1 Adaptive Algorithms

Adaptive algorithms make use of the space characteristics of filtering for high gain in the desired direction and null the interferences. Blind algorithms and nonblind algorithms include least mean square (LMS), recursive least square (RLS), SMI, Least Common Multiple Vector (LCMV), and so on. The SMI algorithm has fast convergence but is computationally complex. The LCMV algorithm has a deep null depth and needs Direction of Arrival (DOA).

8.7.1.1 Least Mean Square Algorithm

The Wiener-Hopf equation is used for LMS simulation. Modification in Wiener-Hopf provides an updated recursive adaptive algorithm known as the LMS algorithm [33]. The steps involved are as follows:

Step 1: Computation of current and processed signal takes place.

Step 2: Generation of error.

Step 3: Adjustments of weights with new error.

Weights affect the settling time and steady state error of LMS. The larger the step size is, the faster the settling time and the poorer the steady state error. The equation below summarizes the above three steps.

$$d^\wedge(n) = w_1(n) * u_1(n) + w_2(n) * u_2(n) + \cdots + w_n(n) * u_t(n) \tag{8.1}$$

Or in matrix form,

$$d^\wedge(n) = w^H(n)u(n) \tag{8.2}$$

$$e(n) = d(n) - d^\wedge(n) \tag{8.3}$$

$$w(n + 1) = w(n) + \mu u(n)e * (n) \tag{8.4}$$

where
  w: vector with whole set of weights (step size parameter)
  H: Hermitian transpose of vector.

Eight elements for each symbol are received at time. The weights are updated by w in each recursion. At time zero, the weights have a value of zero.

8.7.1.2 Recursive Least Square Algorithm

In RLS, the mean square errors are not minimized rather they are summed up by Kalman filter (multi tap transversal filter). The squared errors are sampled in time. The equations below illustrate the steps for the RLS algorithm.

$$k(n) = \frac{\lambda^{-1}p(n-1)u(n)}{1 + \lambda^{-1}u^H(n)p(n-1)u(n)} \tag{8.5}$$

$$\varepsilon(n) = d(n) - w^H(n-1)u(n) \tag{8.6}$$

$$w(n) = w(n-1) + k(n)\varepsilon * (n) \tag{8.7}$$

$$p(n) = \lambda^{-1}p(n-1) - \lambda^{-1}k(n)u^H(n)p(n-1) \tag{8.8}$$

where
  P: $\delta^{-1}I$ positive constant
  I: identity matrix
  K: vector (Kalman gain factor).

The filter in this system does not have a transversal architecture, thus the value left is with a unity coefficient.

8.7.2 Vector Recursive Least Square Algorithm (VRLS)

Vector RLS uses a one rank covariance matrix. The advantages are complexity of order and a high convergence rate of about 2M. Its implementation encounters numerical problems due to rounding off errors. This occurs after a number of iterations, causing instability [33]. VRLS provides more reduction in complexity than the conventional RLS of order O (Nk), where k is the number of processing snapshots. The hardware elements of VRLS operate in a real time environment.

With many numbers of operations per second, VRLS is an algorithm for weight adjustment in smart antennas because of its complexity and the convergence rate of signal to interference noise ratio (SINR).

8.7.2.1 Design of VRLS Beamformer

According to the floating-point operation, the core VRLS beam former block is developed and tested. The beam former block is developed by using Quatrus II for the basic components' design.

Modelsim is used to produce the behavioral simulation. The core block is composed of the basic components, namely, a complex multiplier block, a complex vector multiplier, and an array of complex multipliers. The complex vector multiplier is built using four complex

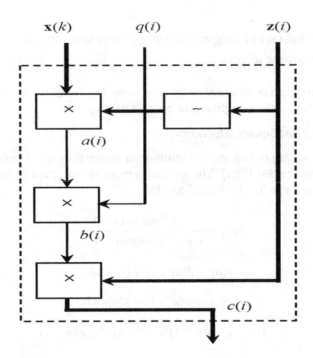

FIGURE 8.7
The VRLS beamformer core block.

multipliers and adding their outputs to form the result of the dot product. The complex elements are built in the same way but without adders. The complex multiplier, which is the most primary component of the core block, is shown in Figure 8.7.

8.8 Simulation Results and Discussion

The presence of embedded soft processor cores within field programmable gate arrays (FPGAs) provides flexibility and portability while maintaining the performance of a parallel hardware implementation. Figure 8.8 shows the computational block of the VRLS beamforming algorithm with Quatrus II. The numerical performance of the VRLS beamformer, including some measures to avoid the rounding off errors; accumulation, is discussed. The basic components of the core block complex multiplier, a complex vector multiplier, and a complex elements multiplier are designed using Quatrus II.

8.8.1 Complex Multiplier

The complex multiplier consists of eight real inputs and eight imaginary inputs, which are then given to multipliers. The output of each multiplier is added to produce the final output as in Figure 8.9.

8.8.2 Complex Vector Multiplier

Figure 8.10 shows that the complex vector multiplier consists of four complex multipliers and each output is added to produce the final output.

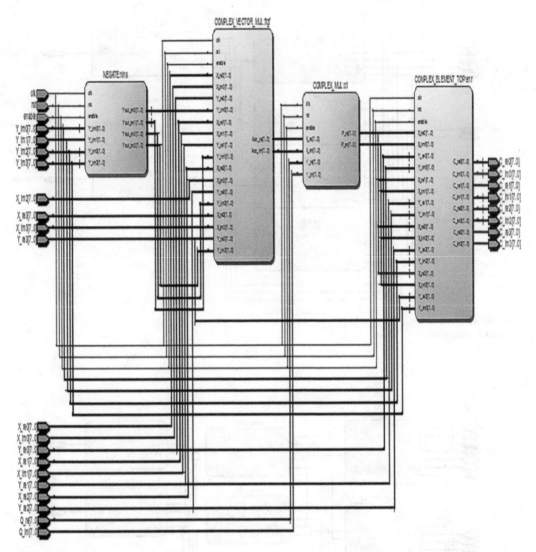

FIGURE 8.8
VRLS beamformer.

8.8.3 Complex Element Multiplier

The complex element multiplier consists of complex multipliers to produce the real and imaginary values as in Figure 8.11.

8.8.4 RTL Simulation for VRLS Beamformer

The diagram in Figure 8.12 shows the resistor transistor logic (RTL) simulation for the OFDM systems.

The ModelSim behavioral is illustrated for four element basic core blocks. It consists of 32 bits of real and 32 bits of imaginary values. Pipelining of both the complex multipliers and complex vector multipliers was proposed. When compared with a fixed point, the floating-point representation yields good accuracy and efficiency.

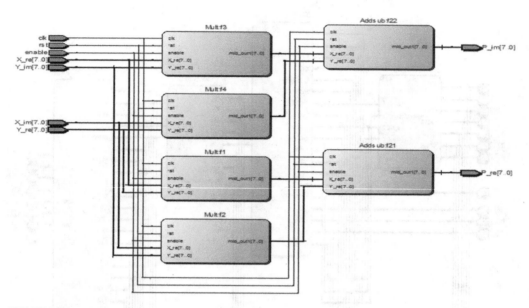

FIGURE 8.9
Complex multiplier.

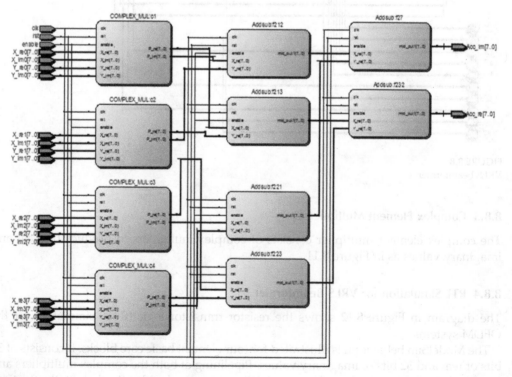

FIGURE 8.10
Complex vector multiplier.

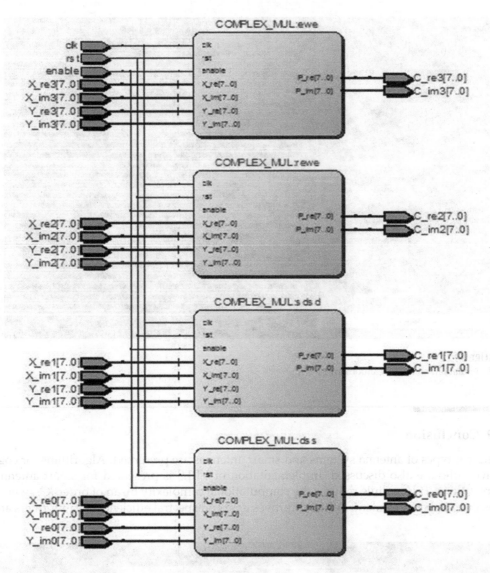

FIGURE 8.11
Complex element multiplier.

8.8.5 Implementation on Cyclone IV E FPGA

The vector RLS system model is implemented on the DE2-115 embedded development tool kit. The Universal Serial Bus (USB) blaster is used to interface the system with Field Programmable Gate Array (FPGA). The output is seen in the DE2-115 FPGA kit in which the real and imaginary count values are seen as in Figure 8.13.

8.8.6 Flow Summary

Table 8.1 explains the outpour generated under different logical values.

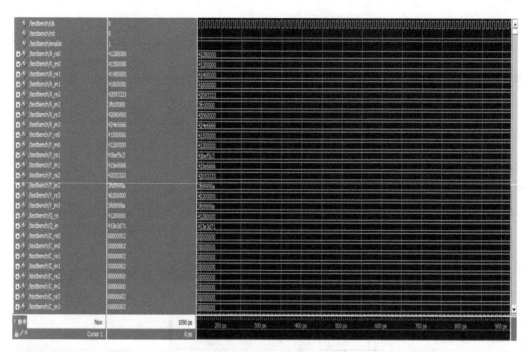

FIGURE 8.12
RTL simulation for VRLS beamformer.

8.9 Conclusion

Different types of antenna systems and smart antennas are presented. Algorithms for cognitive radio are also discussed. Implementation of VRLS is presented for smart antenna applications. This module reduces the computational complexity by an of order K^N, where N is the number of elements. VRLS improves gain and spectral efficiency. Beamformers are

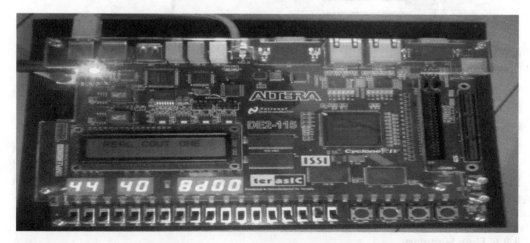

FIGURE 8.13
Implementation of cyclone IV E FPGA.

TABLE 8.1

Flow Summary of Simulation

Flow Summary	
Flow Status	Successful—Wed May 07 10:16:28 2014
Quartus II 32-bit version	11.1 Build 173 11/01/2011 SJ Web Edition
Revision Name	TOP
Top-level Entity Name	DE2_115_Default
Family	Cyclone IV E
Device	EP4CE115F29C7
Timing Models	Final
Total logic elements	3,285/114,480 (3%)
Total combinational functions	3,272/114,480 (3%)
Dedicated logic registers	2,088/114,480 (2%)
Total registers	2,088
Total pins	88/529 (17%)
Total virtual pins	0
Total memory bits	0/3,981,312 (0%)
Embedded Multiplier 9-bit elemnts	0/532 (0%)
Total PLLs	0/4 (0%)

developed using Quatrus II. The running test of the core block for a four element antenna array is shown and discussed. The pipelining of complex multipliers and complex vector multipliers are also proposed.

References

1. Akyildiz, I., Lee, W., Vuran, M. and Mohanty, S., "NeXt Generation/Dynamic Spectrum Access/Cognitive Radio Wireless Networks: A Survey," *Computer Networks*, vol. 50, no. 13, pp. 2127–2159, May 2006.
2. Song, M., Xin, C. and Zhao, Y., "Dynamic Spectrum Access: From Cognitive Radio to Network Radio," *IEEE Wireless Communications*, vol. 19, no. 1, pp. 23–29, February 2012.
3. Haykin, S., "Cognitive Radio: Brain-Empowered Wireless Communications," *IEEE Journal On Selected Areas In Communications*, vol. 23, no. 2, pp. 201–220, February 2005.
4. David Meyer, "4G Auction Winners," GIGAOM, February 2013.
5. Proakis, J., "*Digital Communication*," Tata McGraw Hill, 4th edition, Ch. 5–6, pp. 233–371, 2000.
6. Proakis, J., "*Digital Communications*," Tata McGraw Hill, 5th edition, Ch. 10–11, pp. 689–761, 2008.
7. Zalawadia, K.R., Doshi, T.V. and Dalal, U.D., "Adaptive Beam former Design using RLS algorithm for Smart Antenna Systems," *International Conference on Computational Intelligence and Communication systems*, pp. 102–106.
8. Reboredo, H., Renna, F., Calderbank, R. and Rodrigues, M.R.D., "Bounds on the number of measurements for reliable Compressive Classification," *IEEE Transactions on Signal Processing*, vol. 8, no. 54, pp. 160–176, July 2016.
9. Mubeen, S., Prasad, A.M. and Jhansi Rani, A., "Smart Antenna its Algorithms and Implementation," *International Journal of Advanced Research in Computer Science and Software Engineering*, pp. 97–101, 2012.

10. Akyildiz, I.F., Lee, W.-Y. and Chowdhury, K.R., "CRAHNs: Cognitive Radio Ad Hoc Networks," *Ad Hoc Networks*, vol. 7, no. 5, pp. 810–836, January 2009.
11. Wyglinski, A.M., Nekovee, M. and Hou, T.Y., "Cognitive Radio Communications and Networks: Principles and Practice," *IEEE Journal on Selected Areas in Communications*, vol. 11, no. 5, pp. 211–219, October 2010.
12. Farhang Boroujeny, B., "*Signal Processing Techniques for Software Radios*," Lulu, 2nd edition, Ch. 3–5, pp. 87–124, 2010.
13. Cordeiro, C., Challapali, K., Birru, D. and Sai Shankar, N., "IEEE 802.22: An Introduction to the First Wireless Standard Based on Cognitive Radios," *Journal of Communications*, vol. 1, no. 1, pp. 328–337, April 2006.
14. Gaafar, M., Khafagy, M.G., Amin, O. and Alouini, M.S., "Improper Gaussian Signaling in Full-Duplex Relay Channels with Residual Self-Interference," *Proc. IEEE Int. Conf. Commun. (ICC)*, Kuala Lumpure, May 2016.
15. Lameiro, C., Santamarıa, I. and Schreier, P.J., "Benefits of Improper Signaling for Underlay Cognitive Radio," *IEEE Wireless Communication Letters*, vol. 4, no. 1, pp. 22–25, February 2015.
16. Huang, Y., Al-Qahtani, F.S., Duong, T.Q. and Wang, J., "Secure Transmission in MIMO Wiretap Channels Using General-Order Transmit Antenna Selection with Outdated CSI," *IEEE Transactions on Communications*, vol. 63, no. 8, pp. 2959–2971, August 2015.
17. Wang, L. and de Lamare, R.C., "A Novel Constrained Adaptive Algorithm Using the Conjugate Gradient Method for Smart Antennas," pp. 2243–2245, 2007.
18. Amarasuriya, G., Larsson, E.G. and Poor, H.V., "Wireless Information and Power Transfer in Multiway Massive MIMO Relay Networks," *IEEE Transactions on Wireless Communications*, vol. 15, no. 6, pp. 3837–3855, June 2016.
19. Al-Hraishawi, H. and Baduge, G.A.A., "Wireless Energy Harvesting in Cognitive Massive MIMO Systems with Underlay Spectrum Sharing," *IEEE Wireless Communications Letters*, vol. 6, no. 1, February 2017.
20. Rahman, M.J., Wang, X. and Primak, S.L., "Efficient Mutual Interference Minimization and Power Allocation for OFDM Based Cognitive Radio," *IEEE Communication Society*, vol. 60, no. 4, pp. 1699–1713, June 2009.
21. Chen, R., Teo, K.H. and Farhang, B., "Random Access Protocols for Collaborative Spectrum Sensing in Multi Band Cognitive Radio Networks," *IEEE Journal of Selected Topics in Signal Processing*, vol. 5, no. 1, pp.124–136, February 2011.
22. Mubeen, S., Prasad, A.M. and Jhansi Rani, A., "Smart Antenna Its Algorithms and Implementation," *International Journal of Advanced Research in Computer Science and Software Engineering*, pp. 97–101, 2012.
23. Razia, S., Hossain, T. and Matin, M.A., "Performance Analysis of Adaptive for Smart Antenna System," *IEEE/OSA/IAPR International Conference on Informatics, Electronics & Vision*, pp. 946–949, 2012.
24. Sherman, M., Mody, A.N., Martinez, R. and Rodriguez, C., "IEEE Standards Supporting Cognitive Radio and Networks, Dynamic Spectrum Access, and Coexistence," *IEEE Communications Magazine*, vol. 46, no. 7, pp. 72–79, Jul 2008.
25. Cao, H., Leung, V., Chow, C. and Chan, H., "Enabling Technologies for Wireless Body Area Network: A Survey and Outlook," *IEEE Communication Magazine*, vol. 47, no. 12, pp. 84–93, December 2009.
26. Boulogeorgos, A.A.A., Bany Salameh, H.A. and Karagiannidis, G.K., "Spectrum Sensing in Full-Duplex Cognitive Radio Networks Under Hardware Imperfections," *IEEE Transactions on Vehicular Technology*, vol. 66, no. 3, pp. 2072–2084, 2017.
27. Wu, Y., Hu, F., Zhu, Y.y. and Kumar, S., "Optimal Spectrum Handoff Control for Cognitive Radio Network Based on Hybrid Priority Queuing and Multi-Teacher Apprentice Learning," *IEEE Transactions on Vehicular Technology*, vol. 66, no. 3, pp. 2630–2642, 2017.
28. Yang, J. and Ulukus, S., "Optimal Packet Scheduling in an Energy Harvesting Communication System," *IEEE Transactions on Communications*, vol. 60, no. 1, pp. 220–230, January 2012.

29. Rahaman, M.M., Hossain, M.M. and Rana, M.M., "Least Mean Square (LMS) for Smart Antenna," *Universal Journal of Communications and Network*, vol. 1, pp. 16–21, 2013.
30. Imtiaj, S.K., Misra, I.S. and Biswas, R., "A Comparative Study of Beamforming Technique Using LMS and SMI Algorihm in Smart Antenna," pp. 246–249, 1999.
31. Zalawadia, K.R., Doshi, T.V. and Dalal, U.D., "Adaptive Beam Former Design Using RLS Algorithm for Smart Antenna System," *International Conference on Computational Intelligence and Communication Systems*, pp. 102–106, 2011.
32. Hong, X., Wang, J., Wang, C.X. and Shi, J., "Cognitive Radio in 5G: A Perspective on Energy Spectral Efficiency Trade-Off," *IEEE Communication Magazine*, vol. 52, pp. 46–53, July 2014.
33. "2020: Beyond 4G, Radio Evolution for the Gigabit Experience," Nokia Siemens Networks, August 2011.

Part IV

Energy Efficient Routing Protocols

9

Investigation of Energy Efficient Routing Protocols in Wireless Sensor Networks with Variant Battery Models

Vinod Kumar Verma, Surinder Singh, and N.P. Pathak

CONTENTS

9.1 Introduction

Wireless sensor networks (WSN) have appeared as a uniform valuable and novel platform for wireless communication and in other fields of applications. The future of WSNs includes utilizing wider areas of coverage such as environmental checking, defense technology and surveillance, ecology estimation, industrial goods manufacturing, home instruments, shipping, medical appliances, all-purpose applications, and so on. [1]. Wireless sensors are handy devices integrated with a transmitter and receiver along with low energy sources. Common properties of a wireless sensor node include memory, energy, and an economical processor for computational purposes [2,3]. The main goal of any WSN is to perform a distributed field task. This is achieved by mutual coordination of various sensor nodes with specific applications like sensing, computing, broadcasting, and storage. The parameter nodes' cooperation plays a crucial role in the overall performance determination of any WSN system [4,5]. In common terms, a WSN is a group of sensor nodes linked with each other in a specific way to perform a distributed task. The deployment of WSNs is a serious concern as applications may vary from simple to complicated physical deployment situations. The issues of security and reliability have become important research areas in WSN and have garnered the interest of scientists and researchers [6]. There remains the probability of a collusive node in WSNs as the region of deployment ranges from a close environment to an open environment as well [7]. These malicious nodes may spread incorrect information over the whole network which results in overall system performance degradation. Therefore, it is quite necessary to identify the collusive nodes and alleviate these problems. There are a range of strategies and policies to sense a malicious node in the WSNs. The conventional methods to secure a network include different cipher techniques and approaches. The availability of cipher-based results addresses the general issues such as authentication, access control, confidentiality, integrity, and non-repudiation. But the designing necessities of WSN applications are more serious than those of traditional strategies. In the absence of a sufficient security policy, a node may bypass the traditional security and can convey the wrong information. As a result, the reliability of the complete WSN system may be compromised. The major drawback of cipher-based results is the involvement of complex computations which consumes extra energy resources. This makes the results more difficult for adoption in WSN [8]. Some light weight cryptographic methods do exist in the literature, but they do not serve the ultimate goal. Thus, there remains a need to probe the WSN reliability and search for more means of integrating greater reliability into the overall WSN system. The trust and reputation models are the solutions for problem to adhere to reliability in the WSNs years. In literature, numerous models have been proposed which are focused on secure routing, cluster head selection, data aggregation, and synchronized trust management [7,9,10]. But there is a need to address different issues such as routing protocols, collusion, scalability, portability, and computability in the WSNs. At present, most of the trust estimation frameworks belong to an algorithm-based methodology on which the entire actions of nodes depend in terms of resource usability, accuracy, and energy consumption. More investigation on these problems such as collusion and fraudulent environments are needed. The following sections outline the foundation for the scope, aim, and general character of our research work.

9.2 Literature Review

Sensor arrangement enlargement was organized by the United States during the Cold War. An organization of acoustic sensors was situated at strategic places on the bottom of the sea to sense and track Soviet submarines. This organization of acoustic sensors was known as the Sound Surveillance System (SOSUS). The United States also deployed a larger number of radar systems for air defense. These sensor layouts were organized in hierarchical manner, where information was processed at some distant level until useful data access by the end user; humans played an important role in this network. The sensor networks were wired and did not fulfill the major design challenges such as energy or bandwidth constraints. Recent WSN research was started in the early 1980s by Defense Advanced Research Projects Agency (DARPA) in the United States [4]. The Distributed Sensor Networks (DSN) program was structured with different independent cost effective sensing nodes. These nodes were placed in a collaborative manner and the data were routed to the node. In the middle of the 1980s, Massachusetts Institute of Technology (MIT) developed a DSN and acoustic sensors designed to track low-flying aircraft. The microphones (arranged in arrays of six) were used for acoustic sensing and mobile vehicle nodes consisted of one computer and three processors with a 256 KB memory and 512 KB of shared memory for processing the acoustic signals. Energy was applied by an acoustically quiet generator, which was placed on the back of the vehicle node. The nodes, connected with microwave radio and Ethernet, were used for permanent line broadcasting. Very recently, a WSN project called the Wireless Self-Sustaining Sensor Network (WSSN) was designed at the Vienna University of Technology (TUV) by the Institute of Computer Technology [11] and observed the impacts of various design space approaches regarding energy efficiency in WSNs [12]. This project shows the impact of WSNs in the field of a self-sustaining network. The research paid more attention to the development of cost effective, energy effective hardware and an energy competent medium access control (MAC) protocol. The major features of any sensor node are its processing unit, wireless link, and battery. The wireless interface has a 1 Mbps data rate and a 2.4 GHz transceiver. These nodes work inside a temperature accuracy of a half degree and are integrated with a sensor of ten-bits interface. The energy management shown by these nodes is very meaningful. These nodes use an average 100 µW of power in certain environmental conditions and each node receives and transmits 120 bits of data every five seconds. These nodes would remain active for almost nine years and each node was dressed with a 3200 mAh lithium battery and an input voltage of two volts. This lifetime is attained by energy scavenging and creative energy storage. For storage purposes, the network nodes need ultra-capacitors and lithium accumulators. The benefit of ultra-capacitors is to rapidly absorb huge amounts of energy, but the leakage current increases exponentially as the applied voltage increases. For energy scavenging purposes, nodes use solar cells, specifically the sun, to recharge the energy storage components. This technique produces very small nodes that can work for years by extracting energy from the environment. In the future, more skilled and versatile systems based on the novel microelectromechanical system (MEMS) technology will be expected. The company presently working in MEMS technology is Dust Inc., Berkeley, CA. This company is the result of the Smart Dust research project at the University of California, Berkeley, which was building MEMS sensors in the late 1990s. Such sensors can sense and communicate and are portable enough to fit inside a cubic millimeter. An individual Smart Dust optical mote uses MEMS with submillimeter sized mirrors for communications. Smart Dust [13] sensors can be deployed by using a 3×10 mm^2 "wavelet" shaped like a maple tree seed and dropped to float on the ground. A wireless network with such sensors may be used in many novel applications based on criteria such as ubiquitousness, low-cost, and disposability [4]. To examine the various aspects of sensor networks, the challenges like evolution opportunities, and applications should be considered in the wireless domain. Table 9.1 shows the performance of sensor nodes as reported by Reference 4 and it shows that the state of the technology existing in these is already far beyond that which was accessible in 2003 and will be tentatively available for 2020. The sensor nodes made by TUV already use solar panels and theoretically achieve a life span of a few years. By comparing the conventional MIT nodes in the mid-1980s to the modern TUV WSSN nodes, it is easy to see that there have been tremendous advances in technology during the twenty-year period. The WSSN nodes can use limited energy resources, integrated sensing, processing, and communications. These nodes are low in cost and can use a variety of sensors with an ease of deployment for large numbers.

The MIT nodes needed a generator for energy with individual sensing, processing, and communication systems. These expensive nodes were expressly planned for acoustic sensing and were set up in small numbers. If the dimension of a self-sustaining sensor node decreases from the size of a motor vehicle (MIT node) to the size of a one Euro coin (WSSN node) in a span of twenty years, then how small will be these nodes be twenty years from now? This type of sensor might be five square millimeters within ten years and even smaller in the next twenty years [14]. The observed frugal energy budget of sensor networks predicts that a significant amount of work is needed for energy-aware network protocols. When the size of a sensor node shrinks, there is a continuous need to evaluate the behavior of the node under severe terrain conditions corresponding to the different routing protocols. The ultimate purpose of this research is to achieve optimization and enhancement in existing WSN frameworks. The key components for a typical wireless sensor device are comprised of the following.

TABLE 9.1

Evolution of Sensor Nodes

	1980s–1990s	2000–2005	2010	Upto 2020
Company	Custom contractors	Crossbow Technology Inc.	Sensoria Corp. Ember Corp.	EDust Inc. and others
Dimension	Bulky shoe box	Packed cards into little shoe box	Tiny particle	Dirt particle
Heaviness	Kilograms	Grams	Nanograms	Unimportant
Node structural design	Individual sensing, processing, and communication	Integrated sensing, processing, and communication	Integrated sensing, processing, and communication	Full integrated structure
Topology	Node-to-Node, Star	Client server approach, peer to peer	Peer to peer	Mixed approach
Energy Supply and life span	Big batteries; hours, days, and longer	AA batteries; few Days to few weeks	Solar cells; few months to years	Solar and Battery power; few years and more years
Implementation	Vehicle-placed or air-dropped single sensors	Hand-placed	Embedded, "sprinkled," left behind	Fully integrated and embedded

9.2.1 Low Power Embedded Processor

The computational tasks on a WSN comprise the processing of local information and remote information from other sensors. Due to the economic issues of such processors, these devices typically use specialized components based on operating systems such as TinyOS [13]. A network-based strategy for portable equipment was suggested by Reference 15. This strategy can also be applied to various models in WSNs and different nodes having larger computational power. In the future, Moore's law may provide extremely powerful embedded processors for WSN devices.

9.2.2 Memory/Storage

The random-access memory (RAM) and read only memory (ROM) include the program memory and data memory. The quantity of memory in the wireless sensor node is fixed and it is expected to improve with time.

9.2.3 Radio Transceiver

WSN devices have short range wireless radio with a bit rate 10–100 kbps and a range of less than 100 m. These radios have been improved in terms of spectral efficiency, cost, and immunity to noise and fading. Radio communication being the most power intensive mode and incorporate energy efficient sleep and wake up modes.

9.2.4 Sensors

WSN devices can support low data rate sensing due to bandwidth and power issues. Many applications used for multimodal sensing and each WSN device have different sensors on board. The applications are dependent on the specific sensors' design and may include humidity sensors, light sensors, temperature and pressure sensors, magnetometers, accelerometers, acoustic sensors, chemical sensors, and low-resolution imagers.

9.2.5 Global Positioning System

In WSN, it is necessary for all sensor measurements to be location stamped and to consider sensor locations for deployment. But it can only be feasible in limited deployments, particularly for outdoor operations. Such information can be easily retrieved via satellite-based Global Positioning System (GPS). In some applications, some nodes may be equipped with GPS capability and some are not due to environmental and economic constraints. Every node may get their position indirectly through network localization algorithms. In Reference 16, the impact of local angle information on localization and routing in WSN is reported.

9.2.6 Power Source

The wireless sensor nodes are battery powered and it is possible to recharge the batteries, but most of the nodes have only finite energy. The ideal wireless sensor should be networked, portable, scalable, programmable, and consume a minute amount of energy. This makes it suitable for data acquisition and should have features such as accuracy over the long term, reliability, cost effectiveness, easy installation, and lower maintenance. The ideal wireless sensors and communication links have knowledge of the major design and its application, battery life, weight, size, and sensor update rates.

9.3 WSN Application Areas

The latest wireless sensors have a wide range of applications of WSN compared to conventional sensors. The WSNs perform different tasks such as information collection, storage, processing, and metrology, and broadcast to the base station. At the beginning of an application, a WSN is disseminated in a zone to collect data through sensor nodes. The applications include health monitoring and help for physically disabled persons, addressing goods' safety and supply, scanning disaster regions, monitoring ecological habitats, seismic monitoring, industrial and military applications, structural health monitoring, and so on. Some of the most often used applications are:

9.3.1 Ecological Habitat Monitoring

This is a major application field of the WSNs where temperature acts as variable and is dispersed over a particular area. Sensor networks can be easily applied to the environment and habitat monitoring applications. Reference 17 examined environmental observation and forecasting challenges in WSNs. The hub for Embedded Network Sensing was the first to take the initiative in this field and in Reference 18 future paradigms for WSNs have been demonstrated. Reference 19 explains the concept of WSNs in the avionics sector based on communication, navigation, and surveillance. Scientific studies of ecological habitats like plants, animals, and microorganisms are also followed through ground activities. This study is sometimes referred to as the "observer effect." The presence and the intrusive potential actions of investigators may change the nature of the organisms and bias the results observed. Scattered types of WSNs enable habitat monitoring by using a cleaner remote observer approach. Moreover, sensor networks also supply experimental data of an unprecedented wealth due to their big scale and high temporal density.

9.3.2 Military Surveillance and Targets

The WSNs started primarily in armed forces related research. The controllers of military systems were early in recognizing the benefits of a sensor network because it was directly related to nuclear centric warfare [20]. In other terms, sensors form a base as a hidden weapon for the battlefield as they can be controlled by remote entities. Reference 21 demonstrated a new cooperative engagement capability (CEC) approach. This approach can allow battle systems to share unfiltered sensor data measurements with rapid timing to enable the battle group units to operate as one. The key ingredient of scattered sensor networks in the military is the network central warfare systems. They can be quickly developed for surveillance and providing battlefield intelligence. This includes information regarding position, figures, progress, and the uniqueness of the troops, vehicles, and findings of chemical, biological, and nuclear weapons.

9.3.3 Architectural and Seismic Monitoring

Another potential application of WSNs is to monitor civil structures such as buildings, roads, bridges, and so on. In the present scenario, these civil structures are monitored through manual and visual inspections such as X-rays and ultrasound which are more expensive and time consuming. Wireless sensor networks help in monitoring the health of a structure if deployed properly during the construction of the civil structure, especially during any destructive events such as earthquakes or explosions. Reference 22 introduces a new preface sampling MAC protocol for a mini-powered WSN. A compelling potential use for sensor networks involves the deployment of convenient structures. These have actuators that respond to real time sensor information to carry out "echo cancellation" on seismic waves, so that the configuration is unaffected by any exterior disturbance.

9.3.4 Industrial Utilization

In industrial applications, actuators and sensors are used for controlling and monitoring the different processes. In a synthetic processing and control system, temperature, pressure, and chemical concentration can be controlled by placing the sensors at different points. Real-time monitoring information is used for process control and adjusting the concentration of an ingredient or changing the heat settings. The advantage of WSNs include improving the cost and flexibility associated with maintenance and installation and advances in a wired system. Reference 23 indicate that the trends are moving toward the integration of wireless communications with sensors. Without such a strategy, the life of this new technology can be cut short before its true potential is explored.

9.4 Design Issues

Depending on the application area, specific WSNs are designed. The important design challenges are discussed in the following subsections.

9.4.1 Extended Lifetime

A wireless sensor node is greatly affected by the hindrance of power sources and [24] emphasizes the energy efficient protocol for WSNs. In a huge network, a longer life span is preferred over the expense of the batteries as it is potentially infeasible to monitor and replace batteries rapidly. In practice, many applications provide a guarantee that a network of unattended WSNs will remain working without any substitution of batteries for a long time. The hardware enhancement in the design of batteries and energy harvesting techniques will only provide partial solutions to the problems. Most protocol designs are explicit and energy efficiency is the primary goal in WSNs.

9.4.2 Responsiveness

One of the best solutions to enhance the lifetime of a sensor node is to actuate it in a sleep and wake up manner. The concurrent execution of nodes is hard and an arbitrarily long sleep interval can decrease the responsiveness and usefulness of sensors. In many application areas, it is also critical that certain trials in the environment be sensed and described rapidly. The latency produced by a sleep schedule must be kept inside the application boundaries to avoid network congestion. Reference 25 describes an approach for congestion control and point-dependent multi-path routing in WSNs.

9.4.3 Robustness

The latest version of WSNs provides a great scale and fine-grained treatment for real-time applications. In Reference 26, an optimal polynomial time algorithm for the solution of the worst and best cases associated with coverage in a WSN are examined. This motivates the application of large numbers of inexpensive devices and all of these devices are unreliable and prone to failure. Devices' failure rates will also be high and sensor devices are deployed in harsh or hostile environments. The protocol design must have a built-in mechanism to provide robustness. The global performance of the system is not sensitive to individual device collapse. The performance of the system gradually decreases with respect to component collapse.

9.4.4 Synergy

The term synergy refers to the fact that the whole WSN system exhibits a better result than the sum of the individual nodes' capabilities. Reference 27 demonstrates the impact of Moore's law in the performance evaluation of sensor nodes and enhances the device capability in the form of storage memory, radio transceiver performance, processing power, and accuracy of sensing. However, economic considerations require that the cost per node be reduced. Therefore, a synergistic protocol must be proposed which ensures more system capability and efficient usage of storage and computational resources.

9.4.5 Scalability

The combination of a large coverage area and fine granularity sensing implies that WSNs have the potential to be deployed in extremely large-scale applications. In Reference 26, an optimal polynomial time algorithm has been proposed for solving the best and worst cases associated with coverage in WSNs. Routing protocols should address the criterion of easy distribution and networks and localized communication must use a hierarchical architecture to improve scalability. The vision of many nodes will remain unrealized in practice until some fundamental problems such as failure handling and *in situ* reprogramming are solved. This should be equally true in small settings involving tens to hundreds of nodes. There are some fundamental limitations such as capacity and throughput that affect the scalability of WSNs.

9.4.6 Heterogeneity

The term heterogeneity may be referred to as the WSN system behavior which remains unaffected with the variation of hardware and software issues of individual nodes. There will be heterogeneity capabilities in realistic settings and this has many important design consequences. Reference 28 highlights the specifications of the sensor node to predict its efficiency in WSNs. For instance, low-capability devices use two-tier and cluster-dependent network designs. Multiple sensing modalities need a pertinent sensor fusion method. A major issue is often to determine the right arrangement of heterogeneous devices for a given application.

9.4.7 Self-Configuration

WSNs are naturally unattended due to the nature and scale of their utilization and the autonomous operations of the network is an important design challenge. The WSN nodes must configure their own network topology (localize, synchronize, and calibrate) (coordinate inter-node routing) and determine other vital operating parameters.

9.4.8 Self-Optimization and Adaptation

To operate efficiently in the face of expected or well-modeled operating conditions, all the engineering systems must be optimized. Prior to the development of WSNs, there may be significant uncertainty about operating conditions. It is important that there should be flexible built-in mechanisms to autonomously learn from network and sensor measurements. Further, the built-in mechanisms should be able to collect information over any design methodologies that sacrifice some of the performance. Reference 29 predicts a new flexible and adaptive framework with tiny cubes for WSNs. Performance optimization is very significant because of the severe resource constraints in WSNs. Logical design methodologies, run time adaptation, reuse, and modularity are other constraints that should be addressed by practical considerations.

9.4.9 Privacy and Security

In WSNs, the privacy and security of the collective information from different nodes are key challenges. Reference 30 introduces the concepts of knowledge discovery and data mining for information extraction through sensor nodes in WSNs.

9.5 Selection of Research Domain

Practically, WSNs have multiple problems like communication, data processing, and sensor node management due to ambiguous and dynamic environments. In addition, WSNs have more challenging issues such as network routing protocols, sensor node assessment strategies, energy efficiency, and energy models. There is a need to develop new protocols that can provide efficient network management and extend the network lifetime. The concept of WSNs looks practical and exciting on paper, but the power consumption by an individual node is the main constraint of node performance. Various strategies that can be implemented to reduce the power consumption include (i) reduction in data transmission through data compression, (ii) lower the frequency and duty cycle of the data transmission, (iii) reduce the size of the frame overhead, (iv) efficient power management mechanisms, (v) scheduling an event-driven transmission strategy, and (vi) develop energy efficient routing protocols. There are many authors that have considered the term energy efficiency from different viewpoints, but there are additional issues such as energy models, terrain conditions, mobility, scalability, and so on that still need more consideration to become more and more energy efficient. The foremost goal of this research is to evaluate and enhance the existing WSN frameworks.

9.6 Introduction to WSNs

MIT technology reviewed the listed WSNs as "Top ten technologies that will change the world" [31]. WSN covers a wide variety of applications [32] such as ecological habitat monitoring, military surveillance, seismic and structural monitoring, industrial applications, and so on. With such a huge potential for WSNs, it is still surprising that only a limited number of applications are benefiting from this technology. Moore's law [33] highlights smaller, more economic and energy efficient nodes instead of increasing the available memory or enhancing the central processing unit (CPU) speed. More than a decade has passed since the development of Smart Dust [34], but is still there is a need to tackle the criterion of energy consumption in wireless sensor nodes. Energy constraints are playing a vital role in the performance determination of WSNs and thorough study is required to measure the energy consumption. Hahm et al. [35] have presented the approach of energy consumption based on the concept of fine-granular measurements and this creates demanding requirements for the energy of an individual node in the network. Shnayder et al. [36] have presented the feasibility of power consumption and the pattern of power loads in the wireless networks. Park et al. [37] have proposed a sensing module for mica motes in WSNs. This new module significantly improves the signal to noise ratio. The major challenges for the performance of WSNs are to extend network life times and to consider the criteria of mobility of the nodes in the specified environment. Two energy efficient protocols, asynchronous media access control protocol and asynchronous scheduled-based media access control protocol, were proposed by Ren and Liang [38]. Chou et al. [39] proposed an approach to reduce energy consumption for sensor networks. A more novel approach concerning an energy-efficient virtual multiple input multiple output communication architecture for distributed WSNs was suggested by Jayaweera et al. [40] and a generic model for energy was suggested by Tremley et al. [41] for the dynamic simulation of a hybrid electric vehicle. Jain et al. [42] proposed a model based on generic energy consumption. The per bit energy consumption of power states like on/off/sleep were included in order to accurately measure the power consumption associated with each node. Dhawan et al. [43] reported a novel approach toward the frame work of real-time monitoring of acoustic events. The grouping of micaZ motes and scalable networks ensures the reliability, low energy consumption, and higher data transmission rates in the WSNs. It is expected that the coming generation of computer innovators will focus on how to program and develop applications using WSNs. Recent advancements in technology have allowed us to move toward a future where the scope of WSNs can be broadened to a significant level. Here, we investigated three energy models for transmitting, receiving, and idle modes in the WSNs. The lifetime of the network can be extended by using an adequate energy model. In order to create ideal resultants for energy consumption in generic, mica-mote, and micaZ energy models, we evaluated these models in transmitting, receiving, and idle modes with respect to the dynamic source routing protocol (DSR) [44–48]. DSR is a simple and specifically designed protocol for dynamic wireless networks. In DSR, routing information can be determined by two mechanisms—route discovery and route maintenance. These mechanisms collectively discover and maintain the information about source and designation routes in wireless networks. The use of source routing information makes the packet routing loop free. The protocol is entirely on a demand basis and allows the routing packet overhead to scale automatically.

9.7 Energy Models with Related Work

Three energy models are described by generic, mica-mote, and micaZ. The generic energy model uses generic mote boards [49] which consist of four mono audio jacks. These jacks provide a connection to an analog to digital converter and power to a sensor and digital output can be supplied by changing two of the analog to digital control (ADC) ports. The mote board is not a plug and play, so the signal and power pins have to be set accordingly. The mica-mote energy model uses a mica-mote module, that is, MOT300, which is a product of Crossbow Corporation [50]. The mica-mote is a small and low power consuming module used by the researchers for advancement in WSNs and was invented by the UC Berkeley research group [50]. This mote includes an Atmega 103L processor, 916 MHz radio processor, TinyOS distributed software operating system, and an AA (2) battery pack, and the MPR300CA module is based on Atmel ATmega103L. It is a low power microcontroller that uses an internal flash memory for Tiny opearating System (TOS) execution. The specifications include: (i) a base station that allows the aggregation of WSN data onto a personal computer (PC), (ii) any WSN node module can function as a base station, [51] ad specifications are (i) Institute of Electrical anf Electronics Engineer (IEEE) 802.15.4, intensely embedded sensor networks (ii) data rate of 250 kbps (iii) A globally compatible industrial, scientific, and medical (ISM) radio band of 2.4–2.8 GHz (iv) each node as router capability (v) extension adapter for light, acceleration, relative humidity (RH), temperature, seismic, acoustic, barometric, magnetic, and other weapon sensor boards. Feeney et al. [52] proposed the following linear equation for the energy consumption in these energy models.

$$\text{Energy} = m \times \text{size} + b \tag{9.1}$$

Here, m denotes an incremental component and is proportional to the packet size *and* fixed component associated with channel acquisition overhead (b). For different applications, specific coefficients like m and b can be found in a more particular fashion. Based on the above linear equation, the energy needed for the sending and receiving operations is as follows:

$$\text{Energy}_{(\text{send})} = m_{\text{send}} \times \text{size} + b_{\text{send}} \tag{9.2}$$

$$\text{Energy}_{(\text{receive})} = m_{\text{receive}} \times \text{size} + b_{\text{receive}} \tag{9.3}$$

9.8 Motivation for Current Work

An accurate energy model remains the top most priority for the performance evaluation of WSNs. An optimal energy structure enhances the output of the overall system, but the WSN system may not be dependent on it. A simple energy structure may give a better performance for a single instance, but we have to deploy an efficient energy structure that provides an overall optimal performance. An inefficient energy structure may overload the full network and use more resources both in terms of energy and computation, resulting in entire system performance degradation. There always remains a direct pressure for the energy model on the complete operating environment when evaluating a particular routing protocol. The ultimate goal is to carefully choose and examine the energy model for information that presents an optimal result without compromising any constraints of the expected outcome. Therefore, a typical investigation should include accessing the scope of a particular energy model for the WSNs.

9.9 Problem Definition and System Model

A network consists of 100s of wireless sensor nodes deployed with three energy models. Sensor nodes have a specific radio range that can transmit the data to the cluster head and base station within the entire network. The network implementation focusses on transmitting, receiving, and idle modes. Although any sensor node energy model can be used in our model, we used generic, mica-mote, and micaZ energy models for our proposed framework. The given network with dynamic source routing protocol and energy models has main two problems: (i) the influence of energy models on communication specific node operations in the WSNs, (ii) how the transmitting, receiving, and idle states' specific node operations affect the energy consumption of the WSN.

9.10 Scenario Analysis

The assessment of three energy models with dynamic routing protocols in WSNs is analyzed with the Qualnet version 5.0 simulation platform. Qualnet is a discrete event simulator [53] which can simulate wired or wireless networks from simple to complex conditions. In the designed model, 100 WSN nodes are connected to a common wireless station as shown in Figure 9.1.

The terrain conditions are fixed at 1500 m × 1500 m as a flat region and at sea level remain equal to 1000 m. The coverage area is separated into 225 square-shaped cells and static or dynamic nodes. There is one channel with a 2.4 GHz frequency and 30 s of pause time. The numbers of constant bit rate (CBR) connections were 10 and the mobility interval was set as 100 ms. The entire connection setup was done randomly and the speed of each node varied from 0 to 20 mps with a pause time considered to be 30 sec. In simulation, Internet Protocol version 4 (IPv4) for network layer protocol, Dynamic Source Routing for network routing protocol, IEEE 802.15.4 standard for physical layer protocol, and IEEE 802.11 standard for Media Access Protocol (MAC) layer protocol have been considered. Table 9.2 shows the details of the parameters for these energy models.

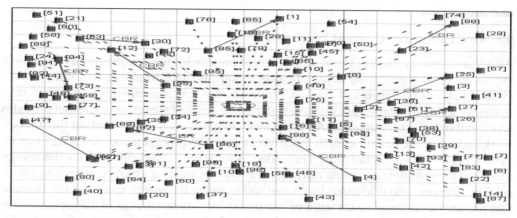

FIGURE 9.1
Simulation setup of 100 WSN nodes connected to common wireless station.

TABLE 9.2

Simulation Parameters

Area Size	1500 m × 1500 m
Simulation Time	300 s
Node Placement	Random
Traffic Type	CBR
Data Rate	2 Mbps
Mobility Model	Random Waypoint
Network Protocol	IPv4
Routing protocol	DSR
No. of Nodes	100
No. of CBRs	10
Temperature (K)	290
Energy Models	Generic, Mica, and MicaZ

After simulating the above scenario, the obtained results are reported in Figures 9.2 through 9.7. The results are revealed by various analyses in transmitting, receiving, and idle modes. The energy consumption of the generic model corresponds to the transmitting mode as shown in Figure 9.2. The energy consumption of the network node is at some distance from the base station and participation with a constant bit rate in the network is maximum whereas the nodes which are not communicating with the constant bit rate consume less energy.

Figure 9.3 show individual node energy consumptions with respect to the receiving mode. The amount of energy consumed by the node is based on the amount of data being transmitted within the networks.

The energy consumption analysis for the mica-mote model corresponding to the transmitting and receiving modes is reported in Figure 9.4 and Figure 9.5. Here, the energy consumption depends on the amount of the information transferred by the individual node.

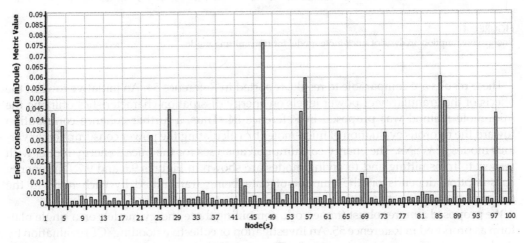

FIGURE 9.2
Generic model of energy consumption analysis for transmitting mode.

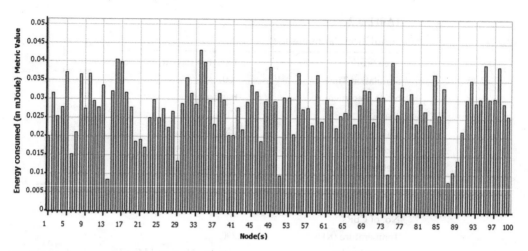

FIGURE 9.3

Energy consumption analysis of generic model for receiving mode.

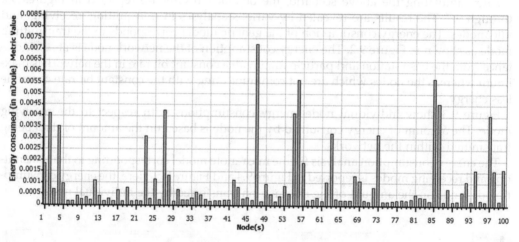

FIGURE 9.4

Energy consumption analysis of mica-mote model for transmitting mode.

These results are comparable to results reported in Reference 54. An initiative toward the effects of the granularity of power levels on energy dissipation characteristics utilizing the mica-mote method was proposed in Reference 54. Thus, a further enhance contribution toward the rigorous evaluation of mica-motes by calculating the power consumption in various modes of WSNs. The energy consumption analyses for the micaZ energy model with respect to transmitting and receiving modes are shown in Figures 9.6 and 9.7. The energy consumption depends on the amount of data being transmitted by each node in the network.

We proposed a more robust framework, combining three energy models on a single platform as proposed in Reference 55. An investigation of collective flooding (CF) evaluation by deploying micaZ motes was reported by Zhu et al. [55]. An emphasis to achieve better reliability for WSNs was presented in Reference 55. Further contributions incorporating

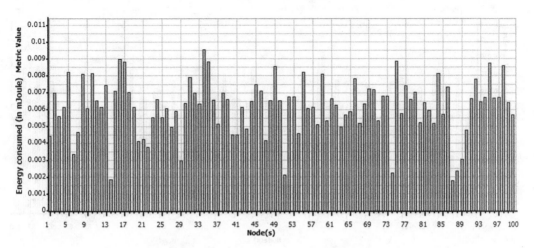

FIGURE 9.5
Energy consumption analysis of mica-mote model for receiving mode.

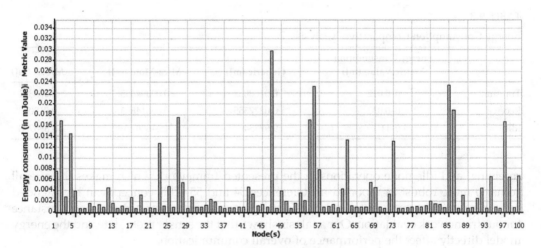

FIGURE 9.6
Energy consumption analysis of micaZ model for transmitting mode.

generic, mica-mote, and micaZ energy models for 100 nodes adds more robustness to our evaluation. The comparison based on the energy consumption in transmitting, receiving, and idle modes corresponding to the generic, mica-mote, and micaZ models is shown in Table 9.3. Here, we compared the energy consumption corresponding to different transmitting, receiving, and idle modes for the above-mentioned energy models. The results show that the mica-mote energy model consumed minimum energy for the transmitting and receiving modes, whereas the micaZ energy model consumed minimum energy for the idle mode.

The entire framework with 100 nodes was analyzed six times to correspond to the three energy models. We observed that power consumption is higher in the transmitting and receiving modes as compared to the idle mode of WSNs. We added a variety of evaluation strategies based on dynamic source routing protocol corresponding to transmitting,

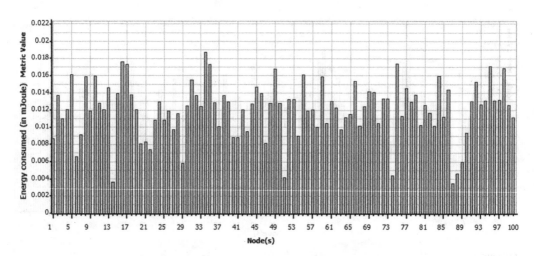

FIGURE 9.7

Energy consumption analysis of micaZ model for receiving mode.

TABLE 9.3

Energy Consumption Comparative Analysis

	Energy Consumption Metric Value (mJ)	Generic (mJ)	Mica-Mote (mJ)	MicaZ (mJ)
Transmit	0–0.012	0.0100002	0.00094655	0.003891
Receive	0–0.032	0.0277555	0.00614893	0.012063
Idle	0–11	9.97354	1.24669	0.896788

receiving, and idle node operations in the presented framework which makes the overall scenario more robust as reported in References 54 and 55. This concept can be extended by adding generic, mica-mote, and micaZ energy models incorporated at a single instance for our framework evaluation. Our analysis shows that the sensor mote state and the energy model directly affect the performance of overall communication.

9.11 Conclusions

This chapter introduced a novel way to realize energy consumption in WSNs and reviewed DSR routing protocol over energy models in the prescribed network scenario. We evaluated dynamic source routing protocol on a power consumption basis in transmitting, receiving, and idle modes. In the transmitting and receiving modes, power consumption was highest in the generic model and lowest in the mica-mote model. On the other hand, in the idle mode, there is a sharp decrease in energy consumption from the generic model to the mica-mote mode and a further decrease in energy consumption for the micaZ model. Finally, we concluded that energy consumption is higher in the case of both transmitting and receiving modes in the generic model, whereas it is lowest in the mica-mote model. Considering the case of idle mode, energy consumption is higher in the generic model and it is lowest in the micaZ model. The energy consumption is a medium value in the mica-mote model. Theses finding are validated by comparing the theoretical predictions with the simulated environment and analysis can be done by considering the parameters such as scalability, terrain conditions, mobility, different routing protocols, temporal enhancement, and so on.

References

1. Wang, X., Ding, L. and Wang, S. 2011. Trust evaluation sensing for WSNs. *IEEE Transactions on Instrumentation and Measurement*. 60(6): 2088–2095.
2. Alkalbani, A.S., Md. Tap, A.O. and Mantoro, T.A. 2012. Improving the lifetime of WSNs based on routing power factors. *4th International Conference, Network Digital Technologies*, Dubai, UAE, April 24–26, pp. 566–576
3. Chen, H., Wu, H., Zhou, X. and Gao, C. 2007. Reputation based trust in WSNs. *International Conference on Multimedia and Ubiquitous Engineering (MUE'07)*, New-York, USA, 0-7695-2777-9/07.2007.
4. Chong, C. and Kumar, S.P. 2003. Sensor networks: Evolution, opportunities, and challenges. *Proceedings of the IEEE*. 91(8): 1247–1256.
5. Akyildiz, I.F., Su, W., Sankarasubramaniam, Y. and Cayirci, E. 2002. A survey on sensor networks. *IEEE Communication Magazine*. 40(8): 102–114.
6. Esch, J. 2010. A survey of trust and reputation management systems in wireless communications. *Proceedings of the IEEE*. 98(10): 1755–1772.
7. Hurt, J., Lee, Y., Yoont, H., Choi, D. and Jin, S. 2005. Trust evaluation model for WSNs. *Proceedings of the 7th International Conference on Advanced Communication Technology (ICACT'05)*, Republic of Korea, pp. 491–496.
8. Jing, Q., Tang, L.Y. and Chen, Z. 2008. Trust management in WSNs. *Journal of Software*. 19(7): 1716–1730.
9. Crosby, G.V., Pissinou, N. and Gadze, J. 2006. A framework for trust-based cluster head election in WSNs. *Proceedings of the 2nd IEEE Workshop on Dependability and Security in Sensor Networks and Systems (DSSNS'06), IEEE Computer Society*, Columbia, MD, USA, pp. 13–22.
10. Sun, Y.L., Yu, W., Han, Z. and Liu, K.J.R. 2006. Information theoretic framework of trust modeling and evaluation for ad hoc networks. *IEEE Journal On Selected Areas In Communications*. 24(2): 305–317.
11. Mahlknecht, S. and Bock, M. 2004. CSMA-MPS: A minimum preamble sampling MAC protocol for low power WSNs. *Proceedings of the IEEE International Workshop on Factory Communication Systems (IWFC)*, Vienna, Austria, pp. 73–80.
12. Mahlknecht, S. 2005. WSSN (Wireless Self-sustaining Sensor Network) Project.
13. University of California, Berkeley. 2003. TinyOS project, DARPA NEST program.
14. Kahn, J.M., Katz, R.H. and Pister, K.S.J. 1999. Mobile networking for Smart Dust. *Proc. ACM/ IEEE International Conference on Mobile Computing and Networking (MobiCom)*, Seattle, WA, pp. 271–278.
15. Culler, D.E., Hill, J., Buonadonna, P., Szewczyk, R. and Woo, A. 2001. A network-centric approach to embedded software for tiny devices privacy. *EMSOFT First International Workshop on Embedded Software*, pp. 114–130.
16. Bruck, J., Gao, J. and Jiang, A. 2005. Localization and routing in sensor networks by local angle information. *Proc. of the 6th ACM International Symposium on Mobile Ad Hoc Networking and Computing (MOBIHOC'05)*, Urbana-Champaign, IL, USA.
17. Steere, D., Baptista, A., McNamee, D., Pu, C. and Walpole, J. 2000. Research challenges in environmental observation and forecasting systems. *Proc. 6th Int. Conf. Mobile Computing and Networking (MOBICOMM)*, pp. 292–299.

18. Charny, B. 2002. Wireless research senses the future. *ZDNet News* [Online] Available: http://zdnet.com.com/2100-1105-976377.html.

19. Jensen, D. 2002. SIVAM: Communication, navigation and surveillance for the Amazon. *Avionics Magazine*. Retrieved October 30, 2006 from http://www.aviationtoday.com/reports/avionics/previous/0602/0602sivam.htm

20. Alberts, D.S., Garstka, J.J. and Stein, F.P. 1999. *Network Centric Warfare, Developing and Leveraging Information Superiority*, Command and Control Research Program (CCRP) Publication (DoD). 2nd edition (Revised).

21. Hopkins, J. 1995. The cooperative engagement capability. *APL Technical Digest*. 16: 377–396.

22. Xu, N., Rangwala, S., Chintalapudi, K., Ganesan, D., Broad, A., Govindam, R. and Estrin, D. 2004. A WSN for structural monitoring. *Proceedings of ACM Conference on Embedded Networked Sensor Systems*, New York, NY, USA, pp. 13–24.

23. Manges, W. W., Allgood, G. O. and Smith, S. F. 1999. Itís time for sensors to go wireless; Part 2: Take a good technology and make it an economic success, *Sensors: The Journal of Applied Sensing Technology* 16(5), 70–80.

24. Heinzelman, R.W., Chandrakasan, A. and Balakrishnan, H. 2000. Energy efficient communication protocol for wireless micro sensor networks. *Proceeding of the 33th Hawaii International Conference on System Sciences*, Maui, HI, USA, pp. 1–10.

25. Paganini, F., Senior Member, IEEE and Mallada, E. 2009. A unified approach to congestion control and node-based multipath routing. *IEEE/ACM Transactions on Networking*. 17(5): 1413–1426.

26. Meguerdichian, S., Koushanfar, F., Potkonjak, M. and Srivastava, M.B. 2001.Coverage problems in wireless ad hoc sensor networks. *IEEE INFOCOM*. 3: 1380–1387.

27. Robert Keyes, W. 2006.The impact of Moore's Law. *Solid State Circuits Newsletter, IEEE*. 20: 25–27.

28. Chakeres, I.D. and Belding-Royer, E.M. 2003. Resource biased path selection in heterogeneous mobile networks. Univ. of California, Santa Barbara, Comp. Sci. Dept. Tech. Report 2003-18.

29. Marron, P.J. et al. 2005. TinyCubus: A flexible and adaptive framework sensor networks. *Proc. of the Second European Workshop on WSNs*, pp. 278–289.

30. Evfimievski, A., Srikant, R., Agrawal, R. and Gehrke, J. 2002. Privacy preserving mining of association rules. *Proceedings of the Eighth ACM SIGKDD International Conference on Knowledge Discovery and Data Mining*, New York, NY, USA, pp. 217–228.

31. MIT Technology Review. Feb 2003. "10 Emerging Technologies That Will Change the World," http://www.Technologyreview.com/read_artical.aspx,id=13060&chinfotech

32. Chong, C.-Y. and Kumar, S.P. 2003. Sensor networks: Evolution, opportunities and challenges. *Proceeding of the IEEE*. 91(8), 1247–1256.

33. Moore, G.E. 1965. Cramming more components onto integrated circuits. *Electr*. 38(8): 114, 117, April [Online], http://dx.doi.org/10.1109/JPROC.1998.658762

34. Kahn, J.M., Katz, R.H. and Pister, K.S.J. 1999. Next century challenges: Mobile networking for "Smart Dust". *MobiCom'99: Proceedings of the 5th Annual ACM/IEEE International Conference on Mobile Computing and Networking*, New York, NY, USA: ACM Press, pp. 271–278 [Online], http://dx.doi.org/10.1145/313451.313558

35. Hahm, O., Adler, S., Schmittberger, N. and Gunes, M. Energy Profiling for WSNs. *Proceedings of the Australasian Telecommunication Networks and Applications Conference (ATNAC 2011)*, http://www.page.mi.fu-berlin.de/schmittb/hahm2011energy-profiling.pdf

36. Shnayder, V., Hempstead, M., Chen, B., Werner-Allen, G. and Wels, M. 2004. Simulating the power consumption of large-scale sensor network applications. *SenSys'04: Proceedings of the 2nd International Conference on Embedded Networked Sensor Systems*, New York, NY, USA: ACM Press, November, pp. 188–200.

37. Park, H., Friedman, J., Srivastava, M.B. and Burke, J. 2005. A new light sensing module for Mica motes, *Sensors, 2005 IEEE Conference*, Irvine, CA, October 30, 2005–November 3, 2005, doi: 10.1109/ICSENS.2005.1597748

38. Ren, Q. and Liang, Q. 2006. Energy-efficient medium access control protocols for WSNs. *EURASIP Journal on Wireless Communications and Networking*. 2006: 039814, doi: 10.1155/WCN/2006/39814

39. Chou, J., Petrovic, D. and Ramachandran, K. 2003. A distributed and adaptive signal processing approach to reducing energy consumption in sensor networks. *Proceedings of 22nd Annual Joint Conference on the IEEE Computer and Communications Societies (INFOCOM'03)*, San Francisco, Calif, USA, March–April, 2, pp. 1054–1062.

40. Jayaweera, S.K. 2004. An energy-efficient virtual MIMO communications architecture based on V-BLAST processing for distributed WSNs. *Proceedings of 1st Annual IEEE Communications Society Conference on Sensor and Ad Hoc Communications and Networks (SECON'04)*, Santa Clara, Calif, USA, October 2004, pp. 299–308.

41. Tremblay, O., Dessaint, L.-A. and Dekkiche, A. 2007. A generic battery model for the dynamic simulation of hybrid electric vehicles. *Vehicle Power and Propulsion Conference, VPPC 2007.* IEEE, Santa Clara, CA, USA, pp. 284–289, doi: 10.1109/VPPC.2007.4544139

42. Jain, V., Parr, G.P., Bustard, D.W. and Morrow, P.J. 2010. Deriving a generic energy consumption model for network enabled devices. *National Conference on Communications (NCC)*, Arlington, pp. 1–5, doi: 10.1109/ NCC.2010. 5430165

43. Dhawan, A., Balasubramanian, R. and Vokkarane, V. 2011. Technologies for homeland security (HST). *2011 IEEE International Conference*, Waltham, MA, USA, pp. 254–261, doi: 10.1109/THS.2011.6107880

44. Johnson, D.B., Maltz, D.A. and Broch, J. "DSR: The Dynamic Source Routing Protocol for Multi-Hop Wireless Ad Hoc Networks," http://www.monarch.cs.cmu.edu/

45. Verma, V.K., Singh, S. and Pathak, N.P. 2011. Effect of temperature on the behavior of dynamic source routing protocol in WSN. *4th National Conference on Communication and Networking (NCCN-11), SLIET*, Longowal, India.

46. Johnson, D.B. 1994. Routing in ad hoc networks of mobile hosts. *Procedding of the IEEE Workshop on Mobile Computing Systems and Applications*, December, pp. 158–163, IEEE Computer Society.

47. Johnson, D.B. and Maltz, D.A. 1996. Dynamic source routing in ad hoc wireless network. In *Mobile Computing*, edited by Imielinski, T. and Korth, H., Kluwer Academic Publisher, Chapter 5, pp. 153–181.

48. Broch, J., Maltz, D.A. and Johnson, D.B. 1999. Supporting hierarchy and heterogeneous interfaces in multi-hop wireelsss ad hoc networks. *Proceedings of "The International Symposium on Parallel Architectures, Algorithms and Networks (ISPAN'99)," Workshop on Mobile Computing*, Perth, Western Australia, June, IEEE Computer Society.

49. Watts, W. Generic Mote Documentation, Mechanical Engineering, UC, Berkeley, http://www.dr.berkeley.edu/dream/hwdocs/generic.pdf

50. Crossbow Technology, Inc. http://www.xbow.com/

51. Memsic, Inc. http://www.memsic.com/

52. Feeney, L.M. and Nilsson, M. 2002. Investigating the energy consumption of a wireless network interface in an adhoc networking environment. *Proceedings of the INFOCOM01 Twentieth Annual Joint Conference of the IEEE Computer and Communication Societies*, August, 3, pp. 1548–1557.

53. Scalable Network Technologies. 2003. "Qualnet Simulator," Software Package, http://www.scalable-networks.com

54. Cotuk, H., Bicakci, K., Tavli, B. and Uzun, E. 2013. The impact of transmission power control strategies on lifetime of WSNs. *IEEE Transactions On Computers*. 99: 2866–2879. doi: 10.1109/TC.2013.151

55. Zhu, T., Zhong, Z., He, T. and Zhang, Z.-L. 2013. Achieving efficient flooding by utilizing link correlationin WSNs. *IEEE/ACM Transactions On Networking*, 21(1): 121–134, doi: 10.1109/TNET.2012.2197689

Part V

Challenges in 5G Networks

10

Challenges Confronting the Next Generation Wireless Networks

R. Narmadha and A. Jayanthiladevi

CONTENTS

10.1 Introduction

Actualizing a practical internetwork [1] is no basic task. Many difficulties must be confronted, particularly in the regions of availability, unwavering quality, organization of administration, and adaptability. Every area is geared toward the build-up of a proficient and compelling internetwork. The main obstacle confronted when associating different frameworks is to help create correspondence between dissimilar techniques. Distinctive locales, for instance, may utilize diverse types of media or they may work at different rates. Another basic area, dependable administration, must be kept up in any internetwork. Singular clients and whole associations rely upon predictable, dependable access in order to organize assets. In addition, various administrations [2,3] must be brought together to assist each other and investigate the capabilities in an internetwork. Arrangement, security, execution, and other issues must be satisfactorily handled for the internetwork to work easily. Adaptability, the last concern, is important for arranging the development of the network, new applications, and the various administrative associations among different components.

The Internet [4,5] is an asset that can be accessed quickly, however, access is not the same all over the world. The speed of accessing the Internet will be as high as it once was until broadband is expanded more and the cost for this is lowered.

For a few, this is cause for concern. We are perhaps excessively wired and more adjusted to this fact, making it difficult for networks and people a large number of miles away to understand what is happening directly in front of us and more inclined to share over cell phones than to utilize our local facilities. Maybe these innovative changes are convincing us to pull back from the physical world, advancing introverted conduct and undermining our actual connections.

World Wide Web (WWW) usage has expanded from a thousand to over a billion. More than ten million individuals worldwide are interfacing with the Internet only through remote access arrangements. The speed of accessing the Internet has developed at an extraordinary pace. Next generation networks [16–19] have been redesigned and normal Internet speeds are presently high in individuals' homes in numerous nations around the world. Availability to the worldwide data stream has turned out to be prevalent to the point that the Internet is even considered by some to be a human right.

The Internet is a huge mosaic of financial actions and communications online, including exchanges and correspondences to cell phone downloads of television (TV). In any case, there is little thought about how the web completely adds to worldwide development, profitability, and business. Portable web clients are the overwhelming section among web clients. Among add up to web endorsers [10–15] wired web supporters are more contrasted with remote web supporters. Remote web users and mobile remote (portable and dongle) supporters have expanded by millions, while stationary remote supporters have expanded very little. For the most part, advanced mobile phones are boosting web utilization all over the web and the use of cell phones have just surpassed that of personal computer's. Less expensive and quicker versatile systems, an increase in the quantity of clients of these systems, and more moderate 3G to 5G handsets will continue to increase Internet access.

It is a fact that the key driver of information development on a worldwide scale is portable applications with billions of gadgets associated each other and the online medicinal services and retail spending are anticipated to develop at an even higher rate [6,7].

The developing web in India is creating new possibilities to share data and administration among a larger number of individuals more quickly and at a lower cost.

There is an unmistakable association between the development of web utilization and the rising standard of living. Our way of life is not only affected by more elevated productivity, but also by the nature of these items and the administrations. "Web of things" transformation is helping associations and specialist organizations to provide more prominent open doors and motivating them to support greater quality for the data to be gathered. It additionally makes it less demanding for associations to plan more modified items and administrations, which are of higher quality since they are all tailored to fit the selections of buyers. In addition, heterogeneous networks help this advance by giving clients a greater a part in molding the advancements, to some extent by making research more synergistic.

Heterogeneous networks have also prompted the creation of many jobs, as web/ ecommerce organizations are enlisting workers from information technology (IT's) experts to administrative experts who convey online items and services. The Internet uses the execution enhancements of expansive multinational company (MNCs), however, the effect of the heterogeneous networks is more unmistakable on small and medium enterprises (SMEs), making it conceivable to reach a huge shopper base with more providers and to tap new resources from day one of a business. Subsequently, organizations can create enormous client bases. This has prompted the rise of small scale multinational businesses.

The greatest development will come in web-based business, which will increase multiple times, while instruction and social insurance by means of the versatile web will grow. Heterogeneous networks would in reality inspire business enterprises and enrich local enterprises because of the colossal capability of the undiscovered Indian market.

Sooner rather than later, the Internet will fundamentally influence each area of our lives, as we see the use of the Internet of things (IoT) increase which makes the regular day-to-day existence of man simpler and more beneficial. Human engagement and work load will be diminished while prompting a superior yield and greater development. Heterogeneous networks have shown that they will be a progressive power in rebuilding the economy and society of this century; we ought not to dismiss the massive capability of the web economy to help economic development across India and the rest of the world.

10.2 Wireless Network Operation and Features

A massive increase in the numbers of cell phones has aided in the development of Internet business. Numerous reports have examined and discussed how the increase in the number of cell phones is driving the appearance of more up-to-date benefits, turning cell phones into an important fixture for the utilization of media and creating new user encounters. With clients able to access an incredible number of goods and purchasing magnificent items and furniture on the web, the prominence of shopping on the Internet continues to develop. Table 10.1 shows the the wireless network architecture and its features.

10.3 Heterogeneous Networks Challenges

There are various difficulties [8–9] that presently limit the execution of heterogeneous systems. Each of these difficulties is related to a subject area that must be considered when building up an expansive structural arrangement.

- *Asset reconciliation and consistency*: Heterogeneous systems are at present less effective and harder to use than homogenous systems because of an absence of asset amalgamation, and clients/applications must work around issues related to the limits and the contrasts between different modalities. Client/application control and flexibility: Heterogeneous systems are now more inflexible and provide a lower level of client/application control than homogenous systems. Clients often encounter limits in a system since reduced asset administration and the absence of consistency prompts static (of limit assignments, prioritizations, routes, etc.) that are mind boggling and hard to change rapidly. The low level of reconciliation between the different systems fundamentally limits the decisions accessible to application creators.
- *Power*: Heterogeneous systems are at present delicate and are attacked more frequently than homogenous systems, because of poor asset administration and static issues.

TABLE 10.1

Wireless Network and Their Features

Networks	Standardization	Operations	Features	Applications
Wireless Local Area Network (WLAN)	WLANs are based on IEEE 802.11 standards. The IEEE 802.11 is operated in two basic modes. Infrastructure mode Mobile nodes communicate with each other through an access point. Ad hoc Mode. Mobile nodes communicate with each other directly, peer to peer communication	It links two or more wireless devices using a wireless distribution method within a limited area. Base station serves as a wireless access point hub, and nodes communicate through the access point hub. The access points are fixed.	The user can move around within the local coverage area of WLAN. Low service cost. Low deployment cost. Protocol used: Extensible Authentication Protocol Transport Layer Security (EAP-TLS)	WLAN can be inside a home, school, computer laboratory or an office building.
Universal Mobile Telecommunications System (UMTS)	It is a wireless mobile communication system for networks. It is based on the Global System for Mobile Communication (GSM) standard. This technology is being used for 3G networks. Developed and maintained by the Third Generation Partnership Project (3GPP)	Node Bs are connected to Radio Network Controller (RNC). The radio resources and the node Bs are controlled by the RNC. Some of the mobility management functions and data encryption/decryption are performed at the RNC. Node B performs resource management along with the RNC as well.	Wide coverage area. High security. UMTS AKA Authentication protocol	Fixed network multimedia services. E-Commerce Transaction based applications.

(Continued)

TABLE 10.1 (Continued)

Wireless Network and Their Features

Networks	Standardization	Operations	Features	Applications
Worldwide Interoperability for Microwave Access (WiMAX)	WiMAX is a wireless technology developed by the WiMAX Forum which is widely used in 4G networks and is based on IEEE standard 802.16.	WiMAX technology can be operated in two modes viz. point to point network and wide area network.	Medium service cost. Medium deployment cost. Medium security. Scalability. IEEE 802.16e supports EAP (Extensible authentication protocol) The authentication protocol recommended by IEEE802.16e is EAP-TLS. The security is high. As Public Key Integrity (PKI) handles the certificate, it is inefficient and costly.	Broadband connections, hotspots and cellular backhaul
Long Term Evolution (LTE)	It is a high-speed wireless mobile communication system being used in 4G and is based on the GSM/Enhanced Data rates for GSM Evolution (EDGE) and UMTS/ High-Speed Packet Access (HSPA) network technologies.	Capacity and speed of this network are increased due to the fact that it uses a different radio interface along with improvements in the core network	High security. High throughput. Low air interference latency compared with 2G/3G systems. High security. High throughput. Low air interference latency compared with 2G/3G systems has proposed an authentication and key agreement (AKA) protocol, named EPS-AKA.	High traffic Broadband connections, Voice over Internet Protocol (VoIP)

- *Deliberation of system points of interest*: There are at present huge difficulties to overcome to drive specific applications on a heterogeneous system. An essential test is to accomplish the applications without requiring the applications to be modified for different systems. Clients and applications who would prefer not to manage the heterogeneity of the system are frequently compelled to adapt to it.

- *Abundance and battery life*: The poor asset management and low flexibility of heterogeneous systems makes them at present devour more power than is practical. It is hard to save battery life when there are required, but often superfluous, segments to negotiate. There is no real way to enhance the utilization of end users with regard to controlling effectiveness.

- *Security, protection, and fidelity*: Heterogeneous systems are as of now less secure than homogenous systems. When there are various heterogeneous administrations or Quality of service (QoS), the expanded framework unpredictability makes it harder to separate typical processes from assaults. The more prominent multifaceted nature of heterogeneous systems makes it harder to control the system to guarantee security approaches are taken before and to re-establish benefits after an assault. In a huge or heterogeneous system, the "assault surface" is bigger. This is the arrangement of different types of applications (e.g., loads, waveform plans) that an aggressor could possibly target and which consequently should be secured. Finally, disavowal of administration assaults can create abuse in heterogeneous systems with the result that assaults can find a way around locations and guard instruments.

- While security issues are not that much different in heterogeneous systems from the current homogenous systems, the natural heterogeneity can create inconspicuous channels for data spillage that are not readily anticipated. Heterogeneous systems ought to be more dependable than homogenous systems, yet without carefully building an overall plan, they can wind up being unreliable.

10.3.1 Internetworking Security

Authentication is a primary security mechanism to verify whether the sources are what they claim to be. The increasing security threats and postings in mobile communication impose the need for a way to authenticate mobile subscribers and networks. At present, there are various approaches used for addressing authentication in heterogeneous networks. An exhaustive literature survey on various approaches used for describing heterogeneous network security is provided below.

Heterogeneous networks have a gap between security and seamless changes. Much quantitative and qualitative analysis of security and changes to new networks exists. The classification of authentication levels is based on identity protection, key functions, and delay sensitivity. Synchronization between entities is also one of the main problems during handovers to heterogeneous systems. This will produce additional delay and complexity because of computational differemces. Existing analyses or current methods do not cover all the security problems. A random number-based authentication protocol bypasses the existing authentication problems. It is necessary to deposit a time stamp when sending and receiving random numbers between entities. In this paper, a thorough analysis is made of user's signal Random (RAND) and attackers' signal (RAND) based on the time stamps.

Due to the nature of heterogeneous security, it is necessary to consider all possible attacks of authentication protocol. Hence to increase the authentication level between heterogeneous networks, a random number-based authentication protocol is proposed. International Mobile Subscriber Identity (IMSI) or Temporary Mobile Subscriber Identity (TMSI) do not solve the problems of replay back attacks. To protect the disclosure of IMSI, a time stamp based on a random number is being employed in the proposed authentication protocol.

10.3.1.1 Authentication Protocols

It is essential to protect the user's identity in the presence of attackers. Attackers can create many attempts to receive a user's credentials. Thus, it is necessary to distinguish between RAND number generation with and without a time stamp. The unique signal (user) can be identified with a time stamp. Unlike the unique signal, the inferior signal (attacker) cannot know the chronological details of the exchange. It cannot compute a random number with the specified time stamp. Figure 10.1 shows the possible attacks on authentication protocol.

10.3.2 Initial Assumption for Future Heterogeneous Base Station

Protection of IMSI

User Equipment (UE): UE and Future Heterogeneous Base Station (FHBS) have a preselected public and private key pair.

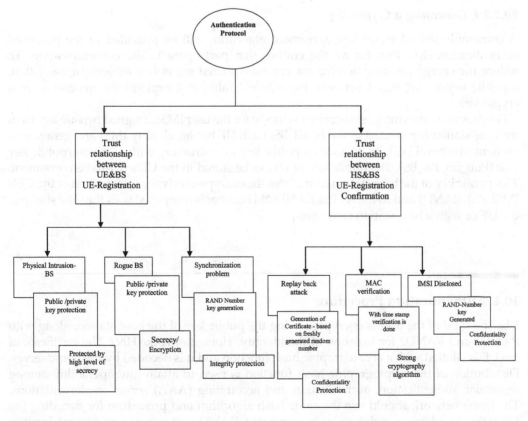

FIGURE 10.1
Possible attacks of authentication protocol.

TABLE 10.2

Generation of Crypto Key

RAND-User Equipment R(UE) = Private Key (PRI_KEY-UE) *Public Key (PUB_KEY-BS)
RAND-Base Station R(BS) = PRI_KEY(BS) *PUB_KEY(UE)
R(UE) = RAND-Base Station R(BS) = Private Key (PK-UE & BS)

Upon reducing the signal complexity, there is no need to produce a signed certificate in the UE. Using the public key Base Station (BS) makes it possible to encrypt the IMSI.

FHET.BS: The future heterogeneous base station (FHBS) stores the certificate authority for the home network and the user equipment.

A pair wise key with a RAND number is generated as Public key (PK, UE, BS). For each and every register UE -IMSI, an equivalent signed certificate is derived with a dynamically generated RAND and time stamp.

HOME SERVER: This computes the pair wise secret key with a RAND number PK (UE, BS). From the equivalent signed certificate, decoding is done with RAND and the identity of the UE -IMSI. Time stamps of the UE and base station are accompanied by a random number. RAND3 is composed on the UE-RAND and FHET BS-RAND.

Decoding of the IMSI has to be done after confirming the public and private keys of the UE and base station.

10.3.2.1 Generating a Crypto Key

A commonly shared secret key agreement/algorithm will be provided in the proposed authentication algorithm for all the entities that participate in the communication. To reduce the energy consumption for the common shared secret key agreement/algorithm, a public key is exchanged between the entities. Table 10.2 explains the generation of a crypto key.

For providing the strongest security exchange for the user IMSI, a signed private key from the base station is provided in the FHET.BS. Each UE has an identity IMSI and generates a random number. FHET.BS provides a public key infrastructure with a private/public key pair (Pub_BS, Pri_BS). The public key of BS can be stored in the UE's trusted environment. This public key of the base station formulates the encrypted privacy information of the UE's IMSI with RAND1 and RAND2. The RANDOM number is composed with the time stamp of the UE or with a base station time stamp.

10.4 Authentication Procedure

UE: The IMSI of the user is encrypted using the public key of the base station, along with RAND1 and RAND2 for isolation of the identity. Home network (HN): The certificate of the UE is allotted with a cryptographic hash function and it is decoded by the home server. Distribution of the cryptographic hash function is used to attain interoperability among dissimilar authentication, authorization and accounting (AAA) server implementations. The home network should use the same hash algorithm and procedure for decoding the UE-IMSI. In addition, a dynamically generated RAND will provide additional identity protection.

TABLE 10.3

Key Negotiation between Entities

UE————RAND1 + RAND2 + IMSI + IK + CK + AUTN—SHA256—RES
FHETBS——RAND3 + IMSI + cert_ID + (nonce = RAND4) —SHA256—XMAC
————RAND1 + RAND2 + IMSI + IK + CK + AUTN—SHA256——XRES
Core Network——Recover ID from RAND3 + cert_ID——IMSI
————RAND3 + RAND4 + cert_ID + (IMSI)—SHA256—MAC

*FHETBS-Future Heterogeneous Base Station
*IK-Integrity Key
*CK-Cipher Key
*AUTN-Authentication Token
*SHA256-Secure Hash Algorithm 256
*SRES-Server Response
*RES-Response
*XRES-Expected Response
*RAND-Random Number Generation
*Cert_ID-Certificate Identity

10.4.1 Negotiation between Entities

Re-authentication methods are used for safe and quick connections in assorted networks and are analyzed at the base station. With the reduction of connectivity operations and message exchanges in the proposed scheme, the delay of re-authentication can be considerably decreased. Apart from that, the suggested re-authentication protocol is more capable as can be observed from the simulation results. These are better than the present re-authentication methods in terms of identification, video/voice communication, throughput, and delay. Table 10.3 shows key negotiations between entities.

The UE will toggle from one base station to another base station during re-authentication linking. In general, the linking delay is reduced when the new base station distributes the credentials of the UE. The delay in communication will be reduced for a comparable amount of traffic.

10.5 Worldwide Interoperability for Microwave Access (WiMAX) Network Simulation

Though a number of units for WiMAX network simulation have been planned for the Network Simulator (NS-2), none of them contain all the medium access control (MAC) equipment as specified by the Institute of Electrical and Electronics Engineers (IEEE 802.16) standard for bandwidth management, security, and QoS support. Justification of a WiMAX module is based on the IEEE 802.16 standard. The unit should include mechanisms for bandwidth request and allocation, as well as for QoS provisions. The simulation parameters are shown in Table 10.4.

By using the sequential key in the handoff process, the UE can competently connect with a target network by executing the planned re-authentication methods. Figure 10.2 shows a WiMAX network with base station re-authentication protocol. The execution of mutual authentication and the pair wise master key are carried out between the base station and the UE without involving any other parties.

TABLE 10.4

Simulation Parameters

Number of Base Station (BS)	7
Number of Ms for each BS	100
Inter BS distance	5 Km
PHYSICAL	Wireless Orthogonal Frequency Division Multiple Access (OFDMA) 5 MHz and OFDM
Medium Access Control (MAC) propagation delay	10 ms
Simulation time	30 Minutes
Traffic channel bandwidth (MHz)	Base frequency (5.8 GHz) and bandwidth (20 MHz).
Frame duration (ms)	5 ms
Path loss model vehicular	Vehicular environment

Figure 10.3 shows that the handover delay is reduced by 0.005 millisecond (ms) with re-authentication protocol and the overall average delay is reduced by 0.0002 ms. In an identical network, Figures 10.4 and 10.5 show a voice/video conference for packet delay variation and the separate curves show the delays that occur between (with and without) re-authentication processes.

Figures 10.6 and 10.7 also show the WiMAX network throughput and load analysis with re-authentication protocol. As per simulation results, the reduction of the re-authentication phase increases throughout and decreases the handoff delay. Re-authentication is supported by base station procedures and programs and quickly reduces the connectivity delay in assorted networks, especially for the MAC layer that is responsible for the authentication process. The average delay and pass over delay with Extensible Authentication Protocol (EAP) are reduced by 0.00032 and 0.006 ms, respectively.

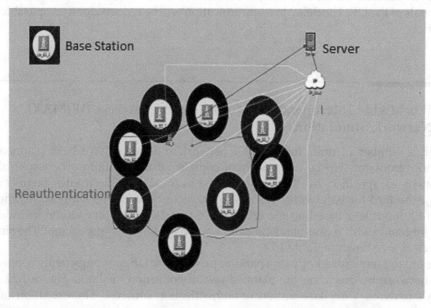

FIGURE 10.2
WiMAX network with base station re-authentication protocol.

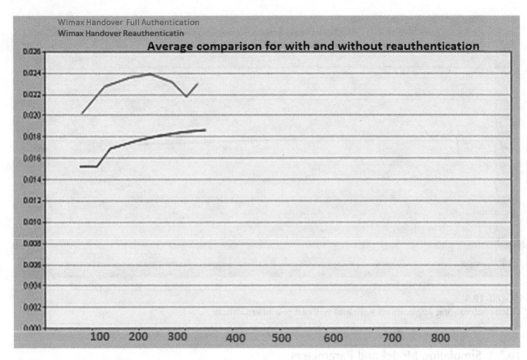

FIGURE 10.3
Handover delay/average comparison for with and without re-authentication.

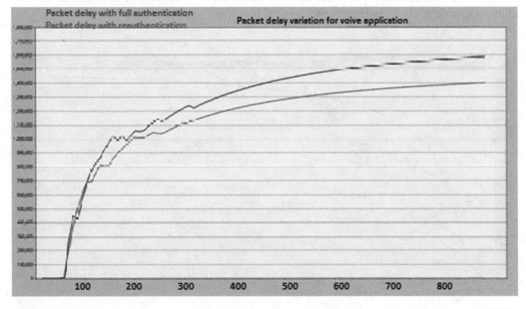

FIGURE 10.4
Packet delay variation for voice application with and without re-authentication.

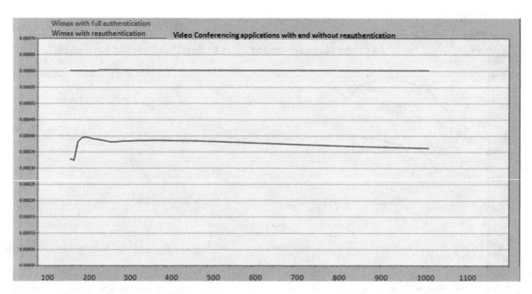

FIGURE 10.5
Video conferencing applications with and without re-authentication.

10.5.1 Simulation Model and Parameters

To simulate the proposed scheme, NS-2 [20] is used. In the simulation, clients Subscriber System (SS) and the BS are deployed in a 500 m × 500 m region for 50 seconds' simulation time. It consists of six base stations, among which BS1 and BS2 are based on 802.16 WiMAX and BS3 and BS4 are based on 802.11 wireless local area network (WLAN). The remaining two base stations BS4 and BS5 are based on Long Term Evolution (LTE) [21]. Each network contains five mobile nodes. All nodes have the same transmission range of 250 m. In our simulation, mobile node 13 performs the vertical handoff.

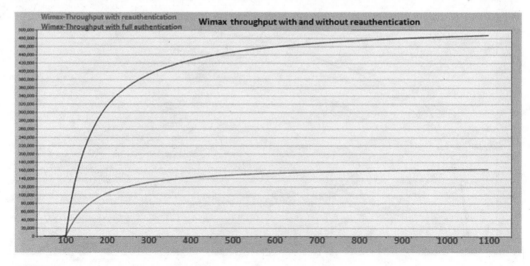

FIGURE 10.6
WiMAX throughput with and without re-authentication.

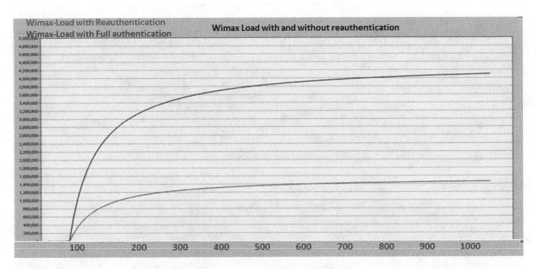

FIGURE 10.7
WiMAX load with and without re-authentication.

10.5.1.1 Performance Metrics

To compare the Extensible Authentication Protocol-Authentication Key Agreement (EAP-AKA) authentication protocol with the Evolved Packet System Authentication Key Agreement (EPS-AKA) authentication scheme, we considered two scenarios: Inter and Intra Handoff. In intra handoff, the mobile node roams into the same network whereas in inter, it moves from WiMAX to LTE and vice versa. The number of service requests is varied from 50 to 250 and the performance is evaluated in terms of authentication delay, packet delivery ratio, and message transaction load. Figures 10.8 through 10.10 show the performances of EAP-AKA and EPS-AKA from the view of message transaction load, authentication delay, and packet delivery ratio (Figures 10.8 through 10.10).

10.6 Conclusion and Future Work

Testing was intended to assess the progress toward the main purpose of the IEEE 802.16 MAC. The results point out that the BS is able to administer medium access both in the downlink and uplink directions, as well as assign support for the transmission of bandwidth requests and data according to the conditions of the standard. Moreover, the subsystems are able to send bandwidth requests and data packets in the range allocated by the BS.

This WiMAX-LTE module can facilitate research on heterogeneous networks, especially those involving bandwidth allocation and security provisions. At present, an Orthogonal Frequency Division Multiplexing (OFDM) channel is under expansion which will contain an unreliable wireless link capability and a location-dependent channel status. In connection to that, we also aimed to study the effects of fragmentation, concatenation, and share the accomplishments of enhancements in internetworking security.

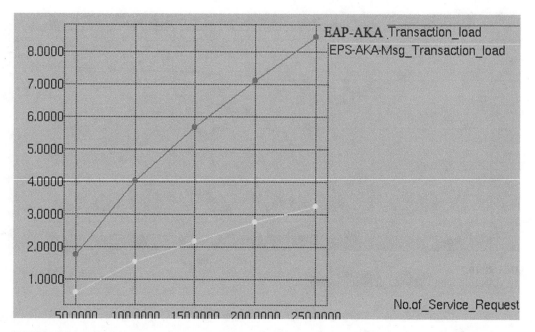

FIGURE 10.8
EAP-AKA and EPS AKA transaction load variations.

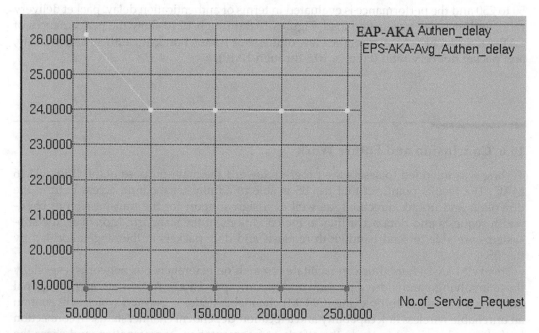

FIGURE 10.9
EAP-AKA and EPS AKA-authentication delay.

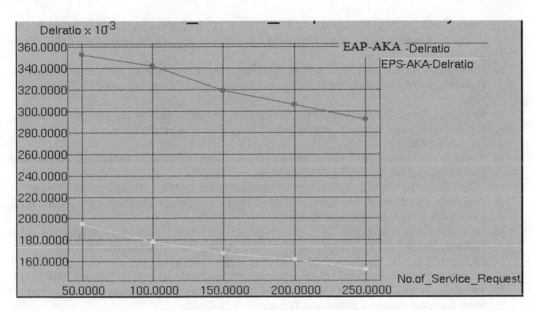

FIGURE 10.10
EAP-AKA and EPS AKA-delivery ratio.

Acknowledgments

We thank our parents for their support and motivation.

References

1. Duda, A. and Sreenan, C.J. 2003. Challenges for quality of service in next generation mobile networks. *Proc. of Information Technology & Telecommunications Conference (IT&T)*, Letterkenny, Ireland.
2. Mousa, A.M. 2012. Prospective of fifth generation mobile communications. *International Journal of Next—Generation Networks (IJNGN)*. 4(3): 1–30.
3. Rappaport, T.S., Roh, W. and Cheun, K. 2014. Wireless engineers long considered high frequencies worthless for cellular systems. They couldn't be more wrong. *IEEE Spectrum*. 51(9): 34–58, September.
4. Patel, S., Malhar, C. and Kapadiya, K. 2012. 5G: Future mobile technology-vision 2020. *International Journal Of Computer Applications*. 54(17): 6–10.
5. Toh, C.K. 2002. *Ad Hoc Mobile Wireless Networks: Protocols and Systems*. Prentice Hall, New Jersey, USA.
6. Shukla, S., Shukla, S. and Pandey, M.C. 2012. Mobile technology in 4G. *International Conference on Recent Trends in Engineering & Technology (ICRTET 2012)*, pp. 107–110, Bangalore, India.
7. Mishra, A. 2004. *Fundamentals of Cellular Network Planning and Optimisation*. John Wiley & Sons.
8. UMTS World 2009. *UMTS/3G History and Future Milestones*, [Online], http://www.umtsworld.com/umts/history.htm
9. Naik, G., Aigal, V., Sehgal, P. and Poojary, J. 2012. Challenges in the implementation of fourth generation wireless systems. *International Journal of Engineering Research and Applications (IJERA)*. 2(2): 1353–1355.

10. Chiang, M., Low, S.H., Calderbank, A.R. and Doyle, J.C. 2007. Layering as optimization decomposition: A mathematical theory of network architectures. *Proceedings of the IEEE.* 95(1): 255–312.

11. Gudipati, A., Li, L.E. and Katti, S. 2014. Radiovisor: A slicing plane for radio access networks. *Proceedings of ACM Workshop on Hot Topics in Software Defined Networking*, pp. 237–238, Helsinki, Finland.

12. Blenk, A., Basta, A., Reisslein, M. and Kellerer, W. 2016. Survey on network virtualization hypervisors for software defined networking. *IEEE Communications Surveys and Tutorials.* 18(1): 655–685.

13. Parikh, J. and Basu, A. 2011. LTE advanced: The 4G mobile broadband technology. *International Journal of Computer Applications.* 13(5): 17–21.

14. 3GPP TR 36.814, V9.0.0 2010. Further Advancements for E-UTRA Physical Layer Aspects.

15. Bangerter, S., Talwar, R. and Arefi, K. S. 2014. Intel networks and devices for the 5G era. *IEEE Communications Magazine.* 52(2): 90–96.

16. Hrikhande, S. and Mulky, E. 2012. Fourth generation wireless technology. *Proceedings of the National Conference "NCNTE-2012" at Fr. C.R.I.T.*, Vashi, Navi Mumbai, pp. 24–25.

17. Pachauri, A.K. and Singh, O. 2012. 5G technology—Redefining wireless communication in upcoming years. *International Journal of Computer Science and Management Research.* 1(1): 12–19.

18. Tudzarov, A. and Janevski, T. 2011. Functional architecture for 5G mobile networks. *International Journal of Advanced Science and Technology.* 3(2): 65–78.

19. Singh, S. and Singh, P. 2012. Key concepts and network architecture for 5G mobile technology. *International Journal of Scientific Research Engineering & Technology (IJSRET).* 1(5): 165–170.

20. Andrews, J.G. et al. 2014. What will 5G be? *IEEE Journal on Selected Areas in Communications.* 32(6): 1065–1082.

21. Holma, H., Toskala, A. and Reunanen, J. 2015. *LTE Small Cell Optimization: 3GPP Evolution to Release 13.* Wiley, Hoboken, NJ, USA.

11

Antennas in Cognitive Radio Systems for 5G Networks: Challenges and Review

M. Hassanein Rabah and Divitha Seetharamdoo

CONTENTS

11.1 Introduction

The main purpose of cognitive radios (CRs) is enabling the exploitation of the unoccupied channels that are possibly spread over a wide bandwidth. Before CRs can be implemented, several challenges that researchers and operators are faced with have to be solved. In CR systems, signal processing is pushed as much as possible toward digital signal processing. This makes the physical interface one of the most challenging parts of the architecture. In this chapter, different CR architectures are described from an antenna point of view. Key components of the radio frequency (RF) front-end are identified with the associated antenna design challenges. Then a state of the art review of the most recent antenna systems proposed for CR is presented. It will be shown that strong constraints make antennas subject to several physical limitations. Metamaterials can prove to be helpful for overcoming these limitations. Finally, one of our recent antenna designs is presented; it is inspired by metamaterials and is a good candidate for spectrum sensing operations.

11.2 Antenna Challenges in CR Systems

Higher data rates requiring greater bandwidth together with a growing number of telecommunication systems have led to a shortage in the radio frequency (RF) spectrum. One of the most important reasons for this shortage is static frequency allocation which has resulted in an underutilization of a large portion of the spectrum. As a result, several dynamic spectrum

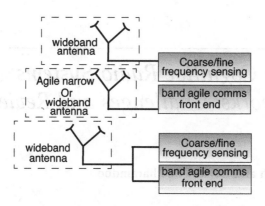

FIGURE 11.1
Interweave cognitive radio architecture with parallel sensing and communications.

access techniques are proposed for a more efficient utilization of the spectrum. The three solutions which have been suggested by the Federal Communications Commission (FCC) to improve spectrum utilization are spectrum reallocation, spectrum leasing, and spectrum sharing.

The frequency ranges needed will be much wider than those covered by antennas in most current communication systems. This implies that extremely-wide-band and frequency reconfigurable antennas will become increasingly important as well as smart and multiple antenna techniques both in base stations and in terminals. The antennas required for two specific techniques: interweave CR and underlay CR, are described in this chapter.

Interweave CR continuously monitors the spectrum usage in a process which runs in parallel with the communication link as shown in Figure 11.1.

The interweave CR radio architecture is based on two antennas [1]. The first antenna is a wideband omnidirectional one. It feeds a receiver having both coarse and fine spectrum sensing functionalities over a wide frequency band. The second antenna is a narrowband one which feeds a frequency agile front-end that can be tuned to the selected band. This category can also include a single antenna system [2]. In this case, a single wideband antenna is used for both the spectrum sensing modules and the frequency agile front-end.

In underlay CR, a single channel is assigned for both spectrum sensing and communication as depicted in Figure 11.2.

The operations are separated by various time frames. Spectrum sensing and radio reconfiguration are performed when the communication link quality falls below defined thresholds. In [3], two thresholds are defined. Link quality falling below the first threshold triggers spectrum sensing such that a better system configuration can be identified thus meeting the link quality requirements. A second threshold is defined such that when the quality falls below this threshold, the system is reconfigured.

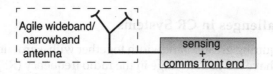

FIGURE 11.2
Underlay cognitive radio architecture with combined sensing module and communications front-end.

Platform integration constraints and available space are the major parameters that determine which one of these techniques will be used. For instance, in a base station, both spatial and spectral sensing may be used, but in the case of handheld terminals, it is more likely that only spectral sensing is used [4]. These issues have been further detailed in [5].

The most (relevant) significant antenna challenges are listed below:

1. In general, wideband antenna dimensions are larger than those of narrowband ones, which will be a significant problem. *Miniaturization of wideband antennas* is a main challenge for CR systems. The fundamental limits of electrically small antennas, in terms of bounds on the Q factor and gain, also limit the instantaneous coverage that can be achieved [6]. Furthermore, the design of wideband arrays results in great difficulties in inter-element spacing in base stations.

2. Combining the two bounds of the gain and Q factor implies that an antenna with an extremely wide band will be very inefficient if it is small compared to the wavelength. Thus, the efficiency of the antenna in the electrically small regime becomes a challenge.

3. The sensing and communication antennas should be enclosed within the same space, thus the colocation of both these antennas requires good isolation.

Antenna designers generally face the above-mentioned challenges. They combine multiple antennas within the same space and try to find a trade-off between the bandwidth, miniaturization, and the isolation. In the next section, we present the most relevant designs proposed in the context of CR.

11.3 Review of Antennas Proposed for CR

The literature is rich in antenna designs dedicated to diverse applications and that can be used in the context of CRs. Table 11.1 lists the presented antennas together with those used for spectrum interweave CR.

It can be deduced from both Tables 11.1 and 11.2 that when the electrical size of the antenna system decreases, a trade-off in terms of bandwidth, gain or efficiency is imposed. In fact, at the smallest operating frequency, the electrical size is the smallest and it is at those frequencies that the other antenna parameters are mostly affected. This trade-off is due to the physical limitations governing these antennas.

11.4 Antennas' Physical Limitations

Antennas' physical limitations depend mainly on the electrical size. Electrically small antennas (ESAs) occupy a volume of the sphere whose radius a is a small fraction of the free-space wavelength of the radiated electromagnetic field (Figure 11.3). The $k \times a$ product is commonly used to describe this relation, where k is the wave vector defined as $k = 2\pi/\lambda$. An antenna is electrically small if:

- $k \times a < 1$ (without a ground-plane)
- $k \times a < 0.5$ (with a ground-plane)

TABLE 11.1

Overview of Proposed Antenna Systems for Spectrum Interweave CR in the Past Years

Ref. Capture	Year	Antenna Operating Frequency in (GHz)	Antenna Dimensions in (mm²)	ϵ_r	Electrical Size	Coupling	Gain/Efficiency	Design Configuration	Reconfigurability
[12]	2009	3.3–11	65.5 × 58	2.2	(0.72 × 0.64)λl	<−20 dB	7 dBi	Slotted monopole in microstrip technology with two positions triangular monopole	Mechanical: two positions triangular monopole
[13]	2010	3.1–11	50 × 50	2.2	(0.74 × 0.74)λl	<−10 dB	4.7 dBi	Egg-shaped monopole fed by a microstrip line	Electrical: Use of lumped element
[14]	2011	2–10	70 × 50	2.2	(0.46 × 0.33)λl	<−10 dB	N.A	Modified egg-shaped monopole fed by a tapered microstrip line	Mechanical: Five rotating shapes
[15]	2013	2.6–11	74 × 59	6	(0.64 × 0.51)λl	<−10 dB	80%	Coplanar Vivaldi monopole	Electrical: Printed dipole with lumped elements
[16]	2015	0.72–3.44	120 × 65	4.4	(0.28 × 0.15)λl	<−11.5 dB	40%	Planar monopole with two meander-line reconfigurable antennas	Electrical: slots in the ground plane controlled by varactor diodes
[17]	2017	2.8–11.4	21 × 9	4.4	(0.16 × 0.15)λl	N.A	60%	Planar patch with stepped slotted ground plane	Electrical: slots in the ground plane controlled by diodes

TABLE 11.2

Overview of Proposed Antennas for Spectrum Underlay and Wideband Sensing Operation in the Past Years

Ref. Capture	Year	Antenna Operating Frequency in (GHz)	Antenna Dimensions in (mm²)	ϵ_r	Electrical Size	Gain/Efficiency	Design Configuration
[18]	2011	1.08–27	124 × 120	3.48	$(0.44 \times 0.43)\lambda l$	6.2 dBi	Printed monopole with trapezoid ground plane and semi-ring feed
[19]	2012	2.4–10.6	50 × 50	4.3	$(0.4 \times 0.4)\lambda l$	70%	Circular printed monopole (Switches OFF for Ultra-Wide-Band [UWB] mode)
[20]	2014	3.1–10.6	40 × 40	4.4	$(0.41 \times 0.41)\lambda l$	N/A	Circular ring patch antenna
[21]	2017	2.5–8	60 × 50	2.55	$(0.8 \times 0.66)\lambda l$	4 dBi	Triangular monopole with optical switching system

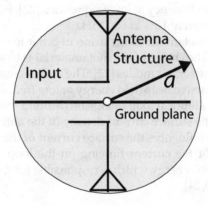

FIGURE 11.3
Illustration of the smallest sphere containing an antenna.

The fundamental limitations of small antennas are still an active research area [6–10]. The physical bounds of ESAs can be estimated with the quality factor Q:

$$Q = \frac{2.\omega.W_{\{elec,\,mag\}}}{P_{rad}}$$

where ω is the angular frequency, $W_{\{elec,\,mag\}}$ is the time-average, non-propagating energy stored by the antenna, and P_{rad} is the radiated power. Q is inversely proportional to a, that is, the antenna dimensions. The smaller the quality factor is, the higher the radiated power by the antenna.

One of the advanced electromagnetic (EM) techniques used for extending the antenna limits relies on using artificial structures called metamaterials (MTMs) [11]. In the next paragraph, we present MTM-inspired antenna designs which can be good candidates for spectrum sensing CRs.

11.5 Novel Metamaterial-Based Antenna Design for CR

This section presents a novel extremely-wide-band antenna dedicated for underlay CR used for spectrum sensing operations based on the designs proposed in [22]. The theory of characteristic modes is used to optimize the antenna in order to meet spectrum sensing requirements taking into account both constraints: bandwidth and radiation pattern stability.

The initial design in [22] presents a wide spectrum sensing bandwidth with stable radiation pattern over the frequency band. Figure 11.4 shows the return losses with respect to the frequency of the initial antenna.

The radiation patterns for E- and H-planes are shown in Figure 11.5 for several frequencies in the operating frequency band.

The radiation pattern in the YZ plane is very stable over the matched frequency range, which guarantees minimum signal distortion over the frequency band. This is a very important antenna factor for spectrum sensing [5]. However, despite the good pattern of the antenna, it suffers from low efficiency at low frequencies [22]. For instance, the antenna radiation efficiency is approximately 15% at 600 MHz.

The use of an additional metamaterial inclusion in order to enhance the radiation characteristics has been studied. The choice of the metamaterial is based on a systematic study by means of the theory of characteristic modes [22]. The authors make an energy-based analysis in order to conjugate the reactive near-field energy at low frequencies. This analysis resulted in the selection of a slotted elliptical loop (inclusion) around the radiator. Figure 11.6 shows the impact of the loop on the surface current density of the antenna.

The presence of the loop influences the surface current of the antenna such that it follows an identical path to that of the current flowing on the loop. Thus, a circulating current enhances the stored magnetic energy which is responsible for the matching of the monopole stored electrical energy [23,24].

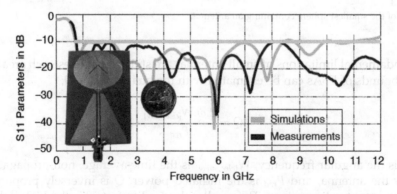

FIGURE 11.4
Comparison between simulated and measured S11 parameters for the antenna.

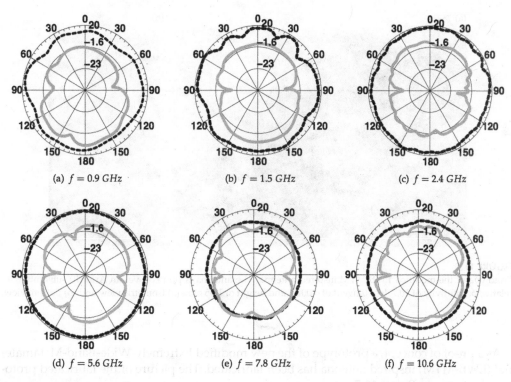

FIGURE 11.5
Measured radiation pattern of the antenna in the XZ plane (--), and YZ plane (—), over the operating frequency band.

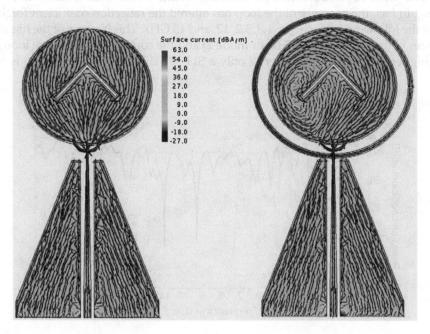

FIGURE 11.6
Impact of the MTM inclusion on the surface current flowing on the antenna at 600 MHz.

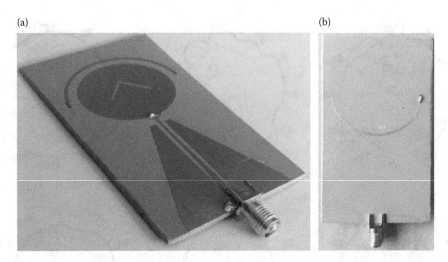

FIGURE 11.7
Prototype of the modified EWB-MTM inspired antenna. The antenna is printed over an Arlon10 substrate with relative permittivity of 10.7, loss tangent of 0.0023, and height of 1.55 mm. (a) Isometric view and (b) Bottom view.

As a proof of concept, a prototype of the new modified Extremely-Wide-Band-Metamaterial (EWB-MTM) inspired antenna has been fabricated. The picture of the fabricated prototype is shown in Figure 11.7.

Figure 11.8 shows a comparison between the simulated and measured S11 of the EWB-MTM inspired antenna over a larger bandwidth (0–18 GHz).

The EWB-MTM inspired antenna presents an extremely wide bandwidth with acceptable matching. In fact, the presence of the loop has altered the reflection coefficient (higher than 10 dB) at the following frequencies: 1.8, 3.2, 12, and 15 GHz. This because of the higher-order resonances of the loop (i.e., 1.8 GHz for mode 2) and the coupling between the loop and the disk at higher frequencies. However, if only a S11 < 6 dB reflection coefficient is required

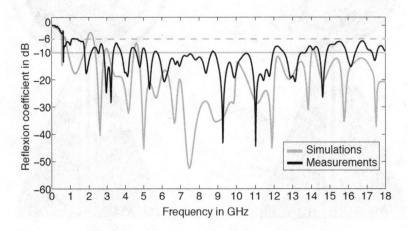

FIGURE 11.8
Comparison between simulation and measurement of the reflection coefficient of the EWB-MTM inspired antenna.

(typical for spectrum sensing [4]), the antenna proves to cover a bandwidth extending from 0.6–18 GHz.

On the other hand, the metamaterial inclusion significantly enhances the realized gain of the antenna at 600 MHz. This enhancement is around 10 dB when averaged over all the angles in the XZ plane. The maximum realized gain of the EWB-MTM inspired antenna is about 0.582 (-3.16 dBi) at 600 MHz while the calculated directivity is around 0.85 (-0.7 dB). This means that the antenna presents a 56.4% radiation efficiency (compared to 15% without the inclusion) which is excellent considering its total dimensions.

11.6 Conclusion and Future Work

In this chapter, a state of the art discussion of CR configurations and associated antennas is presented. An overview on the existing interweave and underlay CR antenna solutions is presented. The design challenges and associated physical limitations were reported. A novel EWB antenna is proposed as a good candidate for spectrum sensing applications in the context of CR systems. The proposed antenna presents a very small form factor given the covered bandwidth. The achieved antenna efficiency at 600 MHz equals 56.4%, which is considered excellent given its small electrical size ($0.146 \times 0.09\lambda_1$). Moreover, the antenna radiation patterns remain stable and omnidirectional in both planes over the whole frequency band.

This is done through the use of characteristic mode (CM) theory in the definition of metrics related to the nature of the stored energy in the structure together with the resonance conditions, and by decomposing the total surface currents onto a set of real orthogonal currents. Providing such tools to analyze antennas and MTM from a physical point of view will be the key to meeting CR antenna systems requirements in terms of cohabitation (i.e., isolation), bandwidth enhancement, and miniaturization.

Acknowledgments

The authors acknowledge partial funding from the Hauts-de-France Regional Council and through the regional project SMARTIES in the framework of the ELSAT 2020 program co-financed by the European Union with the European Regional Development Fund, the French state, and Hauts de France Regional council.

References

1. Y. Hur, J. Park, W. Woo, K. Lim, C.-H. Lee, H.S. Kim, and J. Laskar, "A wideband analog multi-resolution spectrum sensing (MRSS) technique for cognitive radio (CR) systems", in *2006 IEEE International Symposium on Circuits and Systems, 2006*. ISCAS 2006. Proceedings, 2006, 4 pp.
2. J. Laskar, R. Mukhopadhyay, Y. Hur, C.-H. Lee, and K. Lim, "Reconfigurable RFICs and modules for cognitive radio", in *2006 Topical Meeting on Silicon Mono-lithic Integrated Circuits in RF Systems, 2006*. Digest of Papers, 2006, 4 pp.

3. H. Harada, "A software defined cognitive radio prototype", in *IEEE 18th International Symposium on Personal, Indoor and Mobile Radio Communications, 2007. PIMRC 2007*, 2007, pp. 1–5.

4. P.S. Hall, P. Gardner, J. Kelly, E. Ebrahimi, M.R. Hamid, F. Ghanem, F.J. Herraiz-Martinez, and D. Segovia-Vargas, "Reconfigurable antenna challenges for future radio systems", in *3rd European Conference on Antennas and Propagation, 2009. EuCAP 2009*, March 2009, pp. 949–955.

5. P. Gardner, M.R. Hamid, P.S. Hall, J. Kelly, F. Ghanem, and E. Ebrahimi, "Re-configurable antennas for cognitive radio: Requirements and potential design approaches", in *2008 Institution of Engineering and Technology Seminar on Wide-band, Multiband Antennas and Arrays for Defence or Civil Applications*, 2008, pp. 89–94.

6. J.S. McLean, "A re-examination of the fundamental limits on the radiation Q of electrically small antennas", *IEEE Transactions On Antennas And Propagation*, vol. 44, no. 5, pp. 672, 1996.

7. L.J. Chu, "Physical limitations of omni-directional antennas", *Journal Of Applied Physics*, vol. 19, no. 12, pp. 1163, 1948.

8. J.L. Volakis, Chi-Chih-Chen, Ming Lee, B. Kramer, and D. Psychoudakis, "Miniaturization methods for narrowband and ultra wide band antennas", in *IEEE International Workshop on Antenna Technology: Small Antennas and Novel Metamaterials, 2005. IWAT 2005*, March 2005, pp. 119–121.

9. A.D. Yaghjian and S.R. Best, "Impedance, bandwidth, and Q of antennas", *IEEE Transactions On Antennas And Propagation*, vol. 53, no. 4, pp. 1298–1324, April 2005.

10. M. Gustafsson, M. Cismasu, and B. L. G. Jonsson, "Physical bounds and optimal currents on antennas", *IEEE Transactions On Antennas And Propagation*, vol. 60, no. 6, pp. 2672–2681, 2012.

11. E. Lheurette, S. Divitha, and S. Bruno, Metamaterials and wave control Chapter 3: Metamaterials for Non-Radiative Microwave Functions and Antennas, 2013, John Wiley & Sons, pp. 67–86.

12. Y. Tawk, J. Costantine, K. Avery, and C.G. Christodoulou, "Implementation of a cognitive radio front-end using rotatable controlled reconfigurable anten-nas", *IEEE Transactions On Antennas And Propagation*, vol. 59, no. 5, pp. 1773–1778, 2011.

13. M. Al-Husseini, Y. Tawk, C.G. Christodoulou, K.Y. Kabalan, and A. El-Hajj, "A reconfigurable cognitive radio antenna design", in *2010 IEEE Antennas and Propagation Society International Symposium (APSURSI)*, 2010, pp. 1–4.

14. Y. Tawk and C.G. Christodoulou, "A new reconfigurable antenna design for cognitive radio", *IEEE Antennas And Wireless Propagation Letters*, vol. 8, pp. 1378–1381, 2009.

15. G. Augustin and T.A. Denidni, "An integrated ultra wideband/narrow band antenna in uniplanar configuration for cognitive radio systems", *IEEE Trans-actions On Antennas And Propagation*, vol. 60, no. 11, pp. 5479–5484, November 2012.

16. R. Hussain and M.S. Sharawi, "A cognitive radio reconfigurable MIMO and sensing antenna system", *IEEE Antennas And Wireless Propagation Letters*, vol. 14, pp. 257–260, 2015.

17. G. Srivastava, A. Mohan, and A. Chakrabarty, "Compact reconfigurable UWB slot antenna for cognitive radio applications", *IEEE Antennas And Wireless Propagation Letters*, vol. 16, pp. 1139–1142, 2017.

18. J. Liu, K.P. Esselle, S.G. Hay, and S. Zhong, "Achieving ratio band-width of 25:1 from a printed antenna using a tapered semi-ring feed", *IEEE Antennas And Wireless Propagation Letters*, vol. 10, pp. 1333–1336, 2011.

19. T. Aboufoul, A. Alomainy, and C. Parini, "Reconfiguring UWB monopole antenna for cognitive radio applications using GaAs FET switches", *IEEE Antennas And Wireless Propagation Letters*, vol. 11, pp. 392–394, 2012.

20. E.J.B. Rodrigues, H.W.C. Lins, and A.G. D'Assuncao, "Reconfigurable circular ring patch antenna for UWB and cognitive radio applications", in *2014 8th European Conference on Antennas and Propagation (EuCAP)*, April 2014, pp. 2744–2748.

21. A. Andy, P. Alizadeh, K. Z. Rajab, T. Kreouzis, and R. Donnan, "An optically-switched frequency reconfigurable antenna for cognitive radio applications", in *2016 10th European Conference on Antennas and Propagation (EuCAP)*, 2016, pp. 1–4.

22. M.H. Rabah, D. Seetharamdoo, R. Addaci, and M. Berbineau, "Novel miniature extremely-wide-band antenna with stable radiation pattern for spectrum sensing applications", *IEEE Antennas And Wireless Propagation Letters*, vol. PP, no. 99, pp. 1–1, 2015.

23. M.H. Rabah, "Design Methodology of Antennas Based on Metamaterials and the Theory of Characteristic Modes: Application to Cognitive Radio", PhD dissertation, University of Lille, 2015.

24. M.H. Rabah, D. Seetharamdoo, H. Srour, and M. Berbineau, *FR3052920.*

Part VI

5G Networks with Ad hoc Networks

12

Wireless Ad hoc Networks with 5G Technology

Shadab Pasha Khan, M.A. Rizvi, and Anu Mangal

CONTENTS

12.1 Introduction

This age is the information age, where information is very important for every age group of people. The flawless flow of information is possible only when we have robust architecture, backbone, and 24×7 connectivity. In the past, people accessed information with the help of desktop computers, then after a few years, laptops came into the picture.

Now, however, due to the proliferation of wireless devices, almost all applications are available on smart mobile phones and it will become easier to get connected to the real world as and when needed. Wireless technology enables us to think about new dimensions and applications. Wireless technology has changed the way we live. Very soon due to the evolution of mobile generations and internet-enabled Internet of Things (IoT) devices, almost all devices will be connected, controlled, and monitored by mobiles.

12.2 Wireless Ad hoc Networks and Their Characteristics

In the next generation networks, wireless technologies and compact computing are two areas of ad hoc networks. Without any fixed infrastructure, all the nodes of the network communicate by hopping from one site to another. This type of network is spontaneous in nature because it forms and reforms dynamically as per the situation. It is also referred as on-the-fly networks. It is easy to set up because it does not require an access point. Ad hoc wireless networks have multi-hop wireless links that share radio channels and deliver best-effort data traffic. The routing process [1] is also distributed which helps all the nodes to find the best path out of the available paths with minimum overhead. Nodes exhibit the reconfiguration of broken paths in each node in this type of network where each one will behave in two forms; one as a router and the other as a node.

Futuristic customer centric applications have a dynamic nature and mobile ad hoc networks exhibit the same property which makes it ideal for next-generation networks. This kind of network is also suitable in the case of emergencies where quick deployment and minimal configuration are needed. Next generation mobile ad hoc networks will have more scalability, reliability, and availability. These devices include personal digital assistants (PDAs), laptops, cellular phones, personal computers, and various wearable devices. Lightweight, compact, and energy efficient devices will be in more demand in the future. Dynamic wireless ad hoc networks (DAWN) and rich communication services are the two most important contributing factors in next generation mobile ad hoc networks.

12.2.1 Types of Ad hoc Networks

The types of ad hoc networks are as follows:

- *Wireless Mesh Networks*: This is a communication network where all the topologies are used to interconnect the nodes. In this kind of network, wireless access points (AP) play an important role in connectivity. The network infrastructure is decentralized so that each node has to transmit data to the next node only. This offers rich interconnection among nodes. In this type of network, the mobility of the nodes is more static and exhibits better connectivity. The nodes may be laptops, mobile phones, and other wireless equipment.

- *Wireless Sensor Networks*: In this type of communication network, all the communicating nodes are autonomous in behavior and use sensors to monitor the conditions. Changes take place in any physical object or the environment changes. The network must provide asset tracking and the monitoring of machines, building structures, and processes. These are a few applications of wireless sensor nodes.

12.2.2 Characteristics of Ad hoc Networks

- *Wireless*: This does not depend upon media or wire. Communication between nodes occurs through radio waves [2] which share the same media.

- *Ad hoc based*: This is a temporary network which is established dynamically by the nodes as the need arises.

- *Self-configuring and self-organizing network*: This network has the unique capability to configure the nodes dynamically without any external agent. Nodes actively participate in organizing themselves according to the need of the network. All nodes are organized in such a way that best suits the actual condition of the network.

- *Autonomous*: An autonomous network does not depend upon any kind of base network.

- *Infrastructure-less*: Nothing can happen without infrastructure, but the practical scenario of ad hoc network communication is still possible without establishing any infrastructure.

- *Ease of deployment*: The deployment of an ad hoc network does not need any kind of base station which means it is easily deployed without requiring much time.

- *Decentralized administration*: The administration of messages is controlled by nodes themselves as they participate in the communication process. Each node exhibits the properties of a router as well as a node. All the resources such as bandwidth, computing power, and battery life time are managed in a distributed manner by applying peer-to-peer connectivity.

- *Multi-hop routing*: The process of information sharing among the available nodes is performed without dedicated routers. All the nodes in the network behave as routers to perform routing activities as well as data transmission.

- *Mobility*: The topology of this type of network is frequently changing due to the constant movement of existing nodes. Due to this, the communication patterns among the nodes change continuously.

12.3 Issues and Challenges of Wireless Ad hoc Network

There are various issues and challenges associated with wireless ad hoc networks. The network is established without any infrastructures introducing complexities [3] such as routing activity, synchronizing activity bandwidth optimization, power consumption, and control performance.

There are various issues and challenges that need to be addressed.

12.3.1 Medium Access

In wireless ad hoc networks, due to broadcasting and shared transmission, packet collisions and congestions occur. This reduces channel utilization and throughput. There are also other issues such as hidden terminal problems and exposed terminal problems.

12.3.2 Quality of Service

How well the network performs depends upon the various parameters. These parameters are called quality of service parameters. There are various parameters on which the quality of service of mobile ad hoc networks depends including throughput, delay jitter, and packet delivery ratio (PDR), and so on.

12.3.3 Routing

An ad hoc network is an unpredictable network due to its frequent changes in network topologies. Based on the traffic conditions and the requirement of the nodes, routing decisions are made by nodes. Correct and efficient route establishment are the two most important objectives of the routing process in a wireless ad hoc network. When the connection breaks, new route construction should be done. The two parameters that need to be addressed are the routing overhead and bandwidth consumption [4].

There are certain considerations that need to be addressed for future next generation customer-centric applications

1. Ease of implementation
2. Diligent route convergence
3. Lightweight
4. Distributed
5. More scalable
6. Enhanced security

7. Better reliability

8. Aiding quality of service requirements

12.3.4 Security

In an ad hoc network, security is one of the major concerns. All the nodes use different channels at different times. These channels will be called shared broadcast channels because they are more exposed to unwanted users or attackers. To fix this, different respective security solutions are needed. It is comparatively difficult to implement security solutions due to the decentralized administration. Good security solutions always provide confidentiality, authentication, integrity, and non-repudiation. To design and develop relevant security solutions, understanding of the possible forms of attack plays a very prominent role. The nodes of mobile ad hoc networks cannot be trusted for correct execution of critical network services. Authentication of entities can be used to ensure the correct execution of critical functions of the ad hoc network. On the other hand, if the network is large, a need for keys arises for entity authentication. In this scenario, there is a need for a common trusted authority called a managed environment.

Some nodes are selfish nodes and some are cooperative nodes. A reasonable solution is provided by various cooperative security schemes. Due to the insufficiency of *a priori* trust, classical network security mechanisms based on authentication and access control cannot cope with the greediness of some nodes (Figure 12.1).

The ad hoc nature of a wireless ad hoc network brings new challenges to network design.

12.3.5 Nodes Mobility

The movement of the nodes in a wireless ad hoc network plays a key role in the selection of routing protocols which influence the overall performance [5] of the network once it is established. There are various mobility models available in wireless ad hoc networks such as random models, temporal dependency models, and geographic restriction models.

12.3.6 Synchronization

The next generation ubiquitous computing [6] environments are generally based upon ad hoc networks of mobile computing devices. These devices may be equipped with sensor

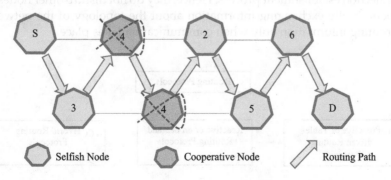

FIGURE 12.1
Selfish node problem.

nodes to learn the real-world facts and need to transfer this data to other nodes. For proper communication, clock synchronization of nodes is essential. However, clock synchronization is crucial and needs smart synchronization algorithms to fulfill the demands of customer-centric future applications.

12.3.7 Power or Energy Consumption

Energy efficient communication is essential due to the limited battery power of all communicating nodes in mobile ad hoc networks. Due to the spontaneous nature of the ad hoc network, all the nodes must have sufficient power to communicate with each other without any interruption. Measuring the energy consumptions of nodes in the transmitting state, receiving state, idle state, and sleep state is required. Based on these, protocols are generated which saves power in the nodes.

12.4 Routing Protocols in Current Scenario and in 5G

Routing protocols in mobile ad hoc network (MANET) are divided into three categories (Figure 12.2).

12.4.1 Proactive Protocols

The entire work of these protocols exhibits the proactive behavior of all the communicating nodes. They update information periodically regarding the status of various routes and topology changes and save all information in the routing table. Nodes exchange routing information periodically with each other by flooding the whole network. A path finding algorithm is executed before transmission of any packet from one node to another.

Examples are distance vector routing protocol (DSDV) and the wireless routing protocol (WRP).

12.4.2 Reactive Protocols

In this kind of protocol, all the communicating nodes do not exchange route information and topology information in advance. They do this only when it is required by using a process called a connection establishment process. Hence, they do not disturb other nodes of the network by periodically exchanging information about the topology of the network. Nodes exchange routing information only when communication takes place.

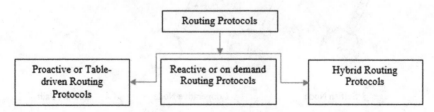

FIGURE 12.2
Categories of routing protocols.

Examples are:

Dynamic source routing protocol (DSR),

Ad hoc on demand distance vector routing protocol (AODV),

Temporally ordered routing algorithm (TORA), and

Location-aided routing (LAR).

12.4.3 Hybrid Protocols

It has been observed that in the real world of routing, both categories of protocols have their own advantages and disadvantages under different scenarios. Therefore, we cannot ignore any of the categories of protocols. The third category of protocols is a combination of attributes demonstrated by the above-mentioned proactive and reactive protocols.
Examples are:

Zone routing protocol (ZRP) and

Zone-based hierarchical link state routing protocol (ZHLS).

12.4.3.1 Expected Routing Protocols in 5G

The next generation network is a high-speed network where users are more data hungry. They need high speed 24×7 connectivity with minimum latency. The 4G network has already introduced Voice over Internet Protocol (VoIP) or Voice over Long Term Evolution (VoLTE) where voice and data both will be treated as single entities. In long term evolution (LTE) , the maximum allowed delay is between 50 and 300 (ms) depending upon the quality of service. Before 4G, in the case of 2G and 3G, voice and SMS were transmitted by Circuit Switched Core and user data was transmitted by Packet Switched Core.

12.4.3.2 Multi-Protocol Label Switching (MPLS)

This is a virtual circuit protocol with circuit switching and packet switching where both concepts are used in the forwarding of data from one node to another. But in the context of the next generation network, it may play a vital role due to its unique traffic controlling ability such as a packet's priority [2] and CoS (Class of Service).

It allows the packet to be forwarded to layer 2 rather than layer 3 and the Internet Service Provider (ISP)uses an ingress router to check and verify the malicious content of a packet, then the ingress router removes the label and forwards it toward the final destination.

It has been observed that MPLS exhibits various benefits over other technologies such as improvement in the quality of service, service classification in different classes (CoS) for service differentiating, and network scalable greater flexibility, and it responds to the rapidly changing needs of the next generation network.

The next version of MPLS is GMPLS, that is, Generalized Multi-Protocol Label Switching (Figure 12.3).

The above figure shows different types of technologies and how these are interconnected with each other to provide next generation network applications, such as Internet Protocol (IP), MPLS, and others.

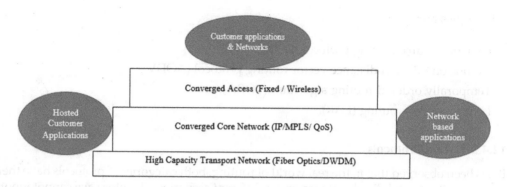

FIGURE 12.3
Classification of services.

12.5 Security in Wireless Ad hoc Networks

12.5.1 Secure Routing

Security is one of the major components of wired as well as wireless networks. It protects user data from unwanted peoples like hackers and attackers. Due to the proliferation of smart phones, people want to access banks online on a smart phone and want shop online, providing the necessary details like credit card number, debit card number, and password.

The performance of on-demand routing protocols such as ad hoc on demand distance vector (AODV) and Dynamic Source Routing (DSR) are more efficient than proactive routing protocols. All security protocols must provide confidentiality, authentication, integrity, and non-repudiation.

- *Confidentiality*: The data is the most important ingredient of communication. If the data is leaked then confidentiality is lost. Hence, we must apply security protocols in such a way that the data which is traveling across the network from one end to another must be confidential.

- *Authentication*: Any packet received by the receiver node in the ad hoc network [7] must be verified through some authentication mechanism by ensuring that the packet is sent by a legitimate sender and not by anyone else.

- *Integrity*: If someone modifies the packet between the transmission and reception, then the impact of the message changes and the response changes. We must apply security protocols to ensure an equal number of bits at the sending end and at the receiving end as well. In other words, not one bit is added or removed by anyone.

- *Non-repudiation*: All security protocols must provide non-repudiation so that the sender node cannot deny that the message has been delivered on the network.

There are three most widely used security protocols (Table 12.1 Encryption Standard). There are various secure routing protocols for ad hoc networks.

- SRP—Secure routing protocol
- ARAIDNE—A secure on demand routing protocol
- ARAN—Authenticated routing for ad hoc networks
- SEAD—Secure efficient ad hoc distance vector routing protocol

TABLE 12.1

Encryption Standard

Encryption Standard	Facts	Working	Remarks
Wired Equivalent Privacy (WEP)	24 bit initialization vector and weak authentication	Static master key must be manually entered. Uses RC4 Stream cipher 24 bit or 128 bit key.	No
Wi-Fi Protected Access (WPA)	Compatible with WEP Devices. Two modes, personal and enterprise.	Longer IVs, uses 252 bit keys. Each client uses Temporal Key Integrity Protocol (TKIP). Strong authentication.	Only if WPA2 is not available.
WPA2	Ensure advanced encryption, doesn't affect performance.	Replaces RC4, TKIP with Counter Mode Cipher Block Chaining Message Authentication Code Protocol (CCMP) and Advanced Encryption Standard (AES) for stronger authentication and encryption	Yes

12.5.2 Participation and Cooperation among Nodes

Basic networking functions in the traditional network are carried out by various networking equipment like switches, routers, and others, but in case of an ad hoc network, all the routing functions are performed by the node itself. The node's behavior, especially in the case of ad hoc networks, is observed and it is known if it exhibits selfishness. The functionality of a selfish node [8] does not affect the other nodes directly, but it saves its own battery to increase its existence for further communication. These types of nodes would not participate in the routing process.

Mechanisms that enforce node cooperation are divided into two categories: currency-based and cooperative security scheme based. Apart from the above, there are some prominent efforts to solve the problem of selfish nodes. These are as follows:

- Nuglets
- CONFIDANT-A strong authentication system in MANET
- CORE-Collaborative reputation mechanism
- Token-based cooperation enforcement

12.5.3 Key Management

Providing security to the ad hoc network is more challenging compared to the wired network because of the intrinsic behavior of the nodes. The implementation of Confidentiality (C), Integrity (I) and Authentication (A) also known as CIA principles along with non-repudiation is the most important task in order to achieve security. The deployment of ad hoc technology depends upon the implementation of basic CIA principles.

Authentication services are divided into two categories:

- Pretty good privacy (PGP)-like architecture
- Polynomial secret sharing technique

Both categories are widely used for authentication services and other security related services.

12.6 Quality of Service Parameters in Wireless Ad hoc Networks

In order to support customer-centric various next generation applications of 5G, the quality of various service parameters plays a key role in the design of next generation networks. These applications are data hungry applications and consume a lot of bandwidth to transfer audio, video, images, text, and so on. To support all these high-density services, the guarantee of QoS [1] parameters is a major objective (Figure 12.4).

To fulfill the requirement of various data-hungry applications in the next generation wireless networks, providing QoS guarantees for these applications is most important.

12.6.1 QoS Parameters

These are the QoS parameters which are frequently used in wireless ad hoc networks:

12.6.1.1 Bandwidth

Bandwidth is one of the most important QoS parameters necessary in order to fulfill the demand of next generation futuristic applications. Bandwidth is directly proportional to the amount of data transmitted or the capacity of the channel (i.e., Radio Access Network capacity). It is measured in bits/s.

12.6.1.2 Throughput

The success of the network depends upon the value of throughput. A higher throughput represents the maximum number of bits that are successfully transmitted out of the total available number of bits in the entire message per unit time. Hardware devices, bandwidth, signal to noise ratio (SNR), and others things affect the value of throughput [6].

Throughput plays a key role in measuring the actual rate of transmission. The entire gamut of applications depends upon higher throughput.

12.6.1.3 Latency

Delay that occurs in a communication network is known as latency. There are two kinds of delay: low delay and high delay. The delay between the two ends from source to destination is known as an end-to-end delay (EED) [2].

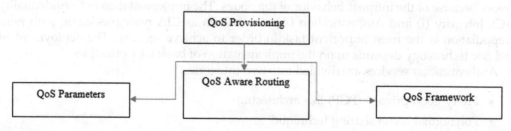

FIGURE 12.4
QoS provisioning.

Latency is dependent upon four components, which are explained by following mathematical equation:

$$Latency = P.T + T.T + Q.T + P.D.$$

where
P.T. is propagation time
T.T. is transmission time
Q.T. is queuing time
P.D. is processing delay

In order to achieve a good quality network, latency must be in the minimum range. This the prime requirement of next generation network applications otherwise users will lose interest.

12.6.1.4 Jitter

Everyone wants continuous transmission of packets without any delay, but jitter is one parameter which hampers the entire communication by introducing a delay between the packets. It is also called packet delay variation (PDV) [2]. Seamless transmission of packets depends upon a minimum delay occurring between packets. This factor must be within the permissible range, especially in the case of next generation video and audio streaming. Jitter is one of the important QoS performance parameters.

12.6.1.5 Bit Error Rate

This is the parameter which identifies the error occurring in the number of bits out of the total available number of bits transferred. It is also known as bit error ratio. It is defined as follows:
It is the ratio between the numbers of bit errors to the total number of transferred bits. Bit error rate (BER) must be minimized to fulfill the requirement of next generation data-hungry applications.

12.6.1.6 Packet Delivery Ratio (PDR)

As the name indicates, this is the ratio of the number of packets delivered out of the total number of packets sent [6] across the network.
PDR decides the efficiency of the next generation network. It must be high.

12.6.1.7 Route Discovery Time

The time taken to determine a route from source to destination is known as route discovery time.
In the case of a mobile ad hoc network, the network changes frequently due to node movements. The routing algorithm discovers the appropriate route before transmitting. The route discovery time should be minimum to connect different nodes. Smart routing algorithms are needed to achieve minimum route discovery times for next generation applications.

12.6.1.8 Route Reconstruction Time

The route reconstruction or repair time of a route depends upon the mobility of nodes and is known as route reconstruction time. However, smart routing algorithms are needed in the case of next generation mobile ad hoc network applications.

12.6.2 QoS-Aware Routing

The initial step to improving the quality of service of a routing protocol is to have a routing protocol that uses QoS parameters for finding the best path out of the available paths. The parameters that can be considered for better routing decisions are PDR, throughput, end-to-end delay, jitter, and path loss.

12.6.3 QoS Framework

A framework is a complete system that provides all services to the user by taking care of all QoS parameters required by the running application. A QoS service model plays a key role in assigning the services such as signaling protocol, routing protocol, and management of resources to each node and also takes care of different states of the nodes when the topology changes abruptly.

12.7 Applications of Wireless Ad hoc Networks in 5G

The need for data-hungry applications is one of the core ideas behind the evolution of 5G technology. The demand of data is increasing day by day. Users' requirements to reduce efforts in managing electronic devices like televisions, refrigerators, air conditioners, and all other devices is increasing. This is possible only when 5G provides efficient and high-speed connectivity between different nodes of the network. Such applications include global positioning system (GPS), geographic information system (GIS), online video streaming, and location-aware services like taxi-cab (CAB) services.

The concept of a Smart City is one in which 24×7 connectivity is entirely dependent upon the high-speed networks and technology is the enabler that makes it possible. The main challenge of smart applications is the mobility. These real-time applications need to transfer the requested information on time with minimum delay; they are called SMART applications.

There are various applications of wireless ad hoc networks like traditional applications, modern applications, and futuristic applications.

12.7.1 Traditional Applications

- Smart phone personal area network
- Short messaging services
- Multimedia messaging services
- Bluetooth and infrared

12.7.2 Modern Applications

- VANET—Vehicle ad hoc network driverless cars
- Wireless mesh network—Wi-Fi ad hoc networking
- Unmanned aerial vehicle (UAV) ad hoc networks

12.7.3 Futuristic Applications

- All smart city applications
- Better mobile connectivity
- Control applications
- Monitoring applications
- Augmented reality applications
- Supported applications for automation
- Drones applications
- Real time 24 × 7 communications
- Tactual internet
- Device applications connected to Internet called IoT
- Wireless sensor-based applications
- Artificial intelligence-based applications
- Exclusive smart applications of next generation network
- Voice-based personal devices
- Alexa, Cortana, Bixby, and a few others

High-speed connectivity among different nodes to run various applications is the core idea behind the development of 5G. Now almost all devices are smart enough to access and communicate with each other and fulfill the user demands for more data. Monitoring and controlling of different applications are now available on a smart phone. IoT-based applications would provide various opportunities to enhance the standard of living (Figure 12.5).

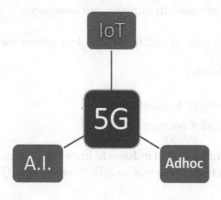

FIGURE 12.5
5G major application areas.

By 2020, Artificial Intelligence (A.I), Internet of Things (IoT), and the ad hoc network will together bring new dimensions in human society. They will rule the entire digital world of smart devices. Various electronic appliances used in a home such as Televisions (TV) Air Conditioners (A.C) and washing machines will be able to communicate with each other through a smart phone. Smart devices will play an important role in the management of these devices.

12.8 Overview of Next Generation Wireless Network Architecture

12.8.1 Introduction

The 5G network architecture is divided into two categories: 5G core functionality and 5G radio access. 5G core functionality includes flexibility in the deployment process for network functions, optimization of service enablers, and utilization of Software Defined Networking (SDN) and Network Function Virtualization (NFV). On the other hand, the biggest challenge for 5G radio access is to integrate all radio access technologies (RATs) [9] in one platform and provide effortless and seamless mobility to the user.

12.8.2 Heterogeneous Network

The next generation wireless network architecture will have multiple folds. Due to the complex and modern high-speed applications, the next generation network must provide higher throughput and lower latency. This will be achieved by applying the concept of a heterogeneous network. To fulfill the demands of the futuristic customer-centric applications where voice, video, and images travel across the globe, the next generation architecture must provide 24 × 7 connectivity and connectivity depends upon the coverage. Now the issue becomes how to increase the cellular coverage. It has been observed that cellular coverage plays a pivotal role in the enhancement of signals. The major issue faced by the network operators today is to provide uniform coverage, especially in metro cities which are filled with high rise buildings. One way is to broaden the existing macro network by adding more *eNodeBs* [10]. However, the installation of macro sites can be very expensive.

By using relay nodes in the heterogeneous network, we can improve the coverage.

The following methods are used to improve cell coverage:

1. Introduction of small cells in addition to the low power base station (eNodeB).

There are two reasons for this:

- To increase the capacity of hotspots.
- To increase the network coverage.

They can be used both outdoors and indoors to improve network performance and service quality by shuffling loads from large macro cells to small cells (Figure 12.6).

1. Introducing relay nodes—Without a wired backhaul connection, the long term evolution (LTE) relay [11] in a fixed relay infrastructure can be introduced (Figure 12.7).

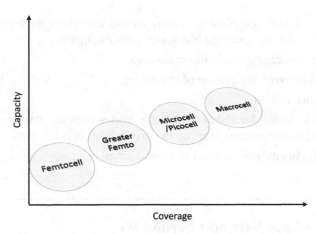

FIGURE 12.6
Cells' capacity vs coverage.

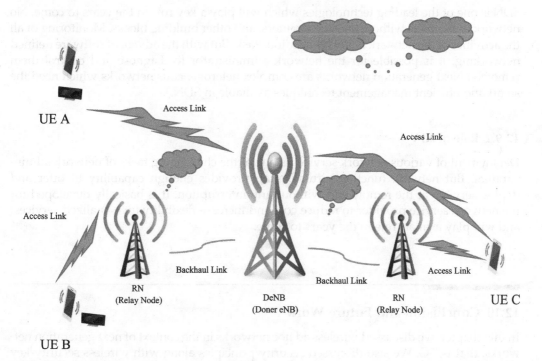

FIGURE 12.7
Heterogeneous network.

The relays supply messages between the base station and mobile stations through multi-hop communication. The relay node is connected to a donor evolved node B (eNB) and from a user equipment (UE) perspective, the relay node will act as an eNB. From a donor perspective, the relay node will be seen as a UE. The advantages of LTE relay nodes are:

- Increased network density to ensure good signal level in all areas.
- Network coverage extension.

- No need to install complete base stations and the relays can be quickly installed so that they fill the coverage blackspot with high gain.
- Increased coverage outside the main area.
- Cascaded network (extension of coverage).
- Rapid network rollout.
  - No need to install backhaul. LTE relay nodes provide a very easy method to extend network coverage during an early rollout of a network.
- Remote radio heads–can be used to extend small cell coverage.

12.9 Wireless Ad hoc Networks beyond 5G

12.9.1 Role of SDN

SDN is one of the leading technologies which will play a key role in the years to come. No network is complete without switches, routers, and other building blocks. Monitoring of all the activities of the network is always a tedious task. But with the advent of software defined networking, it is possible for the network administrator to diagnose and control them remotely. Next generation networks are complex heterogeneous networks which need the smart and efficient management techniques available in SDN.

12.9.2 Role of NFV

Deployment of various network services is one of the challenging tasks of network administrators. But network function virtualization provides enough capability to offer and deploy services at the remote end without any interruption. It is basically developed for the network service provider to reduce cost and increase flexibility (personalized services) and will play a smart role in the years to come.

12.10 Conclusion and Future Work

In this chapter, we discussed wireless ad hoc networks in the context of next generation networks, that is, 5G. We also discussed security principles along with wireless security key management processes. We provide insights into various QoS parameters in an ad hoc network along with different categories of routing protocols with examples. The LTE architecture is discussed, including the recent advantage of VoLTE in using Evolved Packet Core (EPC). Cell coverage is increased by using small cells in a macro cell. The next generation modern, futuristic applications along with traditional applications of the mobile ad hoc network were explained. A key role of SDN and network function virtualization (NFV) was discussed.

In the future, SDN and NFV will play key roles in managing hardware devices like switches, routers, and so on. The next generation network will be a very complex network because it is going to integrate various technologies. Monitoring and controlling are two key management issues which will be handled through software. The diagnostic capability is also very important. We explored all issues of wireless ad hoc networks including routing algorithms, QoS parameters, and security in the context of traditional ad hoc networks and 5G.

Acknowledgments

We thank our parents and family members for their support and motivation. We would also like to thank our colleagues who helped us in the entire process of writing.

References

1. D. Wu. "QoS Provisioning in Wireless Networks," *Wireless Communications and Mobile Computing*, 2005;5:957–969.
2. G. Jisha, P. Samuel and V. Paul. "Role of Gateways in MANET Integration Scenarios," *Indian Journal of Science and Technology*, 2016;9(3), January.
3. Z. Li and H. Shen. "A QoS-Oriented Distributed Routing Protocol for Hybrid Wireless Networks," *IEEE Transactions on Mobile Computing*, 2014;13(3), March.
4. A. Al-Fuqaha, M. Guizani, M. Mohammadi, M. Aledhari and M. Ayyash. "Internet of Things: A Survey on Enabling Technologies, Protocols, and Applications," *IEEE Communication Surveys & Tutorials*, 2015;17(4), Fourth Quarter.
5. S. Hakak, F. Anwar, S.A. Latif, G. Gilkar and M.K. Alam. "Impact of Packet Size and Node Mobility Pause Time on Average End to End Delay and Jitter on MANET's," *ICCCE,IEEE*, 2014. Kualalampur, Malaysia.
6. Z.D. Katheeth and K.K. Raman. "Performance Evaluation with Throughput and Packet Delivery Ratio for Mobile Ad-Hoc Networks," *IJARCCE*, 2014;3(5), May, ISSN (Online): 2278-1021, ISSN (Print): 2319-5940.
7. G. Hasenpfad and M. Iwamura. "NGMN View on 5G Architecture," ©2015 IEEE.
8. A.F. Ibikunle, J.A. Sarumi and E.O. Shonibare. "Comparative Analysis of Routing Technologies in Next Generation Converged IP Network," *International Journal of Engineering & Technology IJET-IJENS*, 2011;11(02), April.
9. A.P. Singh, A.S. Chawla and Surjeet. "Performance Issues and Behavioral Analysis of Routing Protocols in MANETs," *International Journal of Communications, Network And System Sciences*, 2016;9:431–439.
10. T. Xu, D. Gao, P. Dong and H. Zhang. "Defending against New-Flow Attack in SDN-Based Internet of Things," *Special Section on Security and Privacy in Applications and Services for Future Internet of Things*, 2017;5.
11. Z.E. Ankarali, B. Peköz and H. Arslan. "Flexible Radio Access Beyond 5G: A Future Projection on Waveform, Numerology, and Frame Design Principles," *Special Section on Physical and Medium Access Control Layer Advances in 5G Wireless Networks*, 2017;5.

13

Cognitive Radio Sensor Networks: Fundamentals and Applications

P.T.V. Bhuvaneswari

CONTENTS

13.1 Introduction

13.1.1 Wireless Sensor Networks (WSN)

A Wireless Sensor Network (WSN) is a wireless network created with a large number of nodes which possess the capabilities of sensing, processing, and communicating. These nodes are normally battery operated, hence to extend the lifetime of the network, low power wireless communication is adopted. Initially, they found applications in the defense sector. Later, due to the appreciable characteristic features of this network, they were employed in environmental applications, namely pollution monitoring and disaster management. In recent years, they have been used in other applications, namely health care, smart home, smart logistics, and industries [1]. The list of nomenclatures used in this chapter is given in Table 13.1.

Conceptually, a WSN consists of a dense network of nodes as shown in Figure 13.1. The deployment of nodes can be either manual or random and is made on the basis of the application. In manual deployment, to ensure network connectivity, the nodes are placed within the overlapping communication range of other nodes. However, in random deployment, more control overheads may be required to establish connectivity. The standard topologies adopted are star and mesh. In a dense network scenario, a multi-hop mode of communication is employed due to the battery-operated nature of these nodes. Each sensor node can perform several functions, namely sense the physical parameters of the application, process the sensed raw data to extract the feature of interest, and transmit the information to the Base Station (BS) using neighbors as relay nodes. In some applications, additional functions, namely data compression and encryption, may also be incorporated [9]. The BS can be centralized or distributed on the basis of the density of

TABLE 13.1

List of Nomenclatures

Abbreviation	Expansion
CR	Cognitive Radio
CRSN	Cognitive Radio Sensor Network
WSN	Wireless Sensor Network
OSA	Opportunistic Spectrum Access
BS	Base Station
PUs	Primary Users
SUs	Secondary Users
CU	Cognitive Users
QoS	Quality of Service
WLAN	Wireless Local Area Network
CRU	Cognitive Radio Unit
MAC	Medium Access Control
CSN	Cognitive Sensor Node
FC	Fusion Center
SDR	Software-Defined Radio
DLL	Data Link Layer
FEC	Forward Error Correction
ARQ	Automatic Repeat Request
MEMS	Micro Electro Mechanical System
VANETS	Vehicular Ad hoc NETworkS
WAVE	Wireless Access for Vehicular Environments

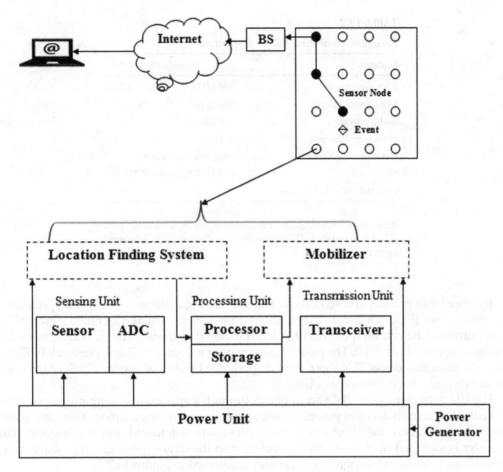

FIGURE 13.1
Deployment scenario of wireless sensor network.

nodes. In time critical applications, to mitigate delay, distributed BS can be used. The technical specifications of WSN prescribed by Institute of Electrical and Electronics Engineers (IEEE) 802.15.4 standard are presented in Table 13.2.

13.1.2 Need for Cognitive Concept in WSN

The applications of WSNs can be categorized into periodic and event-driven. WSNs can be designed to operate in either licensed or unlicensed bands. In the first case, an expensive spectrum is leased; this may significantly impact the cost of deployment. In the latter case, a crowded spectrum problem may be experienced due to the use of unlicensed bands by various devices, namely wireless local area networks (WLAN), Bluetooth, ultra wideband (UWB), and so on, In order to enhance spectrum efficiency, the concept of spectrum sharing has been suggested, in which the spectrum is dynamically shared among WSNs and other wireless systems that have the capability to operate in the industrial, scientific, and medical radio band (ISM band) [2–7]. The concept of Cognitive Radio (CR) introduced by Joseph Mitola [8] can be well applied to tackle the above situation. Here the users are

TABLE 13.2

Specification of IEEE 802.15.4 Standard

Features	Specification
Radio spectrum	868 MHz, 915 MHz, 2.4 GHz
Maximum data rate	250 kbps
Radio power	>1 mW
Maximum Range	1–100 m
Network topologies	Star, tree, and Mesh
Media access	CSMA-CA, optional TDD
Optional security features	AES-128

Abbreviation: CSMA/CA, carrier-sense multiple access with collision avoidance; TDD, time division duplex; AES, Advanced Encryption Standard.

categorized into primary and secondary. The user having a license to access the spectrum is a primary user (PUs) while the other, unlicensed user is known as a secondary user (SUs). The portion of the unused spectrum of PU can be shared by the SU. The SU is also referred to as the Cognitive User (CU). The basic requirement in a Cognitive Radio Network (CRN) is that the transmissions of SUs should not degrade the Quality of Service (QoS) of the operators who have been licensed as PUs.

The CU detects the potential vacant bands through a spectrum sensing procedure, then executes a spectrum decision process to select the channel to be occupied. To enable seamless communication, the spectrum handoff procedure is initiated and the ongoing data transfer is switched over from serving spectrum to the target spectrum. This sequence of operations is known as a cognitive cycle and is depicted in Figure 13.2.

13.1.3 Potential Benefits of Cognitive Radio in WSN

WSNs can be empowered with CR capabilities by allowing sensor nodes to act either as PUs or SUs and thus yield to a new sensor networking paradigm, referred to as

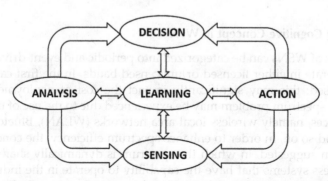

FIGURE 13.2
Cognitive radio cycle.

Cognitive Radio WSN (CRWSN). The salient features of dynamic spectrum access are discussed below:

- *Dynamic spectrum access*: In general, the existing WSN deployments assume fixed spectrum allocation. As per IEEE 802.15.4, three different frequencies of operation are suggested for WSN. They are 868, 915, and 2450 MHz. Most of the applications of WSN use the unlicensed band which is 2.4 GHz. This spectrum is also used by other devices, namely WLAN hotspots, personal digital assistant (PDA), and Bluetooth devices. Due to the wide usage of this band, WSN may experience a crowded spectrum problem. This may degrade the QoS of WSN applications. Hence to alleviate this issue and to maximize the network performance, WSN must use an opportunistic spectrum access scheme wherein the nodes in the sensor network cooperate efficiently with other types of users in the band [9,10].

- *Opportunistic channel access*: In WSN, most of the applications are event-driven. Sensor nodes generate traffic whenever an event is detected. Normally, the traffic is bursty in nature. Moreover, in the dense deployment scenario, a large number of nodes present within the event area might have generated traffic by sensing the event. Hence, they may compete to access the channel. This might introduce collisions in the network which in turn can affect the reliability of the application. Further, retransmission of lost packets may increase bandwidth wastage and repeated transmission of lost packets also leads to excessive power consumption and packet delay. Hence, sensor nodes with CR capability can resolve the above issue by opportunistically accessing the other available channels [11,12].

- *Adaptability to the wireless environment*: The wireless channel used in WSN is time varying in nature. Due to the effect of multipath propagation, fading of the signal can occur. The effect can be further worsened if the application supports node mobility. As discussed earlier, packet loss and retransmission increase energy consumption in the network which may, in turn, affect the lifetime of the application. CR capable sensor nodes can be designed to adapt to the changing channel conditions. This can increase bandwidth efficiency and reduce power consumption in the network.

- *Overlaid concurrent deployment of multiple WSNs*: Due to the battery-operated nature of a WSN, to obtain meta data of the application, dense deployment is preferred in most cases. Further to sense multiple features of the application, it is possible to have an overlapping deployment of concurrent sensor networks. Hence to increase the performance of these overlapping sensor networks, dynamic spectrum management is suggested which enables efficient sharing of the resource among the nodes in the network [13].

- *Support access to different spectrum regulations*: The spectrum regulation rule and availability of band differ in each country. Hence it becomes essential to manufacture different products to adhere to the variations. This may impose an additional cost on deployment. To overcome the above limitation, CR enablement can be the best solution. The WSN works adaptively with the existing bands, thereby minimizing the cost involved in the production.

Hence from the above benefits, it can be concluded that equipping sensor nodes with CR capabilities can definitely enhance the QoS of an application and enhance the longevity of the application. Moreover, it is possible to generalize the product development. Thus, the new networking paradigm which is CRSN will be a promising technology in the next-generationwireless network.

13.1.4 Challenges in CRSN

Despite the potential advantages of CRSN, the realization of these networks in real time imposes several challenges which are detailed in this section. In CRSN, ensuring the QoS of the PU is of great concern as they are the licensed user [14–29].

- *Hardware*: The conventional WSN does sensing, processing, and communicating. When compared to them, the CRSN performs additional functionalities, namely spectrum sensing, spectrum analyzing, spectrum decisions, and spectrum handoff. To accomplish these functionalities, the sensor nodes are equipped with a CR unit. This unit has to dynamically adapt to the communication parameters, namely carrier frequency, transmission power, and modulation. The unit has to select the best available channel, share the spectrum with other users, and manage the spectrum mobility.

- *Adaptability to changing topology*: The topology of WSN is mostly stochastic in nature. This is due to the mobility of the nodes. The mobility model exhibited by the application also makes a significant contribution to the topological changes. The network lifetime is influenced by these changes. As the control overhead involved in ensuring reliability is increased tremendously, this may cause energy depletion. Hardware malfunctioning may also occur due to energy depletion. Further changing topologies can also reflect on the routing mechanism. Hence, an adaptive self-configuration topology mechanism can be introduced in CRSN to resolve all the above limitations.

- *Channel Selection*: In traditional WSN, the Medium Control Access (MAC) protocol devised by IEEE 802.15.4 standard provides resource scheduling to the nodes in the network. By adopting the CR concept in WSN, no dedicated channel can be received to send the data. The nodes negotiate with the neighbors and select a channel for data communication. This does not impose any challenges as long as both PUs and SUs are cooperative. Since the nodes are dynamic, it is cumbersome to attain cooperation among them. Further, the asynchronous operation of PUs and SUs demands intelligence in the channel selection process.

- *Fault Tolerance*: The conventional WSNs are mostly driven by a battery. The energy depletion may result in network partitioning. Sustainability of the applications under this faulty environment can be a major challenge. To address this issue, CRSN needs to possess the properties of self-forming, self-configuration, and self-healing. Whenever any nodes or links fail, an alternative effective path has to be discovered to ensure guaranteed packet delivery. Faults can occur due to various reasons, namely hardware or software malfunctioning and natural calamities (fire, floods, earthquakes, volcanic eruptions, etc.,). Faults are of different types, including node faults, network faults, and sink faults.

- *Scalability*: Some applications deployed by CRSN need to be dense. Thus cooperation among the nodes for sharing the spectrum may be challenging. Due to node mobility and energy depletion, additional topological changes may occur. New nodes can be also added in the network. The above events may result in a heterogeneous CRSN. Hence, algorithms and protocols developed for CRSN should possess the capability to resolve these issues caused by the growing size of the network.

- *Power Consumption*: The conventional WSN is a power constrained network. By enabling CR, energy depletion is further increased by the following mechanisms which include spectrum sensing, channel negotiation, route discovery, transmission and reception of data packets, back—off, data processing, and frequent spectrum handoff. A few reports suggest the use of multiple antennas to monitor the PUs' activities. This may also increase energy consumption. Energy harvesting can be an alternative solution. However, it may not be applicable for all applications. Hence it can be concluded that power consumption needs to be considered as one of the major performance metrics as it directly affects the network lifetime.

- *Quality of Service (QoS)*: The QoS in conventional WSNs can be characterized by four difference parameters, namely bandwidth, delay, jitter, and reliability. Due to resource constraints, achieving acceptable QoS becomes the major challenge. However, most of the applications of WSNs are critical and are in real time, thus QoS cannot be compromised. Equipping CR in sensor nodes may induce additional challenges such as protection of the incumbent PU from the SU. The accuracy of a spectrum sensing algorithm makes a significant contribution in addressing the above issue. By reducing the probability of false alarms and misdetections, this can be achieved.

13.2 CRSN Architecture

The wireless communication architecture of a CRSN is shown Figure 13.3. It consists of PU and the SU, also known as the cognitive sensor node (CSN). The PU is served by the primary BS. The CSN is classified into conventional, mobile, and high power. In the considered scenario, two BS are assumed to serve PUs 1 and 2. The sink node is considered as the destination node for both the PU and CSN. An infrastructure-based communication model is assumed in the considered scenario. The information obtained from the field is conveyed to the sink node by multiple hops.

The main duty of the sensor nodes is to perform sensing on the environment. In addition to this conventional sensing duty, CSN nodes also perform sensing on the spectrum. Depending on the spectrum availability, sensor nodes transmit their readings in an opportunistic manner to their next hop CSN, then to the sink. The BS is connected to a spectrum broker which does spectrum sensing in a cooperative manner to enable opportunistic spectrum access to cognitive secondary nodes. In some cases, the sink node may also be equipped with CR capability. Then it is called a cognitive radio sink. In the assumed scenario, the sensing node, in addition to event sensing, also exchanges information related to group formulation, spectrum allocation, spectrum handover, and route determination for dynamic topology.

The other assumption considered in the presented scenario is that a few CSN nodes have high power [30]. They can perform an additional function, namely local spectrum bargaining, when compared to other types of CSN. Hence, they play an active part in the network

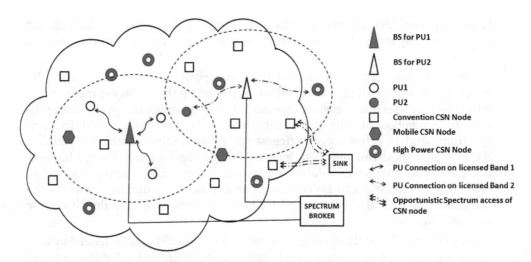

FIGURE 13.3
Architecture of CRSN.

topology. Further, the sink node is assumed to operate with unlimited power to enable uninterrupted reception of events from the application.

13.2.1 CRSN Node Structure

The hardware structure of the CRSN node is presented in Figure 13.4. It mainly consists of a sensing unit, processor unit, memory unit, power unit, and CR transceiver unit. Some applications may demand mobility and location update. Hence the CRSN nodes can have mobilization and localization units as well.

The main difference between conventional sensor nodes [9] and CRSN nodes in terms of the hardware structure is the presence of a CR transceiver in CRSN nodes.

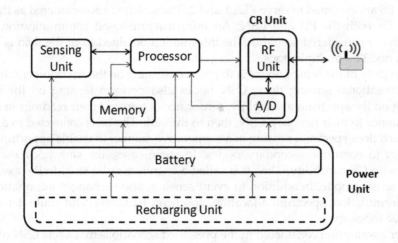

FIGURE 13.4
Hardware structure of CRSN node.

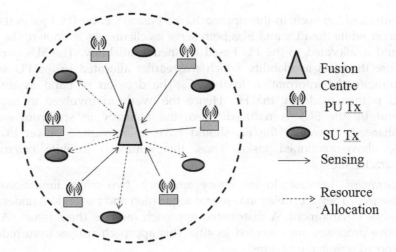

FIGURE 13.5
Centralized approach in CRSN.

Further, the CR unit also enables the sensor nodes to dynamically adapt their communication parameters, namely carrier frequency, transmission power, and modulation. However, the inherit limitations possessed by conventional WSNs, namely power, memory, and bandwidth, also apply for CRSNs. These limitations may impose difficulty in exploiting the features of the CR concept.

13.2.2 CRSN Topology

- *Centralized versus Distributed*: The deployment of nodes in CRSN can be classified into two approaches, namely distributed and centralized, as illustrated in Figures 13.5 and 13.6.

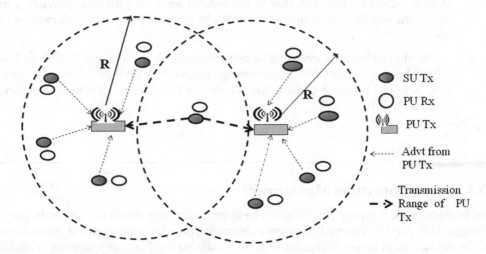

FIGURE 13.6
Distributed approach in CRSN.

- *Centralized Approach*: In this approach, the Fusion Center (FC) plays the role of server while the PUs and SUs both serve as clients. As is known, the licensed band is allocated to the PU based on their availability. The SUs periodically sense the band availability which was earlier allocated to the PU and communicate the information to the FC. The decision of band assignment to SU is then made by the FC. Hence the overhead involved in acquiring a band by the SUs is reduced. Also, the accuracy in spectrum sensing is enhanced. However, the FC should have uninterrupted power to perform the above-mentioned tasks. Thus, this approach exhibits heterogeneous characteristics.

- *Distributed Approach*: In the above approach, two major limitations can be observed. They are: delay in resource acquisition and packet loss under a highly mobile environment. A distributed approach resolves these issues. All of the above processes are executed locally. This approach suffers from hidden and exposed terminal problems.

- *Infrastructure versus Ad hoc*: The network topologies in CRSN are more application specific. They can be categorized into infrastructure and ad hoc. The scenario illustrated in Figure 13.3 falls under the first category while that in Figure 13.5 shows an ad hoc topology.
  - *Infrastructure topology*: In this topology, the BS controls the entire network operation. Network configuration, address assignment, resource scheduling, and data forwarding are the common functions executed in a traditional WSN. In addition to the above, the operations related to the cognitive concept are also performed.
  - *Ad hoc topology*: In this topology, the network operations are accomplished without the infrastructural element. The nodes in the network need to have the intelligence to execute the all of the above-mentioned tasks. Spectrum sensing is performed by each node individually or collaboratively in a distributed way. Similarly, spectrum allocation is also done on the basis of the individual decisions of the sensor nodes. The communication overhead involved in terms of control data is reduced. However, due to the hidden terminal problem, inaccuracy in spectrum sensing can result which may, in turn, degrade the performance of the PU.

  The above classification can also be sub-classified as clustered CRSN, mobile CRSN, homogeneous CRSN, and heterogeneous CRSN on the basis of scalability, mobility, and resource distribution which can be in terms of power, memory, and bandwidth.

13.3 Dynamic Spectrum Management

The benefits of a CR concept in WSN can be appreciated only when the spectrum usage is efficient. This can be achieved through a dynamic spectrum management framework in which the spectrum access is regulated dynamically on the basis of spectrum availability and access demand. It is accomplished with the processes of spectrum sensing, spectrum decision, and spectrum handoff.

13.3.1 Spectrum Sensing

Spectrum sensing is the process by which the presence of a PU is detected in order to opportunistically allocate the licensed band of the PU to an SU. Sensing can be classified into narrow band sensing and wide band sensing on the basis of the spectrum band to be detected. Several sensing methods are presented in the literature. Popular methods are matched filter [31], energy detection [32], feature detection [33], and interference temperature [34]. Most of them are not suitable for CRSN due to the resource-constrained aspect of the sensor nodes. Hybrid sensing and cooperative sensing can be the best alternative methods for CRSN.

13.3.2 Spectrum Decision

Spectrum decision is the process in which the CRSN nodes analyze the sensed information obtained from the previous process to make a decision about the channel and the transmission parameters. This process is tedious, as the channel parameters are stochastic in nature. The existing spectrum decision methods proposed for CR networks cannot be considered for CRSN due to the involvement of high power consumption. As the sensor nodes, which can be either PU or SU, are driven by batteries, the number of extra control packets involved in making the decision is large. This may lead to failure of the nodes. Hence these solutions are not feasible for CRSN. So, a power aware spectrum decision algorithm has to be devised for CRSN. In [35], the authors have a developed distributed spectrum decision scheme based on clustered architecture.

13.3.3 Spectrum Handoff

Spectrum handoff [36] is the process in which the nodes switch the ongoing data transfer from one node to another. This can be done under occurrence of two different circumstances; one, when a CRSN node detects the absence of the PU through the spectrum sensing process and decides to utilize the available channel, and second, the nodes may wish to switch over to an available healthy channel to enhance the communication performance. Several methods are presented in the literature [36–39] for CRN. Since they do not address the limitations of CRSN challenges, it is not feasible to apply them. A central spectrum allocation scheme is developed for CRSN in [40], which aims to minimize spectrum handoff.

13.4 Protocol Stack of CRSN

In this section, the function of each communication layer is presented, including physical, data link, network, transport, and application layers.

13.4.1 Physical Layer

The major function of the physical layer of a conventional WSN is to regulate the interaction between the data link layer and the physical wireless medium. In CRSN, an additional responsibility of this layer is to perform spectrum sensing and dynamically reconfigure the various transmission parameters, namely operating frequency, modulation, channel coding, and output power to ensure the performance of the network. Reconfiguration of parameters is achieved through software-defined radio (SDR) in which the RF front-end transmitters and receivers [41] are designed with a built-in reconfigurable ability. Due to the low cost and resource-constrained nature of sensor nodes, implementing SDR is considered to be a significant challenge in CRSN. Running high computational sensing algorithms to detect the presence of the PU is yet another challenge in CRSN [42].

13.4.2 Data Link Layer

The basic functions of the data link layer (DLL) are resource scheduling, error control, and flow control. The MAC protocol takes care of resource scheduling. As the CRSN works with the principle of dynamic spectrum management, the conventional MAC protocol used in WSN has to be modified. An on—demand MAC protocol that takes into consideration the drastic topological changes is preferred to enhance the QoS of the network [43–46]. The error control schemes, namely Forward Error Correction (FEC) and automatic repeat request (ARQ) used in WSN can also be applied to CRSN due to their simplicity.

13.4.3 Network Layer

Data exchange is the key function of the network layer. CRSN supports both ad hoc and multi-hop networking. Hence it inherits all the major issues of the network layer from WSN. The routing protocols for CRSN need to be energy—aware, data-centric, attribute-based addressing, and location-aware. Several routing schemes [47,48,36] are proposed which aim to provide joint spectrum and routing decisions based on on-demand routing to adhere to the requirements of CRSN.

CRSN is also energy-constrained. Hence the number of hop counts involved in the routing mechanism needs to be kept minimal. Due to spectrum mobility, determination of the hop count is governed by the channel characteristics, namely interference, operating frequency, and bandwidth. Hence the routing protocol of CRSN needs to consider them as additional routing metrics to ensure guaranteed data delivery. The routing algorithms also need to select the minimal channel switching path to reduce delay involved in data forwarding [36]. Determination of an efficient routing path also depends on the spectrum decision process. In this process, the neighboring status of CRSN node changes with respect to the operating frequency [49]. Further, rerouting challenges can also be experienced due to spectrum handoff.

13.4.4 Transport Layer

The main responsibility of the transport layer is to provide end-to-endreliability and congestion control to meet the application-specific QoS requirement [50]. CRSN inherits the transport layer issues from WSN. The dynamic spectrum management adopted in CRSN brings additional challenges when compared to WSN. Lack of a fixed frequency set over the path established between the sensing node and sink node can significantly vary the channel characteristics. The end-to-end delay and packet loss may be influenced by spectrum handoff and spectrum mobility. Due to periodic spectrum sensing, an additional delay can also be introduced which may further degrade the performance. Several transport layer solutions for WSN that aim to provide reliable end-to-end delivery with minimum energy consumption and congestion avoidance are presented in [51–53]. However, they do not consider the dynamic spectrum access.

13.4.5 Application Layer

The major function of the application layer is to generate information by extracting the features of the event being sensed and communicate them to the sink. The supplementary services provided by the application layer include query processing, generation of an event of interest, data dissemination, data aggregation, and fusion [2]. The application layer protocol of CRSN has to support a wide range of applications. Hence the protocol needs to analyze, organize the queries, and perform other services as mentioned above to address the requirements of the application of interest.

13.5 Potential Application

Conventional WSN can be applied to a tremendous number of applications. Initially, they were employed in military applications. Later, the attractive features of WSN led to usage in environmental monitoring, critical health care, home automation, industrial automation, and so on. The resource constraints of WSN, namely power, memory, and bandwidth, prohibit the above applications from attaining the required QoS. This can be resolved to some extent by employing the CR concept in WSN. In this section, major applications are discussed to provide an in-depth understanding of the technology.

13.5.1 Disaster Rescue Operation

The conventional cellular networks fail to provide communication in a disaster situation. The disaster may be natural or man-made. The main reason can be water logging, power failure, and infrastructural damages caused due to disaster. This may slow down the rescue operation. Under such circumstances, WSN can be employed as an alternative. The traffic generated may be unpredicted and will depend on the level of the calamity. Due to the constraints possessed by the WSN in terms of bandwidth, power, and memory, the QoS offered by this network may not be adequate. The dynamic spectrum management of CR provides flexibility in accessing multiple channels. Thus the resource offered to the network by employing CR in WSN can enhance the data rate, throughput, and capacity. Hence CRSN can be a promising solution for this application when compared to WSN.

13.5.2 Health Care

The advancement in Micro-Electro-Mechanical Systems (MEMS) technology has led to the development of wearable sensors and implantable sensors. This has given a new dimension to the use of WSN in critical health care applications. In 2011, the IEEE 802.15 Task Group 6 (BAN) [54] has approved a draft of a standard developed for Body Area Network (BAN) technology. Wireless BAN-assisted health care systems are in practice in some remote areas in Nepal and India [55,56]. They can be used in places where the number of health specialists is relatively low. Yet another application could be an Intensive Care Unit (ICU) which demands continuous monitoring of a patient's vital parameters, namely Electrocardiography (ECG), pulse rate, heart rate, Saturation of Peripheral Oxygen (SpO_2), and so on. Employing manpower for such monitoring may be cumbersome or may provide error data. WSN can be the best alternative, in which patient can be tied into wireless wearable vital parameter sensors that can provide 24×7 monitoring. Further, abnormalities in vital parameters can be set as events in the application, so that whenever they arise, they can be attended to. Since multiple sensors are used in this application, heavy traffic can result in the network. Due to the spectrum crowding problem [11], the QoS of the application may be degraded. To alleviate this issue, CR can be adopted in WSN. Again, the dynamic spectrum management feature of CRN aids in enhancing QoS.

13.5.3 Industrial Automation and Indoor Applications

WSNs also find applications in automation, including home automation, industrial automation, warehousing automation, and so on. An indoor environment can be the common feature for the above applications. Thus, power will not be a constraint, as the sensing nodes can be recharged with an alternative power source [10]. Moreover, nodes in most of the applications are fixed. Hence, table driven routing and fixed resource scheduling can be used. Due to bandwidth and memory constraints, a large volume of data cannot be exchanged in the network. The usage of other ISM-based technology, namely WLAN, Bluetooth, and UWB can also be used along with WSN. Thus it is possible to build a heterogeneous network based on the requirements of the application. Hence employing CRN will definitely improve the performance of the application [57].

13.5.4 Logistics

The ad hoc feature of WSN has produced a new kind of network known as VANETS (Vehicular ad hoc Network). The IEEE 1609.4 standard has proposed multi-channel operations in wireless access for vehicular environments (WAVE). The WAVE system operates on the 75 MHz spectrum in the 5.9 GHz band with one control channel and six service channels. All vehicular users need to contend for channel access and transmit the information in the 5.9 GHz band. However, it still suffers from spectrum insufficiency problems. A study on spectrum scarcity and the requirements of CR in WAVE has been made in [58–60]. The scope of CRSN in logistics is investigated in [61,62].

13.5.5 Multimedia and Surveillance

Reliable and timely delivery of event features can be the prime objective of multimedia applications in which the traffic can be audio, still images, and video [31]. Using resource-constrained sensor networks in such applications can be more challenging. For example, in surveillance, a high bandwidth will be required to monitor real-time traffic. The variations in temporal and spatial characteristics of the channel can also induce additional challenges for the QoS. So CRSN can be used instead of WSN, as it provides the sensor nodes the flexibility to change channels dynamically based on the environmental conditions and application-specific QoS [63,64].

13.6 Conclusion

CRSN is the upcoming technology which embeds the CR concept in WSNs. In this chapter, the fundamentals of CRSN including challenges, requirements, and potential benefits are discussed in detail. Further, the architecture and applications are also presented. The significance of dynamic spectrum management is also discussed.

References

1. J. Yick, B. Mukherjee, D. Ghosal. Wireless sensor network survey, *Elsevier Journal On Computer Networks*, Vol. 52, pp. 2292–2330, 2008.
2. G. Vijay, E. Ben Ali Bdira, M. Ibnkahla, Cognition in wireless sensor networks: A perspective. *IEEE Sens. J.* 2011, 11, 582–592.
3. O.B. Akan, O.B. Karli, O. Ergul, Cognitive radio sensor networks. *IEEE Netw.* 2009, 23, 34–40.
4. A.O. Bicen, V.C. Gungor, O.B. Akan, Delay-sensitive and multimedia communication in cognitive radio sensor networks. *Ad. Hoc. Netw.* 2012, 10, 816–830.
5. B. Atakan, O.B. Akan, Biological foraging-inspired communication in intermittently connected mobile cognitive radio ad hoc networks. *IEEE Trans. Veh. Technol.* 2012, 61, 2651–2658.
6. Z. Liang, D. Zhao, Quality of Service Performance of a Cognitive Radio Sensor Network. In *Proceedings of the IEEE International Conference on Communications (ICC)*, Cape Town, South Africa, May 23–27, 2010; pp. 1–5.
7. J.A. Han, W.S. Jeon, D.G. Jeong, Energy-efficient channel management scheme for cognitive radio sensor networks. *IEEE Trans. Veh. Technol.* 2011, 60, 1905–1910.
8. J. Mitola, G.Q. Maguire, Cognitive radio: Making software radios more personal, *IEEE Personal Communications*, 1999.
9. I.F. Akyildiz, W. Su, Y. Sankarasubramaniam, E. Cayirci, A survey on sensor networks, *IEEE Communications Magazine*, Vol. 40, No. 2, pp. 102–114, Aug. 2002.
10. G. Zhou, J.A. Stankovic, S.H. Son, "Crowded Spectrum in Wireless Sensor Networks," in *Proc. Third Workshop on Embedded Networked Sensors (EmNets 2006)*, 2006.
11. G. Zhou, J.A. Stankovic, S. Son, Crowded Spectrum in Wireless Sensor Networks. In *Proceedings of the Third Workshop on Embedded Networked Sensors (EmNets 2006)*, Cambridge, MA, USA, 30–31 May 2006.
12. FCC. Spectrum policy task force report. Technical Report ET Docket, no. 02-155, Federal Communications Commission, Washington DC, USA, 2002.
13. J. Borms, K. Steenhaut, B. Lemmens, Low-Overhead Dynamic Multi-Channel MAC for Wireless Sensor Networks. In *Proceedings of the Seventh European Conference on Wireless Sensor Networks (EWSN'10)*, Coimbra, Portugal, 17–19 February 2010; pp. 81–96.
14. I.F. Akyildiz, W.Y. Lee, M.C. Vuran, S. Mohanty, A survey on spectrum management in cognitive radio networks. *IEEE Commun. Mag.* 2008, 46, 40–48.
15. B. Wang, K. Liu, Advances in cognitive radio networks: A survey. *IEEE J. Sel. Top. Signal Proc.* 2011, 5, 5–23.
16. A. Umamaheswari, V. Subashini, P. Subhapriya, Survey on Performance, Reliability and Future Proposal of Cognitive Radio under Wireless Computing. In *Proceedings of the Third International Conference on Computing Communication & Networking Technologies (ICCCNT)*, Tamilnadu, India, July 26–28, 2012; pp. 1–6.
17. T. Yucek, H. Arslan, A survey of spectrum sensing algorithms for cognitive radio applications. *IEEE Commun. Surv. Tutor.* 2009, 11, 116–130.
18. A. De Domenico, E.C. Strinati, M. Di Benedetto, A survey on MAC strategies for cognitive radio networks. *IEEE Commun. Surv. Tutor.* 2012, 14, 21–44.
19. A. Attar, H. Tang, A.V. Vasilakos, F.R. Yu, V.C.M. Leung, A survey of security challenges in cognitive radio networks: Solutions and future research directions. *Proc. IEEE* 2012, 100, 3172–3186.
20. T. Zhang, X. Yu, Spectrum Sharing in Cognitive Radio Using Game Theory—A Survey. In *Proceedings of the Sixth International Conference on Wireless Communications Networking and Mobile Computing (WiCOM)*, Chengdu, China, September 23–25, 2010; pp. 1–5.
21. M. Bkassiny, Y. Li, S. Jayaweera, A survey on machine-learning techniques in cognitive radios. *IEEE Commun. Surv. Tutor.* 2013, 15, 1136–1159.
22. H. Wang, Z. Gao, Y. Guo, Y. Huang, A Survey of Range-Based Localization Algorithms for Cognitive Radio Networks. In *Proceedings of the Second International Conference on Consumer*

Electronics, Communications and Networks (CECNet), Hubei, China, April 21–23, 2012; pp. 844–847.

23. M. Masonta, M. Mzyece, N. Ntlatlapa, Spectrum decision in cognitive radio networks: A survey. *IEEE Commun. Surv. Tutor.* 2013, 15, 1088–1107.

24. D.D. Ariananda, M.K. Lakshmanan, H. Nikookar, A Survey on Spectrum Sensing Techniques for Cognitive Radio. In *Proceedings of the Second International Workshop on Cognitive Radio and Advanced Spectrum Management (CogART 2009)*, Aalborg, Denmark, May 18–20, 2009; pp. 74–79.

25. E. Tragos, S. Zeadally, A. Fragkiadakis, V. Siris, Spectrum assignment in cognitive radio networks: A comprehensive survey. *IEEE Commun. Surv. Tutor.* 2013, 15, 1108–1135.

26. H. Wang, H. Qin, L. Zhu, A Survey on MAC Protocols for Opportunistic Spectrum Access in Cognitive Radio Networks. In *Proceedings of the IEEE International Conference on Computer Science and Software Engineering*, Hubei, China, December 12–14, 2008; pp. 214–218.

27. A.G. Fragkiadakis, E.Z. Tragos, I.G. Askoxylakis, A survey on security threats and detection techniques in cognitive radio networks. *IEEE Commun. Surv. Tutor.* 2013, 15, 428–445. Sensors 2013, 13 11224.

28. A. He, K.Y. Bae, T.R. Newman, J. Gaeddert, K.W. Kim, R. Menon, L. Morales-Tirado et al. A survey of artificial intelligence for cognitive radios. *IEEE Trans. Veh. Technol.* 2010, 59, 1578–1592.

29. S. Sengupta, K.P. Subbalakshmi, Open research issues in multi-hop cognitive radio networks. *IEEE Commun. Mag.* 2013, 51, 168–176.

30. I.F. Akyildiz, I.H. Kasimoglu, Wireless sensor and actor networks: Research challenges, *Ad Hoc Networks Journal (Elsevier)*, Vol. 2, No. 4, pp. 351–367, Oct. 2004.

31. A. Sahai, N. Hoven, R. Tandra, "Some Fundamental Limits in Cognitive Radio," In *Proceedings of the Forty-second Allerton Conference on Communication, Control, and Computing 2004*, Oct. 2004.

32. A. Ghasemi, E.S. Sousa, "Collaborative Spectrum Sensing for Opportunistic Access in Fading Environment," In *Proceedings of the IEEE DySPAN 2005*, Nov. 2005; pp. 131–136.

33. A. Fehske, J.D. Gaeddert, J.H. Reed, "A New Approach to Signal Classification Using Spectral Correlation and Neural Networks," In *Proc. IEEE DySPAN 2005*, Nov. 2005; pp. 144–150.

34. FCC, "ET Docket No 03-237 Notice of Inquiry and Notice of Proposed", ET Docket No. 03-237, Nov. 2003.

35. J. Zhao, H. Zheng, G. Yang, "Distributed Coordination in Dynamic Spectrum Allocation Networks," In *Proceedings of the IEEE DySPAN 2005*, Nov. 2005; pp. 259–268.

36. S. Krishnamurthy, M. Thoppian, S. Venkatesan, R. Prakash, "Control Channel based MAC Layer Configuration, Routing and Situation Awareness for Cognitive Radio Networks," in *Proceedings of the IEEE MILCOM 2005*, Oct. 2005.

37. B. Atakan, O.B. Akan, "BIOlogically-inspired Spectrum Sharing in Cognitive Radio Networks," In *Proceedings of the IEEE WCNC 2007*, Mar. 2007; pp. 43–48.

38. L. Wang, C. Anderson, "On the performance of spectrum handoff for link maintenance in cognitive radio," In *Proceedings of the 3rd International Symposium on Wireless Pervasive Computing*, May 2008; pp. 670–674.

39. X. Zhu, L. Shen, T.P. Yum, Analysis of cognitive radio spectrum access with optimal channel reservation, *IEEE Communications Letters*, Vol. 11, No. 4, pp.304–306, Apr. 2007.

40. S. Byun, I. Balasingham, X. Liang, "Dynamic Spectrum Allocation in Wireless Cognitive Sensor Networks: Improving Fairness and Energy Efficiency," In *Proceedings of the IEEE VTC 2008*, Sep. 2008; pp. 1–5.

41. V. Blaschke, S. Nagel, F.K. Jondral, "Mechanisms for the Adaptation of the Physical Layer in a Cognitive Radio," In *Proceedings of the 9th European Conference on Wireless Technology*, Sept. 2006; pp. 41–46.

42. D. Cabric, R.W. Brodersen, Physical layer design issues unique to cognitive radio systems, *Proc. IEEE PIMRC 2005*, Vol. 2, pp. 759–763, Sept. 2005.

43. S. Wu, C. Lin, Y. Tseng, J. Sheu, "A New Multi-Channel MAC Protocol with ON-Demand Channel Assignment for Multi-Hop Mobile Ad Hoc Networks," in *Proc. Int. Symp. Parallel Architectures, Algorithms and Networks (I-SPAN 2000)*, pp. 232–237, 2000.

44. J. So, N. Vaidya, "Multi-Channel MAC for AD-Hoc Networks: Handling Multi-Channel Hidden Terminals Using A Single Transceiver," in *Proc. ACM MOBIHOC 2004*, pp. 222–233, 2004.

45. N. Choi, M. Patel, S. Venkatesan, "A Full Duplex Multi-channel MAC Protocol for Multi-hop Cognitive Radio Networks," in *Proc. 1st Int. Conf.on Cognitive Radio Oriented Wireless Networks and Communications*, pp. 1–5, June 2006.

46. J. N. Al-Karaki, A. E. Kamal, Routing techniques in wireless sensor networks: A survey, *IEEE Wireless Communications*, Vol. 11, No. 6, pp. 6–28, Dec. 2004.

47. C. Xin, "A Novel Layered Graph Model for Topology Formation and Routing in Dynamic Spectrum Access Networks," In *Proceedings of the IEEE DySPAN 2005*, pp. 308–317, Nov. 2005.

48. G. Cheng, W. Liu, Y. Li, W. Cheng, "Spectrum Aware On-Demand Routing in Cognitive Radio Networks," In *Proceedings of the DySPAN 2007*, pp. 571–574, Apr. 2007.

49. P. Kyasanur, N.H. Vaidya, "Protocol Design Challenges for Multi-hop Dynamic Spectrum Access Networks," In *Proceedings of the DySPAN 2005*, pp. 645–648, Nov. 2005.

50. C. Wang, M. Daneshmand, B. Li, K. Sohraby, A survey of transport protocols for wireless sensor networks, *IEEE Network*, Vol. 20, No. 3, pp. 34–40, 2006.

51. S.-J. Park, R. Vedantham, R. Sivakumar, I. F. Akyildiz, "A scalable approach for reliable downstream data delivery in wireless sensor networks," In *Proceedings of the ACM MOBIHOC 2004*, pp. 78–89, May 2004.

52. O.B. Akan, I.F. Akyildiz, Event-to-sink reliable transport in wireless sensor networks, *IEEE/ACM Trans. Networking*, Vol. 13, No. 5, pp.1003–1016, Oct. 2005.

53. C. Wan, S.B. Eisenman, "CODA: Congestion Detection and Avoidance in Sensor Networks," In *Proceedings of the ACM SenSys 2003*, pp. 266–279, Nov. 2003.

54. IEEE 802.15 WPANTM Task Group 6 (TG6) Body Area Networks. IEEE Standards Association. Available online: http://www.ieee802.org/15/pub/TG6.html (accessed May 30, 2013).

55. D. Stoner, Wireless from peak: Telemedicine in Nepal. *Wilderness Med.* Vol. 29, pp. 14–15, 2012. Available online: http://wms.org/magazine/292.pdf (accessed May 7, 2013).

56. S.K. Mishra, L. Kapoor, I.P. Singh, Telemedicine in India: Current scenario and the future. *Telemed. e-Health* 2009, 15, 568–575.

57. A.K.M. Azad, J. Kamruzzaman, "A Framework for Collaborative Multi Class Heterogeneous Wireless Sensor Networks," In *Proceedings of the IEEE ICC 2008*, pp. 4396–4401, May 2008.

58. A.J. Ghandour, K. Fawaz, H. Artail, Data Delivery Guarantees in Congested Vehicular Ad Hoc Networks Using Cognitive Networks. In *Proceedings of the IEEE IWCMC 2011*, Istanbul, Turkey, July 4–8, 2011; pp. 871–876.

59. M. Di Felice, R. Doost-Mohammady, K.R. Chowdhury, L. Bononi, Smart radios for smart vehicles: Cognitive vehicular networks. *IEEE Veh. Technol. Mag.* 2012, 7, 26–33.

60. D.B. Rawat, Y. Zhao, G. Yan, M. Song, CRAVE: Cognitive Radio Enabled Vehicular Communications in Heterogeneous Networks. In *Proceedings of the IEEE Radio and Wireless Symposium (RWS 2013)*, Austin, TX, USA, January 20–23, 2013; pp. 190–192.

61. A. El Mougy, M. Ibnkahla, A Cognitive WSN Framework for Highway Safety based on Weighted Cognitive Maps and Q-learning. In *Proceedings of the Second ACM International Symposium on Design and Analysis of Intelligent Vehicular Networks and Applications, (DIVANet'12)*, Cyprus, October 21–25, 2012; pp. 55–62.

62. F. Aalamifar, G. Vijay, P. Abedi Khoozani, M. Ibnkahla, Cognitive Wireless Sensor Networks for Highway Safety. In *Proceedings of the First ACM International Symposium on Design and Analysis of Intelligent Vehicular Networks and Applications (DIVANet "11)*, Miami Beach, FL, USA, 31 October–4 November 2011; pp. 55–60.

63. B. Gao, Y. Yang, J.M. Park, Channel Aggregation in Cognitive Radio Networks with Practical Considerations. In *Proceedings of the IEEE International Conference on Communications (ICC)*, Kyoto, Japan, June 5–9, 2011; pp. 1–5.

64. G.P. Joshi, S.W. Kim, An Enhanced Synchronized MAC Protocol for Cognitive Radio Networks. In *Proceedings of the 7th International Conference on Wireless Communications, Networking and Mobile Computing (WiCOM)*, Wuhan, China, September 23–25, 2011; pp. 1–4.

14

Cognitive Radio Sensor Networks: A Survey

N. Thirupathi Rao, Debnath Bhattacharyya, and Tai-hoon Kim

CONTENTS

14.1 Introduction to Radios

Cognitive radios are mindful and wise gadgets which can detect changing natural conditions and can change their parameters such as recurrence, adjustment systems, coding strategies, control, and so on [1,2]. This is managed by changing the measurable correspondence ecology and subsequently bringing about effective use of assets [5]. Cognitive radios must learn and choose their working parameters and can change their transmission and gathering parameters to meet execution prerequisites and boost Quality of Service [6]. The operations of a subjective radio are controlled by the cognitive motor (Cognitive Engine).

The cognitive motor carries out the undertakings of detecting, examination, learning, basic leadership, and reconfiguration [3]. Cognitive radio systems are comprised of two types of clients, essential (authorized) and auxiliary (unlicensed or intellectual) clients. Authorized clients have a higher access for the use of the authorized range. However, unlicensed clients can impact the authorized range by changing their correspondence parameters in a versatile way when range gaps are accessible [7]. On the premise of approaching Radio Frequency (RF) signals, the range use can be grouped into three more extensive classes of dark spaces, dim spaces, and void areas. Dark spaces are the mixtures of the authorized range being utilized by essential clients and are characterized by high power signals. Dark spaces are impermanent and possess low power interfaces, while blank areas are free from Radio Frequency obstructions and are simply unutilized segments of the authorized range [2]. White and dim spaces are contenders for the correspondence of optional clients in authorized groups.

The matter of remote correspondence can be settled better using Cognitive Radio. Cognitive radios are made with the particular ultimate objective to give an extremely strong correspondence to all customers of the framework anywhere and at any point necessary and to energize fruitful utilization of the radio spectrum [4]. Figures 14.1 and 14.2 demonstrate, for the most part, low utilization of the approved spectrum which is, all things considered, due to inefficient repeat designations instead of any physical absence of spectrum. This inspection has prompted the managerial bodies to look for procedures where assistant (unlicensed) structures are allowed to adroitly utilize the unused cognitive (approved) bunches of bands (Institute of Electronics and Electrical Engineers Personal Communications: Special issue on Software Radios, vol. 6, no. 4, Aug. 99).

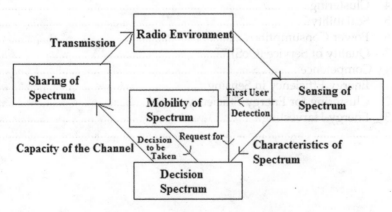

FIGURE 14.1
Cognitive radio cycle.

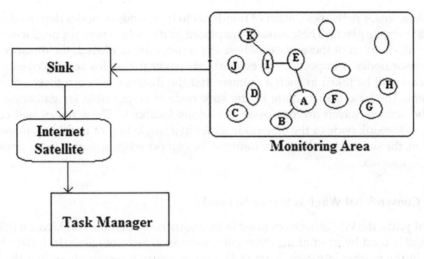

FIGURE 14.2
Architecture of conventional Wireless Sensor Networks.

Subjective radio can change its transmitter parameters in a coordinated effort with changes in the conditions in which it works. Subjective radio consolidates four functions: spectrum identifying, spectrum organization, spectrum sharing, and spectrum flexibility. Cognitive radios mechanism plans to choose spectrum openings and the closeness of the approved customers (generally called basic customers) [2]. Range organization is used to determine to what degree the spectrum openings are likely to stay accessible for use by customers with no proper permission (also called subjective radio customers or helper customers). Range sharing is the process by which spectrum holes are dispersed among the discretionary customers. Range adaptability is used to keep up predictable correspondence requirements in the advance to a better spectrum (Institute of Electronics and Electrical Engineers Personal Communications: Special issue on Software Radios, vol. 6, no. 4, Aug. 99) [4]. The electromagnetic broadcasting distance range variation is a controlled frequent positive feature and receiving swarmed stride by stride since of augmentation in inaccessible widget and submissions.

14.1.1 Traditional Wireless Sensor Networks

Interactions between the users in wireless sensor networks are determined as needed. At any time, an event activates and the wireless sensor nodes produce bursts in the traffic flow in networks [2]. Whenever the network feels or observes the thick flow of communications, the wireless sensor nodes placed at the same place in the environment try to access or contact the available channels [3,6]. Nowadays, these sensor networks are used in order to monitor and observe for identifying the victims and also as proof for various reasons and for various cases. Various types of sensor networks are available for the customers in order to reduce the waiting time in the sensor networks to reduce the delays. In general, these wireless sensor networks or these wireless sensors are deployed in places that are not accessible to human beings. Hence, it is very important for the sensor networks to have features such as organizing themselves and monitoring the life time of the wireless sensor networks. The maintenance of the life time of the sensor network is a very crucial point in terms of the working nature of the sensor networks.

Wireless sensor networks consist of hundreds to thousands of nodes deployed in the networks at various places. These sensors are placed in the field where we need to observe the sensor values. In all of these places where the sensors are deployed, the distance between these sensor nodes is important. In general, whenever the nodes are deployed in various fields, care will be taken in such a manner that the distance between these nodes will be in meters. The base station node or the sink node is responsible for gathering the data from the sensors which are deployed at various locations. These nodes will collect the data from the sink node or the base node either in a single-hop or multi-hop manner. After collection, the sink node will send or transmit the composed information to the customers by using the internet.

14.1.2 Conventional Wireless Sensor Networks

In recent years, the WSNs have operated in the Industrial, Scientific and Medical (ISM) band. This band is used by most of the other communication technologies which have been successful in the market in recent years [2,4]. Recent research results show that the presence of the Industrial, Scientific and Medical band can reduce the performance and quality of functioning of the WSNs. The performance of these WSNs was being reduced due to various reasons such as the deployment of sensors in wider areas or wider places, the power transmission requirements related to larger distances, and the range of the cover of IEEE 802.11 devices. When the data from sensors are being transferred from one set of nodes to another set of nodes, interference is one of the important considerations. The interference will disturb the signals and the noise in the signal will increase. Hence, it can be reduced by using various methods like space, time, and frequency utilizations.

In recent years, the research on these sensor networks has been highly focused on improving the performance of the WSNs [2,3]. Various factors need to be considered for improving the performance of these sensor networks. Some of the features are cost of the network, establishment cost of the network, the amount of energy being consumed, the rate of the data these sensors nodes are able to process, robustness, throughput of the network, quality of service to be provided to the customers or the users of the network, and security to be provided to these nodes in the sensor networks. To increase the performance of the network, several groups are working on research and several hardware and software upgrades are being made to the technology of these sensor networks (IEEE Personal Communications: Special issue on Software Radios, vol. 6, no. 4, Aug. 99). Some of the techniques that are being proposed by various researchers for increasing the performance include a cross-layer design technique, good sensing technique, power aware medium access control (MAC), and some important improvements in the designs of the hardware. However, these techniques have some restrictions of their own.

Huge number of sensor nodes with a similar equipment structure, and poor detecting, handling, and conveying abilities are placed in the observing region. Transmitted and forward data sent by the other sensor hubs to the sink hub utilize a type of multi-bounce with the assistance of different hubs inside remote sensors. The remote sensors are associated with different kinds of organizations by the sink hub. The client can remotely access, question, and deal with the remote sensor arrangement [2]. Most investigation of remote sensor systems are applied to remote sensor organizations, for example, single-jump remote sensor systems [3], multi-bounce remote sensor systems, and so forth. A common arrangement of remote sensors is shown in Figure 14.1.

In a remote sensor arrangement, the bigger the system is, the more information can be lost, and the worse the system execution. In the meantime, a remote sensor prompts halfway hubs for sending information and heterogeneous issues emerge. Thus, there are a substantial number of viable applications where a hierarchical remote sensor arrangement is more suitable, for example, Internet Protocol version6 remote sensor systems [4], half and half remote sensor systems (IEEE Personal Communications: Special issue on Software Radios, vol. 6, no. 4, Aug. 99) [6], various sink remote sensor systems [7], remote sensor systems with portable sinks [8], and so on. Progressive remote sensor organizations are generally made out of a few types of heterogeneous gadgets which mostly consist of sinks that are in charge of assembling and sending information from fundamental sensor hubs. Some of them are rechargeable, some have a greater capacity of correspondence over that of the sensor hubs, and some can even move arbitrarily.

These highlights do not just enhance the system execution. Vitality productivity, throughput, unwavering quality, and adaptability are realized in addition to expanding the potential applications and making them suitable for business uses [9]. In customary remote sensor arrangements, the sink hubs and the sensor hubs are for the most part static. We, as a rule, disregard the effects of the mobility originating from sensor hubs on the system. In a few situations which require that sensor hubs be versatile, the customary system design is not pertinent [5]. In the field of restorative care, the counteractive action of irresistible sicknesses in airplane terminal movement et cetera. In these regions, the sensor hubs can be tattered on the patient's remains, and arbitrarily shift with the development of patients in the checking locale, region whenever, so the number and thickness of system hubs are very extraordinary at various system minutes.

In the meantime, we have to guarantee the continuity of the system and the productivity of sensor hubs. The level remote sensor organization may find it hard to meet these necessities. From one perspective, when the sensor hubs arbitrarily move in the district, they might be detached from other sensor hubs and afterward end up as noticeably separated hubs, which will bring about a huge system delay. Again, with the development of the system estimate, the jump number between the source sensor hub furthermore, the sink hub will increment altogether, which will cause moderate sensor hubs to expand the vitality utilization and drag out information delay. In addition, in light of the fact that the sensor hubs are portable, the likelihood of detecting information will quickly increase during the time spent in transmission, which will likewise create a loss in productivity.

In recent years, the research on these sensor networks has been highly focused on improving the performance of the WSNs. Various factors need to be considered for improving the performance of these sensor networks. Some of the features are cost of the network, establishment cost of the network, the amount of energy being consumed, the rate of the data these sensors nodes are able to process, robustness, throughput of the network, quality of service to be provided to the customers or the users of the network, and security to be provided to these sets of nodes in the sensor networks. To increase the performance of the network, several groups have done research and several hardware and software upgrades are being made to the technology to improve the performance of these sensor networks. Some of the techniques that are being proposed by various research results for increasing the performance include the cross-layer design technique, good sensing technique, power aware Medium Access Control, and some important improvements in the designs of the hardware. Still, these techniques have some restrictions of their own which also affect the sensor networks.

14.1.3 Accepting Cognitive Method in Wireless Sensor Networks

Recently, cognitive methods have been highly used in WSNs to avoid the restrictions encountered by traditional WSNs. is an application which was chosen for the subsequent creation of WSNs. The cognitive method is the procedure of understanding the system/band through awareness, preparation, development, and perception, constantly appraising and advancing the system. If the CR method was combined with the WSNs, many challenges that were being faced in WSNs could be overcome or solved.

CR has the capability to identify unused spectrum in authorized or unauthorized and licensed and unlicensed spectrum bands. This radio model uses the unused spectrum resourcefully. The first users or the main users have the right to use the available spectrum at any time. The secondary users will have the option to utilize the available spectrum only when the first users or the primary users are not using it.

14.1.4 Potential Capabilities of a Wireless Sensor with Cognitive Radio

Cognitive Radio permits the users who have no license to access several channels which are licensed enabled. The users can access multiple licensed channels. This feature of these CR networks provides good advantages and high usefulness to the WSNs. These features will increase the communication consistency and increase the energy efficiency of the network. When the nodes of the sensor networks were given CR capabilities throughout the network, innovative characteristics were observed by the researchers and the research industry and the organizations which led to the development of some new software and hardware units. With the help of these newly developed software and hardware units, the limitations and the restrictions that were present at the sensor networks can be avoided. Utilizing the additional means of access of the spectrum application regulation by the Federal Communications Commission and procedural developments in sensor technology, wireless sensors with Cognitive Radio can alleviate the present matter of spectrum void spots and increase the network productivity with a variety of functions.

14.2 Cognitive Radio Wireless Sensor Networks (CR-WSN)

Cognitive radio wireless sensor networks are a devoted impromptu system of remote sensors which were set up with the abilities of subjective radio. Subjective radio remote sensor systems are quite different when contrasted with the customary remote sensor systems. The accompanying area deals with the contrasts in the angles among specially appointed Cognitive Radio Networks (CRNs), Wireless Sensor Networks (WSNs), and Cognitive Radio-Wireless Sensor Networks (CR-WSNs). Subjective cognitive radio WSN organizations generally involve an incredible number of spatially spread, self-designing, mindful remote sensor hubs with psychological capabilities. This arrangement requires an increased capacity for an incredible number of joint efforts and amendments to complete the required obligations. These systems exchange information bundles as well as safeguard the obligatory enlisted clients. This is a framework that administers the majority of the abilities needed for a psychological radio framework which is characterized for remote sensor systems.

As per the literature, a CR-WSN can be considered as a scattered system of remote cognitive radio wireless sensor (Cognitive Radio Wireless Sensor) hubs which observe the system and participate in open range groups in a multi-jump way, with the end goal being to perform an application's particular necessities. In CR-WSNs, a remote sensor hub picks the most reasonable channel and clears the channel when the absence of an enlisted client on the channel is noted. The intellectual radio technique may be one of the most important strategies for enhancing the profitability of remote sensor systems. Subjective radio remote sensor systems expand the accessible range utilization, increase the system viability, and enhance the available time for remote sensor systems.

14.2.1 Benefits of Using Cognitive Radio in Wireless Sensor Networks

CR-WSN is another example in a WSN ring that observes range sources for burst activities. This kind of framework has the capacity of decreasing the loss of parcels, lessening wasted bands, supporting controls, and has enhanced correspondence. The next section discussed the advantages of utilizing subjective radios in Wireless Sensor Networks.

14.2.2 Effective Spectrum Application and Spaces for New Technologies

The accessibility of the electromagnetic range is a benefit of our environment. The measure of available operational range groups cannot be increased, but they can be used more ingeniously. In general, one needs an approval from the administration of a specific nation to work the radio groups. Because the cost related to range authorization is high, a few specialists, equipment manufacturers, and organizations have focused on applications for industrial, scientific, and medical groups. Therefore, these accessible groups currently control the extension and change of new and existing advancements. Subsequently, these CR remote sensors may utilize the unutilized part of the range known as the blank areas, without upsetting the current enlisted and authorized clients. Unlicensed clients can have the capacity to utilize those groups with small or no cost, so more new devices can be built for these kinds of groups.

14.2.3 Various Channels' Usage

The vast majority of the customary remote sensor systems utilize a solitary channel for correspondence. In these sensor nodes, subsequent to recognizing an event, the hubs used in the sensor system will produce movement in the system with parcels of data. After this, greater numbers of hubs are sent to the remote sensor organize, extremely colossal number of hubs in a similar system will attempt to possess or utilize a similar normal channel at same time interim. Because of this, the impact of events decreases the reliability of the system. As a result of this, the power utilization by the system increases a great deal and parcel conveyance likewise increases. Subjective radio remote sensor systems will facilitate different channels to ease this problem.

14.2.4 Energy Efficiency

In general, power consumption is very high and the waste of power is high in general sensor networks. This over consumption is the result of packet resending or retransmitting due to packet losses in the networks. CR wireless sensors might use less energy or less power because these sensors scan their own parameters or use features that consume less power. Hence, as a result of this, the energy consumption in the networks due to packet retransmission and packet collision can be reduced.

14.2.5 Universal Operability

Every nation in the world has its own spectrum allocation and spectrum monitoring and utilizing regulations. A spectrum band available for one network may not be same in another nation for the same application. Hence, the problem arises that whenever the sensors are used in certain regions or countries, the sensors might not work well because the frequency spectrum band is different from that where the sensors are manufactured. In contrast to this, if the nodes are prepared with CR capability, they can overcome the spectrum inconsistency difficulty by altering their communication frequency band. Hence, Cognitive Radio wireless sensors function in almost every place in the world.

14.2.6 Application Explicit Spectrum Band Operation

The number of wireless sensors positioned for different applications has gradually increased. In Wireless Sensor Networks, data traffic is frequently associated both temporally and spatially. In WSNs, the networks will generate packet bursts whenever an event occurs and the networks remain silent if no event occurs. These sequential and longitudinal associations present design challenges for the communication protocols for WSNs. Due to the presence of smart communication protocols in CR-WSNs, it is probable that the wireless sensors may use the spectrum of various occupants in spatially overlying areas.

14.2.7 Financial Returns to the Occupants by Renting or Leasing

While using these networks, whenever there is no requirement for licensed spectrum bands, then there is a chance for the occupant or the people who have the licensed spectrum to lease their spectrum to others who are in need. The charges for such types of rental or leasing purposes can be very low and they might obtain good profits by utilizing such facilities. This process can be done by providing the facility to the existing users and providing the facility to the other users without causing any problems to the existing users. This is a good opportunity for the users who cannot spend much money or who cannot afford high prices for purchasing the spectrum for their applications or their uses.

14.3 Differences between Ad Hoc CRNs, WSNs, and CR-WSNs

This section shows some of the differences between the ad hoc CRNs, WSNs, and CR-WSNs (Table 14.1).

14.4 Prospective Application Areas of CR-WSNs

CR-WSNs might use an extensive variety of bands/requests. They can be positioned anywhere in the WSNs. This section discusses some of the prospective areas where CR-WSNs can be positioned with examples.

TABLE 14.1

Compares Several Factors among ad hoc Cognitive Radio Networks, Conventional Wireless Sensor Networks, and Cognitive Radio-Wireless Sensor Networks

Aspect	Ad Hoc CRNs	WSNs	CR-WSNs
Channel type: Wireless	Proficient spectrum bands (data channels) Proficient band (control channels)	ISM Bands	Authorized spectrum bands (data channels) authorized band (control channel)
Movement	Arbitrary	One to many, many to one, many to many	One to many, many to one, many to many
Bandwidth lacking	Occurs regularly	Occurs sometimes	Occurs regularly
Fault recognition	Low error leniency need	High error leniency essential	High error leniency essential
Communication choice	Extended	Tiny range	Tiny range
Communication	Transmit	Point-to-point	Point-to-point
Failure rate	Little	Tall	Reasonable
Topology changes	Communal	Fewer common	Fewer common
Application specific	Normally not specific	Yes, specific	Yes, specific
Energy maintenance	Concern	High concern	High concern

14.4.1 Military and Public Safety Applications

Customary remote sensor systems are utilized as a part of a few military and open well-being applications, for example, (a) biochemical, natural radiological, and atomic assault acknowledgment and examination; (b) charge control; (c) accumulation of gear-harmful data from the front lines, (d) perceptions from the combat zone, (e) help partners, (f) pointing, and so forth. In the war areas, the controlling specialist may sends signals to change the current radio correspondence channels. In such circumstances, because of the presence of Cognitive Radio-Wireless Sensor Networks, frequencies can change over a shifted extent as these CR-WSNs are ready to use different recurring groups (Figure 14.3).

14.4.2 Real-Time Surveillance Applications

Continuous reconnaissance applications such as movement checking, biodiversity mapping, natural surroundings observations, ecological observations, natural conditions' checks that influence harvests and domesticated animals, water systems, submerged WSNs, vehicle following, stock following, catastrophe help operations, and scaffolds or passages observations require low access and wait times. Some on going observation applications are profoundly delay-delicate and require a high unwavering quality. A postponement because of a connection delay can likewise happen in multi-hop WSNs if the control state is not great. Then again, WS hubs can bounce to another channel in the event that they locate another site with superior conditions in CR-WSNs. Channel conglomeration and the simultaneous utilization of different sites are conceivable in CR-WSNs to increase the channel transmission capacity.

14.4.3 Transportation and Vehicular Networks

The IEEE 1609.4 standard suggests multi-occupancy procedures in remote settings for vehicles. The present structure of IEEE 1609.4 chips away at the 75 MHz range in the

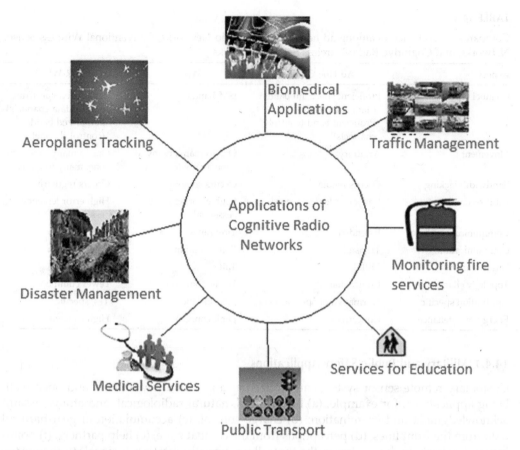

FIGURE 14.3
Application areas of cognitive radio networks.

5.9 GHz band with one managing guide and six organization channels. Each and every vehicular customer will have to fight for a channel to broadcast data in the 5.9 GHz band. This range deficiency topic and the necessities of intellectual radio in WAVE should be considered. Some preliminary works in CR-enabled vehicular correspondences have recently been done. Vehicular remote sensor frameworks are another framework perspective for proactively checking data to be considered under urban conditions. CR-WSNs are most likely going to be more noteworthy in this field. Although this area ought to be examined more carefully, a couple of applications for interstate security using CR-WSNs are projected.

14.5 Challenges Affecting the Design of a CR-WSN

CR-WSNs are different from ordinary WSNs in numerous ways. Since securing the use for essential clients is the fundamental worry in CR-WSN, it has numerous new difficulties that incorporate the difficulties in regular WSNs. This segment examines the difficulties influencing the design of a CR-WSN.

14.5.1 Hardware

Cognitive Radio remote sensors have equipment requirements regarding computational power, stockpiling, and vitality. Unlike regular remote sensors, these sensors have a duty to detect channels, break down the observations, choose a response, and act. Cognitive Radio remote sensors ought to be able to change the parameter or transmitters in light of different conditions. Detecting units contain sensors and simple to program converters. The simple flag seen by the sensor is changed to a computerized flag and sent to the handling unit. The CRWS ought to have the capacity to utilize cutting edge manmade innovations. This ability is required in the Cognitive Radio unit. The Cognitive Radio unit needs to quickly adjust the correspondence parameters, for example, bearer recurrence, transmission power, and balance. The unit needs to choose the best accessible channel, share the range with different clients, and deal with the range versatility, that is, immediately abandon the utilization when the primary users needs to utilize that channel. A handset unit is in charge of getting and sending information. Since the gathering methods in remote sensor hubs have grown quickly, the collecting or reviving units are discretionary, particularly the sensors.

14.5.2 Topology Adjustments

Topology particularly impacts the framework lifetime in WSNs. Dependent upon the application, Cognitive Radio remote sensors may be sent statically or dynamically. In a WSN, gear frustration is typical as a result of hardware separating and equipment wear. The topologies for CR-WSNs may be as that for customary WSNs, but they are geared to change more frequently than CRNs. Regardless, there is not ordinarily the potential to discover such a course in static sensor frameworks' topology. Along these lines, a flexible self-setup topology is basic for CR-WSNs for achieving robustness, reducing usage, and fulfilling better framework execution. A flexible self-setup topology framework performs better than any static topology, in spite of the fact that it is difficult to layout and execute. This range has not been the subject of much research.

14.5.3 Fault Tolerance

CR-WSNs ought to exhibiy self-setup and self-recuperating properties. At the end of the day, at the point where a few hubs or connections fizzle, a method that maintains a strategic distance from the broken hub or connection must be determined. In CR-WSNs, shortcomings can happen for an assortment of reasons, for example, equipment or programming break down or normal disasters, for example, fire, surges, seismic tremors, volcanic ejections or waves and so forth. A CR-WSN ought to be set up to manage such circumstances. There are a few sorts of deficiencies like hub blame, organize blame, and sink blame and so on.

14.5.4 Clustering

Coherently gathering and sorting out comparable Cognitive Radio remote sensors for their nearness has a few favorable advantages. Gathering sensor hubs into groups has attempted in Wireless Sensor Networks to accomplish system adaptability, decrease utilization, and diminish the correspondence overhead. A few types of methods for bunching sensors exist, for example, stationary, lively, solitary bound, multi-hop, standardized, and varied.

14.5.5 Scalability

For a few applications, Cognitive Radio remote sensors ought to be placed in tremendous numbers. Not at all like ordinary Wireless Sensor hubs that have Cognitive Radio remote sensors, larger numbers of sensors are required for participation among hubs for range data sharing. This is exceptionally hard to organize in heterogeneous CR remote sensor conditions. Calculations and conventions produced for CR-WSNs ought to be equipped for tackling these issues because of the developing size of the system.

14.5.6 Power Consumption

Numerous applications require various reception apparatuses to screen the primary users exercises, thus more power is devoured. In spite of the fact that there are a few recommendations for power savings, these methods have their own particular restrictions. In some applications, energy reaping or the renewal of energy assets is not conceivable. Such confinements are contemplated. In specially appointed CRNs, control utilization is a vital factor, however, it is not the essential objective. In any case, in CR-WSNs, it is one of the fundamental execution measurements that influence the system lifetime.

14.5.7 Quality of Service (QoS)

In customary WSNs, the QoS is for the most part portrayed by four parameters: transmission capacity, postponement, jitter, and unwavering quality. To avoid dangerous outcomes in basic applications, WSNs require consistently keeping an acceptable level of QoS. Providing QoS is a testing issue since the cause of advantage necessities, for example, organizing strength, recollection, and supremacy foundation in remote sensor hubs. This is all the more difficult in CR-WSNs because notwithstanding the difficulties in WSNs, they have more supplementary tests to ensure the privileges of primary users to get to the licensed spectra. Primary userss correspondence ought to be without impedance by the secondary users. This is all the more difficult on the grounds that it is hard to anticipate the primary users PU's access of the channel. A misidentification of essential flags and fake alerts can also introduce extra difficulties.

14.6 Energy Competence

As the significance of energy protection in CR-WSNs has been discussed, a few plans for energy effectiveness have been proposed. They utilize assorted methods, yet the objective of these plans is to monitor energy consumption. Some of these strategies are discussed here.

14.6.1 Energy Efficiency in Sensing

An effective energy range detecting strategy is a fundamental necessity for CR-WSNs. Not at all like the traditional multi resolution spectrum sensing (MRSS) methods, which expend significant power and is included in fundamentally simple circuits in the detecting data transfer, capacity, and detecting affectability which are changed by a simple variable channel, the plan proposed in this paper does flag these occurrences in a computerized space and can distinguish recurrence groups at numerous resolutions and with low power utilization.

14.6.2 Clustering for Energy Efficiency

The courses with additional bounces and smaller jump separations can be more proficient than those with fewer bounces and longer jump separations. Along these lines, bunching is one of the answers for control protection in CR-WSNs. Grouping plans for WSNs cannot be utilized straightforwardly in CR-WSNs in light of the fact that to frame a bunch, the sensors need to detect and choose the group head in an unexpected way in comparison to the regular WSNs.

14.6.3 Energy Harvesting

Radio Frequency vitality reaping empowers the remote sensor hub to work with a basically unending lifetime. Celebi et al. [6] inspected an ideal mode choice approach for CR-WSNs fueled by radio frequency energy collecting. Accepting that the remote sensor hub captures the Radio frequency energy obtained from the essential system, remote sensor hubs can exploit the ranges occupied in the essential system. All things considered, Cognitive Radio remote sensors are requirements and the system lifetime essentially relies on the energy available. The majority of the energy effective plans concentrate on energy productivity in a particular operation, for example, channel detecting or information transmission and so on. To expand energy productivity, energy preservation in a few areas of system operation ought to be considered, including a channel detecting plan, bunching and topology administration calculations, steering calculations, Medium Access Control conventions, channel choice, information gathering, and so on.

References

1. O.B. Akan, O.B. Karli, O. Ergul. Cognitive radio sensor networks, *IEEE Netw.* 2009, 23, 34–40.
2. R. Qiu et al. A unified multi-functional dynamic spectrum access framework: Tutorial, theory and multi-ghz wideband test bed, *Sensors*, vol. 9, no. 8, pp. 6530–6603, 2009.
3. S. Haykin. Cognitive radio: Brain-empowered wireless communications, *IEEE Journal on Selected Areas in Communications*, vol. 23, no. 2, pp. 201–20, 2005.
4. J. Walko. Cognitive radio, *IEEE Review*, vol. 51, no. 5, pp. 34–37, May 2005.
5. K. Akkaya, M. Younis. A survey on routing protocols for wireless sensor networks, *Ad Hoc Networks*, vol. 3, no. 3, pp. 325–349. 2005.
6. H. Celebi et al. Enabling location and environment awareness in cognitive radios, *Elsevier Computer Communications-Special Issue on Advanced Location-Based Services*, vol. 31, no. 6, pp. 1114–1125, 2008.
7. H. Celebi et al. Cognitive positioning systems, *IEEE Transactions on Wireless Communications*, vol. 6, no. 12, pp. 4475–4483, Dec. 2007.
8. H. Celebi, H. Arslan. Utilization of location information in cognitive wireless networks, *IEEE Wireless Communications Magazine-Special Issue on Cognitive Wireless Networks*, vol. 14, no. 4, pp. 6–13, Aug. 2007.
9. A. A. Abbasi, M. Younis. A survey on clustering algorithms for wireless sensor networks, *Computer Communications*, vol. 30, no. 14–15, pp. 2826–2841, 2007.

Part VII

Applications of 5G Networks

15

5G Technology

Pooja Joshi, Ashish Bagwari, and Ashish Negi

CONTENTS

15.1 Introduction

Change in generations is inevitable whether it is related to mankind or technology. How good it would be for all the researchers, students, business people, doctors, and disaster management teams to have clear and strong communication connections for their various activities without interruptions such as call drops, internet time outs, network band issues, high battery consumption, and noise during calls. 5G is evolving as a unique revolution in wireless communication technology. Further, the unexpected growth of wireless devices, numbers of users, and high data transfer has actually motivated 5G development. This technology is completely dedicated to high speed internet, voluminous data, sufficient bandwidth, high speed data transfer, and can accommodate billions of devices such as computers, smart phones, home appliances, wearables, sensors, and many more devices in order to achieve smooth and uninterrupted communication services. 5G is opening the door for those users who really want to experience better quality of services by the end of 2020. In the next section, we consider the major technical requirements proposed by 5G technology which are mentioned below [1,2].

1. *Anytime Anywhere Continuous Connectivity*: In the succeeding years, a large number of devices will be able to achieve reliable connections even in remote places using 5G.

2. *Virtually Nil (Zero) Latency*: The 5G network will support zero or extremely low latency for life-line communication systems, a transportation safety system, massive IoT (internet of things), big data, widespread and reliable videos, extreme real-time services, logistic applications, and smart grids. Nil latency will also facilitate intelligent handover by reducing the call drop problems.

3. *Rapid and High-Speed Gigabit Connection*: The zero-latency property can be achieved using a high-speed connection for concurrent and instantaneous transmission and reception of upto10 Gbps for high end computing machines and users regardless of their geographic region.

4. *Spectrum Utilization*: The spectrum crisis is one of the major issues today. 5G is dedicated to utilize the spectrum white band to resolve this matter.

5. *Crowded Areas also have Reliable Service*: In the present network scenario, users are facing denial of services because of overloaded networks, but the upcoming 5G is committed to providing the best connectivity with high data rates for tens of thousands of users in crowded places like shopping malls, football stadiums, open air festivals, and so on. It is also expected to generate 100,000 s of simultaneous connections per square km. Tens of workers on the same office floor can concurrently enjoy 1 Gbps speeds.

6. *Efficient Energy Usage Delivers High Battery Life*: Different standard bodies are considering the development of green technology so that signaling and energy consumption can be efficiently adapted for various applications. This emerging technology will lead to a significant increase in battery life due to low consumption of power by smart phones and low cost machine type communication (MTC) devices [3–5].

The next section of this chapter is dedicated to background history and how technology has evolved from one generation to the next including their key features. We will first provide a brief overview of 5G history.

15.2 Background Study

5G is a voluntary progression in comparison to previous technology. In this section, there is a quick overview of the comparison of various generations from 1G to5G (see Figure 15.1 for year of inception, facilities, data bandwidth, technology, services, standards, deployment, etc.). In the sequence of this here, (Figure 15.2) represents background history of 5G activities since 2008, at different loction all over the world. The current 4G system is providing heterogeneous network connectivity with low power nodes, but it also has some limits such as high energy consumption, huge interference and overhead, frequent handover overhead, signaling overhead, and so on.

We have highlighted some of the astonishing tests of 5G that have been performed by many companies.

15.3 Latest Achievements in 5G Trials

Many countries, companies, and universities want to stay competitive in the global economy by adapting 5G technology, so they are participating in the research work and

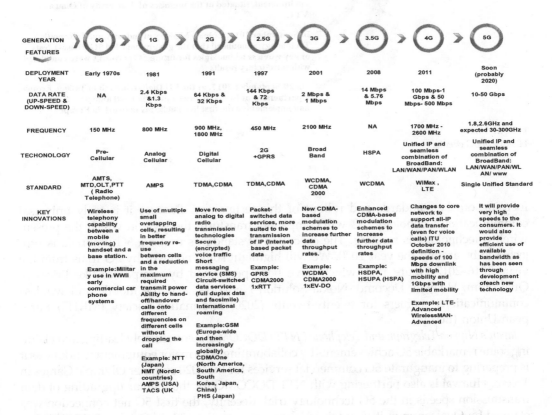

GENERATION FEATURES	0G	1G	2G	2.5G	3G	3.5G	4G	5G
DEPLOYMENT YEAR	Early 1970s	1981	1991	1997	2001	2008	2011	Soon (probably 2020)
DATA RATE (UP-SPEED & DOWN-SPEED)	NA	2.4 Kbps &1.3 Kbps	64 Kbps & 32 Kbps	144 Kbps & 72 Kbps	2 Mbps & 1 Mbps	14 Mbps & 5.76 Mbps	100 Mbps-1 Gbps & 50 Mbps- 500 Mbps	10-50 Gbps
FREQUENCY	150 MHz	800 MHz	900 MHz, 1800 MHz	450 MHz	2100 MHz	NA	1700 MHz - 2600 MHz	1.8,2.6GHz and expected 30-300GHz
TECHONOLOGY	Pre-Cellular	Analog Cellular	Digital Cellular	2G +GPRS	Broad Band	HSPA	Unified IP and seamless combination of BroadBand: LAN/WAN/PAN/WLAN	Unified IP and seamless combination of BroadBand: LAN/WAN/PAN/WLAN/ www
STANDARD	AMTS, MTD,OLT,PTT (Radio Telephone)	AMPS	TDMA,CDMA	TDMA,CDMA	WCDMA, CDMA 2000	WCDMA	WiMax , LTE	Single Unified Standard
KEY INNOVATIONS	Wireless telephony capability between a mobile (moving) handset and a base station. Example:Militar y use in WWII early commercial car phone systems	Use of multiple small overlapping cells, resulting in better frequency re-use between cells and a reduction in the maximum required transmit power Ability to hand-off/handover calls onto different frequencies on different cells without dropping the call Example: NTT (Japan) NMT (Nordic countries) AMPS (USA) TACS (UK	Move from analog to digital radio transmission technologies Secure (encrypted) voice traffic Short messaging service (SMS) Circuit-switched data services (full duplex data and facsimile) International roaming Example:GSM (Europe-wide and then increasingly globally) CDMAOne (North America, South America, South Korea, Japan, China) PHS (Japan)	Packet-switched data services, more suited to the transmission of IP (Internet) based packet data Example: GPRS CDMA2000 1xRTT	New CDMA-based modulation schemes to increase further data throughput rates. Example: WCDMA CDMA2000 1xEV-DO	Enhanced CDMA-based modulation schemes to increase further data throughput rates Example: HSDPA, HSUPA (HSPA)	Changes to core network to support all-IP data transfer (even for voice calls) ITU October 2010 definition - speeds of 100 Mbps downlink with high mobility and 1Gbps with limited mobility Example: LTE-Advanced WirelessMAN-Advanced	It will provide very high speeds to the consumers. It would also provide efficient use of available bandwidth as has been seen through development ofeach new technology

FIGURE 15.1
Comparison of 1G to 5G technology.

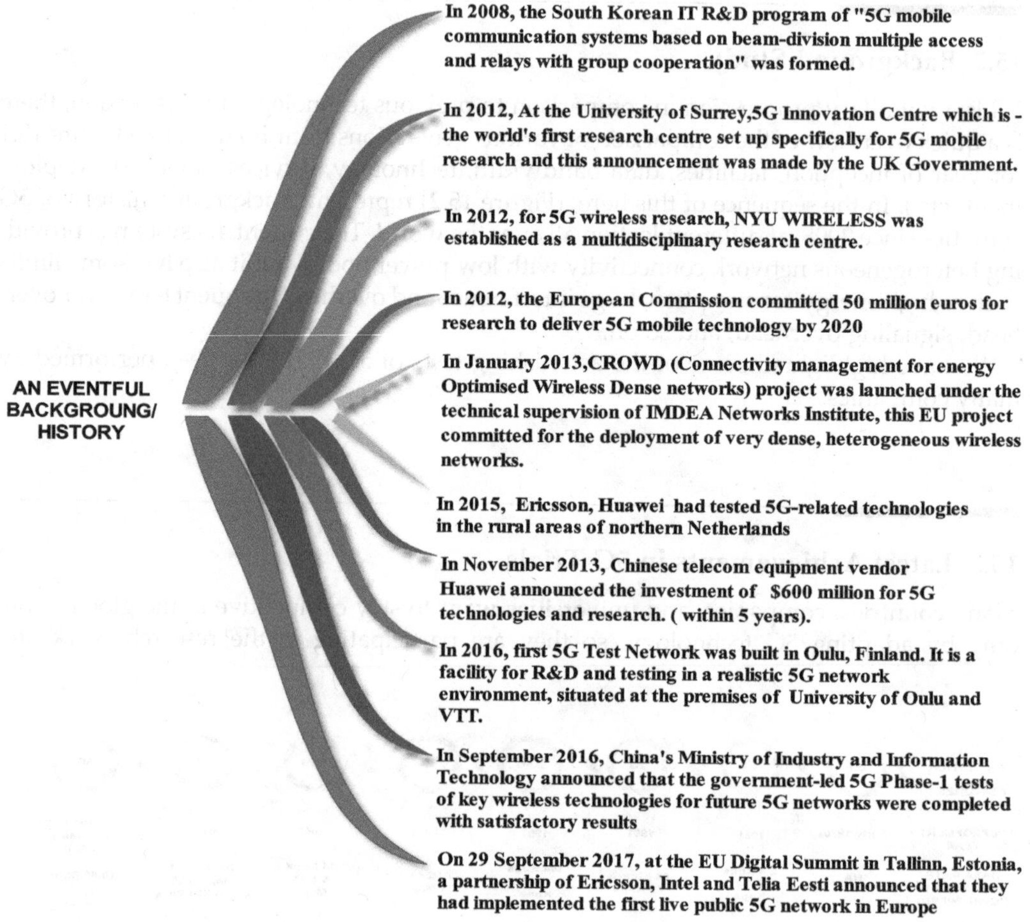

In 2008, the South Korean IT R&D program of "5G mobile communication systems based on beam-division multiple access and relays with group cooperation" was formed.

In 2012, At the University of Surrey, 5G Innovation Centre which is - the world's first research centre set up specifically for 5G mobile research and this announcement was made by the UK Government.

In 2012, for 5G wireless research, NYU WIRELESS was established as a multidisciplinary research centre.

In 2012, the European Commission committed 50 million euros for research to deliver 5G mobile technology by 2020

In January 2013, CROWD (Connectivity management for energy Optimised Wireless Dense networks) project was launched under the technical supervision of IMDEA Networks Institute, this EU project committed for the deployment of very dense, heterogeneous wireless networks.

In 2015, Ericsson, Huawei had tested 5G-related technologies in the rural areas of northern Netherlands

In November 2013, Chinese telecom equipment vendor Huawei announced the investment of $600 million for 5G technologies and research. (within 5 years).

In 2016, first 5G Test Network was built in Oulu, Finland. It is a facility for R&D and testing in a realistic 5G network environment, situated at the premises of University of Oulu and VTT.

In September 2016, China's Ministry of Industry and Information Technology announced that the government-led 5G Phase-1 tests of key wireless technologies for future 5G networks were completed with satisfactory results

On 29 September 2017, at the EU Digital Summit in Tallinn, Estonia, a partnership of Ericsson, Intel and Telia Eesti announced that they had implemented the first live public 5G network in Europe

AN EVENTFUL BACKGROUNG/ HISTORY

FIGURE 15.2
History of 5G events.

focusing on the standards and rollout of this technology. Because it is truly universal communication technology, 5G will completely transform the style in which the present wireless technology is running. The execution of standards under a 5G umbrella is projected to be around the year 2020. We will highlight some noteworthy 5G trials from the years 2016–2017 Figure 15.3, which have been performed by companies like Ericsson, Qualcomm, Huawei, Docomo, Nokia Solution Networks, and the mobile and wireless communications enablers for twenty-twenty (2020) information society (METIS) European Union (EU) [6].

Japan's Nippon Telegraph and Telephone (NTT) DOCOMO is conceivably leading and claiming some remarkable 5G achievements by collaborating with major equipment vendors, as it is preparing to inaugurate 5G commercial services for the 2020 summer Olympic Games in Tokyo. Huawai is also partnering with NTT DOCOMO for the regular upgrading of data transmission speeds in the 5G technology trial. Recently, the first 5G net connection was claimed by Qualcomm in its San Diego laboratories on the 17th of October 2017. This is a noticeable achievement where the company performs its demonstration using a 5G protocol

5G Trials (Test Environment To Real World)

Japan's NTT DOCOMO	Ericsson	Huawei	Nokia
November 2016, in partnership with Samsung, it achieved a data speed of over 2.5Gbps in a vehicle travelling 150km/h, demonstrating the viability of stable connectivity for 5G mobile devices in fast-moving vehicles.	February 2017, in partnership with Korea's SK Telecom and BMW Korea, realised a peak downlink data speed of 3.6Gbps for a connected vehicle travelling at 170km/hr, and maintained throughput of over 1.5Gbps while data transmission was switched from one transmission point to another.	March 2017, achieved maximum speeds of 70Gbps in a 5G demo conducted with Norway's Telenor in the E-band, which acts as a supplementary low frequency band to enhance the user experience.	Nokia is also heavily invested in 5G development, but has been coyer about the speeds of any tests it's participated in. Its AirScale radio platform is 5G-ready and on the market, and in October 2016 U.S. Cellular tested fixed wireless services in outdoor and indoor environments using AirScale, achieving speeds of up to 5Gbps.
October 2016, with Huawei, it notched up a cumulative 11.29Gbps of data throughput (and sub 0.5ms latency) in an outdoor trial using 23 simultaneously connected devices.	December 2016, AT&T launched what it claimed was the first 5G business customer trial in the US, taking the technology it worked on with Ericsson and Intel into the field. It had reached speeds above 10Gbps in early tests with Ericsson.	February 2017, with China Mobile, published the results of their 5G Dual Connectivity work claiming user throughput of over 22Gbps.	Nokia claims to have successfully carried out the world's first connection based on Verizon's 5GTF pre-standard, in December 2016, and early in 2017 it completed fixed wireless 5G tests with DIRECTV NOW, AT&T's internet TV streaming service, also claimed to be a world first.
May 2016, with Nokia, successfully tested live streaming of 8K video over a 5G network (the transmission rates weren't disclosed).	December 2016, implemented what it claimed was the first end-to-end 5G trial system and, in collaboration with Telefonica, demonstrated end-to-end data rates of over 1Gbps.	February 2017, unveiled its 5G New Radio (NR) solution which, in tests of three scenarios, achieved over 10Gbps throughput for over one million simultaneous connections with latency under 1ms.	
February 2016, with Ericsson, it achieved a cumulative 20Gbps of data throughput in an outdoor environment with two simultaneously connected devices, with a downlink bit rate of over 10Gbps each. In separate tests the two companies achieved data throughput of over 10Gbps at a distance of 70m from the base station, and of over 9Gbps at a distance of 120m.	October 2016, in partnership with Telia, demonstrated 5G capabilities in a real-world environment over a live outdoor network with peak rates of 15Gbps per user.		
	September 2016, demonstrated 5G capabilities in a real-world environment over a live network in Australia with Telstra, achieving aggregate speeds in excess of 20Gbps		

FIGURE 15.3
5G trials performed by different vendors [6].

research and development (R&D) toolset and user experience manager emulator UXM's 5G wireless test platform in addition to Qualcomm's Snapdragon X50 modem (using the 28 GHz millimeter wave spectrum band) [7,8]. In November 2017, Verizon Communications, Inc. announced that it will deploy 5G wireless residential broadband services in five U.S. cities in the early second half of 2018 [9].

15.4 Limitations of Conventional Cellular Networks

1. *Out-pouring of data traffic*: In the present era, innumerable wireless services and applications demand very high data transfer rates within a few seconds and consume more battery power in mobile devices. This unexpected traffic growth may affect the performance of the core network because the current network is dedicated

only for a single kind of signalling or control mechanism. This is responsible for generating excessive overhead for bursty traffic.

2. *Ineffective use of base stations (BSs') capabilities*: In current cellular networks, the processing power of base stations is only being utilized by its affiliated user's equipment. This aspect can be improved by utilizing the same processing power in a sharing mode. For example, BSs in office areas are overloaded during the daytime while they are idle during the late night. Similarly, BSs in residential areas are almost oversubscribed on weekends but remain relatively idle during daylight. Therefore, the power consumption of those idle BSs will increase the overall cost of the network.

3. *Interference between co-channels*: The existing cellular network uses two channels, that is, UL (uplink) and DL (download link), for transmission between the users' equipment and the base station, but the allocation of two different channels does not provide efficient utilization of frequency bands. Another matter of concern in 4G networks is high channel interference if the UL and DL channels have identical frequencies.

4. *Bogus indoor communication*: In conventional cellular networks, the preferable position for BS installation is the center of the cell. The BS's signal is used by indoor and outdoor users regardless of their locations. Research proves that 80% of the time, user equipment stays inside and the remaining 20% of the time, the user equipments (UEs) stays outdoors. Network coverage and services for indoor user equipment are not good compared to outdoor areas. Indoor services are not very efficient with regard to data transfer rates, efficient spectrum utilization, energy efficiency, signal loss, or penetration loss due to obstacles [10–13].

15.5 Technical Components and Essential Technologies/Methodology of 5G

The mission of 5G technology is to handle the above-mentioned limitations by providing high frequency bands, a large volume of data, a high data transfer rate, and expansion in network capacity via maintaining the cost and power consumption. Although implementation of all these factors is not an easy task, various solutions have been suggested for 5G technology. In this segment, the various features and fundamental technologies which will play a vital role in the development of the 5G mobile communication system are discussed.

15.5.1 OFDM (Orthogonal Frequency Division Multiplexing)

In 1966, this technique was first suggested by R.W. Chang at Bell Labs. This modulation technique uncouples the channel bandwidth into numerous narrow band subcarriers to carry information. Unlike conventional FDM systems, OFDM prevents spectrum wastage by removing the guard band and introducing the unique subcarriers that are orthogonal to each other [14]. This technique is achieved by utilizing FFT (Fast Fourier Transform) at the transmitter and IFFT (Inverse Fast Fourier Transform) at the receiver. 4G LTE (long-term evolution) prefers this technique in order to enhance the data rate, throughput, and capacity, but in the case of 5G, OFDM will have some drawbacks such as PAPR (Peak Average Power Ratio) and CP (Cycle Prefix). Signal proximity will cause noise, so CP is introduced to help reduce ISI (Inter Symbol Reference). But inclusion of CP also creates the issue of 9% bandwidth loss. OFDM is not a very suitable modulation technique for 5G, therefore, much research is in progress all around the world for a new modulation technique that will meet the 5G requirements [15–17].

15.5.2 FBMC (Filter Band Multi Carrier)

This modulation technique uses an array of filters at the receiver and transmitter instead of CP and delivers a higher quality performance than OFDM. This technique is more suitable for 5G to transmit sets of parallel data through a bank of filters. The adjacent discharge and localization of the frequency can be managed by applying a suitable prototype filter. FBMC is more appropriate for the television white spectrum because it provides flexibility in its frequency domain. It can easily access the fragmented spectrum and control channel delay [18,19].

15.5.3 UFMC (Universal Filter Multi Carrier)

This novel modulation scheme is completely based on OFDM and a filter bank multicarrier. In FBMC, the filtering operation is achieved at each subcarrier, whereas in the UFMC technique, the filtering operation is conducted only for a certain class of subcarrier. This technique also enhances the system's throughput, because it is capable of reducing side lobes. Usually, its short length filters support short bursts of communication. In this scheme, the bandwidth splits into sub-bands, which are further allocated to the number of subcarriers. In this modulation technique, at the receiver end, an N-point IFFT operation permutates time domain signals to a frequency domain, whereas at the receiver end, the FFT operation converts the frequency domain of the signal into a time domain [20].

15.5.4 GFDM (Generalized Frequency Domain Multiplexing)

This modulation technique registers itself as a first non-orthogonalwaveform for 5G technology. In this scheme, filtering for each subcarrier reduces the side lobes and PAPR. It utilizes the Balian low theorem and Poisson summation algorithm for transmission and reception, respectively [21,22].

15.5.5 OFBMC (Orthogonal Frequency Band Multi Carrier)

In this modulation technique, utilization of bandwidth is efficient and results are more robust for the system. As with OFDM, the bandwidth is sliced up into subcarriers which are orthogonal in nature and do not use CP. This technique is compatible with Space Time Block Code(STBC), Spatial Division Multiplexing(SDM), Space time Trellis Codes (SPTC), and boosts system performance. OFBMC also gets rid of impairments such as ISI [23].

15.5.6 Cognitive Radio

This is an intelligent device that senses and understands the outside or surrounding radio frequency (RF) environment by utilizing a specific methodology and then changes or settles its own internal statics and parameters (carrier frequency, modulation strategy, transmitting power) according to what is has sensed. The fundamental advantage of this system is to recognize the existing white spectrum spaces (from the primary user's [PU's] signal) and utilize them in order to reduce spectrum wastage and deficiencies. The operations performed by cognitive radio [CR] are as follows: (C. I. Badoi, N. Prasad, V. Croitiru, and R. Prasad, "5G Based on Cognitive Radio" Wireless Pers Communication, 2011.)

1. Spectrum sensing is the ability of CR to detect the free channel from the existing licensed bands. There is an obligation to respect the priority of the PU's signal in order to avoid interference, therefore, under this condition, a CR has to cease its transmission activity in any channel where it registers the presence of a PU's signal. CR first checks for the presence of a signal without knowing its type or nature. Once the signal is detected, the second step is to classify the signal by extracting its features and then determining the availability of the channel.

2. Once the CR identifies a free channel, its next step is to share the spectrum with other CR devices. Spectrum sharing among different CRs can be performed by using techniques like horizontal spectrum sharing, vertical spectrum sharing, and hierarchical sharing.

3. Spectrum handover is also an important operation where the CR will dynamically maintain the transmission. This means that when a PU appears or performance degradation takes place for any reason, the secondary user should be able to switch channels dynamically or seamlessly without affecting the performance.

15.5.6.1 5G Terminal Itself a CR Terminal

A CR radio terminal is smart enough to select the appropriate network, support all data types, and maintain quality of service and data transmission rate with the help of its knowledge, reasoning, and decision-making properties. This section presents the three important predecessors of CR terminals. A CR device is a reconfigurable, self-contained component that condenses all the radio features into a single device. Thus, it can be concluded that a CR terminal, as shown in Figure 15.4a, is the best type of terminal for *5th Generation (5G)*.

A CR-based 5G communication system is appropriate for responding to greater user demands by integrating the different system architectures and technologies. CR technology is the best tool to provide more tightly combined architecture as shown in Figure 15.4b below.

Hence, it can be stated that the proposed 5G network is not like traditional access network or (core communication network). The major goal of 5G using CR is to homogenize wireless diversity.

15.5.7 Massive Multiple Input Multiple Output (MIMO)

A MIMO system consists of an array of 100 antennas at the Mobile base station (MBS) in order to serve a large number of users concurrently with a single antenna in same frequency and time. A MIMO system is also called a full dimension MIMO and many other names. This system depends on spatial multiplexing (multi-user), which depends on the channel knowledge found at the MBS on both downlink and uplink channels. A massive MIMO structure helps to consume less energy and reduces the latency. It also removes the complexity of an medium access control (MAC) layer. This system is much more

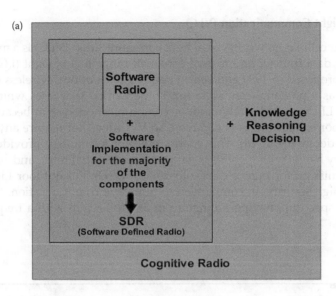

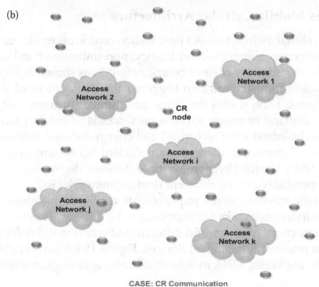

CASE: CR Communication

FIGURE 15.4
(a) Cognitive radio. (b) Cognitive radio communication.

capable of handling interference caused by a jammer's signals during moderate transmission [25,26].

15.5.8 Millimeter Waves

Modern day communication requires a wider microwave spectrum. Milimeter mmwave communication is basically introduced to achieve a high-speed data transmission rate in the 30–300 GHz frequency band for a large number of users. However, sensitivity to blockage is also an issue which demands adaptive array processing algorithms for an mmwave system [27].

15.5.9 Visual Light Communication (VLC)

In the upcoming cellular network, visual light communication (VLC) is a medium that convey high-speed data transfer and is used for small range line of sight (LOS) optical links. VLC was first proposed in 1999 and is also referred to as optical wireless communication. It is presented as a potential candidate for 5G networks. VLC uses white light emitting diodes, that is, LEDs, as a desirable indoor communication system because the presence of LEDs in indoor environments is common, so VLC does not require any additional cost and power for deployment [28]. This energy efficient technology provides a wide range of free frequency bands with gigabits/s data rates and spatial reuse and supports interference-free transmission for indoor device-to-device (D2D) and outdoor Light Fidelity (Li-Fi) users with high security. In comparison to mmwave communication, the VLC band is much richer in spectrum, having a range from 380 to 780 nm with a frequency range up to 790 THz [29].

15.6 5G-Futures Mobile Cellular Architecture

The conventional cellular architecture is a base station centric network, but the requirements of ubiquitous connections, submillisecond latency, and unlimited bandwidth are inspiring researchers to shift toward a device/user centric network, as shown in Figure 15.5a. Intense growth in the wireless industry has also triggered the deployment of small, micro, pico, and femto cells. Figure 15.5b shows the range and number of users that exist in different types of cells. The demand of future wireless networks is to connect multiple nodes with various proximities by introducing sectorized and energy-focused antennas in place of outdated omnidirectional antennas. Therefore, an efficient 5G system demands a systematic antenna design, SDMA (Space Division Multiple Access), decoupling of user and control planes, and interoperability among different devices/network [30].

This section draws attention to the requirements for 5G architecture and its emerging technologies. 5G wireless networks are supposed to be a fusion of network tiers of various sizes, backhaul connections, powers, and different radio access technologies, and will integrate an enormous number of intelligent devices. Figure 15.6 represents 5G multitier architecture along with small cells, D2D, mobile small cells, and cognitive radio network CRN communications.

15.6.1 Two-Tier Architecture

For the 5G network, several two-tier architectures have been suggested, where the macro-cell base station, that is, MBS, is positioned at the top tier and small cell base stations, that is, SBSs, are in the lower tier under the control of the MBS. Two-tier architecture is utilized as a procedure for network densification that is a mixture of spatial densification (each user is aided by a number of antennas and heavy placement of small cells) and spectral aggregation (frequency bands greater than 3 GHz). A trade-off exists between the coverage area of small cells and transmission power of the cell, that is, if the transmission power of the macro cell becomes high then it will compel the adjacent user equipment in small cells to fall into the service area of the macro cell, thus the size of the small cell will shrink. Conversely, if the transmission power of the macro cell decreases

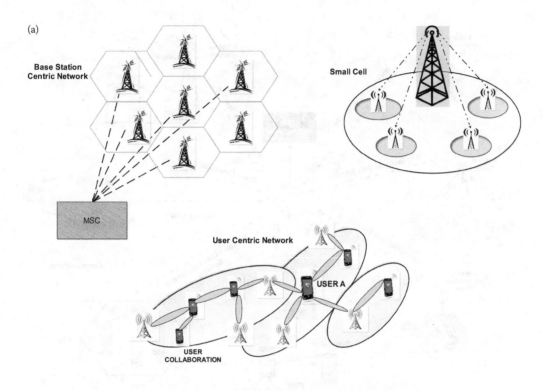

FIGURE 15.5
(a) Conventional base station centric network and user centric network. (b) Different cell types and their comparison.

then the coverage area of small cells will expand. Therefore, the expansion of cell range should be carried out in order to benefit users depending on the small cell to which they are closer [31].

Deployment of small cells provides several benefits like high data rates, efficient spectrum utilization, energy saving, money saving, less congestion, and smooth hand-off, but frequent authentications and sudden topological changes are also some realistic issues of using small cells in a two-tier architecture.

15.6.1.1 Issues with Two-Tier Architecture Using Small Cells

1. *Handling of interference*: The use of small cells creates different types of inter- and intra-tier interference, for example inter-tier interference occurs from MBS to SBS,

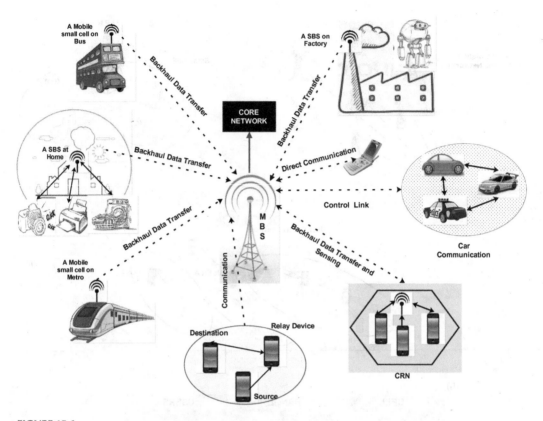

FIGURE 15.6
5G multitier architecture along with small cells, D2D, mobile small cells, and CRN communications.

MBS to UEs of SBS, and SBS to UEs of MBS. Intra-tier interference from the SBS to users of other SBSs occurs, so it is necessary to design appropriate models and methods to handle this interference.

2. *Backhaul data transfer*: This technique uses three methods (wired fiber optical, wireless point to point, wireless point to multipoint) to carry data from the SBS to the core network. Heavy deployment of small cells demands a large amount of data transfer, which is quite a challenging task.

15.6.1.2 Self-Healing Property of Two-Tier Architecture

In densely deployed two-tier architecture, automatic recovery and detection of failed small cells is really an issue, which can be resolved using the approaches mentioned below [32]

1. *Centralized Approach*: In this approach, a centralized dedicated server detects the failed cells by analyzing the problematic behavior of users. It also contains global information used to reconfigure the failed cell, but this method also requires immense communication overhead and computational cost.

2. *Distributed Approach*: Each SBS can identify the failed small cells in its neighborhood by analyzing two things. The first is a user's hand-off behavior, and the second is small cells' signals. SBS has to increase its transmitting power in order to cooperate with failed cells' users. This approach may suffer, particularly in the case where the users are scattered.

3. *Hybrid Approach*: This approach is much better than the previously mentioned methods, as it follows two steps. The first step is the distributed trigger, in which each SBS collects the information of its users' activity and eventually sends the message to the dedicated server if the received information falls below a defined threshold. Thus, it does not require communication among small cells. Another step is cooperation detection, where a devoted server makes the final decision after observing the received information from several small cells. This results in an increase in accuracy and a decline in latency.

15.6.2 Device-to-Device Communication Architecture

D2D communication supports the close proximity of users to communicate with each other on a licensed band without or with limited assistance from the MBS. It operates on in-band and out-band D2D modes [33]. This communication architecture was first implemented by Qualcomm's FlashLinQ in their cellular network, where OFDM/OFMA technologies and distributed scheduling have been used for time synchronization, peer discovery, and link management [34]. Figure 15.7 presents the D2D use cases such as

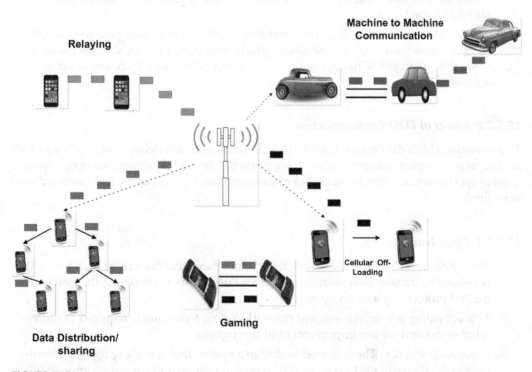

FIGURE 15.7
Device-to-device use case.

multicasting, peer to peer communication, machine to machine communication, cellular off-loading, and so on.

15.6.2.1 Issues in D2D Communication

    i. Interference Management

       1. *Interference explored while using downlink channel*: (i) Interference received from the BSs in the same cell, (ii) Interference from other cochannel D2D UEs in the same cell, and (iii) Interference from BSs and co-channel D2D UEs from other cells.

       2. *Interference explored while using uplink channel*: (i) Interference from all co-channel cellular-UEs in the same cell and other cells, and (ii) Interference from all co-channel D2D UEs in the same cell and other cells.

         Solution proposed: The above-mentioned interference problems can be solved by implementing cognitive radio networks in D2D communications, where D2D UEs are considered secondary users and do not interfere with cellular UEs who are considered to be primary users [35].

    ii. *Resource Management*: It is necessary to provide a significant amount of bandwidth and channel allocation to all users involved in device-to-device communication. The main challenge is the allocation of optimum resources and the establishment of efficient communication by the D2D user equipment without causing any interference to the cellular users [36].

        Solution proposed: Slot by slot and frame by frame channel allocation methods should be used.

    iii. *Delay sensitive processing*: Real time and delay sensitive processing are required for (audio, video streaming, online games) the applications used by various users.

        Solution Proposed: Channel state information (CSI) and QoS are used as a solution [37].

15.6.2.2 Merits of D2D Communication

This provides a high data rate, reliability to D2D users, and also delivers an easy way of file sharing in peer to peer communication. It supports fast and quick communication, improvement of spectrum efficiency, reduces power consumption for D2D users, and traffic off-load from the MBS.

15.6.2.3 Open Issue

    1. *Privacy and security*: D2D users seek help from other users (as a relay node), so it is necessary to transfer data secretly and in a secure manner. Therefore, the design of trusted protocols is also an open issue.

    2. *Network coding scheme*: An efficient network coding technique is required to utilize relay nodes and for the improvement of throughput.

    3. *Multi-mode selection*: There is need to design a system that can allow users to simultaneously engage in the two types (D2D communication and communication to BS) of communication modes.

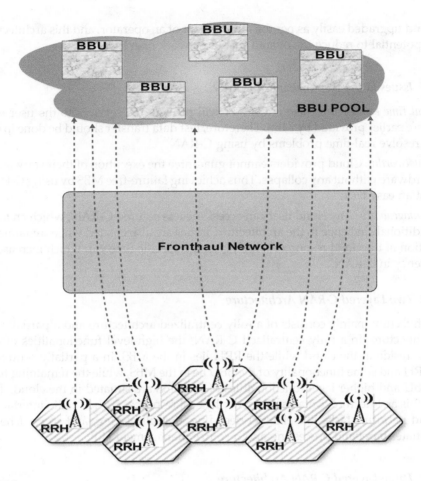

FIGURE 15.8
C-RAN architecture.

15.6.3 Cloud Based Radio Access Network (C-RAN)

C-RAN has the capability to support a dynamic service allocation scheme for scaling the network without worrying about the management of resources. The first C-RAN was proposed by the China Mobile Research Onstitute in April 2010. Many other operators such as American telephone and telegraph (AT&T), Orange, Sunkyong (SK) Telecom, Softbank Corp, and NTT Docomo are planning for the deployment of C-RAN in the 2018–2020 time frame. The main objective of C-RAN is to implement all the functions of MBS in the cloud and further divide these functions between the data layer and control layer. In C-RAN, MBS contains two important components; the baseband unit (placed in cloud) and the remote radio head (placed in MBSs).

The base band unit (BBU) is used for baseband processing and the remote radio head (RRH) performs radio functions. Figure 15.8 shows a typical C-RAN architecture with BBUs from many remote sites centralized at a virtual BBU pool [38].

C-RAN architecture is well prepared to accept non-uniform traffic so fewer baseband unit BBUs are required in this architecture in comparison to the conventional one. BBUs can be added and upgraded easily as per the requirement of an operator, and this architecture also has the potential to reduce the overall cost of network operation [39].

15.6.3.1 Issues in the Deployment of C-RAN

1. *Real time execution capability*: C-RAN will provide the services to the user which were earlier provided by MBS. Therefore, fast data transfer should be done in order to resolve real-time problems by using C-RAN.

2. *Trustworthy*: Cloud providers cannot guarantee the execution of their software and hardware without any collapse. Thus achieving failure-free MBS by using C-RAN is not an easy task.

3. *Manageability*: Any cloud user can access the less secured C-RAN, which creates an additional challenge in the architecture. Issues are also created when dynamic allocation of the cloud resources takes place at a specific time gap which increases the latency in C-RAN.

15.6.3.2 Two Layered C-RAN Architecture

This architecture mainly consists of a fully centralized architecture and a partially centralized architecture. In a fully centralized C-RAN, the high-level functionalities of an MBS and BBU reside in the cloud while the RRH lies in the MBS. In a partially centralized C-RAN, RRH and some functionality of the BBU lie in the MBS, while the remaining functions of the BBU and higher level functionalities of the MBS are situated in the cloud. The data layer of this architecture contains different physical resources such as radio interface equipment and performs tasks like channel decoding, demultiplexing, and so on. The control layer initiates baseband processing and resource management [40].

15.6.3.3 Three-Layered C-RAN Architecture

In this architecture, one more layer, that is, a software-defined service layer, is also added along with data and control layers. The software-defined service layer handles the processing delay that occurs in fully centralized C-RAN architecture where the data and control layers are usually far from each other. This problem can be handled in a three-layered architecture also called convergence of the cloud and cellular system (CONCERT) [41].

15.6.3.4 Potential Advantages of C-RAN

1. *Low deployment and operating cost*: C-RAN architecture uses RRH entities which consume less power than regular base stations. Therefore, it enables a significant cut in capital expenditure of the telecom service provider. The standard base stations, which consume high power, negatively affect the environment and this issue is also considered under C-RAN architecture, so it is also referred to as GREEN RAN.

2. *Overall systems' throughput improvement*: It is cheaper and simpler to form small cells with low transmitting power in dense areas to satisfy customers' throughput by using MIMO techniques, modulation techniques, and frequency channels (20 MHz) in advanced LTE. In C-RAN, however, the gap between customers' needs and operator capabilities is solved by deploying dense RRH schemes in the areas where high throughput is required.

3. *Optimized resource utilization*: It is known that an end user mostly moves across different cell sites in a certain manner and because of that, base stations' resources remain unused for a significant amount of time on a daily basis. The wasting of radio resources is a major issue faced by operators, which is why in C-RAN, a virtual base station entity, that is, BBU, is introduced inside the cloud to provide the same coverage area with fewer virtual base stations (VBSs) than a regular base station.

4. *Co-existence with other standards*: New standards should accept the expensive existing old standard equipment and make an effort to generate profits with them. The C-RAN equipment, such as a universal RRH and virtual base stations, can easily be implemented on reprogrammable hardware. This also supports the unification of various standards/technologies with minimum cost.

15.7 Emerging Applications

1. *Transportation*: In the future, we will use self-driving vehicles which also share information or communicate with other vehicles in order to generate a safe and integrated environment which helps cars to become more advanced and faster and to make decisions about any problem related to road safety, routes, weather, and so on. Basically, the 5G network will provide an intelligent transportation system with very low latency to all the vehicle-to-vehicle and vehicle-to-infrastructure systems.

2. *Health System*: Patients can self-monitor their health issues such as pulse rate, blood pressure, and breathing rate by wearing smart devices which are capable of transmitting all these real time data to health care centers or the cloud. This service also helps to reduce cost by facilitating the patients to stay at home without going to hospitals.

3. *Tactile Internet*: Tactile internet applications lead to secure and fast medical diagnosis for medical treatment. A rapid and valid mobile communication can facilitate medical facilities and services in any corner of the world. Tactile internet also helps in reducing both medical services' cost and time. Here, users experience only milliseconds of interaction latency for futuristic applications.

4. *Smart Cities*: Smart cities' applications are varied because it acquires a huge amount of data from multiple domains (traffic management, parking, shipping, energy management, waste management, water services, lighting, etc.) and brings them together in an *information technology* (IT) system. Rio de Janerio is the second largest city of Brazil and has a large integrated information technologyIT system with deep sensor networks to capture and analyze thousands of data streams [42].

5. *Industry*: Manufacturing industries are going to be revolutionized using 5G connectivity, where super intelligent robots manage and operate the industrial functions [43]

6. *Tracking and Logistics*: 5G connection gives full accountability and better tracking services to the supplier and customer both by installing 5G connected sensors on every single object so that the supplier need not require any manual checkpoints or can easily create a transparent and optimized supply of items without damaging them [44,24].

15.8 Conclusion

This chapter discussed essential technologies, components, and architecture required for the deployment of the future 5G communication system. Recent trials and ongoing projects of 5G technology conducted by different operators and vendors have also been discussed. A 5G communication system truly yields better flexibility, improved spectral efficiency, omnipresent connectivity, and reliability. Two–tier architecture, C-RAN, and Device-To-Device communication are incorporated in 5G in order to push back the limitations of conventional cellular systems. In this chapter, we have also examined some open issues and advantages associated with different architectures.

Acknowledgments

We thank our parents for their support and motivation.

References

1. N. Panwar, S. Sharma and A. K. Singh, "A survey on 5g: The next generation of mobile communication," *Physical Communication*, vol. 18, Part 2, pp. 64–84, 2016.
2. NGMN Alliance, "5G White Paper—Executive Version," NGMN White Paper, December 2014.
3. A. Naha and P. Whale, *Essentials of Mobile Handset Design.* Cambridge: Cambridge University Press, 2012.
4. M. M. Siddiqui, "Vision of 5G communication," *High Performance Architecture And Grid Computing*, vol. 169, pp. 252–256, 2011.
5. G. Caso, M. T. P. Le, L. De Nardis, M.-G. Di Benedetto and W. Zhang, Non-cooperative and cooperative spectrum sensing in 5G cognitive networks, in: Zhang W. (ed) *Handbook of Cognitive Radio*, Singapore: Springer, pp. 1–21, 2017.
6. S. Kavanagh, "5G guides: How fast is 5G?," 5G.co.uk. [Online]. Available: https://5g.co.uk/guides/how-fast-is-5g/ [Accessed: November 23, 2017].
7. BBC News, First 5G mobile net connection' claimed by Qualcomm. [Online]. Available: http://www.bbc.com/news/technology-41652967 [Accessed: October 17, 2017].
8. J. Carter, "5G News: Qualcomm's first 5G smartphone chip scores gigabit speeds," 5G.co.uk, 23 October 2017. [Online]. Available: https://5g.co.uk/news/first-5g-smartphone-chip/4214/ [Accessed: November 25, 2017].
9. B. McDermid, "Verizon plan to launch 5G broadband lifts shares," Business News, November 30, 2017. [Online]. Available: https://www.reuters.com/article/us-verizon-stocks/verizon-plan-to-launch-5g-broadband-lifts-shares-idUSKBN1DU2IP.
10. X. Zhou et al., "Toward 5G: When explosive bursts meet soft cloud," *IEEE Network*, vol. 28, no. 6, pp. 12–17, Nov.-Dec. 2014.
11. E. Oh, K. Son and B. Krishnamachari, "Dynamic base station switching-on/off strategies for green cellular networks," *IEEE Transactions On Wireless Communications*, vol. 12, no. 5, pp. 2126–2136, May 2013.
12. W. Nam, D. Bai, J. Lee and I. Kang, "Advanced interference management for 5G cellular networks," *IEEE Communications Magazine*, vol. 52, no. 5, pp. 52–60, May 2014.
13. C. X. Wang et al., "Cellular architecture and key technologies for 5G wireless communication networks," *IEEE Communications Magazine*, vol. 52, no. 2, pp. 122–130, February 2014.

14. Nutaq, An Introduction To Orthogonal Frequency Division Multiplex (OFDM). [Online]. Available: https://www.nutaq.com/blog/introduction-orthogonal-frequency-division-multi-plex-ofdm [Accessed: November 3, 2017].

15. A. Kumar and M. Gupta, "Design of OFDM and PAPR reduction using clipping method," *Artificial Intelligence And Network Security, Desidoc DRDO Delhi*, vol. 1, no. 1, pp. 221–229, 2015.

16. A. Kumar and M. Gupta, "A review on OFDM and PAPR reduction techniques," *Am. J. Eng. Appl. Sci. (AJEAS)*, vol. 8, no. 2, pp. 202. 209, 2015.

17. A. Kumar and M. Gupta, "Design and comparison of MIMO OFDM for different transmission schemes," *Electronics World Monthly*, vol. 121, pp. 16–22, 2015.

18. I. Estella, A.P. Iserte, M. Payar, OFDM and FBMCperformance comparison for multi-stream MIMO systems, in: P. Cunningham, M. Cunningham (Eds.), *Future Network and Mobile Summit Conference Proceedings*, IIMCInternational Information Management Corporation, Florence, Italy, pp. 1–8, 2008.

19. J. Fang, Z. You, I. T. Lu, J. Li and R. Yang, "Comparisons of filter bank multicarrier systems," *2013 IEEE Long Island Systems, Applications and Technology Conference (LISAT)*, Farmingdale, NY, 2013, pp. 1–6.

20. V. Vakilian, T. Wild, F. Schaich, S. Brink and J-F Frigon, "Universal filter multi carrier technique for wireless system beyond LTE," *Global Workshop Broadband Wireless Access*, Atlanta, GA, USA 2008, pp. 223–228.

21. I. Gaspar, M. Matthe´, N. Michailow, LL. Mendes, D. Zhang and G. Fettweis, "GFDM trans-ceiver using precoded data and low-complexity multiplication in time domain," pp. 1–4, June 2015, [online] Available: http://arxiv.org/abs/1506.03350.

22. A. Aminjavaheri, A. Farhang, A. RezazadehReyhani and B. Farhang-Boroujeny, "Impact of timing and frequency offsets on multicarrier waveform candidates for 5G," *2015 IEEE Signal Processing and Signal Processing Education Workshop (SP/SPE)*, Salt Lake City, UT, 2015, pp. 178–183.

23. D. Roque and C. Siclet, "Performances of weighted cyclic prefix OFDM with low-complexity equalization, *IEEE Communications Letters*, vol. 17, no. 3, pp. 439–442, March 2013.

24. 5G network technology: Putting Europe at the leading edge. European Parliament ThinkTank, January 4, 2016. [Online]. Available: http://www.europarl.europa.eu/thinktank/en/document.html?reference=EPRS_BRI(2016)573892 [Accessed: October 30, 2017].

25. Y. H. Nam et al., "Full-dimension MIMO (FD-MIMO) for next generation cellular technology," *IEEE Communications Magazine*, vol. 51, no. 6, pp. 172–179, June 2013.

26. E. G. Larsson, O. Edfors, F. Tufvesson and T. L. Marzetta, "Massive MIMO for next generation wireless systems," *IEEE Communications Magazine*, vol. 52, no. 2, pp. 186–195, February 2014.

27. F. Hu, *Opportunities in 5G Networks: A Research and Development Perspective*, Boca Raton, FL, USA: CRC Press, 2016.

28. A. Jovicic, J. Li and T. Richardson, "Visible light communication: Opportunities, challenges and the path to market," *IEEE Communications Magazine*, vol. 51, no. 12, pp. 26–32, December 2013

29. L. Feng, R. Q. Hu, J. Wang, P. Xu and Y. Qian, "Applying VLC in 5G networks: Architectures and key technologies," *IEEE Network*, vol. 30, no. 6, pp. 77–83, November-December 2016.

30. M. Agiwal, A. Roy and N. Saxena, "Next generation 5G wireless networks: A comprehensive sur-vey," *IEEE Communications Surveys & Tutorials*, vol. 18, no. 3, pp. 1617–1655, thirdquarter 2016.

31. N. Panwar, S. Sharma and A. K. Singh, "A survey on 5G: The next generation of mobile com-munication," *Phys. Commun.*, vol. 18, pp. 64–84, March 2016.

32. W. Wang and Q. Zhang, "Local cooperation architecture for self-healing femtocell networks", *IEEE Wireless Communications*, vol. 21, no. 2, pp. 42–49, April 2014.

33. A. Asadi, Q. Wang and V. Mancuso, "A survey on device-to-device communication in cellular networks," *IEEE Commun. Surveys & Tutorials*, vol. 16, no. 4, pp. 1801–1819, 2014.

34. X. Wu et al., "FlashLinQ: A synchronous distributed scheduler for peer-to-peer ad hoc net-works," *Proceedings Allerton Conference Communications Control Computing*, Allerton, IL, USA, pp. 514–521, 2010.

35. L. Wei, R. Q. Hu, Y. Qian and G. Wu, "Enable device-to-device communications underlaying cellular networks: Challenges and research aspects." *IEEE Communications Magazine*, vol. 52, no. 6, pp. 90–96, June 2014.

36. Y. Li, T. Wu, P. Hui, D. Jin and S. Chen, "Social-aware D2D communications: Qualitative insights and quantitative analysis," *IEEE Communications Magazine*, vol. 52, no. 6, pp. 150–158, June 2014.

37. W. Wang and V. K. N. Lau, "Delay-aware cross-layer design for device-to-device communications in future cellular systems," *IEEE Communications Magazine*, vol. 52, no. 6, pp. 133–139, June 2014.

38. A. Checko et al., "Cloud RAN for mobile networks—A technology overview," *IEEE Commun. Surveys Tuts.*, vol. 17, no. 1, pp. 405–426, 1st Quart. 2015.(A. Checko, "Cloud radio access network architecture. Towards 5G mobile networks", 2016)

39. R. Wang, H. Hu and X. Yang, "Potentials and challenges of C-RAN supporting multi-RATs toward 5G mobile networks," *IEEE Access*, vol. 2, pp. 1187–1195, 2014.

40. China Mobile,"C-RAN: The road towards green ran," White Paper, ver. 2.5, China mobile Research Institute,Beijing, China, October 2011.

41. J. Liu, T. Zhao, S. Zhou, Y. Cheng and Z. Niu, "CONCERT: A cloud-based architecture for next-generation cellular systems," *IEEE Wireless Communications*, vol. 21, no. 6, pp. 14–22, December 2014.

42. T. Newcombe, "The Rise of the Sensor-Based Smart City, "Government Technology, June 2, 2014. [Online]. Available: http://www.govtech.com/data/the-rise-of-the-sensor-based-city.html [Accessed: October 11, 2017].

43. Global Mobile Suppliers Assiociation. The Road to 5G: Drivers, Applications, Requirements and Technical Development, November 19, 2015. [Online]. Available: https://gsacom.com/paper/the-road-to-5g-drivers-applications-requirements-and-technical-development/ [Accessed: November 20, 2017].

44. A. Tøgard, "The impact of 5G: How will 5G affect supply chain & logistics?," *Wallenius Welhelmsen Logistics*, August 18, 2017. [Online]. Available: https://www.2wglobal.com/news-and-insights/articles/features/the-impact-of-5g/ [Accessed: September 27, 2017].

16

Wireless Internet Offloading Techniques: Based on 802.21 Medium Access Control

Bilal Muhammad Khan and Rabia Bilal

CONTENTS

16.1 Overview of Wi-Fi Offloading

Wireless Internet (Wi-Fi) offloading or simply offloading technology means releasing congestion in the licensed spectrum, that is, from cellular networks toward the unlicensed band of Wi-Fi. The latter is achieved through a vertical handover supported by mobile devices, thus creating a balance in data usage with no additional infrastructure.

This also releases bandwidth in the cellular frequency band and attempts to load share with the unlicensed Wi-Fi band, which means the data destined for the cellular network is processed by Wi-Fi links. This is an attempt to create equilibrium in the network utilization of both bands. Offloading is not limited to handover between long term evolution (LTE) and Wi-Fi, in fact, it is flexible enough for all radio access technology (RAT) types specified for licensed and unlicensed spectrum. Institute of electrical electronic engineering (IEEE) standard 802.21 controls this. In this work, we focus on the offloading of data between LTE and Wi-Fi.

Each technology comes with its pros and cons. Here in this work, we analyze on Wi-Fi offloading and our contributions to offloading.

16.2 Background Information

The increases in technological advances and emerging technologies such as 3G and LTE networks have led to the increased use of data services and easy access as well. With the availability of sophisticated handheld devices, this has also paved the way for increased usage of mobile data. Wi-Fi technology is already widely available and with the ready availability of mobile wireless technologies, the concept of offloading is quite feasible.

The adaptation of Wi-Fi offloading for our technology-hungry society would not be a challenging matter as data traffic need is on the rise in every are of life, including science, education, entertainment, navigation, disaster management, health information systems, and so on. The need for the ready availability of data connections at all times and at all places is already an accepted reality. Hence, offloading theories can soon be implemented not only in the modernized world, but in the third world countries as well.

The idea of Wi-Fi offloading is still new to researchers and various techniques and algorithms are being proposed for this technology. Our motive here is to present an overview of the Wi-Fi offloading techniques, focusing on the algorithms and keeping the existing infrastructure in view while also discussing the positive impact on society for the adaptation of offloading technology, hence motivating new and as well as established researchers to invest their efforts in a field which has a direct social impact on society is a priority. In this paper, we will discuss the different aspects of Wi-Fi offloading with respect to economics, technical, and social impacts and its available techniques.

16.3 Underlying Concept of Wi-Fi Offloading: Always Best Connected

The concept behind the use of 802.21 lies in it being in the best interest of the user for to be always best connected (ABC) taking into consideration the mobility factors, coverage area for a particular access network, and the data capacity for each network to check for the throughputs that could be achieved. The concept of ABC has originated to provide the best data services to the user where multiple access technologies are available from which to choose . Hence the challenge lies in designing a user transparent heterogeneous wireless network that best serves the users' needs, keeping in view the data necessities. The concept of ABC was proposed in [2].

With global reachability and ABC mechanisms in place, mobile devices will be able to selectively connect to different access networks depending on certain pre-defined criteria. For the efficient usage of network resources, there is a need to collect relevant network information at periodic intervals as governed by some policy or in a standardized way regardless of the access technology. The periodically gathered information can then to be used for the handover decision.

16.4 Aspects of Wi-Fi Offloading

16.4.1 Economic Aspects

Before getting into the technical specifications of Wi-Fi offloading, we need to justify it economically. This can be best done by referring to the Coase theorem, although a detailed discussion is beyond scope of this work. However, for the sake of clarification, the Coase theorem [3] refers to the frequency band to be effectively utilized and a guarantee that no external user other than licensed one uses the services. This reduces the impact of interference. It is also a guarantee that the frequency bands for any service provider are allocated and governed by the regulatory authorities, which leads to the efficient use of resources.

16.4.2 Technical Aspects of Offloading

The inspiration for this work is based on the fact of data explosion in the modern environment and the heavy utilization of Internet services. The use of Wi-Fi as an alternate technology along with cellular data is unavoidable. This technique is more commonly known as Wi-Fi offloading. This means if a third generation partnership project (3GPP) network gets congested due to an increase in network utilization or some other reason, data traffic may need to be offloaded to Wi-Fi and vice versa. This handover of services would remain transparent to the subscriber. Offloading is implemented by using vertical handover algorithms on the medium access control (MAC) layer of the open system interconnection (OSI) model. In cities in developed countries, wide deployment of Wi-Fi networks is becoming a trend which this supports the idea of Wi-Fi offloading. Such deployments are being done in developing countries. Hence, the idea of offloading and its practical implementations is soon to become a reality not only in the developed countries, but also in the third world countries.

The important aspect of Wi-Fi offloading depends upon the handover trigger conditions. These mainly are based upon network conditions, link utilization, and signal strength, more precisely the received signal strength indication (RSSI). The IEEE standard developed for vertical handover is 802.21. It provides a structure for processing the handover in a heterogeneous environment. A heterogeneous network environment is a network which has multiple devices under its coverage using multiple radio access technologies. A pictorial view of such a network is shown in Figure 16.1.

There are multiple issues of management in such networks to provide high quality services to the user. A few of these issues include the mobility issues, quality of experience for the user, interference between RATs, interoperability, and most importantly, the inter RAT handovers. In a crowded environment, the deployment of new cell eNodeBs becomes impractical. Operators need to think about heterogeneous networks so that enhanced services can be provided with the same network capacity.

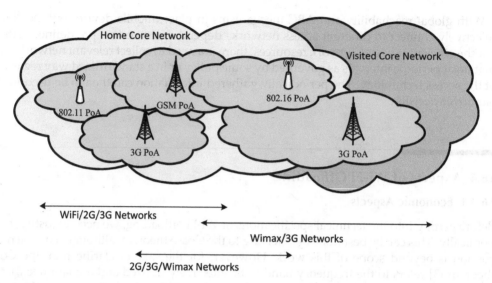

FIGURE 16.1
Heterogeneous network environment pictorial overview.

16.5 Application: Pros and Cons of Wi-Fi Offloading

Wi-Fi offloading can find its applications in multiple scenarios that are present every day. It can find its applications in the reporting of seismic incidents, health information systems like patient care and reporting, crime reporting, disaster management, emergency incidents, and so on. To accomplish Wi-Fi offloading, all that is required is a heterogeneous network environment as described in the technical description section of this paper, that is, there must be availability of infrastructures of both Wi-Fi and cellular data. The following section discusses the advantages and disadvantages of Wi-Fi offloading with respect to the applications and their impact on society.

Figure 16.2 shows a heterogeneous network environment which is a common picture of crowded deployment in today's world. As can be clearly observed, there is an overlap between the coverage areas of multiple access technologies. Hence the implementation of media independent handover (MIH) protocol is feasible and calls for a better quality of experience.

In an urban environment, due to skyscrapers and high-rise buildings, an effective cellular network requires deployment of micro and nano sites to overcome loss of signal issues. If the Wi-Fi offloading option is available in the network, heavy savings could be achieved by avoiding the purchase and deployment of new sites. The alternate Wi-Fi networks serve the purpose of data connectivity. Figure 16.2 explains this scenario.

The effectiveness of Wi-Fi offloading can also be utilized in a rural environment. In a rural environment, network quality is not up to the standards for both Wi-Fi and cellular data. However, if multiple access technologies can be made available with the use of offloading technology, a better user experience can be achieved. Hence in this way underprivileged, under developed areas get the same facilities as developed areas.

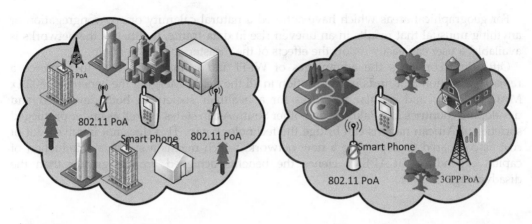

FIGURE 16.2
Urban environment versus rural environment.

A user who has a network compatible with offloading has more access to the Internet than the ones without it. Hence those users can avail the numerous advantages offered by Wi-Fi offloading.

Crime reporting or emergency reporting is an important aspect and yet one that is rarely used. A probable application scenario of this could be in case of a network outage on cellular data when a Wi-Fi base station continues to be operational or vice versa. Hence, there is always an available data connection for reporting incidents. A crime incident occurs at some XYZ place, but the dynamics of the place is such that it has poor cellular coverage and an acceptable Wi-Fi service. Provided the mobile operator supports Wi-Fi offloading, reporting the incident is more convenient. Thus, it is a contribution to our society as a whole. If an accident occurs in a densely populated area where the cellular network is facing congestion, an alternate access to data services without changing mobile devices would be extremely advantageous. If an emergency situation and the network suddenly become choked, there will be an urgent need for extra network resources which can be best fulfilled with the use of Wi-Fi offloading.

Hence, there is an immediate call for providers to incorporate Wi-Fi offloading in existing network deployments.

Although there are many advantages for offloading technology, the seamless connectivity may give an extra edge to the subscriber regardless of their usage. Such technology may be used for criminal activities as well. However, this is not such a huge disadvantage that development work should be halted. This can be circumvented by applying proper security features in the network such as authentication and other measures as per the network standards.

Such facilities are available in the developed countries of the world. However, all of the above scenarios are equally valid for developing countries such as Pakistan, where there is a definite need for such facilities. However, resources for implementing this requires the same infrastructure as is found in developed which is not feasible in the near future. Hence, Wi-Fi offloading serves the same purpose with the existing infrastructure in a heterogeneous network environment where there is no stable network condition, meaning in some areas the cellular infrastructure has better services than Wi-Fi and in others, Wi-Fi provides a better user experience.

For geographical areas which have suffered a natural calamity or any congregation or anything unusual that results in an uneven rise in data traffic, if either of the networks is available, a user can easily report the effects of the disaster and call for help.

Offloading combines the advantages of Wi-Fi and cellular networks to reinforce a research direction that finds its application in all the fields. Merging the benefits of 802.1x MAC protocols and cellular networks for a healthier society in both developed and developing countries like Pakistan and other South Asian states as well as under privileged societies of African nations can bridge the technology gap. This does not involve a lot of cost as compared to deploying a new network, which means a significant reduction of capital expenditure (CAPEX). Hence the benefits achieved are far greater than the disadvantages.

16.6 Scope of WI-FI Offloading

It is very important to understand the scope of Wi-Fi offloading to ensure research is for the betterment of the user experience and makes a socially positive impact on society. The scope of Wi-Fi offloading can be explained with respect to a mobile device. For a multi-access mobile node, a simultaneous connection may exist with each access network, hence maintaining multiple internet protocol (IP) flows is commonly known as IP Flow Mobility-IFOM. The 3GPP standard for this purpose is 23.261 [4] while 23.861 [5] addresses the standardization process for IFOM. Depending upon the network condition, a particular IP flow could be offloaded or a complete session could be to provide uninterrupted services to the user, hence being seamless and transparent to the user. This is tackled at the core network, however, it is transmitted to the access network to make sure the user remains transparent. With this, data transmission and reception to multiple IP flows remain unified during handover or vertical handover in our case. Vertical handovers can be precisely defined as inter technology handovers which are described later in the text.

16.7 Model for Wi-Fi Offloading: Heterogenous Network

The basic pictorial view explaining the difference between vertical and horizontal handovers is shown in Figure 16.3. The implementation of a vertical handover scenario is different for each of the above network models. However, in each case, the network model remains transparent to the user. Such handovers between different Radio Access Technologies (RAT) are commonly known as vertical handovers, that is, a handover between cellular and Wi-Fi can be one example in a heterogeneous network environment.

When Wi-Fi and cellular share the same core network, it is considered to be the simplest case as it involves the least amount of interworking. The 3GPP standard 23.402 [4] specifies the interworking between 3GPP and non-3GPP access. In universal mobile telecommunication system (UMTS), flat architectures are introduced. LTE or long term evolution advance (LTE-A) are the access part and the EPC (Evolved Packet Core) is the core part. They are collectively called the Evolved Packet System (EPS). The protocol is supported by Proxy Mobile Internet Protocol (PMIP). There are defined interfaces for each access network to reach the EPC as specified in the standard.

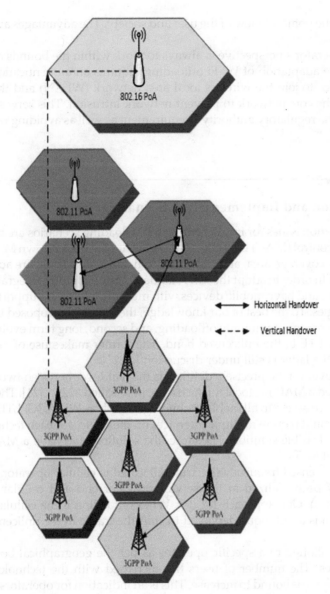

FIGURE 16.3
Pictorial view for a vertical handover.

16.8 Challenges to the Adaptation of Wi-Fi Offloading

Although Wi-Fi offloading seems to be an attractive technology to adopt when analyzed with respect to the user perspective, it needs more development from operator side, we will highlight the challenges of Wi-Fi offloading implementation and its solution.

In a real-world scenario, a major concern of an operator is to be a market leader with the minimum possible investment in the operation expenditure (OPEX). Wi-Fi offloading facilitates from the points of view of the user and society. The advantages are described later in the section.

Second, an operator's perspective is always to work within the bounds of the regulatory authority. Hence adaptation of Wi-Fi offloading requires an authentication procedure for the mobile device to join the wireless local area network (WLAN) and the availability of this feature on the core network to prevent network intrusion. This serves a two-fold purpose; fulfilling the regulatory authority's requirement as well as avoiding revenue leakages.

16.9 Integration and Implementation Scenarios

The basic integration issues for implementing the offloading scenarios are how to tackle the medium access control (MAC) Layer; each access technology has its own MAC layer, quality of service (QoS), coverage area, and data rates to name a few. These are addressed in IEEE 802.21 standard. In order to adopt the MIH standard, they should be integrated in a common core environment and have mobile devices with multiple interfaces supporting the multiple access technologies. To the best of our knowledge, there are two proposed techniques. First, Wi-Fi offloading or more commonly offloading, and second, long term evolution unlicensed (LTE-U), that is, LTE in the unlicensed band. The former makes use of vertical handover techniques and the latter is still under discussion [20,22].

Vertical handover can be precisely defined as the handover between two different RATs. IEEE has designed a MAC protocol for such a purpose called 802.21 [21]. The purpose of this is for a user to have access to all mobile technologies such as Wi-Fi, 3G, LTE, and Bluetooth. However, this would require multiple interfaces on the device for each technology, which is not a practically feasible solution. Therefore, the solution is to have a MAC protocol that could support all RATs.

The supply of licensed frequency spectrum allocated to cellular operators is very limited; this has already been realized at the service provider end and cellular operators have been working on it. One approach for it is Wi-Fi offloading if the cellular networks gets congested, which is a technique deployed to shift the traffic to the unlicensed band of the Wi-Fi [23,24].

Bandwidth is allotted to a specific operator as per the geographical boundaries by the regulatory bodies. The number of users has increased with the technological advances, hence, the data usage is bound to increase. This is an indication for operators to continuously work for expansion of the bandwidth and to look for alternatives. This, however, impacts the OPEX/CAPEX, so being sure of the availability of bandwidth is as important as the cost. An alternative to 3G and LTE can be a cheaper technology such as Wi-Fi. To overcome the scarcity on the uplink and fulfill the high data needs, the idea of Wi-Fi offloading has been proposed, that is, utilizing the abundant unlicensed frequency spectrum [25–27]. Handing over data traffic to the Wi-Fi helps overcome congestion in the access layer.

Wi-Fi is an unlicensed spectrum resource which makes efficient use of the spectrum by listening before talking. Wi-Fi is a cheap deployment solution as compared to cellular data (Global System for Mobile communication [GSM], 3G, LTE, LTE-A and so forth).

Limitation of the spectrum and debate over the use of licensed and unlicensed spectrum is one point of discussion for the selection of technology for data transmission. The growth of data traffic is also showing an exponential trend. Mobile networks are suffering from the limitation of Capital Expenditures (CAPEX) and Operating Expenditure (OPEX).

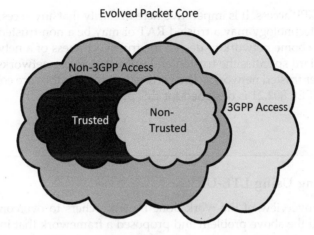

FIGURE 16.4
EPC overview of heterogenous network environment.

16.10 Problem Description

Today, there are over 350 million cellular subscribers in the U.S. and 70% of them possess smartphones [6]. The data traffic carried by these subscribers has exceeded 4.8 exabytes per year and is growing at 50% annually, as described by computer information system company (CISCO) annual reports [7]. However, we all know the radio frequency spectrum used for communication for cellular networks and specifically for data traffic is a limited and extremely valuable resource. With the explosion of new wireless applications, the use of the radio spectrum has increased to the point that new spectrum policies are inevitable.

The concept of allowing cellular over the unlicensed spectrum is important for cellular operators as it allows them to enhance network dimensions without paying additional money to do so. This attractive option has already been accepted by multiple operators around the world [1]. The Figure 16.4 above shows the user trend. As per the Ericsson Data user forecast, there has been an exponential increase in data user subscribers. Hence, the total data usage is bound to increase. Also, all emerging technologies make use of active data sessions. Hence, an alternative means for data must be made available and kept online all the time.

In this chapter, we will present the notable work reported in literature on Wi-Fi offloading. This chapter is organized as follows: first, we present the 3GPP standards supporting Wi-Fi offloading followed by Wi-Fi offloading simulation scenarios proposed by different researchers. For the sake of simplicity, we divide the offloading into two categories, first on the basis of LTE and LTE-U, and second by core definition of Wi-Fi offloading, that is, the vertical handover.

16.11 3GPP Standard for Wi-Fi Offloading

The Wi-Fi offloading standardization process and its technical specifications are defined through 3GPP technical specification (TS) 23.402. This specifies the interoperability in

3GPP and non-3GPP access. It is imperative here to clarify that any access technology other than the cellular technology may a trusted RAT or may be a non-trusted RAT. So, it is the jurisdiction of the home network to decide the trustworthiness of a network in non-3GPP access. This standard specifies the trusted and untrusted access networks, and cellular networks come under trusted networks. The vertical handover is the core concept of Wi-Fi offloading. Hence, IEEE 802.21 is designed for this purpose.

16.12 Offloading Using LTE-U

We first give an overview of the work done by researchers to overcome this. In [1], the authors presented the above problem and proposed a framework that includes the human perspective. The authors proposed three spectrum sharing techniques; static sharing, adaptive sharing, and semiadaptive sharing.

The paper uses a mathematical modeling approach to simulate the spectrum sharing techniques based upon Boolean and Poisson processes. However, the paper considers the human satisfaction factor. The cost affordability is taken as a probabilistic model and does not consider the user application criteria. Adaptive spectrum sharing has been reported as a technique that gives significant advantages in comparison to static partitioning. Semi-adaptive partitioning has been proposed as being highly competitive. Another approach for spectrum sharing was proposed in [2] based upon the fact of spectrum sharing by strategic operators based on PSD. The power spectral density (PSD) of the signal describes the power present in the signal as a function of frequency, per unit frequency. The paper describes two models of sharing—a static sharing scheme and dynamic sharing scheme. For the static sharing scheme, the proposed model is shown to be an subgame perfect nash equilibrium (SPNE) while for dynamic sharing, the proposed model is shown to be Bayesian Equilibrium. The static sharing scheme proposed by the authors is described as the traffic behaviors remaining unchanged with varying PSD, while the dynamic sharing scheme is vice versa. This is based on the logic that at a particular time, some operator may have higher traffic. The one with the higher traffic may be short of spectrum. This scenario leads to trade off spectrum in each slot, hence, dynamic sharing. This study aims to provide a theoretical foundation for LTE-U standardization and deployment. The proposed spectrum sharing schemes are simple and may serve as the basis for a practical design. The authors evaluated the proposed models through numerical results by evaluating the performance in terms of cost and number of operators. Also shown are the results in terms of revenue and power. The paper provides a base mark for the spectrum sharing of LTE-U based upon a theoretical game model. However, the paper focuses on only the economic aspects and the total revenue. The impact on existing Wi-Fi users in the spectrum and performance counters of LTE-U are not addressed. These should be considered in a future work. In [3], the authors attempt to evaluate the performance 802.11 of Wi-Fi, with the scenario of LTE-U existing in the same spectrum. The authors obtained results in a fully controlled environment using open-source equipment for both LTE and Wi-Fi networks. The paper has shown through numerical results the impact of Wi-Fi traffic when LTE-U exists in same spectrum. The performance of Wi-Fi is seen as degraded due to the control signals of LTE-U, and the major point in the paper is the simulation technique based upon a fully controlled environment using real equipment. As shown through the results, the Wi-Fi performance metric deviated a lot. This should alert the advocators of LTE-U. Research

TABLE 16.1

Summary of Offloading to LTE-U

	Offloading Technique	Proposed Algorithm/Key	Performance Metric	Approach
[1]		Spectrum partitioning algorithm	User satisfaction factor	User centric
[2]	Offloading	Probablistic model	Total revenue	User centric
[3]	using LTE-U	Effect on Wi-Fi with LTE-U	Power	Network centric
[4]		Duet	Throughput	Network centric

development work is in process by 3GPP to overcome the gaps highlighted in this paper, such as scheduling blank frames in LTE-U and enhancement of LTE with clear channel access (CCA).

The author in [4] begins by explaining the LTE-U Wi-Fi coexistence problem which we have already described. The authors later present the proposed algorithm Duet whose base line is on channel utilization estimation and duty cycle adaptation. The context of this paper is the coexistence between a wireless network with a centralized MAC (e.g., LTE-U) and a wireless network with distributed MAC (e.g., Wi-Fi). An algorithm to adaptively tackle the coexistence problem of LTE-U and Wi-Fi uses an enhanced ON/OFF duty cycle mechanism, in which LTE-U transmissions are allowed during the LTE-U ON period and Wi-Fi transmissions are allowed during the LTE-U OFF period. Duet can be applied to both fully and partially connected networks with either static or dynamic network loads. The authors evaluated Duet through ns-3 simulations in various scenarios and showed that it can improve the overall network throughput while maintaining channel utilization and fairness among LTE-U and Wi-Fi. The authors performed simulation using ns3. Table 16.1 summarizes the work done on LTE-U used for offloading.

16.13 Architecture of Mobile IP Based Mobility Management in Heterogenous Networks

In this section, we will present the architecture of mobile IP-based mobility management in heterogenous networks. The best work in literature supporting and giving a comprehensive view of it is presented in [6].

16.13.1 Mobility Management Protocols

The major task in tackling offloading and implementing it efficiently depends upon the mobility factor. There is a multiple mobility management protocol described in the following section.

16.13.1.1 Mobile IP

The proposed idea of offloading comes into play when asking why not offload some of the traffic to other access technologies like worldwide interoperability for microwave access (WiMAX) and, more commonly, Wi-Fi? In technical terms, offloading some traffic means routing some of the IP flows to Wi-Fi. This type of offloading is called IP flow mobility and is being standardized within 3GPP networks. IFOM uses proxy mobile IP. The task of maintaining a different IP flow calls upon the use of effective mobility management protocols. One of the key concepts in understanding and implementing the Wi-Fi offload solution is mobile IP [9]. This is being standardized in the internet engineering task force—network-based mobility extensions (IETF NETEXT) Working Group [8] which works with offloading. If the process of shifting IP flows is done at the network side, it is referred to as proxy mobile IPv6 [10,14]. If it is done on the client side, the protocol is mobile IP. The implementation of IFOM standards makes use of mobile IP and proxy mobile IP.

A key concept leading to the implementation of offloading is the point of attachment. Offloading or a media independent handover requires a change of access technology for a mobile device that is more precisely called a change of Point of Attachment (PoA). In Internet protocol terminology, a mobile node associates a unique IP address with its PoA, hence if a node changes its location, the PoA is going to change. This change in location calls upon the need for mobile IP, which plays an important part in handling mobility related issues in a heterogeneous mobile environment. Mobile IP protocol is defined in internet engineering task force- request for comments (IETF RFC) 5944 [11]. The implementation of Mobile IP protocol requires implementation on the mobile node, hence it may not be transparent to the user. To obtain a more user transparent solution to tackle the mobility issue calls for the use of a proxy mobile IP as defined in IETF RFC 5213 [12].

To overcome this issue, proxy mobile IP has been introduced in IETF RFC 5213 for internet protocol version 6 (IPv6), [10,14] and IETF RFC 5563 [13] for internet protocol version 4 (IPv4). The major difference between mobile IP and proxy mobile IP is the transparency to the mobile device. Hence in a proxy mobile IP, network mobility management issues are handled at the network side where a proxy mobility agent (PMA) performs this action. PMA is responsible for tracking the movements of the host, initiating the required mobility, and performing the required signaling on behalf of the mobile host. However, in case the mobility involves different network interfaces, that is, multiple RATs, the mobile host requires modifications similar to mobile IP in order to maintain the same IP address across different interfaces.

16.13.1.2 GTP (GPRS Tunneling Protocol) Is Another Mobility Management Protocol

This is a network-based mobility management protocol as described in 3GPP standard TS 29.060 [1] and TS29.281 [1]. It is an alternative to proxy mobile IP. However, it has its limitations with respect to offloading in a heterogeneous network environment. InterRAT handover (2g↔3g) is commonly implemented commercially. This makes use of the general packet radio service (GPRS) tunneling protocol, more known commonly as GPRS Tunneling Protocol (GTP). GTP does not support vertical handover, that is, handovers with non-3GPP modes as such Wi-Fi, WiMAX, and Bluetooth. For implementing handovers between Wi-Fi and LTE, the mobility management protocol proposed is the proxy mobile IP and its various extensions as described below. Proxy mobile IP is selected as it supports multiple access technologies and most importantly the Wi-Fi. 3GPP standard 23.402 [15] describes the integration of non-3GPP access to the 3GPP networks for the sake of an offloading scenario, incorporating high data traffic needs.

16.14 Implementation of MIH Using 802.21

In this section, we will present the work contributed for the implementation of IEEE 802.21, but before that we will present an overview of IEEE 802.21

16.14.1 Overview of IEEE 802.21

IEEE 802.21 MIH protocol stack is imperative for efficient and seamless mobility management in heterogeneous networks [16–19].

The vital entity for the 802.21 standard is the MIH function commonly known as media independent handover function (MIHF). This is a virtual element that exists between the MIH user and layer 2, hence provisioning the cross layer control information required for the handover decision and execution process. The key role of the MIHF is to provide all the necessary information that will be required for the execution of the handover and the handover decision-making process. This information is to be used by the MIH users which may be the mobility management protocol at the network layer. Hence MIHF does not make any decision with respect to the network selection. Media independent handover users (MIHUs) are assigned to make the handover and link-selection decisions based on their internal policies and the information received from the MIHF. The services offered by MIHF are used by the MIH users at the network layer according to the defined primitives given in the 802.21 standard. These sets of primitives are grouped in service access points (SAPs) acting as a communication interface between the MIHF and the upper layer MIH users. The MIH users are basically the handover management protocols at the upper layers, that is, the network, transport, and application layers. IEEE 802.21 protocol standard for vertical handover is also known as media independent handover services and is a set of rules specifying the handover process for heterogeneous networks. The sole purpose behind the development of this protocol standard is to ensure seamless service availability as the mobility factor varies. The 802.21 standard gathers information from various available networks for vertical handover purposes. The collected information is comprised of the link state (its availability), its reliability, and its capacity under different mobility conditions. The collection of information is a continuous process. IEEE facilitates both types of vertical handover, that is, a soft handover known as make-before-break and a hard handover known as break-before-make. In a soft handover, the mobile node remains connected with the backup purchase order acceptance (PoA) while the data transmission continues from the serving PoA and complete transition occurs upon meeting the requirements. A hard handover normally infers a sudden switch between two access points, base stations or, generally speaking, PoAs. The main design elements of IEEE 802.21 are classified into three categories: a framework for enabling transparent service continuity while handing over between heterogeneous access technologies; a set of handover-enabling functions; and a set of Service Access Points (SAPs). The gathering of essential information for a vertical handover is necessary and all these requirements exist in the IEEE 802.21 standard. This is needed to ensure the connectivity is seamless to the end user, that is, there is no disruption in the service, specifically for the soft handover case. The IEEE 802.21 continuously examines the access network conditions for all the networks in range. Reference [1] explains the information exchanged between heterogeneous systems in view of IEEE 802.21 (MIH) standard and shows how it is adapted for handover among UMTS and WLAN systems. This is characterized as a system for giving handover related data streams to a resource manager that is accountable for grasping the handover choices and approving it by utilizing an altered Recieved Signal Strength (RSS)-based handover. Results have demonstrated that when a portable hub moves between a UMTS and a nearby WLAN system, the application experiences a drop in the overall network parameters because of the contrasts between the two systems. It is recommend that better information be acquired when the portable hub changes from the UMTS system to the WLAN. The execution assessment has shown jitter, packet delay, and lowered throughput. The creators in [2] proposed another handover activating component consistent with IEEE 802.21. The proposed protocol is called DR-HTM (data rate-based vertical handover triggering mechanism). This enhances the limits of LTE as well as those of general systems by embracing a Time-to-Trigger (TTT) option in the vertical handover among WLAN and cell systems for proficient handover activation. By applying DR-HTM technique, a handover is activated only if a competitor WLAN can give preferable information rates over right now joined evolved node B (eNB), wasteful handovers can be forestalled. In addition, DR-HTM decreases the number of MNs having low recurrence proficiency in LTE and increases the aggregate limits of LTE and WLAN. From the execution assessment, it was concluded that the DR-HTM with a TTT component enhances the performance of both LTE and WLANs by increasing the precision and effectiveness of handover choices. The paper in [3] focused on the features based upon the IEEE 802.21 framework that built upon mobile IPv6 protocol. The authors defined a model which proposed that an entity be added to the MIH layer of 802.21. This added entity implements mobile IP functionalities. The proposed way to deal with the layer 3 handover exploits the nearness of the MIH between layers. Portable IPv6, which oversees associations, does not bolster two concurrent associations. Therefore, another element is added to MIH between the layers to deal with the second association with the new system. This additional entity (AE) can speak with layer 3 and the MIHF. The additional element actualizes mobile IP functionalities. It facilitates the augmentation of mobile IP to the inter layer. One of the benefits of this model is that it does not require an arrangement of new complex frameworks to upgrade handovers. This additional entity lessens the packet loss and handover latency when the user equipment moves in heterogeneous network conditions. The method given in [5] is the mix of uplink/downlink signal to interference ratio (SINR) estimation and is considered to be a foundation for handover in LTE. The work was finished by considering lopsided network conditions. Under this supposition, the calculation could accomplish little pick up in the normal throughput under high irregularities in the cell. Thus, if there should be an occurrence of low lopsidedness in the underlying serving cell, the calculation did not enhance client throughput.

16.15 Fuzzy Logic-Based Vertical Handover Trigger

Further extending the scope of the literature review, we found a method that focuses on vertical handover using MIH and exploiting LTE in the unlicensed spectrum, that is, LTE-U [28]. We found some researchers designing algorithms for vertical handover trigger using fuzzy logic. The following section gives a brief overview of fuzzy logic-based algorithms.

In [10], the researchers gave an overview of the two main interworking frameworks which were proposed by IEEE Group and 3GPP for integration between different types of technologies (3GPP and non-3GPP); namely, MIH and internet protocol multimdeia subsystem (IMS). They emphasized the pros and cons of handover in a heterogenous network, particularly the vertical handover, that is, in 3GPP and non-3GPP. The proposed algorithm based on MIH and built upon fuzzy logic illustrates the notable improvements in reducing connection failures and reducing signaling cost in heterogeneous wireless networks compared to the previous works found in the literature [29].

The authors presented the Imperative Alternative MIH for Vertical Handover (I AM 4 VHO) algorithm built upon an MIH framework which has a lower probability of connection failure as a result of using the best available prioritized access technologies, hence reducing the signaling cost. The algorithm defines two main types of VHO: Automatically Imperative VHO (AIVHO) and Alternative VHO (AVHO). The AVHO consists of Automatically Alternative VHO (AAVHO) and Manually Alternative VHO (MAVHO). The imperative request will have high priority, for example, if there are two VHO sessions at the same time, one due to the RSS going down (imperative) and the other due to a user preference change (alternative), the first request will be responded to as high priority and the second request will be considered only if there is not any imperative VHO session underway. Otherwise, the second request will have to wait in queue.

In [7] in this work, the authors proposed a fuzzy logic-based vertical handoff decision algorithm that is capable of switching between different radio access technologies. According to the obtained simulation results, the proposed vertical handoff decision algorithm is able to select the best candidate access network with a lower delay and with less complexity.

It is also observed that artificial intelligence based vertical handoff algorithms as well as newly proposed approaches noticeably reduce the number of handoffs compared to classic algorithms. Together with the number of handoffs, handoff latency, algorithm complexity, and handoff blocking probability are other important metrics that affect the performance of the system.

Many classic Multiple Attribute Decision Making (MADM) methods exist in literature. One of the most well-known is TOPSIS (Technique for Order Preference by Similarity to Ideal Solution). It was first developed by Hwang and Yoon based on the idea that the chosen alternative should have the shortest distance from the Positive Ideal Solution (PIS), and on the other side, the farthest distance from the Negative Ideal Solution (NIS). The PIS maximizes the benefit criteria and minimizes the cost criteria, whereas the NIS maximizes the cost criteria and minimizes the benefit criteria.

Reference [8] increased the quality of service in mobile systems based on efficient network and radio utilization of resources of heterogeneous networks and an optimal procedure of intellectual vertical handover based on cloud technology and fuzzy logic. Thus, a novel network selection mechanism using intelligent agents has been proposed which select the best network based on QoS parameters using the theory of fuzzy sets. The imitation model has been developed to investigate the functioning of real heterogeneous wireless networks under conditions of high user mobility. This imitation model includes a wide number of different wireless access network parameters and uses mathematical and prognostic models. The process of service provisioning to users of a heterogeneous network based on the developed model has been investigated when providing the service of video-conferencing. The optimal cell of the heterogeneous network has been determined based on the evaluation of access node characteristics using fuzzy logic.

The most important issue in a heterogeneous environment is the Always Best Connected (ABC) concept allowing the best connectivity to applications anywhere at any time. The work contributed in [9] used the fuzzy logic tool box of MATLAB® and uses input parameters such as bandwidth (BW), RSSI, packet rejection ratio (PR) and which particular protocol, that is, of 802.11a, 802.11b/g, 802.11e, and 802.11h, shows the best output. So, by checking this, it will be easier and faster to make a decision for the handover of a radio resource to the strongest protocol. This presents an analytical model for Wi-Fi offloading.

Handover decisions, particularly within heterogeneous environments, play an important role in mobility management [9]. There are several open issues that need to be further investigated in the integration of heterogeneous wireless networks. Examples include load balancing and traffic management among networks, quality of service support during vertical handover, resource sharing and resource allocation, security and authentication, billing and operator agreements, and implementation details. Our proposal is useful whenever there are many users using individual protocols according to their needs and whenever there needs to be a handover between them. More parameters like security, authentication, password protection, multivendor interoperability, and so on can also be included. This concept is also applicable to the IEEE 802.21 working group activities which work with media independent handover functions that will help mobile devices to seamlessly roam across heterogeneous access networks.

16.16 Conclusion

In this chapter, Wi-Fi offloading techniques have been discussed. We tried to build an approach that facilitates the user and is also transparent, achieving a win—win situation for both the service provider as well as the end user. Hence, we can call it a user-centric approach. In other words, we attempted to propose a user-centric approach that is both energy aware and maintains a balance in the network load.

References

1. http://www.cisco.com/c/en/us/solutions/collateral/service-provider/visual-networking-index-vni/white_paper_c11-520862.html.
2. J. Kellokoski, J. Koskinen, T. Hämäläinen. *Always Best Connected Heterogeneous Network Concept.* Springer Science+Business Media: New York, 2013.
3. 3GPP TS 23.261. IP flow mobility and seamless Wireless Local Area Network (WLAN) offload; Stage 2. http://www.3gpp.org/DynaReport/23261.htm
4. 3GPP TR 23.861. Network based IP flow mobility (3GPP). http://www.3gpp.org/DynaReport/23861.htm
5. 3GPP TS 29.281. General Packet Radio System (GPRS) Tunnelling Protocol User Plane (GTPv1-U). http://www.3gpp.org/DynaReport/29281.htm
6. 3GPP TS 29.060. General Packet Radio Service (GPRS); GPRS Tunnelling Protocol (GTP) across the Gn and Gp interface. http://www.3gpp.org/DynaReport/29060.htm
7. Network-Based Mobility Extensions (netext). https://datatracker.ietf.org/wg/netext/charter/
8. Architecture enhancements for non-3GPP accesses. http://www.3gpp.org/DynaReport/23402.htm
9. C. Perkins, Ed. IP Mobility Support for IPv4, Revised. http://www.rfc-editor.org/info/rfc5944
10. D. Johnson, C. Perkins, and J. Arkko. Mobility Support in IPv6. http://www.rfc-editor.org/info/rfc3775
11. K. Leung, G. Dommety, P. Yegani, and K. Chowdhury. WiMAX Forum/3GPP2 Proxy Mobile IPv4. http://www.rfc-editor.org/info/rfc5563
12. S. Gundavelli, Ed., K. Leung, V. Devarapalli, K. Chowdhury, and B. Patil. Proxy Mobile IPv6.
13. R. Koodli and C. Perkins. Mobile IPv4 Fast Handovers. http://www.rfc-editor.org/info/rfc4988
14. R. Koodli, Ed. Mobile IPv6 Fast Handovers. http://www.rfc-editor.org/info/rfc5568
15. H. Soliman, C. Castelluccia, K. ElMalki, and L. Bellier. Hierarchical Mobile IPv6 (HMIPv6) Mobility Management. http://www.rfc-editor.org/info/rfc5380
16. S. Budiyanto, M. Asvial, and D. Gunawan. Implementation of genetic zone routing protocol. *TENCON 2013—2013 IEEE Region 10 Conference*
17. S. Budiyanto, M. Asvial, and D. Gunawan. Performance analysis of genetic zone routing protocol combined with vertical handover algorithm for 3G-Wi-Fi offload. *J. ICT Res. Appl.*, Vol. 8, No. 1, 2014, 49–63.

18. S. Budiyanto, M. Asvial, and D. Gunawan. Implementation dedicated sensing receiver (DSR) in 3G—Wi-Fi offload. *ICSGTEIS 2014.*

19. E. Piri and K. Pentikousis. IEEE 802.21. *The Internet Protocol Journal*, Vol. 12, No. 2

20. 3GPP TS 23.402. *Architecture enhancements for non-3GPP accesses.* http://www.3gpp.org/DynaReport/23402.htm

21. F. Firmin. The Evolved Packet Core, http://www.3gpp.org/technologies/keywords-acronyms/100-the-evolved-packet-core

22. F. Liu, E. Bala, E. Erkip, M.C. Beluri, and R. Yang. Small cell traffic balancing over licensed and unlicensed bands. *IEEE Transactions on Vehicular Technology*

23. http://www.ieee802.org/21/

24. https://www.ericsson.com/assets/local/mobility-report/documents/2016/ericsson-mobility-report-november-2016.pdf

25. https://www.cisco.com/c/en/us/solutions/service-provider/visual-networking-index-vni/index.html

26. X. Yuan, X. Qin, F. Tian, Y. Thomas Hou, W. Lou, S.F. Midkiff, and J.H. Reed. Coexistence between Wi-Fi and LTE on unlicensed spectrum: A human-centric approach, *IEEE Journal on Selected Areas in Communications* Vol. 35, No. 4, April 2017, ISSN: 0733-8716.

27. F. Teng, D. Guo, and M.L. Honig. Sharing of unlicensed spectrum by strategic operators, signal and information processing (GlobalSIP), *2014 IEEE Global Conference*, ISBN: 978-1-4799-7088-9

28. V. Maglogiannis, D. Naudts, P. Willemen, and I. Moerman. Impact of LTE operating in unlicensed spectrum on Wi-Fi using real equipment, *Global Communications Conference (GLOBECOM), 2016 IEEE*, ISBN: 978-1-5090-1328-9

29. Y. Jian, U.P. Moravapalle, C.-F. Shih, and R. Sivakumar. Duet: An adaptive algorithm for the coexistence of LTE-U and WiFi in unlicensed spectrum, computing, networking and communications (ICNC), *2017 International Conference*, ISBN: 978-1-5090-4588-4

17

Visible Light Communication for Advanced Wireless 5G Light-Fidelity Networks

G. Nagarajan and P. Magesh Kannan

CONTENTS

17.1 Introduction

Light Fidelity or Li-Fi is an amazing invention in 5G visible light communication systems and the forthcoming wireless Internet access techniques. In recent years, white Light Emitting Diodes (LEDs) have been considered as an encouraging technology for next generation lighting due to their longer lifespan, low power requirement, and very high efficiency. White LEDs have high speed modulation characteristics when compared with traditional incandescent and fluorescent lighting sources. Hence these devices can be employed concurrently for illumination and communication. Currently, communication through visible light waves (380–780 nm) is gaining attention in the research and development world, motivated by advances in LED technologies for next generation Solid-State-Lighting (SSL). Optical

Wireless Communication (OWC) also known as Visible Light Communication (VLC) or Light-Fidelity (Li-Fi) has numerous attractive benefits [1,2].

VLC is an evolving technology for forthcoming high data rate communication interfaces in the visible range of the electromagnetic spectrum utilizing LEDs which simultaneously provide data transmission and room illumination. The modulation speed of the LEDs is in terms of MHz and this is the major challenge in VLC. First, VLC can able provide extra facility at a comparably very low extra cost since the same lighting infrastructure can be reused. Second, it has a free spectrum, specifically from 400 to 800 THz. This offers a massive communication bandwidth to deliver license-free extremely high data rate services.

Third, the VLC spectrum can be spatially reused in neighboring communication cells. Fourth, VLC offers high security. Its narrow beam width and Line-of-Sight(LoS) constraint protect the communication from snooping. Moreover, VLC has immunity to Radio Frequency (RF) interference. The RF based wireless communication has become a bottleneck because of the unavailability of more RF spectrum, limited potential to exploit this spectrum, and huge power consumption. VLC is well thought out as a possible access choice for upcoming 5G wireless communications because of its advantages [3]. Visible-Local-Area-Network (VLAN) or the Li-Fi network has been validated by researchers all over the world [4,5]. VLC technology can also be used in high precision indoor-positioning and navigation systems [6–8], underwater communication, vehicle to traffic light, vehicle to vehicle communication, and information broadcasting [9]. VLC is an emerging technology in OWC which stimulates international research. These facts result in an increasing throughput for the next generation 5G communication networks, which are anticipated to be deployed in 2020.

17.2 Improvements in VLC Technology

The first known use of visible light based wireless communication was by Alexander Graham Bell, who developed a photo-phone in 1880, which transmitted voice data over 200 m using beams of sunlight [10,11]. The perception of using LEDs for VLC was first presented by Pang et al. in 1999 [12,13]. In the early 2000s, white LEDs based indoor wireless communication was projected by Tanaka et al. at Keio University, Japan [14,15].

The Visible-Light-Communication-Consortium (VLCC) was founded in November 2003 in Japan. The VLCC is targeting the advertisement and standardization of the VLC technology [16]. In 2008, the home gigabit access project (OMEGA) in Europe is intended to develop a user-friendly home access system proficient at providing high-bandwidth facilities at one gigabit per second data transmission rates. The important features of Li-Fi networks are license-free spectrum, unlimited channel bandwidth, high data rate interfaces, and energy efficiency. Li-Fi is a subdivision of the VLC which provides access networks with several users.

The VLC transmitting part consists of LEDs either singularly or in an array. These LEDs are intensity modulated at a frequency above which the human eye cannot perceive. The visible range of the electromagnetic spectrum is utilized in VLC since full room illumination is required. Two types of LEDs are being used to produce white light: (i) inorganic metal alloy semiconductor LEDs (usually a blue light emitting gallium-nitride(GaN) interface with a cerium doped yttrium-aluminum-garnet (Ce:YAG)) and (ii) organic LEDs (OLEDs) made from small molecules of polymers, using epitaxial or wet processing methods [17,18]. Inorganic LEDs are normally used in VLC, while generic OLEDs are drawing significant consideration for upcoming VLC systems. Polymer based OLEDs offer numerous major benefits over inorganic devices such as large size and arbitrarily shaped photoactive areas.

The cross-disciplinary project consortium consists of 20 European associates from industry and academia, such as Siemens and France Telecom. A100 Megabits per second video broadcasting based on visible LEDs in ceiling lighting was realized in 2011 [19].

17.3 High-Speed VLC Systems

High-speed VLC schemes can be classified into two types: one is real-time VLC systems and the other one is off-line VLC systems. When Discrete-Multi-Tone (DMT) or Orthogonal Frequency Division Multiplexing (OFDM) modulation schemes are used, a real-time oscilloscope is employed to record and save the received signal, then perform an off-line process on the personal computer. It is essential for researchers to analyze new technology in VLC using off-line processing.

Additionally, it is an interesting but tough engineering problem to implement hundreds of megahertz or gigabit data rate OFDM or DMT, VLC systems by utilizing complex hardware such as Analog-to-Digital Converters (ADC), Digital-to-Analog Converters (DAC), Field-Programmable Gate Arrays (FPGA), and Digital Signal Processors (DSP). If On-Off shift Keying (OOK) modulation is adopted, hardware design becomes easy and acceptable without the expensive hardware modules mentioned earlier. Hence, the transmitted data by OOK modulation can be easily detected. The OOK-VLC systems are real-time VLC systems and could transmit and receive information at the same time.

17.4 Design Challenges in VLC

The VLC for indoor applications can be categorized into two categories: Line-of-Sight (LoS) and Non-Line-of-Sight (NLoS) [20]. Interference from ambient light sources affects both categories of VLC. Inter-Symbol Interference (ISI) from multipath dispersion and synchronization at the receiver is the main problem. The Signal to Noise Ratio (SNR) of an optical wireless interface is proportional to the square of the average receiver optical signal power. This means that a higher power level transmission is required compared to an electrical channel [21,22]. There are many design challenges to implementing VLC hardware for different applications. A specific modulation scheme has to be selected for any particular application.

17.4.1 Types of Modulation Schemes for VLC

VLC uses different types of modulation schemes based on the requirements for various applications such as Li-Fi, vehicle-to-vehicle communication, under-water communication, visible light Identification (ID) systems, and Wireless Local Area Networks (WLANs). A spectrally efficient modulation scheme such as OFDM is a more widespread method to improve the VLC link capacity. For instance, Gigabits/s transmissions [23,24] can be achieved by a VLC system. Power efficient schemes such as low Peak-to-Average Power Ratio (PAPR) and Single-Carrier Frequency Domain -Equalization (SC-FDE) [25] can be applied to improve the throughput of the VLC system. Further, spectral efficiency improvements can be accomplished by implementing novel OFDM and SC-FDE modulation schemes. Different types of modulation schemes used for VLC are as follows:

17.4.1.1 Carrierless Amplitude and Phase Modulation (CAP)

In recent years, Carrierless Amplitude and Phase modulation (CAP) has been considered for optical systems because it outperforms the OFDM channel for the same experimental setup [26]. CAP schemes do need Fourier transform or a local oscillator unlike OFDM.

CAP uses digital Finite Impulse Response filters (FIR) to generate carrier frequencies.

The available bandwidth is divided into a multiband CAP (m-CAP) modulation scheme for an optical fiber channel. The available system bandwidth is allocated into "m" sub-bands [27]. Less bandwidth will be occupied by a single subcarrier if more sub-bands are employed. This will result in a reduced attenuation caused by the LEDs' low-pass frequency response.

17.4.1.2 Single Carrier Modulation (SCM)

Under a doubly selective channel, the performance of the SCM scheme may be easily overwhelmed by the interference of ISI due to the multi-path transmitting arrangement. At the end of the SCM system, channel equalization is carried out. Researchers employed the Single Carrier Modulation-Frequency Domain Equalization (SCM-FDE) in 1973 [28]. The Inverse Fast Fourier Transform (IFFT) unit of SCM-FDE is one of the blocks of the receiver, whereas in the OFDM scheme, it is in the transmitter side. However, the PAPR of the SCM is lower than that of the OFDM.

17.4.1.3 On-Off Keying (OOK)

On-off keying (OOK) is a very common modulation scheme because of its ease of implementation and compatibility with equalizers. Several equalizers had been verified on a commercially available Digital Signal Processing (DSP) board [29]. The modulation bandwidth is 4.5 MHz and the transmission speed of the LED is up to 170 Mb/s. FPGAs' implementation of data processing will be the next stage to build a fully real-time system.

17.4.1.4 Pulse Position Modulation (PPM)

Recently, VLC has played an important role in our daily life due to the fast switching ability of LEDs, hence it has attracted an increasing amount of attention in the literature. In order to solve the flickering effect and dimming control problems, several modulation techniques have already been proposed in the visible band such as OOK, PPM, variable PPM, and Pulse Width Modulation (PWM) [30]. The Overlapping PPM (OPPM) is one of the PPM types. In several papers, H.M.H. Shalaby proved that the OPPM technique can be adopted in Optical Code Division Multiple Access (OCDMA) systems [31,32].

In an OPPM scheme, all "1's must be adjacent in a code word. Hence, OPPM has fewer code words than the MPPM (Multiple Pulse Position Modulation). In OPPM, a symbol interval is divided into subintervals. The number of the subintervals is NQ when the symbol interval is T seconds. "N" and "Q" represent the indices of overlap and the number of non-overlapping adjacent ones, respectively [33].

17.4.1.5 Pulse Amplitude Modulation (PAM)

Pulse Amplitude Modulation is one of the important modulation schemes employed in signal transmission. PAM has a very simple method of modulation in which analog to digital conversion has been performed and the information is encoded into the amplitude of the series of pulses. Pulse amplitude modulation is a method in which the amplitude of each pulse depends on the instantaneous value of the modulating signal. This technique transmits the data by encoding in the amplitude of a series of signal pulses.

The PAM-4 technique allows data transmission at the same bandwidth, doubling the data bit rate compared to Non-Return Zero (NRZ) binary modulation [34]. Using more level PAM, for example, PAM-8 or PAM-16, a higher data bit rate can be achieved but the smaller difference between the amplitude of the grid can lead to a higher data bit error rate. The amplitude of the PAM-4 signal varies according to the input signal.

17.4.2 Applications of VLC

There are numerous inspiring areas for exact deployment of VLC systems as the technology has evolved with the rapid increase of mobile data requirements. VLC has a high bandwidth, low power consumption, and non-licensed channels with no health hazards which makes it the more attractive method of communication for practical applications. Different applications of VLC are highlighted as follows:

17.4.2.1 VLC for Internet of Things (IoT)

One of the advantages of VLC, besides the potentially high bandwidth, is the possibility to leverage the existing infrastructure. In almost any modern device requiring human interaction, there is at least one status LED or an LED indicating the power state of the device. This paper proposes to multiplex their purposes with VLC to allow unidirectional communication for the distribution of device related metadata. As a receiver of this metadata, a camera mounted on a smart phone will be used. Cameras are present on almost every contemporary smart phone. Therefore, it is very easy to make the VLC technology and its application proposed herein accessible to a wide range of users.

The communication system consists of single or multiple IoT nodes (such as temperature sensors, humidity sensors, Wi-Fi access points, etc.) and single or multiple smart devices with a camera and Graphical Processing Unit (GPU). The number of IoT nodes being captured by a receiver is given by the number of devices visible to the device camera. The communication task can be split in two parts. The first part is the detection of devices in the picture (in the signal from the camera) and the second consists of demodulation and decoding of the transmitted data. The most critical part of the chain is the receiver camera. A common frame rate is 30 fps, which in case of a single red or green LED with OOK provides only 15 bps. In more recent smart phones, there are cameras capable of shooting slow-motion video with a frame rate of up to 240 fps and a resolution of 720 p (e.g., Samsung Galaxy S7 or Apple iPhone 6S). This would enable a maximum bit rate of 120 bps [35].

17.4.2.2 Vehicle-to-Vehicle Communication

The outdoor applications, such as the public transportation, utilize VLC to communicate between vehicles. LED lighting has replaced the use of incandescent lamps across whole cities. For example, over 140,000 existing streetlights were replaced in Los Angeles by the LED Streetlight Replacement Program. This brought energy savings of 68 GWh/yr and money savings of $10M/year [36]. Numerous experimental results have been published for a vehicular VLC network consisting of vehicles and road side units, that is, traffic lights, street lamps, and so on. Vehicles fitted with LED-based front and back lights will be able to communicate with each other and with the Road Side Units (RSUs) through the VLC scheme. Moreover, LED-based RSUs can be employed for both signaling and broadcasting safety related information to vehicles on the road.

The performance analysis of VLC-based vehicle-to-vehicle communications for a range of communication for both the LoS and NLoS paths over a link distance of 20 m at a data rate of 2 Mbps was discussed in Reference 37. Optical wireless communications systems based on an LED transmitter and camera receiver were suggested for automotive applications in Reference 38. The signal reception experiment has been performed for static and moving camera receivers. The error-free throughput under fixed conditions was sustained up to 15 Mb/s. The receiver in the driving situation can detect and accurately track an LED transmitter array with error-free communication over distances of 25–80 m and this is proven in Reference 39.

17.4.2.3 Underwater Communication

Underwater Optical Communication (UWOC) has gained a lot of attention during the last decade. This is considered an alternative technique to the existing acoustic and RF methods for underwater wireless communication. UWOC can deliver orders of magnitude more bandwidth and achieve much higher data rates for short and moderate ranges (<100 m) [40,41] using efficient and low-cost light sources such as LEDs [42] and Laser Diodes (LD) [43] in the low absorption 400–550 nm window of the electromagnetic spectrum in seawater. The primary factors that degrade the system performance in UWOC interfaces are absorption, scattering, and turbulence. The photon energy is lost due to the interaction of light with water molecules and other particulates in absorption.

Scattering is the phenomenon whereby the photons are dispersed away from the initial path after interacting with particles and bubbles in the water. Underwater Optical Turbulence (UOT) is defined as random variations of the index of refraction which affect the beam as it propagates through a water column [44].

There has been significant progress in the research on UWOC both theoretically and experimentally in recent years. Nevertheless, many appropriate studies have mostly concentrated on the effects of absorption and scattering by particles in the optical channel [45–48], system level design and demonstrations [49–52], and underwater turbulence [53–55]. There is little study on the effect of air bubbles in UWOC channels [56].

Breaking surface waves and rain produce air bubbles in the oceans [57]. They originate in different sizes and take on a spherical shape in water as reported by several authors [58–60]. The propagation and scattering of acoustic waves generate air bubbles [61] which contribute to many oceanographic processes such as organic-particle formation and bacteria transport [62]. The signal's amplitude is distorted due to reflection and refraction at the water-bubble interface, when the optical signal propagates through a bubbly underwater channel. This causes the light to stray into various directions. Thus, the scattering properties of the water body are significantly affected in the presence of air bubbles.

17.4.2.4 Visible Light ID System

Numerous locating or positioning systems have been verified in recent years. A digital camera was deployed as a receiver to capture the images of an LED-based positioning beacon transmitter [63]. The system was able to decode the location information which is encoded in the visual patterns transmitted by the LEDs by applying image processing algorithms. A system for localization of vehicles using the Global Positioning System (GPS) along with a light beacon device attached to the vehicle to receive the information from transmitters which are positioned at the road intersections was developed and tested by Honda Motors Co., Ltd in 2010 [64].

Another challenge is utilizing the localization within an indoor scenario where standard GPS signals cannot be received. The research and development in optical based Indoor Positioning Schemes (IPS) offers numerous advantages including smaller transceiver size and immunity to electromagnetic interference along with essential security [65].

VLC-IPS provides the advantages of LED and VLC such as omnipresent coverage, static channel, multiple lighting elements, and so on [66]. By applying VLC with synchronization between the transmitter and receiver, the boundaries on position estimation accuracy are typically in the order of millimeters or centimeters. This depends on the frequency, geometry of the room, power of the transmitted signal, and the properties of the LED and the photo-receiver [67]. VLC-IPS is a highly accurate positioning system which provides an average positioning error of about 1.6 cm, which is much less than that of many existing IPSs.

17.5 Enhancing the Speed of Modulation for VLC

A VLC system deploys LEDs to communicate and blink at the speed of light in terms of Giga bits per second (Gbps). The modulation speed of the LEDs is restricted by the residual charge carriers in the depletion region during the reverse bias condition of the LEDs. The switching speed of the LEDs is reduced during the reverse biased condition of the LEDs.

A carrier sweep-out method during reverse bias to enhance the operating frequency of the LEDs was considered as an effective method, so that a higher data transfer rate can be achieved. The switching speed or the modulation speed of the LEDs should be improved to enhance the data transfer rate. The remaining carriers in the depletion region can be swept outside by connecting the leads of the LEDs for a moment.

During the reverse biased condition of the LED, the depletion-capacitance due to the remaining charge carriers increases the discharge-time constant. This limits the operating frequency of the LEDs. Therefore, extinguishing the remaining charge carriers from the LED takes a long time. The sweep-out mechanism to remove the remaining charge carriers for high-speed LED driver design to improve the data transfer rate for VLC was discussed [68].

An analog modulator for visible light data transfer based on On-Off Keying-Non-Return to Zero (OOK-NRZ) modulation was investigated in Reference 69. A buck converter-based double purpose off-line LED driving circuit for brightness control and VLC to improve the dimming performance was discussed in Reference 70. A high-speed transmitter for VLC of up to 50 Mbps speed was discussed in Reference 71. A wide range of modulation techniques for a VLC transmitter were investigated in Reference 72. VLC using a Complementary Metal-Oxide Semiconductor (CMOS) regulated micro-LED array with high frequency modulation for a high data rate was examined in Reference 73.

An LED-based optical pulse generator array which is used for a fluorescence lifetime imaging system was discussed in Reference 74. Temperature and modulation features of Resonant-Cavity LED (RC-LED) were studied in Reference 75. A digitally regulated micro-LED array-based VLC transmitter for a very high data rate was explained in Reference 76. A hybrid version of RF and VLC systems to improve the user data rate for Access Points (AP) in wireless communication was investigated in Reference 77. A fully integrated high efficiency on-chip boosted LED driver for a VLC transmitter for broadcasting was described in Reference 78. An m-CAP for bandlimited VLC systems for high data rates was explained in Reference 79.

A one-bit SDM for nonlinear VLC using an OOK signal for modulation and broadcasting was discussed in Reference 80. A burst-mode resonant Inductor-Inductor-Capacitor (LLC) Direct Current-Direct Current (DC-DC) regulator for LED light with incorporated with VLC for intelligent buildings both for ambient lighting and for high speed transmission of sensor data was investigated in Reference 81. A buck converter-based LED driver performance comparison for illumination and VLC using a VPPM was discussed in Reference 82.

17.5.1 Simulation Results and Discussion

In the recommended LED driving circuit, a dual supply voltage-based carrier sweep-out mechanism has been implemented to enhance the switching speed of LEDs. The minimum applied voltage will increase the thickness of the depletion layer. Hence the extinction time of the charge carriers will be considerably reduced, so the modulation speed will be increased to a greater extent.

An LED driving circuit using a CMOS inverting circuit has been implemented to minimize the energy consumption of the LED driving circuit. In this arrangement, a p-type Metal-Oxide Semiconductor Field Effect Transistor (pMOSFET) is used to sweep out the remaining charge carriers [68].

The proposed single supply voltage based high speed LED driver without carrier sweep-out and with carrier sweep-out is illustrated in Figures 17.1 and 17.2, respectively. A DC-DC boost regulator is employed to deliver DC voltage to the proposed LED driver. The Pulse Width Modulation (PWM) signal to the DC-DC regulator is generated by the proposed digitally controlled DAC along with a comparator circuit. The proposed digitally controlled PWM circuit generates PWM pulses with accurate duty cycle and outperforms existing PWM pulse generating circuits. These PWM pulses are used to regulate the brightness of the LEDs as per the requirement.

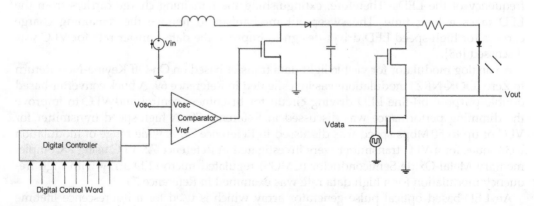

FIGURE 17.1
Schematic diagram of single supply-based LED driver with sweep-out.

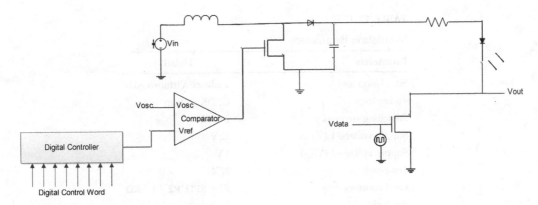

FIGURE 17.2
Schematic of single supply-based LED driver without sweep-out.

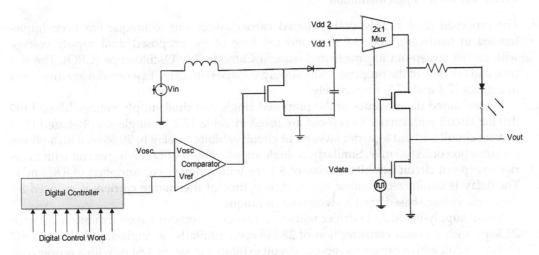

FIGURE 17.3
Schematic of proposed dual supply-based LED driver with sweep-out.

Similarly, the proposed dual supply voltage-based LED driver for VLC applications is designed, implemented, and analyzed in this chapter. The proposed dual supply voltage-based high speed LED driving circuit with carrier sweep-out circuit is depicted in Figure 17.3. There are two voltage sources which are connected to sweep out the circuit.

The high supply voltage is applied for normal operation whereas the low supply voltage, which will be less than or equal to threshold voltage of Metal-Oxide Semiconductor Field Effect Transistor (MOSFET), will be connected during the reverse bias condition of the LEDs. This operation will remove the remaining charge carriers from the depletion layer at a faster rate and the delay is minimized. Hence the switching speed of the LEDs is increased by the proposed dual supply-based high speed LED driver for VLC systems.

The characteristics of the recommended scheme are validated by the simulations executed in the Cadence Virtuoso Analog Design Environment (ADE) using a 180 nm CMOS process from Generic Process Design Kit (GPDK). The simulation parameters of the proposed circuit have been listed in Table 17.1.

TABLE 17.1

Simulation Parameters

Parameters	Details
Simulation tool	Cadence Virtuoso ADE
Technology	GPDK 180 nm
Switching frequency	2.5 MHz
Supply voltage-1 (V_{dd1})	12 V
Supply voltage-2 (V_{dd2})	1 V
Temperature	27°C
Load resistors	R1 = 51 Ω, R2 = 1.5 KΩ
Analysis	Transient

17.5.2 Hardware Implementation

The proposed dual supply voltage-based carrier sweep-out technique has been implemented in hardware. The rise time and fall time of the proposed dual supply voltage with carrier sweep-out are measured using a Cathode Ray Oscilloscope (CRO). The rise time and fall time of the proposed dual supply voltage with carrier sweep-out are displayed in Figures 17.4 and 17.5, respectively.

The measured delay values of the proposed single and dual supply voltage-based LED driving circuit with carrier sweep-out are listed in Table 17.2. A single supply-based LED driving circuit without a carrier sweep-out circuit exhibits a delay of 20.36 ps with a power consumption of 28.845 mW. Similarly, a single supply -based LED driving circuit with a carrier sweep-out circuit exhibits a delay of 8.25 ps with a power consumption of 8.857 mW. The delay is minimized because the extinction time of the charge carriers is reduced by the single voltage-based carrier sweep-out technique.

A dual supply-based LED driver without a carrier sweep-out circuit exhibits a delay of 20.36 ps with a power consumption of 28.845 mW. Similarly, a single supply-based LED driving circuit with a carrier sweep-out circuit exhibits a delay of 4.84 ps with a power consumption of 33.466 mW. The delay is minimized because the extinction time of the charge

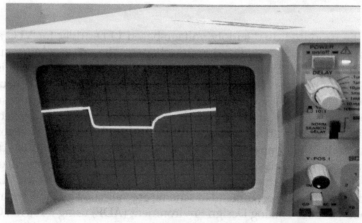

FIGURE 17.4
Rise time of dual supply-based LED driving circuit without carrier sweep-out.

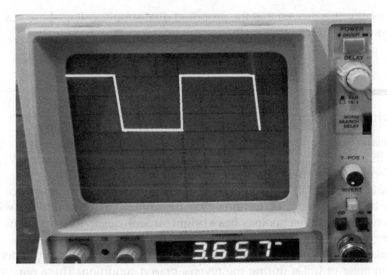

FIGURE 17.5
Fall time of dual supply-based LED driving circuit with carrier sweep-out.

carriers is reduced by the dual supply voltage-based carrier sweep-out technique. The dual supply-based carrier sweep-out technique performs well in terms of both delay and energy requirement. The power consumption is minimized because the reverse bias capacitance is greatly reduced by the proposed technique.

The percentages of improvement of the single supply voltage-based carrier sweep-out and dual supply voltage-based carrier sweep-out are listed and compared in Table 17.3. The single supply voltage-based carrier sweep-out technique exhibits 59.47% improvement in delay minimization and 28.84% improvement in power minimization. Similarly, the dual supply voltage-based carrier sweep-out technique exhibits 76.22% improvement in delay minimization and 68.77% improvement in power minimization. From the analysis of the

TABLE 17.2

Comparative Analysis of Delay and Power Consumption

Technique	Delay (ps)	Power (mW)
Single supply without carrier sweep-out	20.36	28.845
Single supply with carrier sweep-out	8.25	8.857
Dual supply without carrier sweep-out	20.36	33.466
Dual supply with carrier sweep-out	4.84	10.451

TABLE 17.3

Comparative Analysis of Improvements in Delay and Power

Parameter	Technique	Improvement (%)
Delay (ps)	Single supply with carrier sweep-out	59.47
Power (mW)	Single supply with carrier sweep-out	28.84
Delay (ps)	Dual supply with carrier sweep-out	76.22
Power (mW)	Dual supply with carrier sweep-out	68.77

simulation results, it is proven that the proposed dual supply voltage-based carrier sweep-out technique outperforms other methods.

17.6 Conclusion

From the analysis, it is determined that VLC is a promising technology to increase the capacity of indoor wireless communication, but also preserve the security. VLC provides the cost-effective technique of duplex communication for home users, but also satisfies the requirements of a small WLAN. In this chapter, numerous significant recent advances in VLC have been analyzed. VLC technology will be utilized in the near future wireless communication systems. VLC technology has a bright outlook due to its essential merits and the ever-growing reputation of white LEDs.

The modulation speed of the LEDs is restricted by the remaining charge carriers present in the depletion layer of LEDs during the reverse biased condition. These remaining charge carriers can be removed to enhance the operating frequency or modulation speed of the LEDs. The single and dual supply voltage-based carrier sweep-out techniques for high speed LC systems are proposed in this chapter. The single supply voltage-based carrier sweep-out technique exhibits 59.47% improvement in delay minimization and 28.84% improvement in power minimization. Similarly, the dual supply voltage-based carrier sweep-out technique exhibits 76.22%. From the simulation results and analysis, it is evident that the dual supply voltage-based carrier sweep-out technique outperforms the other in terms of both energy requirement and switching speed.

References

1. J. Vucic and K. D. Langer, "High-speed visible light communications," *State-of-the-art. Optical Fiber Communication Conference and Exposition (OFC/NFOEC)*, March 4–8, 2012.
2. K. D. Langer, J. Vucic, and C. Kottke, "Advances and prospects in high-speed information broadcast using phosphorescent white light LEDs," *11th International Conference on Transparent Optical Networks (ICTON)*, June 28–July 2, 2009.
3. S. Wu, H. Wang, and C. H. Youn, "Visible light communications for 5G wireless networking systems: from fixed to mobile communications," *IEEE Network*, vol. 28, no. 6, pp. 41–45, December 2014.
4. L. Grobe, A. Parakevopoulos, and J. Hilt, "High-speed visible light communication systems," *IEEE Communications Magazine*, vol. 51, no. 12, pp. 60–66, December 2013.
5. H. Burchardt, N. Serafimovski, and D. Tsonev, "VLC: beyond point-to-point communication," *IEEE Communication Magazine*, vol. 52, no. 7, pp. 98–105, July 2014.
6. Y. U. Lee and M. Kavehrad, "Long-range indoor hybrid localization system design with visible light communication and wireless network," *IEEE Photonics Society Summer Topical Meeting Series*, July 9–11, 2012.
7. W. Zhang and M. Kavehrad, "A 2-D indoor localization system based on visible light LED," *IEEE Photonics Society Summer Topical Meeting Series*, July 9–11, 2012.
8. K. Okuda, S. Oda, and T. Nakamura, "Information delivery tactile pavings using visible light communication," *IEEE International Conference on Consumer Electronics (ICCE)*, January 10–13, 2014.

9. H. Elgaga, R. Mesleh, and H. Haas, "Indoor broadcasting via white LEDs and OFDM," *IEEE Transactions On Consumer Electronics*, vol. 55, no. 3, October 2009.

10. A. G. Bell , W. G. Adams, and Tyndall, "Discussion on the photo-phone and the conversion of radiant energy into sound," *Journal Of the Society Of Telegraph Engineers*, vol. 9, no. 34, June 2011.

11. D. Karunatilaka, F. Zafar, and V. Kalavally, "LED based indoor visible light communications: state of the art," *IEEE Communication Surveys & Tutorials*, vol. 17, no. 3, pp. 1649–1678, March 2015.

12. G. Pang, T. Kwan, and H. Liu, "Optical wireless based on high brightness visible LEDs," *Industry Applications Conference*, October 1999.

13. G. Pang, T. Kwan, and H. Liu, "LED traffic light as a communications devices," *IEEE/IEEJ/JSAI International Conference on Intelligent Transportation Systems*, October 5–8.

14. Y. Tanaka, S. Haruyama, and M. Nakagawa, "Wireless optical transmissions with white colored LED for wireless home links," *13th IEEE International Symposium on Indoor and Mobile Radio Communications*, September 18–21, 2000.

15. T. Komine and M. Nakagawa, "Integrated system of white LED visible-light communication and power-line communication," *IEEE Transactions On Consumer Electronics*, vol. 49, no. 1, pp. 71–79, February 2003.

16. M. Nakagawa. Visible light communication consortium (VLCC). Retrieved from http://www. vlcc.net/modules/xpage1/, (September 13, 2018).

17. J. H. Burroughes et al., "Light-emitting diodes based on conjugated polymers," *Nature*, vol. 347, pp. 539–541, October 1990.

18. C. W. Tang and S. A. VanSlyke, "Organic electroluminescent diodes," *Applied Physics Letters*, vol. 51, pp. 913–915, 1987.

19. Home gigabit access project (OMEGA): http://www.ictomega.eu/home.html

20. S. Jivkova and M. Kavehrad, "Transceiver design concept for cellular and multispot diffusing regimes of transmission," *EURASIP Journal on Applied Signal Processing*, vol. 1, pp. 30–38, 2005.

21. R. J. Green, H. Joshi, and M. D. Higgins, "Recent developments in indoor optical wireless systems," *IET Communication*, vol. 2, no. 1, pp. 3–10, 2008.

22. J. M. Kahn and R. You, "Imaging diversity receivers for high-speed infrared wireless communication," *IEEE Communication Magazine*, vol. 36, no. 12, pp. 88–94, December 1998.

23. G. Cossu, A. M. Khalid, P. Choudhury, R. Corsini, and E. Ciaramella, "3.4 Gbit/s visible optical wireless transmission based on RGB LED," *Optics Express*, vol. 20, pp. B501–B506, December 2012.

24. A. H. Azhar, T. Tran, and D. O'Brien, "A gigabit/s indoor wireless transmission using MIMO-OFDM visible-light communications," *IEEE Photonics Technology Letters*, vol. 25, no. 2, pp. 171–174, January 2013.

25. V. S. C. Teichmann, A. N. Barreto, T. T. Pham, R. Rodes, I. T. Monroy, and D. A. A. Mello, "SC-FDE for MMF short reach optical interconnects using directly modulated 850 nm VCSELs," *Optics Express*, vol. 20, pp. 25369–25377, November 2012.

26. F. M. Wu et al., "Performance comparison of OFDM signal and CAP signal over high capacity RGB-LED-Based WDM visible light communication," *IEEE Photonics Journal*, vol. 5, no. 4, pp. 7901501–7901507, August 2013.

27. M. I. Olmedo et al., "Multiband carrier-less amplitude phase modulation for high capacity optical data links," *Journal of Lightwave Technology*, vol. 32, no. 4, pp. 798–804, February 2014.

28. F. Pancaldi et al., "Single-carrier frequency domain equalization: A focus on wireless applications," *IEEE Signal Processing Magzine*, vol. 25, no. 5, pp. 37–56, January 2008.

29. P. A. Haigh, Z. Ghassemlooy, S. Rajbhandari, I. Papakonstantinou, and W. Popoola, "Visible light communications: 170 Mb/s using an artificial neural network equalizer in a low bandwidth white light configuration," *Journal Of Lightwave Technology*, vol. 32, no. 9, pp. 1807–1813, April 2014.

30. H. Elgala, R. Mesleh, and H. Haas, "Indoor optical wireless communication: Potential and state-of-the-art," *IEEE Communications Magazine*, vol. 49, no. 9, pp. 56–62, September 2011.

31. H. M. H. Shalaby, "A performance analysis of optical overlapping PPM-CDMA communication systems," *Journal Of Lightwave Technology*, vol. 17, no. 3, pp. 426–433, March 1999.

32. H. M. H. Shalaby, "Performance analysis of SAC-OCDMA systems adopting overlapping PPM schemes," *Journal Of Lightwave Technology*, vol. 31, no. 12, pp. 1856–1866, June 2013.
33. C. N. Georghiades, "Some implications of TCM for optical direct-detection channels," *IEEE Transactions On Communications*, vol. 37, no. 5, pp. 481–487, May 1989.
34. J.-Y. Li, J.-J. Jou, T.-T. Shih, C.-L. Chiu, J.-C. Liou, and H.-W. Ting, "Design of 20-Gb/s four-level pulse amplitute modulation VCSEL driver in 90-nm CMOS technology," *IEEE International Conference on Electron Devices and Solid-State Circuits (EDSSC)*, pp. 195–198, August 3–5, 2016.
35. M. Novak, O. Wilfert, and T. Simicek, "Visible light communication beacon system for internet of things," *Conference on Microwave Techniques (COMITE)*, pp. 1–5, April 20–21, 2017.
36. The LED Streetlight Replacement Program. Available: http://bsl.lacity.org/led.html, (February 10, 2014).
37. P. Luo, Z. Ghassemlooy, H. L. Minh, E. Bentley, A. Burton, and X. Tang, "Performance analysis of a car-to-car visible light communication system," *Applied Optics*, vol. 54, no. 7, pp. 1696–1706, March 2015.
38. I. Takai, S. Ito, K. Yasutomi, K. Kagawa, M. Andoh, and S. Kawahito, "LED and CMOS image sensor based optical wireless communication system for automotive applications," *IEEE Photonics Journal*, vol. 5, no. 5, pp. 6801418–6801424, October 2013.
39. T. Nagura, T. Yamazato, M. Katayama, T. Yendo, T. Fujii, and H. Okada, "Tracking an LED array transmitter for visible light communications in the driving situation," *7th International Symposium on Wireless Communication Systems (ISWCS)*, pp. 765–769, September 19–22, 2010.
40. C. Shen, Y. Guo, H. M. Oubei, T. K. Ng, G. Liu, K.-H. Park, K.-T. Ho, M.-S. Alouini, and B. S. Ooi, "20-meter underwater wireless optical communication link with 1.5 Gbps data rate," *Optics Express*, vol. 24, no. 22, pp. 25502–25509, July 2016.
41. H. H. Lu et al., "An 8 m/9.6 Gbps underwater Wireless optical communication system," *IEEE Photonics Journal*, vol. 8, no. 5, pp. 1–7, October 2016.
42. D. Tsonev et al., "A 3-Gb/s single-LED OFDM-based wireless VLC link using a Gallium Nitride μLED," *IEEE Photonics Technology Letters*, vol. 26, no. 7, pp. 637–640, April 2014.
43. Y.-C. Chi, D.-H. Hsieh, C.-T. Tsai, H.-Y. Chen, H.-C. Kuo, and G.-R. Lin, "450-nm GaN laser diode enables high-speed visible light communication with 9-Gbps QAM-OFDM," *Optics Express*, vol. 23, no. 10, pp. 13051–13059, May 2015.
44. W. Lu, L. Liu, and J. Sun, "Influence of temperature and salinity fluctuations on propagation behaviour of partially coherent beams in oceanic turbulence," *Journal Of Optics A: Pure And Applied Optics*, vol. 8, no. 12, pp. 1052–1058, 2006.
45. B. M. Cochenour and L. J. Mullen, "Free-space optical communications underwater," *Advanced Optical Wireless Communication System*, Eds. S. Arnon, J. Barry, G. Karagiannidis, R. Schober and M. Uysal, Cambridge University Press, pp. 201–239, 2012.
46. A. Laux, R. Billmers, L. Mullen, B. Concannon, J. Davis, J. Prentice, and V. Contarino, "The a, b, c's of oceanographic LIDAR predictions: A significant step toward closing the loop between theory and experiment," *Journal Of Modern Optics*, vol. 49, pp. 439–451, December 2010.
47. W. Cox and J. Muth, "Simulating channel losses in an underwater optical communication system," *Journal Of the Optical Society Of America A*, vol. 31, no. 5, pp. 920–934, May 2014.
48. B. Cochenour, L. Mullen, and J. Muth, "Effect of scattering albedo on attenuation and polarization of light underwater," *Optics Letters*, vol. 35, no. 12, pp. 2088–2090, June 2010.
49. H. M. Oubei, C. Li, K.-H. Park, T. K. Ng, M.-S. Alouini, and B. S. Ooi, "2.3 Gbit/s underwater wireless optical communications using directly modulated 520 nm laser diode," *Optics Express*, vol. 23, no. 16, pp. 20743–20748, July 2015.
50. K. Nakamura, I. Mizukoshi, and M. Hanawa, "Optical wireless transmission of 405 nm, 1.45 Gbit/s optical IM/DD-OFDM signals through a 4.8 m underwater channel," *Optics Express*, vol. 23, no. 2, pp. 1558–1566, January 2015.
51. F. Hanson and S. Radic, "High bandwidth underwater optical communication," *Applied Optics*, vol. 47, no. 2, pp. 277–283, March 2008.

52. H. M. Oubei et al., "4.8 Gbit/s 16-QAM-OFDM transmission based on compact 450-nm laser for underwater wireless optical communication," *Optics Express*, vol. 23, no. 18, pp. 23302–23309, October 2015.

53. F. Hanson and M. Lasher, "Effects of underwater turbulence on laser beam propagation and coupling into single-mode optical fiber," *Applied Optics*, vol. 49, no. 16, pp. 3224–3230, 2010.

54. D. J. Bogucki et al., "Comparison of near-forward light scattering on oceanic turbulence and particles," *Applied Optics*, vol. 37, no. 21, pp. 4669–4677, December 1998.

55. M. V. Jamali et al., "Statistical distribution of intensity fluctuations for underwater wireless optical channels in the presence of air bubbles," *Iran Workshop on Communication and Information Theory (IWCIT)*, Tehran, Iran, pp. 1–6, January 2016.

56. R. M. Hagem, D. V. Thiel, S. G. O'Keefe, and T. Fickenscher, "The effect of air bubbles on an underwater optical communications system for wireless sensor network applications," *Microwave And Optical Technology Letters*, vol. 54, no. 3, pp. 729–732, January 2012.

57. D. K. Woolf, Bubbles, *Encyclopedia of ocean sciences*, Eds J. H. Steele, S. A. Thorpe and K. K. Turekian, Academic Press, pp. 352–357, March 2001.

58. H. Medwin, "In situ acoustic measurements of bubble populations in coastal ocean waters," *Journal Of Geophysical Research*, vol. 75, pp. 599–611, January 1970.

59. D. A. Kolovayev, "Investigation of the concentration and statistical size distribution of wind-produced bubbles in the near-surface ocean," *Oceanology, English Translation*, vol. 15, pp. 659–661, July 1976.

60. B. D. Johnson and R. C. Cooke, "Bubble populations and spectra in coastal waters: A photographic approach," *Journal Of Geophysical Research*, vol. 84, pp. 3761–3766, October 1979.

61. D. M. Farmer and D. D Lemon, "The influence of bubbles on ambient noise in the ocean at high wind speeds," *Journal Of Physical Oceanography*, vol. 14, no. 11, pp. 1762–1778, November 1984.

62. D. C. Blanchard and L. D. Syzdek, "Concentration of bacteria in jet drops from bursting bubbles," *Journal of Geophysical Research*, vol. 77, pp. 5087–5099, March 1972.

63. L. Hugh Sing and G. Pang, "Positioning beacon system using digital camera and LEDs," *IEEE Transactions on Vehicular Technology*, vol. 52, no. 2, pp. 406–419, March 2003.

64. M. Katayama, M. Kazuyuki, and K. Kazumitsu, "Vehicle position detection system," Patent- EP 1906202 A1, 2010.

65. A. Arafa, J. Xian, and R. Klukas, "Wireless indoor optical positioning with a differential photo-sensor," *IEEE Photonics Technology Letters*, vol. 24, pp. 1027–1029, 2012.

66. L. Pengfei et al., "Experimental demonstration of an indoor visible light communication positioning system using dual-tone multi-frequency technique," *3rd International Workshop on Optical Wireless Communications (IWOW)*, pp. 55–59, September 2014.

67. T. Q. Wang, Y. A. Sekercioglu, A. Neild, and J. Armstrong, "Position accuracy of time-of-arrival based ranging using visible light with application in indoor localization systems," *Journal Of Lightwave Technology*, vol. 31, no. 20, pp. 3302–3308, 2013.

68. T. Kishi., H. Tanaka., Y. Umeda, and O. Takyu, "A high-speed LED driver that sweeps out the remaining carriers for visible light communications," *Journal Of Light Wave Technology*, vol. 32, no. 2, pp. 239–439, January 2014.

69. H. Li., X. Chen, J. Guo, Z. Gaoa, and H. Chen, "An analog modulator for 460 Mb/S visible light data transmission based on OOK-NRZ modulation," *IEEE Wireless Communications*, vol. 22, no. 2, pp. 68–73, April 2015.

70. K. Modepalli and L. Parsa, "Dual-Purpose offline LED driver for illumination and visible light communication," *IEEE Transactions On Industry Applications*, vol. 51, no. 5, pp. 406–419, February 2015.

71. A. Ahmed, J. A. Khan, and U. Younis, "A high speed transmitter for visible light communications up to 50 Mbps," *International Conference on Emerging Technologies (ICET)*, pp. 153–157, December 2014.

72. S. De Lausnay., L. De Strycker., J.-P. Goemaere, B. Nauwelaers, and N. Stevens, "Design of a visible light communication transmitter for the evaluation of a wide range of modulation techniques," *2nd International Workshop on Optical Wireless Communications (IWOW)*, pp. 30–34, October 2013.

73. J. J. D. McKendry, D. Massoubre, S. Zhang, B. R. Rae., R. P. Green, E. Gu., R. K. Henderson, A. E. Kelly, and M. D. Dawson, "Visible light communications using a CMOS-controlled micro-light-emiting-diode array," *Journal Of Light Wave Technology*, vol. 30, no. 1, pp. 61–67, January 2012.

74. B. R. Rae, J. McKendry, Z. Gong, E. Gu, D. Renshaw, M. D. Dawson, and R. K. Henderson, "A 200 MHz 300 ps 0.5 pJ/ns optical pulse generator array in 0.35 μm CMOS," *IEEE International Solid-State Circuits Conference—(ISSCC)*, pp. 322–323, Februry 2010.

75. E. F. Schubert., N. E. J. Hunt., R. J. Malik., M. Micovic, and D. L. Miller, "Temperature and modulation characteristics of resonant-cavity light emitting diodes," *Journal Of Light Wave Technology*, vol. 14, no. 7, pp. 1721–1729, July 1996.

76. H. Qian., S. Zhao., S. Z. Cai, and T. Zhou, "Digitally controlled micro-LED array for linear visible light communication systems," *IEEE Photonics Journal*, vol. 7, no. 3, pp. 1–9, June 2015.

77. D. A. Basnayaka and H. Haas, "Hybrid RF and VLC systems: Improving user data rate performance of VLC systems," *81st Vehicular Technology Conference (VTC Spring)*, pp. 1–5, May 2015.

78. F. Che, L. Wu, B. Hussain., X. Li, and C. Patrick Yue, "A fully integrated IEEE 802.15.7 visible light communication transmitter with On-Chip 8-W 85% efficiency boost LED driver," *Symposium on VLSI Circuits (VLSI Circuits)*, pp. C216–C217, June 2015.

79. P. A. Haigh et al., "Multi-band carrier-less amplitude and phase modulation for band limited visible light communications systems," *IEEE Wireless Communications*, vol. 22, no. 2, pp. 46–53, April 2015.

80. H. Qian, J. Chen, S. Yao, Z. Yu, H. Zhang, and W. Xu, "One-bit Sigma-delta modulator for nonlinear visible light communication systems," *IEEE Photonics Technology Letters*, vol. 27, no. 4, pp. 419–422, February 2015.

81. S. Zhao, J. Xu, and O. Trescases, "Burst-mode resonant LLC converter for an LED luminaire with integrated visible light communication for smart buildings," *IEEE Transactions On Power Electronics*, vol. 29, no. 8, pp. 4392–4402, August 2014.

82. X. Deng, Y. Wu, K. Arulandu., G. Zhou, and J.-P. M. G. Linnartz, "Performance comparison for illumination and visible light communication system using buck converters," *Globecom, 2014 Workshop—Optical Wireless Communications*, pp. 547–552, December 2014.

Index

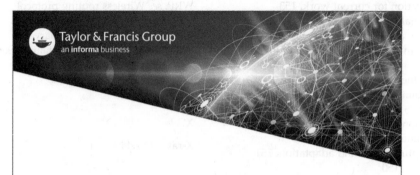